On and Off the Field

Anthony Waine · Kristian Naglo (Hrsg.)

On and Off the Field

Fußballkultur in England
und Deutschland | Football
Culture in England and Germany

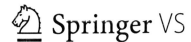 Springer VS

Herausgeber
Dr. Anthony Waine
Morecambe, Großbritannien

Dr. Kristian Naglo
Institut für Soziologie
Justus-Liebig-Universität Gießen
Deutschland

ISBN 978-3-658-00132-2   ISBN 978-3-658-00133-9 (eBook)
DOI 10.1007/978-3-658-00133-9

Die Deutsche Nationalbibliothek verzeichnet diese Publikation in der Deutschen Natio-
nalbibliografie; detaillierte bibliografische Daten sind im Internet über http://dnb.d-nb.de
abrufbar.

Springer VS
© Springer Fachmedien Wiesbaden 2014

Lektorat: Dr. Cori Mackrodt, Yvonne Homann

Gedruckt auf säurefreiem und chlorfrei gebleichtem Papier

Springer VS ist eine Marke von Springer DE. Springer DE ist Teil der Fachverlagsgruppe
Springer Science+Business Media.
www.springer-vs.de

Burnden Park, circa 1952 © Françoise Taylor
Reproduced by kind permission of the estate and heirs of Françoise Taylor.

Inhaltsverzeichnis/Contents

Kristian Naglo & Anthony Waine

1   Imagining Football Nations in the Postmodern Age

The nations of England and Germany lend themselves ideally to a comparative analysis of the kind which this volume is offering. Sport has occupied for both a central place in their society and ideology for at least one hundred and fifty years, though with frequently quite distinct emphases (cf. Eisenberg 1999). It is, however, the game of football where, historically, the relationship between England and Germany has become a space filled with an ever changing admixture of rational and irrational dialogues, legends, moods and truly iconic moments, fixed in the individual's psyche and embedded in the nation's competing historical narratives (see Wagg and Porter / Wagner in this volume). To help the readers of our volume to gain a clearer understanding of the social context, we have appended, in the form of a bi-lingual comparative timeline, an overview of these historical narratives mainly concerning the football related developments of both nations (see Stolz and Waine in this volume). By simply browsing this appendix several of the key moments will gain greater factual substance. Crucially, in the spaces away from the sports fields, the reader will also become aware of striking dissimilarities between England and Germany. For example, Germany's achievement of nationhood comes late in the nineteenth century, as does its transformation from a relatively under-industrialised continental European state into a modern, technologically advanced economy capable of competing with the established imperial powers such as Great Britain. What begins as economic rivalry from approximately the 1870s onwards ends in full-scale political and military enmity by 1914. And inevitably and sadly this enmity is not assuaged by the international treaties, newly established institutions and dialogues of the twenties and thirties, but resumes even more aggressively in 1939.

One could justifiably claim that, at least in the popular English imagination, this historical legacy formed a vital constituent of all international games between the two nations until the end of the twentieth century. Arguably it was only in 2006 when Germany hosted the World Cup that a new, un-blinkered generation of English football fans, metaphorically accompanied by a conspicuously less partisan and backward-looking media, physically encountered a host country magnanimously open to all fans and visitors. A kind of closure was effected there in the stadia and especially the huge open squares of German towns and cities in which English fans (and many other nationalities) enjoyed a football fest together with their German hosts.

Nevertheless, sporting encounters – and in our book especially international football matches – have generally served with regard to the classic modern game as a substitute for military engagement (Elias), or as a unifying factor constituting the nation as an 'imagined community' (Anderson 1991). We therefore adhere to the idea that the *national team* represents right through to the present day the 'homogenous nation', and that it does so in spite of obvious social heterogeneity and the development in the area of playing tactics of global strategies, or at least adaptation to, global patterns. The national side's style of playing is still identified with a specific, historical (football) culture, i.e. it has acquired certain symbolic meanings during the course through modern history which the imagined individual nation has taken (Pyta 2006: 2). The 'arch rivals' England and Germany can be used here as an especially appropriate yardstick for gauging these modern aspects of the game[1].

This book will try to do justice to the sheer breadth of the local relationship between our two countries in the north west of Europe, whilst at the same time intentionally stepping outside of the terrain of what might loosely be called a 'local derby' to consider how the two nations also interact with the global changes in politics, economics, leisure consumption and popular culture. Indeed, the latter two domains of leisure consumption and popular culture have changed quite dramatically over the past fifty years as older patterns of work and communal living have been gradually eroded. Technology and the instant accessibility of the media have facilitated a shift from collective participation in publicly organised forms

---

1   Although we recognize that "certain aspects of football in Britain retained a crucial 'British' dimension" (Taylor 2008:12), our general approach will focus on the nation of England instead of the whole of the United Kingdom.

of 'free time' activity and entertainment to those where the individual receives and processes entertainment and information in their own personally structured private sphere. As part of these paradigmatic shifts, which have assumed global dimensions, individual tastes have come to predominate over those validated previously by revered authorities, so that such subjective preferences and passions of the individual can be, and frequently are, chosen from a potpourri of local, regional, national and global stimuli. In this increasingly jumbled-up world of individualistic passions, privatised lifestyle capsules, and the severance of binding ties to traditional, certainty-bolstering agencies and institutions, our closer-to-home national affiliations have been weakened. How 'our' national game and 'our' national team are then perceived within these postmodern contours is a matter of social and of psychological import, which the book will seek to illuminate.

Thus, in this account of nationality, modernity in its multiple forms is based on different forms of the imaginary, which allows for perceived connections to be drawn among strangers, with the aid of mass mediation. According to this approach, "readers of narratives disseminated translocally through print identify with both the audience addressed by the narrator and the narrated-about characters, and become aware of the existence of like-minded readers who share similar identifications. The 'We' of nationalism is the tropic embodiment of these two identifications" (Lee / LiPuma 2002: 195f.). Whereas Anderson in his famous study focusses on *print capitalism* as the major trigger in the creation of imagined communities, today it is certainly what we could call *media capitalism* which helps to create new perceptions of imagined worlds, including "the appropriation of agonistic bodily skills that can then further lend passion and purpose to the community so imagined" (Appadurai 1996: 112). Thus everyday football routines, (media) discourses on those routines and corresponding narratives, form the basis for what we believe to be the cultural-linguistic spaces of football which help to define national or local imaginary borders.

In a thoroughly mixed international football league as found in England since the early 1990s, footballers and ex-footballers themselves contribute quite substantially to these routines, discourses and narratives. To take one of many possible examples of this phenomenon: Uwe Rösler (who incidentally is far more popular in England than in Germany). This German striker from Leipzig became one of Manchester's foreign heroes playing for City whilst the Frenchman Eric Cantona was at the heart of United's great nineties revival. Shortly after becoming Brentford's manager in June 2011 he stated in a *Guardian* interview (The Guardian, 2.9.2011): "I loved it when I came here. English football is poor. It is honest. It is fast and direct. In the 90s it was not so much about tactics, it was like two boxers hitting each other until one fell down. As a striker, I knew I would get a lot of chances. In Germany there was a lot of man-marking and sweepers, it was much harder to score". Rösler not only identified the perceived differences in the playing styles and mentalities of the two nations from an insider perspective in this piece, but he also spoke appreciatively of the social landscape and cultural space surrounding the field of play: "It's how football started in England, back to the roots, an old-fashioned stadium with the houses on either side. Also, when we play good football and get good results, we fill the stadium and it can be intimidating in here[2]."

Accordingly, our focus in this volume is not only on football as a sporting but also as a spatial experience (cf. Schroer 2008) which takes place *on and off the field*, and consequently is to be viewed as one which is positioned predominantly within a national landscape and which is, in addition, contingent upon other significant fields involving social and economic enterprise. We are aiming to depict these assumed national spaces in a comparative fashion by placing them within a framework characterised by particular actors, fans, forms of capitalism, and markets specifically devoted to football, as well as to teams and sports associations. Our comparative analysis will furthermore incorporate the (spectacular) presentation of the professional game in the media through newspapers (see Kautt in this volume), television, and the radio, and the role played by mythical narratives within the mediatised space. Especially this mediatised space is one which has come to occupy much of our *everyday culture*. Other areas impinging on broader social and cultural fields which form motifs within the book's broader investigation are women's football (see Gros in this volume), amateur football (see Naglo in this volume), the historical awareness of crises in the evolution of the modern and especially post-modern game (see Elliott in this volume), sexual identity and masculinity (see Degele in this volume).

At the same time as assumed national paradigms are being compared to and contrasted with global models we will refer to discussions that are currently taking place throughout Europe and globally, and which centre around the keyword heterogeneity. These identity related discussions are concerned, for example, with a changing fan culture (see Fürtjes in this volume), the perception of the role of sexuality (see Degele and Gros in this volume) or the question of economic ethics in football (see Schraten in this volume). In connection with these private and inner spaces, we are conscious of some of the central actors in post-modern football attempting to break down the *old tribal connections* between predominantly male

---

2   This semi-mythical representation of the aggressively charged atmosphere of a minor club's stadium shows how sports topophilia (Bale) can be experienced by individuals, and it also shows how they work in the context of narratives (cf. Giulianotti 2005, 122).

fans off the field and hyper-masculine players on the field which can be traced back to the deep roots of the game in the industrial working class where certainty and uniformity of both behaviour and cognitive processes were expected. One of the very few central actors in English football (apart from the tragic Justin Fashanu) to confront this tribal connection is the United States international player, Robbie Rogers, who had latterly played for Leeds United and publicly announced he was gay in March 2013. In a long article and interview with Rogers to accompany his coming out, the *Guardian* (29.3.2013) reminded its readers of how historically "the backdrop for a professional sportsman is so harsh that coming out usually feels impossible. There have been notable exceptions – from the Welsh rugby player Gareth Thomas to the Puerto Rican boxer Orlando Cruz. Yet even those hard and violent trades are more forgiving than the tribal world of football". Rogers himself speculated that there were perhaps 'lots of fans' who are not "homophobic. But, in a stadium, sometimes they want to destroy you." In short, it is, in Rogers's view, the ingrained culture of fans *en masse* and not the possibly more enlightened and tolerant attitudes of the individual fan which sustain the macho tribalism generated within the ghettoised spaces of both old and new stadia.

Rogers's public announcement is at present one courageous yet very isolated sign of an individual moving with the support of segments of the media into the space between private freedom and public prejudice. At the same time one can see in men's football how figures like David Beckham both on and off the pitch (see Waine / Hacker in this volume), together with fashionable clothes, hair-cuts or tattoos have come to represent different patterns of behaviour amongst players in recent years. Footballers today are not only athletes but celebrities indicating "the commodification of sports charisma through merchandise endorsement" by which "sport moves away from the impersonality of athletic strengths (...), and towards the commodified personalization of sporting performance" (Giulianotti 2005, 118). Examples of these different patterns include the increasingly ecstatic individualistic celebration of a goal (see Turner in this volume), the progressive professionalization in the 'marketing' of players or the admission of crises in the player's private life. Here we are confronted with the issue of a new generation of players entering the much broader public spaces than of old which football has now created (and indeed been granted by societies globally) and their followers, and these can be read as examples of potential change in the system of football and the widened social context in which it is played out. These developments and specific examples point to the global aspects of a post-modern game strongly moulded by the media. This raises the central question of how and on which levels potentially significant discourses, constructions, and practices are taking place, and this will in turn enable processes of re-connection to be made back to the respective national spaces of both England and Germany – but crucially to re-connect to these national spaces as constructed within imagined boundaries.

We believe as academics that football is an ideal subject with which to analyse how symbolic points of cultural, social and political thinking are being created, which bring together global and local manifestations and allow for links to be made back to national constructs. Viewed against the background of the globalised, post-modern game of football, represented, as we have already claimed, by a new generation of players and attendant symptoms of change in public allegiances, two major questions within this context arise: is it still possible to speak of (imagined) national football cultures in the context of a globalised, post-modern game and, secondly, can they be distinguished from one another? If the answer to the first question is affirmative, then precisely how does one imagine them? With respect to these hypotheses, the bilingual approach of the present book represents an important preliminary methodological decision. From our perspective, national cultures are constructed through the combination of specific media discourses, practices, images, histories, narratives, myths, collective tales and invented traditions. The socially conservative, i.e. self-reiterating ritual of football (e.g. pre-season, League, National Cup, European Cup and so on) can be viewed as an excellent case study in this respect.

2   Locating Culture

Indeed, the joint editors began to develop their ideas for such a volume on sport and culture in their respective countries whilst working on the very concept of 'culture' itself for a collection of essays entitled *Europe in a Global Context* (cf. Krossa 2011). Our chapter's ideas for the first section of that volume, devoted to the 'Culture and History' of Europe, grew in a quite dialectical way out of our discussions about the differing ways in which historically our two societies have approached and dealt with the meanings of this complex, multi-dimensional term – right through to the present day. In particular we observed how England and Germany have had to come to grips with the gradual pluralisation and democratisation of cultural participation and taste in the twentieth century, a process encompassing all classes and both their traditional and their newer areas of play and recreation. We have already highlighted in the first section of our Introduction how significant these areas have become in the postmodern age. It will be helpful to the reader of our present book, therefore, to be familiarised in the first instance with our own definition of popular culture. We claimed in our chapter in *Europe in a Global Context* that the definition which follows gradually became acceptable to more and more educated members of both societies (and of course those beyond this corner of Europe) who had hitherto consciously discriminated between High Culture (the product of the creative, cultivated mind, and the repository of eternal values for mankind) on the one hand, and the allegedly lower pursuits, festivities and traditions of anonymous social collectives (and implicitly therefore ephemeral and superficial) on the other hand. We maintain that:

"From the 1960s onwards this openness to 'culture from below' and 'culture from the here and now' grew and the concept of popular culture gained acceptance. Modern popular culture embraces a vast range of individual performers, sub-cultural genres, technological traditions, increasingly mixed media, and generational movements especially spawned by youth culture. These multifarious talents, fashions and styles articulate the real as well as synthetic longings, feelings and moods of the broad mass of people, and communicate them in ways which give *pleasure* and identity to ordinary people in their everyday lives. Culture has slowly become synonymous with the socialized imagination of the whole community at local, regional and national level" (Naglo / Waine 2011: 13).

To recapitulate and to summarise then our own position, we would contend that, in contrast to traditional, exclusive and class-bound definitions, present day usages of *Kultur* or *culture* generally include discussions about how all humans produce sense and meaning in life in their subjective attempts to understand the world. These attempts to give meaning to, and thereby comprehend the world, are inevitably embedded in collective systems of interpretation and have reference to a full range of human actions (Pyta 2006: 1). Viewed in this way culture is to be understood as contributing to social cohesiveness and unity, rather than, as in the past, to the erection of social boundaries and systems of discriminatory thinking. In the process of constructing our sense of what communities actually are, interpretations of cultural phenomena such as football have the capacity to "carry and transmit non-sporting webs of meaning and become the focal point of processes of socialisation" (Pyta 2006: 2). These collective interpretations can and do vary strongly across perceived cultures. Thus football is very much part of the *glocalised* world (Robertson 1992) in which social actors interpret global processes and phenomena according to their local beliefs and their particular local needs. Despite obvious moves towards global organization and standardization, football is in fact still predominantly organized at a national or local level in specifically defined systems (Giulianotti/Robertson 2009).

However, the definitions, interpretations and contextualisation of cultural phenomena are linguistically contingent, as they can only become a remembered experience through the mediation of a spoken or written language (cf. Koselleck 2004). The production of cultural knowledge in this sense is invariably bound to individual (national) languages and to "the history knowledge has taken in these discourse communities (...)" (Ehlich 2004, 179). As a consequence, it is important in the process of constructing national cultural spaces to consider how – and in which language – people talk about the game. Thus the discourses become very much a matter of national cultural-linguistic interpretation and identity building. Our preliminary conclusion in respect of the present project is as follows: by comparing national football cultures in England and Germany two different dimensions of thought become evident. Firstly, the essays, written in English and German in this volume, display discrete academic and linguistic/semantic approaches to and styles of dealing with the subject of culture and football[3]. Secondly and more specifically, the British scholars integrate more consciously biography and (social) history into their analyses and accord the individual and the team of individuals greater space and weighting, whilst the German scholars are especially sensitive towards the broader themes of commercialisation, commodification, mediatisation, and modernisation and their collective influence on how football culture at home and abroad is subjectively constructed.

3   Subjective Constructions of National Football Cultures

As we have already stated in our introductory remarks the seeds of this particular volume were planted when we, the editors, collaborated on a scholarly project concerned with the meanings and the history of culture. But there was a second, much more tangible autobiographical rapport with the subject. Both of us have played football for various teams in different divisions of English and German football leagues, as well as in the case of Kristian Naglo of also having years of experience training and running teams. The genesis of this particular book is therefore not just a product of dispassionate theoretical interest in, or intellectual passion for the subject but also of the sweat, toil and soil of matches at grass roots level in the two countries, albeit at quite different periods in time. In this section of the Introduction we are therefore going to select some of the first-hand insights gained into the everyday reality of the game, especially since joining a team in a foreign country – Naglo in England, and Waine in Germany – is likely to trigger

---

3   Part of the more implicitly addressed cultural-semantic framework in this respect are for instance opposing concepts and dualisms in both languages like Kultur vs. Culture, Zivilisation vs. Civilization, Kulturindustrie vs. Cultural Industry or Volkskultur vs. Popular Culture (cf. Naglo/Waine 2011; Waine 2007; Koselleck 2006; Fisch 1992).

an often purely sub-conscious thought process of comparing and contrasting the game *on and off the field* at home and abroad – if nothing else then for purposes of self-orientation and social acclimatisation.

Tony Waine spent the year 1966-1967 teaching English as an assistant at a grammar school in a small town in North Germany. He had attended a grammar school himself in the large industrial city of Leicester in the East Midlands, where soccer was, in a manner of speaking, out-lawed. Unlike most other schools in the Midlands and elsewhere which would be involved in weekly games against local schools organised in official inter-school leagues and with the full involvement of teachers (and usually also keen parents), Wyggeston Boys Grammar School only allowed rugby football to be played. And all fixtures were against other independent boys' grammar schools and public schools (i.e. private boarding schools) throughout the Midlands. Ideologically speaking, rugby identified you and your school as middle to upper middle class and, implicitly, part of the private independent sector, whilst soccer was the preserve of the secondary state educational system. As this book's Timeline shows, this was in fact the very opposite of how soccer had begun as an organised game for 'gentlemen' at very good schools in nineteenth century England. At the Gymnasium Westerstede in North Germany where Waine taught, there were no school teams and no school leagues either, but not for any (dubious) reasons of social class allegiance or aspiration. All football, indeed all sport, was organised outside the school system within and through a uniquely German social institution called the 'Verein' (cf. for instance Müller-Jentsch 2008 and Nathaus 2012). The word is derived from the verb 'vereinen' meaning to bring the individual person together with other like-minded people, and the noun 'Verein' designates a legally constituted grouping of individuals sharing a common purpose, pastime or passion. In short, sport together with myriad other communal activities was a highly organised civic affair in Germany, right down to the village level.

Thus the team Waine turned out for in the so-called 'Bezirksliga' (or 'area league') was the 'Fussball-Sportverein Westerstede'. The Football Sports Club was rooted in the community and strongly supported by it. It was overseen by an executive committee which included local town dignitaries. It played its games in front of up to 500 spectators, with the players enjoying civilised changing facilities in a modern building. Indeed everything surrounding the club and the ground, be it the physical environment or the social infrastructure appeared modern, and furthermore everything was approached with a refreshing professional involvement. Coming from mid-sixties England this was an alien experience. Local football there was cheerfully shambolic. It was in the hands of lots of good-hearted, enthusiastic individuals, and who invariably came from working class backgrounds.

Westerstede Football Sports Club, on the other hand, hired a professionally qualified trainer from the next big town's club, Oldenburg, who trained the team twice
a week in tactics and 'Technik' (a concept referring not only to individual skills
but to overall playing strategies and the intelligent application thereof), a word
which would gradually filter into the football consciousness as well as the football
lexis of Britain from the 1980s onwards. The predominant sense gained of sport
and football in particular at a local level in mid-sixties Germany was of a classlessness in the way it was organised, managed, spoken and written about, and
as it manifested itself in the composition of its teams and players' backgrounds.
Even at the microcosmic level of a small town's football sports club in Northern
Germany this New World classlessness was a pointer to the ways in which football
in the decidedly Old World of Great Britain would gradually break away from its
organic affiliations with the popular culture of working class communities. That
Old World order would symbolically and literally disintegrate in the course of
the eighties with two major disasters: the Bradford City stadium fire (1985) and
the Hillsborough stadium tragedy (1989), quite apart from the riots of the Heysel
Stadium European Cup Final (1985) and their consequences.

Kristian Naglo's involvement as a competitive footballer in Germany includes
the Final of the Under-19 German Championships against VFB Stuttgart playing
for the 1. FC Kaiserslautern in the 1990/91 season. He has played over a period
of many years in different German 'Landesverbände' (Regional Associations) in
various amateur leagues, both at a relatively high level (the so-called 'Oberliga',
third tier from the top at the time of competing) to the lowest ('Kreisliga'). He is
still involved in amateur football as a manager, also in the youth league.

Naglo spent the academic year 2008 / 2009 as a teaching assistant in German
studies at Lancaster University. There, he started playing – later on becoming a
player manager – for a local football club (Storeys Football Club) in the neighborhood where he lived. Waine had played for the same works team in the early
seventies and can corroborate everything that Naglo goes on to document! Little
had changed in the intervening thirty years.

The experiences he gained from playing in English football were quite mixed.
While the relatively high standard of English local football in the North Lancashire region impressed him in general, he was quite astonished at the aggression
dominating the game, with referees (in his perception) only blowing the whistle
to start and to end the game – as well as to indicate that it was time for the 'half-
time brew' (a mug of tea). As these initial observations already show, he was able
to confirm all the existing stereotypes held by Germans about English football.

A further observation concerned the rundown state of the mostly local authority pitches and the facilities, i.e changing rooms, as well as the team members

leaving as quickly as possible after the game in the direction of the local pub to have their pints, chips, sausages, bread and butter. This ritual differs greatly from behavior patterns in German football, where team members and spectators stay on at the 'Vereinsheim' (the club house) close to the pitch in which there is a bar where they can have their beer or snacks.

Naglo's main impression was that German football clubs playing in the lower tiers and indeed the whole system of local / amateur football seem to be much better organized, with a lot more money invested to maintain the system. The downside is the often considerable influence wielded by local dignitaries in Germany, who regularly use the club to reinforce and uphold the hierarchies of the respective village or town. In contrast, the English local football Naglo became acquainted with tended to be chaotically organized on the one hand, but perhaps partly because of this transported very positive elements of communal closeness, neighborhood roots and fun for their own sake. These elements are often influenced by 'pseudo-professional discourses' in Germany where even the lowest levels of amateur football are somehow more closely bound up with the corresponding regional association or the national federation.

These brief reflections on personal experiences are of course mere subjective cultural snapshots of local / amateur football in the two countries. Nevertheless, mirroring insider perspectives in different times at different places, they are a legitimate physical starting point for the comparison of the two countries in question. It also means for the editors, that speaking about the cultural dimensions of football on the one hand always comprises the spectacular and mediatised professional game and, on the other hand, the local club game played at the grass roots, even though the latter one is more difficult to grasp for obvious reasons.

4   Conclusion: Comparing English and German Contours Hypothetically

We will conclude our introductory remarks by listing six comparative points concerning the ways in which we, the editors, have subjectively experienced football on and off the field in the two countries, and the more subliminal ways in which our respective national imaginations have been shaped by our media to view 'our' game and 'their' game. The list is therefore intended to be a mildly provocative challenge to the reader of the following eleven chapters to think both critically as well as self-critically about the degree to which national football cultures are constructed and by whom they are created, including by the twelve authors involved in this cross-cultural project.

Firstly, from an English perspective the game is literally driven (forward) by the fighting spirit of the players who derive pleasure from seeking physical confrontations with opponents. The preferred style of playing is to push forwards. This style and its underlying philosophy contrasts markedly with the pronounced deployment of tactical terminology in the German game, such as 'Vierer-Kette' and 'Doppel-Sechs'. These and many other descriptive terms and formulas are indicative of more scientific and intellectual discourses about the game in Germany.

Integrally linked with this first point is, secondly, the far greater emphasis in Germany on different aspects of players' training and preparation. Medical expertise and scientific methodologies are not only taken seriously but systematically applied by team staff who have themselves undergone closely monitored training and gained recognized qualifications before being allowed to exercise their professional skills and use their knowledge. The English game on the other hand has traditionally relied on far fewer fully qualified individuals, who instead draw on the sagacity of personal experience, intuition, sentiment, and who will sacrifice serious planning for pleasure and spontaneous excitement – which are after all the ingredients expected by the fans in the ground and the millions of television spectators wanting to be entertained at home.

Live performance is therefore – our third hypothesis – the product which is the most popular in the English game. The notion of 'performance' suggests and evokes glamour, romance, nostalgia and drama, and it is these emotions which the mass of people attending live matches seek. Hence this justifies the applicability of the term 'popular culture' for describing the inter-play of player and spectator in the gladiatorial arena. In contrast to this the German game is dictated by an emphasis on, and preference for a controlled style of playing in which the emotionally charged elements of glamour, romance, nostalgia and drama are certainly present but reduced in their significance and impact. Semantically, there is no clear German equivalent of 'live performance'. Instead the Germans take the English word 'live' and append it to an existing German noun.

Fourthly, whilst every professional club side in the world has its fan base, English clubs have fans whose loyalty to that club is almost elemental. Their chants, jibes, banter and songs are frequently offensive, obscene and full of visceral hatred for the Other. These gut instincts have been exported, at the very latest in the 1980s, through the supporters of the English national team, and it is no accident that the term 'hooligan' originates in the British Isles and has been borrowed by almost every other major world language. In Germany a generally more critical public attitude is expressed towards fans, especially towards the *Ultras*, and towards the commercial exploitation of fans. Fans themselves should play their part in helping their club to be run in an economically healthy fashion. That is to say,

German fans, however passionate, proud and fiercely loyal, are called upon to show a sense of responsibility and self-discipline.

The fifth supposition we would make concerns the size and the sheer power of the English-language media, especially in view of the fact that the culture of the everyday (the German equivalent of what we call popular culture) is precisely the space in most of our lives where the media exert the greatest influence. The German media, on the other hand, exercise as a rule greater self-restraint and neutrality in the reporting of sporting events and it is fair to assume that this behaviour is in part a consequence of the emotionalism, jingoism and the irresponsibility of the media in the Third Reich. In addition, the country sees itself as being at the heart of the New Europe and therefore committed to relatively sober, informative analyses, even where sport-generated patriotic emotions are involved.

Finally, Germany's self-projection as a thoroughly modern (European) state is manifest in the processes of standardization and modernization which the whole system of football is subjected to. They have been applied as much to the structuring of amateur football, the training of coaching and sports medical staff, the building of stadia, as they are to the playing styles of the clubs and national team. Whilst it is true that the above changes have been taken note of, and some carried out in England, they have most certainly not been applied uniformly nor according to agreed standards, as they have in Germany. Instead, within the modernization processes taking place on the island, especially since the late eighties, one detects the still powerful historical attraction to legendary clubs and stadia and the mythologizing narratives about them. In this respect the metropolitan centres of both early industrial and of postmodern capitalism and, consequently, of cultural production, namely London and Manchester, have played right through to this day a dominant role in the typically English dialectic of myth-making and modernity.

5   An Epilogue

The English media greeted the Champions League final of 2013 between Borussia Dortmund and Bayern Munich with grace, humility and good humour. Several magazines and newspapers mixed and matched the two countries' language and popular culture with references to 'Fussball Comes Home'. More seriously, however, several media reports used the domination by Bundesliga clubs (and therefore by implication German footballing philosophy) of a final played in a stadium, Wembley, epitomizing England's erstwhile glories, to point to wider lessons to be drawn from this historic achievement. Sporting success was equated with progressive social, political and economic thinking. For example, under the headline 'Germany shows how to score on and off the football pitch' the *Financial Times* (24.5.2013) stated in their opening paragraph: "Football is not so much coming home as the country who invented the game is being shown a thing or two by its German rival about fostering young talent, learning from mistakes and planning for the long term." On the same day *The Guardian* asked whether "Britain can learn from the German model?" with a two page feature headlined 'So how did Germany become the new champion of Europe?'

In a country such as England where over roughly the last ten years several major clubs had been bought by wealthy foreign individuals, many of the same publications, along with television and radio programmes, critically compared the English model with that obtaining in Germany. They drew attention to the 50+1 principle requiring that non-profit-making supporters' groups must retain a majority stake in their Bundesliga club, as well as stressing how low ticket prices were kept and how high the average attendance at a game in Germany was. Maurice Glasman, a Labour peer, drew political lessons from this: "We have a Champions League final between two supporter-owned and democratically governed football clubs. Tradition and the preservation of institutional virtue are a source of energy and modernization precisely because change and continuity work together." All of these comments point to important exchanges between England and Germany taking place as a result of a sporting encounter involving two German teams and a famous English setting, thus underlining once again how football carries our gaze from the actual field of play to critically reflect on the socio-cultural networks and structures off the pitch and how the game in the modern era provokes us to imagine our nations not as fixed, definite and homogenous organisms but as dynamic, open and heterogeneous.

Bibliography

Anderson, B. (1991): Die Erfindung der Nation. Zur Karriere eines folgenreichen Konzepts. Erweiterte Neuausgabe. Frankfurt a. M.: Campus.

Appadurai, A. (1996): Modernity at Large. Cultural Dimensions of Globalization. Minneapolis: University of Minnesota Press.

Ehlich, K. (2004): The Future of German and Other Non-English Languages for Acadamic Communication. In: Andreas, G. / Hüppauf, B. (eds.): Globalization and the Future of German. Berlin: De Gruyter, 173-184.

Eisenberg, C. (1999): ‚English Sports' und deutsche Bürger. Eine Gesellschaftsgeschichte 1800-1939. Paderborn: Schöningh.

Financial Times.

Fisch, J. (1992): Zivilisation, Kultur. In: Brunner, O. et al. (eds): Geschichtliche Grund-begriffe. Historisches Lexikon zur politisch-sozialen Sprache in Deutschland, Vol. 7. Stuttgart: Klett-Cotta, 679-774.

Giulianotti, R. (2005): Sport. A Critical Sociology. Cambridge: Polity.

Giulianotti, R. / Robertson, R. (2009): Globalization & Football. London: Sage.

Guardian, The.

Koselleck, R. (2004): Futures Past. On the Semantics of Historical Time (new ed.). Translated and with an Introduction by Keith Tribe. New York: Columbia University Press.

Koselleck, R. (2006): Begriffsgeschichten. Studien zur Semantik und Pragmatik der politischen und sozialen Sprache. Frankfurt a.M.: Suhrkamp.

Krossa, A. S. (Hg.) (2011): Europe in a Global Context. Basingstoke: Palgrave.

Lee, B. / Li Puma, E. (2002): Cultures of circulation: the imaginations of modernity. Public Culture, 14, 191-213.

Müller-Jentsch, W. (2008): Der Verein – ein blinder Fleck der Organisationssoziologie. In: Berliner Journal für Soziologie, 3, 2008, 476-502.

Naglo, K. / Waine, A. (2011): Culture. In: Krossa, A. S. (Hg.): Europe in a Global Context. Basingstoke: Palgrave, 12-23.

Nathaus, K. (2012): Between Club and Commerce: Comparing the Organisation of Sports in Britain and Germany from the Late Nineteenth to the Early Twentieth Century. In: Eisenberg, C. / Gestrich, A. (Hg.): Cultural Industries in Britain and Germany. Sport, Music and Entertainment from the Eighteenth to the Twentieth Century. Augsburg: Wißner Verlag.

Pyta, W. (2006): German Football: a Cultural History. In: Tomlinson, A. / Young, C. (Hg.): German Football. History, Culture, Society. London: Routledge.

Robertson, R. (1992): Globalization: Social Theory and Global Culture. London: Sage.

Schroer, M. (2008): Vom ‚Bolzplatz‘ zum ‚Fußballtempel‘. Was sagt die Architektur der neuen Fußballstadien über die Gesellschaft der Gegenwart aus? In: Klein, G. / Meuser, M. (Hg.): Ernste Spiele. Zur politischen Soziologie des Fußballs. Bielefeld: transcript.

Taylor, M. (2008): The Association Game. A History of British Football. Harlow: Pearson.

Waine, A. (2007): Changing Cultural Tastes. Writers and the Popular in Modern Germany. New York: Berghahn.

"That German Boy who Played for Manchester": Bert Trautmann – Biography, History and Politics

„Dieser deutsche Junge, der für Manchester spielte":
Bert Trautmann – Biographie, Geschichte und
politischer Kontext

Stephen Wagg

Abstract

This essay examines the life and the social and political significance of the German footballer Bernhard 'Bert' Trautmann. Trautmann came to England as a Prisoner of War in 1945 and played League football there between 1949 and 1964. A talented sportsman, he was discovered, while in his prisoner-of-war camp, to be an especially talented goalkeeper and soon established a reputation in North West England. A number of top English clubs hoped to recruit him and he became a Manchester City player in 1949. He achieved something verging on global fame when he kept goal for City in the FA Cup Final of 1956 and finished the game despite having, as doctors discovered later, sustained a broken neck.

A number of myths have formed around Trautmann since the 1950s. Two are scrutinised in this essay. One is that, as the fabled 'good German', he won over an angry populace in Manchester, thousands of whom had turned out in a massive demonstration against his signing and, through force of personality and heroic performances on the field, almost single-handedly effected a post-war reconciliation. The essay argues instead that Trautmann was already integrated into working class life in the area by the time he came to Manchester; that the widely-cited demonstration against him almost certainly did not take place; and that the reconciliation myth was fashioned retrospectively to celebrate a purportedly special British capacity for tolerance. The second myth concerns Bert Trautmann's recent honours for services to Anglo-German relations. The essay suggests that Trautmann's re-emergence has been to do, not with Anglo-German relations, but with the attractiveness of his life – and, in particular his Second World War and football experiences – in relation to the burgeoning media-heritage industry.

Zusammenfassung

Der Aufsatz untersucht das Leben und die soziale bzw. politische Bedeutung des deutschen Fußballers Bernhard 'Bert' Trautmann. Trautmann kam als Kriegsgefangener im Jahr 1945 nach England und spielte dort zwischen 1949 und 1964 professionell Fußball. Noch im Gefangenenlager wurde er als außerordentlich talentierter Torhüter entdeckt. Schnell erarbeitete er sich einen Ruf in den einschlägigen Fußballkreisen Nordwestenglands, woraufhin eine Reihe von Spitzenmannschaften versuchte, ihn zu verpflichten. 1949 wurde er schließlich Spieler von Manchester City. Sein nahezu weltweiter Bekanntheitsgrad geht auf das FA Cup-Finale aus dem Jahr 1956 zurück, als er für Manchester City das Spiel bis zum Ende bestritt, obwohl die Ärzte später feststellten, dass er sich während der Partie einen Genickbruch zugezogen hatte.

Um die Person Trautmann ranken sich seit den 1950er Jahren mehrere Mythen, wobei der vorliegende Essay zwei von ihnen nachgeht. In einem Mythos gilt Trautmann als der legendäre 'gute Deutsche', der in Manchester eine aufgebrachte Bevölkerung umstimmte, die in Demonstrationen mit tausenden Teilnehmern gegen seine Verpflichtung protestiert hatten – und dies nur aufgrund seiner Persönlichkeit sowie seiner heroischen Leistungen als Torwart. Demnach bewirkte er gleichsam im Alleingang eine Versöhnung der beiden Länder in der Nachkriegszeit. Der Artikel argumentiert demgegenüber, dass Trautmann bereits in das Arbeiterleben in der Großregion integriert war, als er nach Manchester kam. Weiterhin wird angenommen, dass die berüchtigte Demonstration gegen ihn sehr wahrscheinlich niemals stattfand. Auch geht der Beitrag davon aus, dass der Versöhnungsmythos erst im Nachhinein Ver-

breitung fand, um eine vermeintlich spezielle britische Toleranz hervorzuheben. Der zweite Mythos bezieht sich auf Bert Trautmanns jüngste Auszeich-
nungen im Dienst der englisch-deutschen Beziehungen. Hier argumentiert der
Beitrag, dass das neuerliche Interesse an Trautmann nicht mit den englisch-
deutschen Beziehungen in Zusammenhang steht, sondern vor allem mit der
Attraktivität seiner Lebensgeschichte, also der Mischung aus II. Weltkriegs-
und Fußballerfahrung, und dies insbesondere im Kontext der aufkommenden
medialen *Heritage*-Industrie.

Football people, especially those of a certain age (say, 50 and over), commonly regard the Soviet Russian Lev Yashin (1929-1990) as the best goalkeeper ever to have
played the game. Yashin himself, not given to false modesty, publicly endorsed
this verdict, adding that the only player to challenge his place in the pantheon of
top keepers was "that German boy who played for Manchester" (Ramsden 2006:
325). This essay considers the German boy in question, Bernhard 'Bert' Trautmann, who came to England as a Prisoner of War in 1945 and signed for Manchester City four years later. It is concerned not with his claims to greatness, but
with his political and social significance. This significance was considerable in
the 1940s and 50s, has grown once again in recent times and has varied in nature
according to time and place. The essay looks critically, therefore, not so much at
what Trautmann was or was not, but at what he was, at various times, taken to represent and it is guided by two noted exhortations – C. Wright Mills' much quoted
insistence that sociology should prove an explanatory bridge between history and
biography[1] and Roland Barthes' equally influential call for myths to be properly
scrutinised. Barthes was, of course, using the word 'myth' to mean not legends, as
such, but 'depoliticised speech' (Barthes 1973: 142) – accounts of events that are
simply taken for granted and not open to critical appraisal.

At the time of writing Trautmann is in his late eighties and living in retirement
in Spain. A great deal of what has been written about him has been published in
the last twenty five years or so. Alan Rowlands, a writer with a principal interest
in the history of football, published a biography of Trautmann in 1990, re-issuing
it, in an updated version, in 2005 (Rowlands 2005/1990).The following year, John
Ramsden, a professor of modern history, devoted virtually a whole chapter to
Trautmann in his study of British-German relations since 1890 (Ramsden 2006:

---

1   Mills (1970: 12) states: "The sociological imagination enables us to grasp history and
    biography and the relations between the two within society. That is its task and its pro-
    mise".

325-362). In 2010, Catrine Clay, a former producer in the BBC's History Unit who had made documentary films about Nazi Germany, published a life of Traut- mann which concentrated principally on the period before her subject became the Manchester City goalkeeper in 1949 (Clay 2010) and in 2011 the accomplished documentary filmmakers Testimony Films produced *The Bert Trautmann Story*[2]. These revisitations of the man have brought renewed press interest in Trautmann, including a number of recent stories available on the internet, which have in turn prompted reminiscences of Trautmann and his time. I draw on much of this ma- terial, as well as contemporary newspaper reports and Trautmann's own 'ghosted' autobiography of 1956 (Trautmann 1956), in this essay.

The essay has two principal purposes and is divided accordingly into two sec- tions. The first aim is to discuss the popular view of Bert as the 'good German' who, with the Second World War fresh in people's minds, won over a doubting English football public with his genial personality and sterling performances: Fred Eyre and Roy Cavanagh have for example, suggested that Trautmann "de- fied British chauvinism and won British hearts with talent and good manners", making him, effectively, "a Teutonic one-man United Nations" (Quoted in Rams- den 2006: 328). The hope here will be to present a more nuanced account. Second, there will be discussion of Trautmann's re-emergence as a public figure during the last decade or so. Here again, the argument will be somewhat contrary to the popular view (expressed for example, in the citation for the OBE awarded to him in 2004) that it constituted (apparently belated) recognition of "his work for Anglo-German relations"[3]. Without wishing either to dispute or disparage any work that Bert Trautmann may have done in this regard, the essay will suggest that his re-discovery was to do with other factors – related chiefly to globalisation and the burgeoning interest, especially (but not solely) among media organisa- tions, with 'heritage'.

---

2   http://www.testimonyfilms.com/index.php?option=com_content&view=catego-
    ry&layout=blog&id=23&Itemid=9. Access: 28th October 2012.
3   "Football Star Trautmann given OBE". http://news.bbc.co.uk/1/hi/england/manches-
    ter/3972309.stm. Access: 29th October 2012.

1   "Rows and Rows of Tiny Terraced Houses": Bert Trautmann, Social Class and the North West of England

A revisionist cloud has recently hovered over the notion of Bert Trautmann as a/ the 'Good German'. In 2006 John Ramsden described the Trautmann family as "not particularly unwilling collaborators in the Nazi regime", adding that Trautmann was classified as a Nazi on capture in 1945 and claiming that Trautmann had joined the Hitler Youth apparently before Hitler came to power (Ramsden 2006: 331). (If this is true, Bert would have been nine. He himself, not entirely without justification, likened the Hitler-Jugend to the Boy Scouts (Trautmann 1956: 16). Moreover, when Clay's biography of Trautmann was published in 2010, reviewers, while generally guarded about the book, were considerably less so about its subject. In *The Observer*, Simon Hattenstone asked: "Why did Trautmann agree to collaborate with this book? To ease his conscience, get the truth out there, or did he simply feel he had nothing to hide?"[4] Paul Croughton in *The Sunday Times* accused Clay of having given Trautmann "a relatively easy ride"[5] and, in *The Times*, Sir Howard Davies (then Director of the London School of Economics and a supporter of Manchester City) went further. "My father", he wrote, " – a D-Day veteran – told me all about Trautmann. I have a very clear recollection of the story he recounted. How Trautmann was a good German, not a Nazi, how he had been captured early in the war and spent a long time in a prisoner-of-war camp on the Isle of Man. How he was a gentle giant who never hurt a fly... The only problem is that none of the above description of his life is true... This book is an interesting tale. But I wish that I had never read it"[6].

However, sifting through accounts of Trautmann's experiences growing up in Nazi Germany (he was ten years old when the National Socialists took power and Hitler became Chancellor) and his engagement both with the north west of England and the culture of the Football League, it is hard to credit either the notion of Trautmann as a "one-man United Nations" or as being "soaked in the blood and horror of the Holocaust" as he is depicted elsewhere in Hattenstone's

---

4   Simon Hattenstone: "Trautmann's Journey: From Hitler Youth to FA Cup Legend", The Observer 4th April 2010. http://www.guardian.co.uk/football/2010/apr/04/trautmanns-journey-from-hitler-youth. Access: 29th October 2012.

5   http://www.theomnivore.co.uk/Book/Classification/Non_fiction/Genre/Sports_Hobbies_Games/5565-Trautmann_s_Journey_From_Hitler_Youth_to_FA_Cup_Legend/Default.aspx. Access: 29th October 2012.

6   Ibid.

review[7]. To quote Mills again, "When wars happen, an insurance man becomes a rocket launcher; a store clerk a radar man [...] Neither the life of an individual nor the history of a society can be understood without understanding both" (Mills 1970: 9).

Bernhard Trautmann was born in the port of Bremen in northern Germany in 1923. His father was a qualified electrician (Trautmann 1956: 13) who worked on the docks for the Kali chemical company (Clay 2010: 13) and is described by Rowlands as a social democrat, notwithstanding the rise of Hitler (Rowlands 2005/1990). In *Steppes to Wembley*, the routinely stylised sports biography written for him by *Guardian* football journalist Eric Todd, Trautmann acknowledges membership of the Hitler Youth, which he joined as a ten year old in 1933; his enlistment at 17 in the *Luftwaffe* in 1941, having trained as a motor mechanic; and his participation in Operation Barbarossa (the German invasion of the Soviet Union) the following year (Trautmann 1956: 16). Both Trautmann's biographers give a strong contextualisation to Trautmann's early life, showing the tentacular growth of the totalitarian state in Germany in the late 1930s. Rowlands notes how by this time the *Kraft durch Freude* (Strength Through Joy) movement was operating in all German cities, how in 1937 all teachers in Germany had to take an oath of loyalty to the Führer, and Trautmann's induction as a teenager into the *Landjahr* programme of sport and militaristic training in rural camps (Rowlands 2005/1990: 24-27). Clay, somewhat of a specialist on life in Nazi Germany, likewise gives a detailed account of the prevailing political circumstances, which were not, of course, of Trautmann's own choosing, or the choosing of many like him: she talks at length about increasingly compulsory National socialist youth programmes (see, for example, Clay 2010: 24-26, 52); the dissolution of trade unions in 1933 and the confiscation of all the assets of the German Communist Party (ibid: 35); and observes that by the eve of the Second World War "only football remained relatively free of state intervention" (ibid: 41). So, remembering Mills and contra the revisionists, one is inclined to agree with a web correspondent called 'sammer' who replied to Hattenstone's review thus:

"Trautmann fought in the Ukraine which was a nasty theatre of war, but I don't think there is evidence to link him with 'genocidal reality', as this article does. Like many footballers Trautmann's politics would be largely nondescript: To be drawn into the HJ [Hitler-Jugend – Hitler Youth] as a 10 year old hardly marks him out from other German boys at that time. As a keen athlete and a character

---

7   Hattenstone "Trautmann's Journey...", see footnote 4.

who obviously relished challenges it's hardly surprising he embraced the macho military ethos of Nazi Germany"[8].

Similarly, two further notions need a degree of correction: one, as we've seen, of Bert Trautmann as some kind of Pied Piper figure trailing an enchanted English football public in his wake and the other of Trautmann's acceptance being evidence of some special British capacity for forgiveness. The latter idea was certainly encouraged by Bert himself when, in the summer of 2012, he told an interviewer from Saga magazine: "I've always said my education began in the UK. The way I was treated - with fairness, kindness, tolerance - even as a prisoner of war - by the people of Lancashire, Mancunians and Great Britain. I am more English than German, even though I was born German. You are a special kind of people, and this is a special kind of island"[9]. But, looked at the round, Trautmann's experiences and his recollections of them, are more inflected by social class – an increasingly inadmissible social difference in post-war Britain – than nationality, ethnicity or any other factor.

As we saw, Trautmann was brought to England as a Prisoner of War in 1945 and was held in various camps. It is certainly the case that, when British intelligence came to categorise German PoWs politically as A (for anti-Nazi), B (for the apolitical) or C (for pro-Nazi), Trautmann was classified as C. Moreover, at a subsequent camp at Northwich in Cheshire, prisoners were divided into East (anti-Nazi) and West (pro-Nazi) contingents and Trautmann was allocated to West. However, C was a broad grouping which embraced both members of the SS and young soldiers who had known no adult life other than under the Third Reich. Trautmann was still only 22 in 1945 and this, or the fact that he had ended the war as a paratrooper, could explain his initial C grading; soon, because of his youth, perhaps, or his lack of political fervour, he was reclassified as a B prisoner (Rowlands 2005/1990: 63). On the other hand, as Clay makes clear, the fiercest friction was not with the English public but between prisoners. Many inmates of the Marbury Hall transit camp in Cheshire who were designated as Category C and 'West' were unreconstructed Nazis who saw the 'East' prisoners as traitors: men who failed to give the Nazi salute or spoke disparagingly of the fuehrer were tried in secret kangaroo courts and, perhaps, found hanging in the toilets the following day (Clay 2010: 191). A and B category PoWs by contrast began to be

---

8   http://www.guardian.co.uk/football/2010/apr/04/trautmanns-journey-from-hitler-youth. Posted 4th April 2010. Access: 30th October 2012.

9   Andy Stevens: "From the Iron Cross to the OBE – Bert Trautmann talks to Saga". http://www.saga.co.uk/lifestyle/people/real-lives/from-the-iron-cross-to-the-obe-bert-trautmann-talks-to-sag.aspx. 10th July 2012. Access: 30th October 2012.

assimilated into local communities. In 1946, Trautmann was among a batch of prisoners to be redeployed to a camp near Ashton-in-Makerfield, a town in what was then the south Lancashire coalfield. Here they got up a football team to play charity matches against local sides; they got passes to go dancing on a Saturday night (they aroused considerable female interest – Clay records that nearly 800 young Englishwomen married German PoWs, ibid: 235); and they were invited into people's homes, on Sundays and at Christmas (Trautmann 1956: 35; Rowlands 2005/1990: 67).

These latter gestures were not, of course, confined to Bert Trautmann; nor can they be attributable to the charm of a one-man United Nations. Rowlands is at pains to attribute them to regional and ethnic factors. The labour force of this predominantly mining and agricultural area, he argues, had avoided conscription because they were in reserved occupations, deemed essential to the war effort; they therefore lacked the bitterness often generated by combat. Besides, they preferred the German prisoners, whom they saw as hardworking, to the Italians, who were seen as skivers (Rowlands 2005/1990: 65). But, aside from rehearsing some very weary national stereotypes, this may underestimate the desire of many people in a predominantly working class area simply to have done with the war. Certainly his experiences in Lancashire in the late 1940s enhanced Trautmann's strong sense of class and community. He was, after all, a working class man from a working class family, a motor mechanic and the son of an electrician. And, whatever else may be said of his war record, it did not diminish his sense that war was something inflicted on the common people. Reflecting on his experiences in Operation Barbarossa, Trautmann wrote in his autobiography "I am convinced the 'man-in-the-street' in any country wants no part in war. War is dictated by a higher authority and the soldier, sailor and airman come inevitably under that authority" (Trautmann 1956: 27).

When Bert Trautmann arrived in the north of England, one of the first things he noticed was the condition of the working classes: staring from the train window at the "rows and rows of tiny terraced houses all backing onto the railway line" he and his fellow PoWs asked "how did they ever win the war?" (Clay 2010: 189). Later, in a camp football game, Trautmann was asked to go in goal; he immediately excelled and rapidly gained a reputation in local football circles. This brought him to the attention of St Helens FC, which was in the process of being re-established, chiefly at the instigation of the manager of the local Cooperative grocery store, the 'Co-op', of course, being an historic bulwark of the British labour movement. Trautmann signed for St Helens in 1946. St Helens Town FC was sited in Sutton, an area of St Helens dominated by one of the biggest coal mines in Lancashire, opened in 1909. Trautmann stressed the importance to him of class and community when he spoke to the St Helens Star in 2009: "St Helens gave me a new life – the five years in the war and three years as a POW took eight years out of my life. I came out and was welcomed in to a beautiful community in Sutton. It was a mining district – miners are the same the world over and very warm-hearted and they took to me"[10]. The community embrace of Trautmann was, it seems, strong enough to transcend grievous personal loss: George Houghton, whose father-in-law Dick Kitts was trainer and groundsman at the St Helens club said recently: "My wife remembers Bert Trautmann coming to her home when there was still some resentment from certain people about him being German and her mother welcomed him saying 'Well he is some mother's son'. Despite losing a son of her own in the conflict, they became very friendly with Bert and they regularly went to see him play at Manchester City" (ibid). Trautmann, then, soon became part of this working class community, drinking in the Junction Inn on Junction Lane[11] and wearing the cloth cap and muffler that still characterised the northern working class male (Ramsden 2006: 339). In January 1949, with Trautmann due to visit his family in Bremen, St Helens supporters presented him with a trunk full of groceries (donated via their own ration books) and an envelope containing fifty £1 notes – a considerable sum in those days (Rowlands 2005/1990: 81). When he received the Footballer of the Year in 1956 Trautmann made a brief, predictably humble speech, in which he paid tribute to "the man who represents the backbone of your national game – the chap on the popular side with his cloth cap and muffler, and penetrating voice. To him and his lady I owe more than I can hope to repay" (Ramsden 2006: 339f.). By that time, though, he had long since been integrated into the northern English working class. He wore his own cap and muffler. He could very easily have said '*our* national game'. On his visit to Bremen back in 1949, his brother had told him "You're a bloody Englishman now" (Rowlands 2005/1990: 82).

In October of 1949 Bert Trautmann moved into what might be called the aristocracy of sporting labour[12] when he signed for Manchester City. As he himself

---

10 http://www.suttonbeauty.org.uk/suttonhistory/sport.html. Access: 31st October 2011.

11 http://www.suttonbeauty.org.uk/suttonhistory/suttonpubs.html. Access: 31st October 2012.

12 I'm aware that historians have used the term 'aristocracy of labour' somewhat differently. As R.J. Morris puts it: "The labour aristocracy were a section of the 19th century working class who were relatively better paid, more secure, better treated at work and more able to control the organisation of their work". See his "The Labour Aristocracy and the British Class Struggle". In: *ReFresh: Recent Findings of Research in Social and Economic History*, Autumn 7, 1988: http://www.ehs.org.uk/ehs/refresh/assets/Morris7a.pdf. Access: 8th November 2012. English League footballers in the 1940s did not, of

reflected, this could be a test of his assimilation into northern football culture
since he was leaving St Helens "for the less parochial atmosphere of Manchester
and Salford with their combined populations of over a million people" (Rowlands
2005/1990: 102). According to a number of popular accounts, he was right to be
apprehensive. Indeed, it is a central element in the Trautmann myth that he won
over an angry Manchester football public calling for City not to sign this German.
Ramsden suggests that, when Trautmann's signing was mooted "all hell broke
out" (although, paradoxically he appears to offer several reasons why it did not)
(Ramsden 2006: 327-331). Clay suggests that 25,000 people demonstrated outside
City's Maine Road ground in the working class district of Moss Side and that the
local papers were deluged with abusive letters (Clay 2010: 274). Similarly, a number of contemporary websites carry the assertion that there was a demonstration
of 20,000 people in Manchester against the deal. Most of these accounts repeat the
phrase "The club's decision to sign a former Axis paratrooper sparked protests,
with 20,000 people attending a demonstration", which appears in Trautmann's
Wikipedia entry[13] and seems to have been cut and pasted by writers posting elsewhere on the web, perhaps with minor alterations to the wording. One site says
simply that 20,000 people "took to the streets"[14] and another that the same streets
were thronged by 40,000[15]. A further version has it that City received 20,000 letters of protest[16] and the most recent suggestion is a march of 25,000 by the writer
Anthony Clavane (2012: 89)[17]. In his autobiography Trautmann refers only to the
"hundreds of letters" that poured into the offices of the local press and to others apparently destroyed by his father-in-law (Trautmann 1956: 45). Rowlands
provides some good historical detail on Jewish Manchester, reports that the City
was divided (with the Jewish community and the Gentile ex-servicemen's club op-
posed to the transfer) and quotes Trautmann as saying that, given the controversy,
he wished at the time that he'd never left St Helens (Rowlands 2005/1990: 92f.).
But the local papers do not mention the actual demonstration and it is possible

course, fit this description; they became 'aristocrats' through social honour, as celebrity
exponents of 'the people's game'.

13 http://en.wikipedia.org/wiki/Bert_Trautmann. Access: 31st October 2012.

14 http://soccernet.espn.go.com/columns/story?id=344190&root=england&cc=5739. Access: 1st November 2012.

15 http://news.bbc.co.uk/1/hi/england/manchester/3972309.stm. Access: 3rd November
2012.

16 http://www.twohundredpercent.net/?refsite=www.nlads.com&ref=alexa-traffic-
rank&paged=545. Access: 1st November 2012.

17 I'm grateful to Anthony for assistance via email on this issue, between 2nd and 6th November 2012.

that it never took place[18]. Manchester City were resolved to sign Trautmann and wished to close the deal before any of a number of other clubs approached; it is highly unlikely that they would have permitted their ground to be used for a huge event aimed at protesting the transfer, so the demonstration would have had to take place in the neighbouring streets, creating chaos and, if the figure of 25,000 is to be believed, temporarily almost doubling the population of Moss Side.

It is also difficult to gauge the scale of opposition to Trautmann. Certainly there had been disquiet in Manchester, just as there had been taunts on the football fields of south Lancashire and reservations, as we've seen, in St Helens and elsewhere. There would be intermittent talk of angry letters and death threats. But those who proposed to organise a boycott of Manchester City, should Trautmann sign, seem in the end, as the record suggests, to have garnered little support. Certainly contemporary press reports suggest this.

On 6th October 1949, the day That Bert Trautmann had actually put pen to paper, the *Manchester Evening News* carried the following letter:

> "As a Jew, I feel very sore that Manchester City should contemplate signing a German (*Manchester Evening News* October 4th). The Germans killed six million of my brothers and sisters in the last war and the English public must have very short memories if they can forget the thousands of women and children killed in air raids in this country.
> I served in the First World War and was in Civil Defence in the Second World War. I have sent a telegram to the directors of Manchester City Football Club informing them that if they sign this German goalkeeper I will organise a boycott among the thousands of men belonging to the Jewish ex-servicemen's club who are City supporters, and also among British Legion members of the Cheetham branch. I am a member of both these organisations. I myself have been a City supporter for 45 years.
> Jewish City Supporter
> Manchester"

There were other letters of disapproval from men citing their military service[19]. The following day, however, the correspondence column of the *Evening News* carried a robust response. "Has 'Jewish City Supporter' previously complained about German women coming to this country to do nursing and domestic work in hos-

---

18 I'm very grateful to Gary James, the leading historian of Manchester City, for confirming this assessment to me in an email 1st November 2012. Similarly, Steve Humphries of Testimony Films, makers of *The Bert Trautmann Story*, told me that his research had found no evidence of a demonstration: email 8th December 2012.

19 *Manchester Evening News*, 6th October 2012: 2.

pitals? I suggest he is biased. Must we hate the whole German race? Would we have poured the money into the [Berlin] airlift as we did if this were so?" asked 'D.W.', another City supporter. "It doesn't matter two hoots", wrote L. Ball of Manchester 14, "if City's goalkeeper is German or English, black or white, Catholic or Protestant, Jewish or Gentile. It would only matter if he were a Fascist – or a poor goalie! The war was not fought against Germans, but against Fascists, whatever their nationality". Better an 'honest German', the writer added, than a member of the British Union of Fascists who had been interned during the war under Defence Regulation 18b. And a letter from Mrs F.M. Sutherland of Manchester 13 drew attention to post-war Jewish politics:

> "'Jewish City Supporter' accuses the Englishman of having a very short memory if he can forget what the Germans did during the war. Our memory is even shorter if we can forget many hundreds of British soldiers tortured and killed in Palestine after the war was over. [...] The war is over. As the wife of a British soldier I say let us forget and forgive both Germans and Jews"[20].

This latter was a particularly powerful intervention. Manchester had (and retains) a strong Jewish community and has been called 'the cradle of Zionism'[21], the Zionist tradition in the city dating back to the mid-1880s (see, for example, Williams 2008: 103-111). Militant Jewish groups such as the Lehi (or Stern Gang) had fought a guerrilla campaign against British forces in Mandatory Palestine after the Second World War, and there had been anti-Jewish riots in British cities, including Manchester, in 1947. These riots, as Tony Kushner pithily notes, "were an indication of who did and did not belong to British society" (Kushner 1993: 152). The guerrilla campaign had, of course, culminated in the establishment of the state of Israel the year before Trautmann came to Manchester and Chaim Weizmann, Israel's first president, was a former lecturer at Manchester University. Dr Alexander Altmann, Manchester's communal rabbi and a professional philosopher, stated that there was "no concerted action inside the community" in favour of a boycott of City (Trautmann 1956: 46). As Ramsden remarks: "The last thing Manchester's Jews wanted so soon after Israel's successful establishment was to be forced to choose between Britishness and Jewishness" (Ramsden 2006: 330). A further correspondence page favourable to Trautmann appeared the next

---

20 *Manchester Evening News*, 7th October 1949: 6.
21 'Manchester and the birth of Israel'. http://www.bbc.co.uk/manchester/content/articles/2008/05/12/140508_israel_weizmann_feature.shtml. Access: 1st November 2012.

day[22] and on the 10thOctober a sponsor of the boycott told the *Evening News*: "We have been thinking over the position and have decided to let the occasion pass"[23]. Four days later *The Jewish Chronicle* carried a short paragraph, noting the "choosing of a German to be goalkeeper for Manchester City Football Club has caused controversy in Manchester". A Jewish businessman had threatened a boycott "and will enlist the aid of Jewish ex-service organisations to support him. The organisations, however, have not taken any action".

The sole references to Trautmann in the *Manchester Guardian* at this time are similarly matter-of-fact: "Trautmann is given his first chance in goal…" (on the morning of his first team debut on 19th November[24]) and (following a draw at home to West Bromwich Albion on 10th December) "City are fortunate, so soon after Swift's retirement, to find a personality like Trautmann to guard their goal. […] For a six-footer, Trautmann gets down to low shots with remarkable ease and grace, but his manner of dealing with high ones calls for some adjustment"[25]. Even allowing for the comparative lack of interest shown by the national sports press of the time in events off the field of play, this does not read like the description of a man at the eye of a political storm.

This episode shows a preparedness of strands of public opinion, once again, to distinguish between invocations of nationality and/or ethnicity ('the Germans') and political philosophy (fascism) - the Second World War had, after all, been promoted and popularly seen as a 'people's war' against fascism, and not against 'the Hun', as with the First[26]. Moreover, there was a recognition that world politics had moved on from the Second World War and that new conflicts were now in play. Most significantly it showed that, in capitalist Europe, labour markets were free of wartime emergency measures and back in operation. Just as German nurses were now welcome to fill vacancies in the British National Health Service, the resumption of League football (and its transfer system) in 1946 meant that a conspicuously talented German goalkeeper who just happened to be living nearby and, as an amateur, was available for next to nothing, was a prime candi-

---

22 *Manchester Evening News*, 8th October 1949: 5.

23 *Manchester Evening News*, 10th October 1949: 1.

24 Manchester Guardian, 19th November 1949: 3.

25 "City 1 West Bromwich Albion 1 NO IMPROVEMENT AT MOSS SIDE", by an Old International, *Manchester Guardian*, 12th December 1949: 6.

26 I'm grateful to Tony Collins for this suggestion. For discussion of this issue see, for example Angus Calder (1971) and Donny Gluckstein (2012). Calder argues that public opinion was, of course, diverse; Gluckstein that, for Britain, there were, in effect, parallel wars – a popular one against fascism and a ruling class one in defence of the British Empire.

date to staff the vacancy between the goalposts at Manchester City. Trautmann was a valuable *asset* on the football labour market – a number of other clubs were known to be after him – and this trumped any other considerations. Within hours of the publication of 'Jewish City Supporter's' proposal of a boycott, and whatever the feelings of Manchester's Jewish and Gentile ex-servicemen, City had his signature. Trautmann was publicly welcomed at Maine Road by club captain Eric Westwood with the words "there is no war in this dressing room". Rowlands suggests that Westwood had been briefed by Smith and describes the phrase as "well rehearsed" (Rowlands 2005/1990: 96f.). It is said that Westwood, who had been in the British army during the war, was privately distressed by Trautmann's arrival[27]. But it is also worth noting that the Second World War had been over for four years by this time and, as Clay suggests, animosity toward German PoWs had been 'virtually gone' for three of those (Clay 2010: 224). Moreover, the historian Sophie Jackson notes that, for many German PoWs in England, "the fears of reprisals and hatred they had assumed would greet them were unfounded" (Jackson 2010: 173).

So, if life in St Helens had cemented Trautmann's *subjective* working class identity, his experience at City confirmed, and somewhat adjusted, his *objective* class position. As a professional footballer he became a member of a skilled, often privileged, but uniquely *tied* working class elite. English clubs still operated the retain-and-transfer system, instituted in 1893, whereby clubs retained their players' registrations and would not permit them to work elsewhere if they didn't want them to. In late 1952, having been approached by the German club Gelsenkirchen-Schalke 04 and concerned about the wellbeing of his family, Trautmann asked to leave Manchester City and go back to Germany. Schalke offered what was, in the predominantly amateur German system, a large sum of money but City refused to release the player. Bert was given the front page of the Manchester *Evening Chronicle* on which to put his case. Pictured with his wife, he wrote of his need to go home, despite his reluctance to "leave a country where I have received nothing but friendliness and kindness, especially from Manchester City and their supporters"[28]. City chairman Robert Smith responded in the *Evening News* two days later. Trautmann, he said, had turned down the offer of a house (which would, nevertheless, have belonged to Manchester City); taking outside jobs into consideration (Trautmann worked as a motor mechanic in Hulme in Manchester) he was City's top earner; Schalke had only offered £432 and two friendly matches,

---

27 Thanks to Colin Shindler, another chronicler of Manchester City matters, for suggesting this to me in an email, 1st November 2012.
28 Bert Trautmann: "Why I have to leave Manchester City". Manchester *Evening Chronicle*, 3rd December 1952: 1.

and so on. "We have had some unfortunate experiences with goalkeepers", he said, "and just because we are sufficiently alert to discover one at small cost some folk think our valuation should remain the same, but they do not understand the economics of the game"[29]. Trautmann remained a Manchester City player until his retirement in 1964. The point here is that, whatever the 'good German' did to melt the hearts of the Manchester football public, his thrilling performances and personal charm in no way mitigated his position as tied football worker. If Manchester City had (as they almost certainly had) reflected local opinion when they had taken Trautmann on, they just as certainly defied it now. "City's directors owe him more than he owes them", wrote 'D.B.' of Cheetham Hill to the *Manchester Evening News*[30]; letters to the *Evening Chronicle* on the matter, meanwhile, ran 90% in the player's favour[31].

2   "Last week I got a letter from China. Unbelievable!"[32]: Bert Trautmann, Heritage and Globalisation

It seems, then, that the notion of Bert Trautmann as a one-man United Nations gained ground some time *after* the business of disposing of wartime enmities had actually been transacted, certainly in the North West of England. It has been suggested that London, much bombed in the Blitz of 1940-1, was a hurdle of acceptance that he still had to clear and much is made of his performance for City at Fulham in January 1950. Trautmann himself, prompted by his father-in-law, supposed that the national press and Londoners generally would regard him with suspicion: "All round the ground I could imagine people taking stock of me and saying: 'So that's him. That's the so-and-so Nazi, is it?' But I misjudged the people of Fulham…" (Trautmann 1956: 49f.). Trautmann put in a memorable performance (although City lost 0-1) and the players formed an avenue of congratulation for him at full-time. They may well have been applauding simply a very good goalkeeper, rather than, as he supposed, a now-forgiven German ex-soldier.

In 1956 what became the central fact of Trautmann's public life occurred. He represented Manchester City against Birmingham City in the FA Cup Final of

---

29 'Trautmann: City state THE FACTS'. *Manchester Evening News*, 5th December 1952: 32.

30 *Manchester Evening News*, 8th December 1952: 13.

31 "'Let him go a free man" plea to City'. Manchester *Evening Chronicle*, 9th December 1952: 13.

32 Bert Trautmann in conversation with Catrine Clay, Manchester, October 2007. See Clay 2010: 2.

1956 and, toward the end of the game, damaged his neck diving at the feet of Birmingham forward Peter Murphy. Although badly hurt he played on and finished
the game, which Manchester won. Days later he was found to have broken several
vertebrae. This has become the most famous injury in football history, dwarfing
others, just as dramatic and more serious, such as the death of Glasgow Celtic
goalkeeper John Thomson in similar circumstances in a match against Rangers in
1931[33]. At the time, the Cup final was seen as a national event and it was broadcast
live every year on BBC television. The audience for the Final of 1956 was around
5 million[34], many of whom may well not have been regular followers of football
(working class people, the bedrock of football spectatorship, tended not to have
television sets in the mid-1950s) or have heard of Bert Trautmann. His nationality
will have raised eyebrows, partly because foreign players were rare in the Football League and partly because he was German, and his injury, and his plucky
response to it, became imprinted on the national memory. Indeed, during the
1950s, Trautmann seems to have become a suitable repository for English national
myths: as Ramsden puts it, it was now widely assumed that: "Trautmann had
healed war wounds between the two countries, but in part this reflected the splendid tolerance of the English" (Ramsden 2006: 339)[35]. The myth was frequently
corroborated by his ghostwriters and the ever-grateful keeper himself. Significantly, Trautmann's autobiography, a standard 'as-told-to' volume published in
1956[36] and carrying an addendum informing readers of his broken neck, went to
several editions and made him the (then) extraordinary sum of £3,350 – enough
money for him to pay for a house in cash (Clay 2010: 304). In the foreword to the
book, Sir Stanley Rous, Secretary of the FA, wrote: "It is typical of football in this
country that not only have we accepted Trautmann as a player, but we have come
to praise his splendid goalkeeping and admire his rich personality" (Trautmann
1956: 9).

Trautmann retired as a player in 1964 and was invited to manage Stockport
County. After less than two years in the job (1965-6) he returned to Germany
and had short spells as trainer to two clubs there - Preussen Munster (1967-8) and

---

33 The incident can be seen on Youtube, http://www.youtube.com/watch?v=juUG-
NUfCpSc. Posted 4th December 2010. Access 2nd November 2012.

34 http://en.wikipedia.org/wiki/1956_FA_Cup_Final. Access: 2nd November 2012.

35 Ramsden's account of Trautmann is well researched and documented but he does not,
so far as I can see, attempt a coherent argument about Trautmann and myth.

36 *Steppes to Wembley* was re-published in London by the Sportsman's Book Club in 1957
and by Panther Books, also in London, in 1958. Robert Hale, the original publishers,
were unable, given the passage of time, to provide sales figures.

Opel Russelsheim (1968-9) – before disappearing from public (that's to say European) view in the early 1970s. After a well-publicised business failure, the remainder of Bert Trautmann's working life was spent working for the German Football Association, chiefly as a football coach in emergent nations where the GFA or the German government were perceived to have strategic interests. He coached in Burma, Tanzania, Liberia, Pakistan, North Yemen and Malta successively, before retiring to live in Spain in 1988.

Bert Trautmann re-emerged as a public figure in 2004. That year the seal was set on his oft-proclaimed Englishness by the award of an OBE, conferred at the British embassy in Berlin, the citation being his promotion of Anglo-German understanding through football. Earlier that year, at the instigation of three German football writers, the Bert Trautmann Foundation was established in Berlin and news of the OBE usually accompanied news of the Foundation[37]. One account has it that the Foundation was Trautmann's idea[38], another that the initiative came from the three (anglophile) football journalists (Rowlands 2005/1990: 250). The purpose of the Foundation was said to be to combat the persistence in the UK of negative stereotypes about German people, evidenced by "regular physical attacks on German schoolchildren visiting the UK". Trautmann, apparently still in demand for charity, trade and sporting functions both in Manchester and Germany, seemed the ideal figurehead. The Foundation would seek, according to its website, to impart "positive values to young people' and 'also contribute positively to European integration, and especially the German-British relationship" by funding camps and placements for youngsters from the two countries, each of whom would receive the Trautmann Award[39]. There would be sponsors and there was interest from the two governments.

It's fair to say, however, that, appraising his long life, Bert Trautmann's most powerful cultural presence was in the North West of England; he became, in Ramsden's words, "a revered figure" in Manchester (Ramsden 2006: 325). His relationship to the country of his birth has been tenuous by comparison. Manchester City toured Germany several times in the early 1950s and Trautmann is said to have been the main draw (although the visit of an English club attracted a lot of British servicemen still stationed in Germany). Trautmann never played for Germany, largely because coaches in the 1950s seldom considered players not

---

37 See, for example, BBC website http://news.bbc.co.uk/1/hi/england/manchester/3972309.stm. Posted 1st November 2004. Access: 3rd November 2012.

38 http://mcivta.com/mcivta/10/40.html. Access: 4th November 2012.

39 http://www.trautmann-foundation.org/index2.html. Access: 21st February 2012. By autumn 2012 the website had been taken down.

playing in their own home league. In December of 1953 the Manchester *Evening Chronicle* carried a story by Eric Todd about German pools companies organising a fund to bring Trautmann back to Germany, but nothing further was heard of this[40]. In the early 1960s Bert became consultant to some Anglo-German businesses (Rowlands 2005/1990: 209), but does not appear to have had a business career. Apart from his brief tenure at Munster and Russelsheim, Trautmann spent the remainder of his working life abroad. Aside from the ephemeral nature of the process itself – the novelist John Updike one referred to "that mostly imaginary activity termed 'cultural exchange'" (Updike 1972:12) – for much of this latter period his scope for promoting Anglo-German football relations will have been limited and, on its own, this seems an improbable basis either for the rediscovery of Bert Trautmann in the early twenty first century or for the honours bestowed on him – in addition to his OBE, Bert was guest of honour when England played Germany in Berlin in 2008, receiving an award from the German FA.

Trautmann's re-emergence seems to be to do with the upsurge in interest in, and the commodification of, history. As Paul Armstrong and Janet Coles observe, "Fascination with the past is an increasingly fashionable theme in popular culture" and they refer, aptly, to "the way we consume our yesterdays" (Armstrong / Collins 2008: 65, 69). This process has had several dimensions which are important here. First there is the widespread desire, in an increasingly individualised age[41], of people to explore their own history (as evidenced by the popularity of TV programmes such *Who Do you Think You Are?*, a popular genealogy documentary series begun by the BBC in 2004) as well as that of their communities, pleasures and affiliations. A website celebrating the history of the Sutton district of St Helens, for example, was begun in 2006 by a local resident and web designer in his mid-50s[42]. Similar history sites for football clubs have begun to proliferate and there has been a rash of club histories and football biographies, most of them written in the last twenty years. In England this trend has run roughly parallel to the founding of the Premier League in 1992 and part of its impulse has, arguably, been to salvage a sense of the 'people's game' amid the encroachments of commercialisation, branding, television and globalisation. The same clubs, we are reminded, whose

40 Eric Todd "German pools plan to pay £25,000 fee for Trautmann". Manchester: *Evening Chronicle*, 10th December 1953: 1-2.

41 As argued by leading contemporary social theorists such as Zygmunt Bauman and Ulrich Beck. See, for example, Zygmunt Bauman 2001 and Ulrich Beck and Elisabeth Beck-Gernsheim 2002.

42 http://www.suttonbeauty.org.uk/about.html. Access: 6th November 2012. Telephone interview with the site designer Stephen Wainwright, 6th November 2012.

players are now multimillionaires recruited from around the world, were once represented on the field by ordinary working class blokes, who parted their hair down the middle, were paid £15 a week and worked part-time as electricians or painters and decorators[43]. The clubs themselves, eager perhaps to embrace the past in order to endorse the present, have followed this trend, erecting statues to former players and managers and making sure that their spanking new stadia show a sense of heritage. For example, at Bolton Wanderers' Reebok Stadium, opened in 1997, there is a conference hall named 'The Lion of Vienna Suite', a reference to the Bolton player Nat Lofthouse, a local man and former miner (he was conscripted as a 'Bevin Boy in 1943), who scored for England against Austria in Vienna in 1952. (Lofthouse later managed – as a caretaker – and became president of the club, but the suite's name prefers him in the early 1950s.) Like any other club, Manchester City have been subject to this heritage work. They have a prolific independent historian[44] and, City's past has been fully excavated. Trautmann, his transition from Bremen to Lancashire and, in particular, his fabled injury have been an expectable part of this process. In 1995, as Ramsden notes, the Manchester City supporters' fanzine changed its name from *Electric Blue* to *Bert Trautmann's Helmet* - an ironic reference to the long-running joke among Manchester United Supporters that this was the only thing in City's trophy cabinet (Ramsden 2006: 325); perhaps inevitably, there is now a fan blog called *Bert Trautmann's Neck*[45].

But it will also have been clear to various media personnel that the Trautmann odyssey held strong possibilities for the wider media-history market. After all, as recent commentary has observed, using a time-honoured simile, Trautmann's life could now be seen as "an incredible tale of *Boys Own* heroism"[46]. More specifically, for filmmakers, biographers and, beyond them, a mass audience, Trautmann offered attractive themes: football (by now enjoying the status of a global preoccupation), heroism (Bert's injury) and heritage. Added to this was the vital element of the Second World War[47] – archive footage and depictions of which abound on contemporary, globalised multi-channel television and is likely be seen by viewers with no direct experience of it (now the majority) as an adventure. In this context Trautmann's life might be received in a variety of ways. Bert has recently said, for example, that most of his copious postbag while a player came from communist

---

43 See Gary Imlach (2005) for an excellent evocation of this vanished social world.

44 Gary James. See, for example, his club history (James 2012).

45 http://manuruinedme.blogspot.co.uk/. Access: 7th November 2012.

46 Stevens "From Iron Cross....", see footnote 9.

47 For a discussion of the dominance of war in television history see Roger Smither 2007: 51-66.

East Germany: "I can't explain it. I imagine that people liked my story. They were locked in. Perhaps they liked the fact that a former prisoner of war was allowed to experience freedom"[48]. Besides which he offered a happy ending – comfortable retirement in Spain, via the brutality of wartime Ukraine and improbable redemption in south Lancashire.

It does seem now that the widely cited demonstration by twenty (or twenty five, or forty) thousand people against Trautmann's coming to Manchester City did not take place. It's quite possible that it is an urban myth. If so, it is a self-serving myth fashioned retrospectively during the 1950s to exalt the notion of British tolerance: when Trautmann appeared between the sticks in the Cup Final of 1956, a collective impulse insisted that the very presence of a German attested to the forgiving nature of the British. Equally, the thousands cited in the demonstration story may be seen as a metaphor for the Jewish presence in Manchester football culture: Manchester City, after all, had a big Jewish following, which had been building since the 1920s[49]. Moreover, the initial proposal for a boycott, besides using the word 'thousands', had invoked the Holocaust and, since the Holocaust remained at the heart of Jewish politics, these thousands of Jewish City supporters were, in a sense, an aggrieved *immanence* in the affair– an implied demonstration that lacked simply the rabbi's permission for it to take place. Whatever their prior feelings or actions, they, like the rest of the City crowd, soon warmed to Bert. In the powerful Trautmann myth they too may therefore have been regarded as having been 'won over' – winning over the demonstrators, that's to say, without their actually having demonstrated.

Bert Trautmann's OBE, then, seems to have been a reward for embodying his own myth, for being an intriguing historical figure, who was born German but became English (and thus a *de facto* motif for transaction between the two countries) and, unlike most of his contemporaries, was still alive. Once again he became a repository for reactionary notions of Britishness. In November 2011 the English football team played Spain and were rebuked by FIFA for wearing Remembrance Day poppies. The right wing *Daily Mail* consulted Trautmann, who obliged the paper by saying: "I always wear a poppy when I'm in England in November. Who objects to it? It doesn't cause offence to anybody. Germans have

---

48 http://www.11freunde.de/interview/bernd-trautmann-ueber-seine-grosse-karriere-england. Access: 3rd February 2013. Translation by Shirley Wagg.

49 I'm grateful to Dave Dee for this information: email 7th November 2012. See David Dee 'Jews and British Sport: Integration, Ethnicity and Anti-Semitism c.1880-1960' PhD Thesis, De Montfort University, 2011. Available online at http://www.academia.edu/731943/Jews_and_British_Sport_Integration_Ethnicity_and_anti-Semitism_c1880-c1960.

no problem with it. It's important to remember what happened in the past"[50]. The same year he similarly obliged the populist tabloid the *Sun* by saying "I played the FA Cup Final with a broken neck but my biggest achievement was just being accepted by my teammates"[51].

P.S.

Bert Trautmann passed away on 19th July 2013 at his home in Spain, while this book was in press.

Bibliography

Armstrong, P. / Coles, J. (2008): Repackaging the Past: Commodification, Consumerism and the Study of History. In: Convergence, Volume XLI No.1, 63-76.

Barthes, R. (1973): Mythologies. St Albans: Paladin.

Bauman, Z. (2001): The Individualized Society. Cambridge: Polity Press.

Beck, U. / Beck-Gernsheim, E. (2002): Individualization. London: Sage.

Calder, A. (1971): The People's War. London: Panther Books.

Clavane, A. (2012): Does Your Rabbi Know You're Here: The Story of English Football's Forgotten Tribe. London: Quercus.

Clay, C. (2010): Trautmann's Journey: from Hitler Youth to FA Cup Legend. London: Yellow Jersey Press.

Gluckstein, D. (2012): A People's History of the Second World War. London: Pluto Press.

Imlach, G. (2005): My Father and Other Working Class Football Heroes. London: Yellow Jersey Press.

Jackson, S. (2010): Churchill's Uninvited Guests: Prisoners of War in Britain in World War II. Port Stroud: The History Press.

James, G. (2012): Manchester. The City Years Halifax: James Ward.

Kushner, T. (1993): Anti-Semitism and austerity: the August 1947 riots in Britain. In: Panikos, P. (ed.): Racial Violence in Britain 1840-1950 London: Leicester University Press, 149-168.

Mills, C. W. (1970): The Sociological Imagination. Harmondsworth: Penguin.

---

50 Chris Wheeler: "Legendary German stopper Trautmann backs poppy cause", http://www.dailymail.co.uk/sport/football/article-2059628/Bert-Trautmann-backs-poppy-cause.html. Posted 9th November 2011. Access: 7th November 2012.

51 Martin Phillips: "I played the FA Cup Final with a broken neck but my biggest achievement was just being accepted by my teammates". http://www.thesun.co.uk/sol/homepage/sport/football/3488602/Bert-Trautmann-The-Nazi-who-became-a-Man-City-star.html Posted 24th March 2011. Access: 7th November 2012.

Ramsden, J. (2006): Don't Mention the War: The British and the Germans since 1890. London: Little, Brown.

Rowlands, A. (2005) [1990]: Trautmann: The Biography. Derby: Breedon Books.

Smither, R. (2007): Why Is So Much Television History About War? In: Cannadine, D. (ed.): History and the Media. Basingstoke: Palgrave Macmillan, 51-66.

Trautmann, B. (1956): Steppes to Wembley. London: Robert Hale.

Updike, J. (1972): Bech: A Book. Harmondsworth: Penguin.

Williams, B. (2008): Jewish Manchester: An Illustrated History. Derby: Breedon Books.

Acknowledgements Thanks to Kristian Naglo and Tony Waine for their invitation to write this essay and for their supportive engagement with it, once written. Thanks also to Peter Bramham, Ron Greenall and David Dee who were kind enough to read the first draft of this essay and to make helpful comments on it. Thanks likewise to Anthony Clavane, Tony Collins, Robert Hale of Robert Hale publishers, Steve Humphries, Gary James, Colin Shindler, Shirley Wagg and Stephen Wainwright for their help in the preparation of the essay.

The Phenomenon of David Beckham: Incorporating Cultural Mobility and Cosmopolitanism

Das Phänomen David Beckham: Kulturelle Mobilität und Kosmopolitismus

Anthony Waine & Vivien Hacker

Abstract

Drawing on the holistic footballing philosophy of the former West German team coach Helmut Schön, the authors apply Schön's contention, that the true 'Meisterspieler' must undergo a learning process as much off the field as on it, to David Beckham. Our essay stresses Beckham's exceptional ability to adapt to different cultures in Europe and the United States, and contrasts his versatility and therefore cultural mobility with that of many other British players who have ventured abroad in the past. His successful personal journey, from very ordinary suburban roots via the northern heartlands of English football, to becoming most recently a globally recognised ambassador for Great Britain at the 2012 Olympic Games, underlines not only his charismatic personality but also his acquired cosmopolitan identity. These qualities, coupled with his extraordinary talents as a footballer and a uniquely global appeal, help to explain the post-modern cultural significance and phenomenon of the Englishman.

Zusammenfassung

Ausgehend von der holistischen Fußball-Philosophie des ehemaligen Bundestrainers Westdeutschlands, Helmut Schön, wenden die Autoren dessen Argument, dass der wahre 'Meisterspieler' sich einem Lernprozess sowohl außerhalb des Stadions als auch auf dem Spielfeld unterziehen muss, auf David Beckham an. Unser Beitrag betont Beckhams außergewöhnliche Fähigkeit, sich unterschiedlichen Kulturen in Europa und den Vereinigten Staaten anzupassen, und stellt seine Flexibilität und damit kulturelle Beweglichkeit der mangelnden Anpassungsfähigkeit vieler anderer britischer Spieler gegenüber,

die in der Vergangenheit den Schritt ins Ausland wagten. Sein Lebensweg
führte ihn von relativ einfachen, vorstädtischen Wurzeln über das nördliche
Kerngebiet (sozusagen Mutterland) des englischen Fußballs hin zu einem
global anerkannten Botschafter für Großbritannien, wie unlängst bei den
Olympischen Spielen im Jahr 2012. Nicht nur seine charismatische Persönlichkeit, sondern auch seine erworbene kosmopolitische Identität werden
durch den erfolgreichen persönlichen Werdegang unterstrichen. Diese Eigenschaften, in Verbindung mit seinem außergewöhnlichen Talent als Fußballer
und einer einzigartigen globalen Anziehungskraft, tragen dazu bei, das postmoderne Phänomen Beckham sowie die kulturelle Bedeutung des Engländers
zu erklären.

1   The 'Spielerpersönlichkeit': A Holistic Approach

*A player's personality will only ever reach the highest degree of maturity if he has
experienced all the highs and lows in his sporting career and learned how to adapt to
the manifold realities on the field of play and outside the stadium. An apprenticeship
is necessary, the outcomes of which cannot be achieved on the training field alone.*
Helmut Schön[1]

*I am personally very grateful to writers like Böttiger or Schulze-Marmeling who look
at football in a different way. But one mustn't turn football into a science. The best one
can do is to throw light on individual phenomena and try and see what's behind them.*
Günter Netzer[2]

The name of Helmut Schön is inextricably linked with one of the greatest
eras in European and indeed world football. In 1964, aged 49, Schön became
'Bundestrainer' ('federal team coach'), i.e. manager of West Germany. He remained in that post until 1978, making him one of the longest serving international coaches of any major national team. In the course of the fourteen years in
charge of the team he took them to the final of the World Cup at Wembley in 1966,
followed by a Third Place four years later in Mexico. In 1972 West Germany won
the European Championships, and were duly crowned World Champions in 1974.
Two years on from this triumph and he once more guided his team through to the

---

1   Schön 1974: 45. This quotation and all other original German quotations in the chapter
    have been translated into English by Anthony Waine and Vivien Hacker.
2   As quoted in the preface to Schulze-Marmeling 2000: 8.

final of the European Championships. Helmut Schön has probably been the most successful international manager in the history of the game.

He had also been a very good player himself, representing his country on sixteen occasions and scoring seventeen goals. Not untypically for continental football development in the earlier part of the twentieth century, there had been an important British connection and influence on him when still a youth. Schön was 13 years old when Jimmy Hogan became the coach of Dresden FC[3], and he learned from Hogan the importance of skills training, the one-two passing game and 'springing surprises during play'. Decades later Schön referred to Hogan as "mein leuchtendes Vorbild" ("my shining role model") (Biermann 2012: 51). Whilst in charge of a succession of West German team formations he guided the international career of Uwe Seeler, Gerd Müller, Wolfgang Overath, Paul Breitner, Berti Vogts, and most notably that of two of the most gifted individual players ever to grace European football pitches, Günter Netzer and Franz Beckenbauer. Schön's style of management was non-hierarchical (giving key players considerable personal responsibility in games), liberal and intellectual, and emphasising creative thinking and playing, especially one generated from the mid-field spaces. Typical of his eschewing of dogma and dictatorial attitudes as well as of his sociological conception of the game as a microcosm of social dynamics is his belief that: "Football is in its own way a playful model of our social relationships. So straightforward that everyone can understand it, and so full of variations that, as in life, ever new constellations can arise" (Schulze-Marmeling 2005: 164).

Bearing in mind Schön's own illustrious career both as player and international team coach, we will briefly summarise his thoughts on what actually makes a great player. In an essay published in 1974 and appearing in the anthology *Netzer kam aus der Tiefe des Raumes* (*Netzer Appeared out of Nowhere*) the West German coach distinguishes between the semi-anonymous yet valuable player serving his fellow players whom he called the 'water carrier', and the individual capable of imposing his will on the team and on the style of the entire game whom he deems a 'Spielerpersönlichkeit'. Regarding the English equivalent of this term, typically encased inside a German compound noun, it is impossible to make an idiomatic translation of it. Literally it translates as 'player personality' and this mechanical rendition does at least emphasise how a player's personality is as decisive as

---

3   Jimmy Hogan was one of the pioneers of continental European football between 1910 and 1934. He spent one season at Dresden FC in 1928. The German football magazine, *11 Freunde Spezial*, devoted to 'Football's coming home. Die Geschichte des Britischen Fußballs' pays tribute to him and 'The Missionaries of the Holy British Football'; see edition of September 2012: 48-51.

his playing abilities. Such a player's ensemble of qualities (and skills) will radiate outwards and mobilise his fellow players and implicitly of course mobilise the spectators too. To do a little more justice therefore in English to the semantics of the word 'Spielerpersönlichkeit' and the connotations Schön imbues it with, one might speak of a 'charismatic playing personality'.

An aura or mystique therefore surrounds this exceptional individual. Schön's essay draws attention to how he "pulls the strings" on the pitch, how he knows when to "improvise" in "critical phases of the game", moving literally against the run of play (Schön 1974: 44). He "adapts his behaviour" technically and tactically to cope with "all situations" (ibid: 45). To be an inspiration to his fellow players he also has to display a readiness to give the greatest degree of physical commitment and show "leadership qualities" (ibid). In particular the notion of "adaptability" is crucial to Schön's inventory of gifts and qualities embodied by the "greats of football" (ibid). The truly great player not only adapts to the ever changing patterns of play on the field but, crucially, to the social dynamics off the field too. Modestly Schön claims that no coach can "train" or "breed" this personality, but he can create the space in which talent grows and attains maturity (ibid). He is suggesting, we believe, that such individuals possess talent that is given and cannot "be acquired through the labours performed on the training pitch alone" (ibid). The real crux for Schön is this: talent resides in the entirety of a player's being, in his corporeal but also equally in his "intellectual-spiritual" ("geistig-seelisch") assets (ibid). In short, Schön's philosophy is holistic, seeking to encompass the totality of an individual player's being, and viewing the outstanding player as being the true incorporation of all our human parts, that is to say their em–bodi–ment. Schön's ideas pointed to important changes in future thinking about how coaches at both club and international level should treat their players as rounded human beings. In his chapter on the changing sub-culture of football players and their clubs, Giulianotti observes precisely such a philosophy being embraced by certain continental club sides in the eighties and nineties: "Modernist coaching techniques presume that the club is responsible only for teaching the player football skills, thus tolerating his personal failure in elementary social skills. Conversely, the more post-modern coaching techniques of Ajax (latterly) and Inter adopt a holistic educational strategy, cultivating a more rounded and cerebral individuality within each player... A post-modern, holistic educational strategy prepares players for life outside of football" (Giulianotti 1999: 115).

Schön's thoughts as summarised in our introduction were formulated most likely in the late sixties or early seventies as he took stock of the first twenty years of post-war football in a Europe still divided by the Iron Curtain. He asks rhetorically whether charismatic playing personalities have become rare, and admits that he cannot answer his own question with a clear yes or no: "In today's football it is more difficult to develop into a charismatic playing personality and to prove oneself in this role. In many respects the demands have become greater than in previous eras. More than ever before, ability, qualities of leadership and adaptability play a role in addition to the possession of outstanding intellectual-spiritual merits" (Schön 1974: 45). Schön concludes his cogent portrait of the modern soccer player by referring us to cycle racing such as the Tour de France where the "water carriers" enable the "Meisterfahrer" or "master cyclist" to be victorious (ibid: 46). In football the "less fully fledged playing personalities with their undaunted work-rate and fighting spirit" (ibid: 46) help complete the "show directed by" the person whom he, in conclusion, fittingly calls the "Meisterspieler" (ibid: 46). This image of the "master player" is indeed redolent of German social and educational values, for the term "Meister" refers to the master craftsman who has completed his own apprenticeship and possesses the authority to train and guide those under him, but the term also has the sense of "champion". Furthermore, his usage of the word "inszenieren" ("directing the show") to express the dominance of the great play maker implicitly captures the theatrical nature of the compelling and thrilling sporting spectacle of two teams engaged in an unfolding drama. The role of the charismatic 'master player' pulling the strings on centre stage is certainly a productive one for us as we now move towards analysing the character and the achievements of a player who represented his country on 115 occasions between 1996 and 2009, and, even more pertinently, captained England 59 times.

2   Football, Post-Modern Culture, Words and Their Import

Beckham's playing career takes place effectively a good two to three decades later than the era being described by the former West German coach, and the social, cultural and economic context has changed in almost every respect. "The demands", as Schön said, have indeed "become greater than in previous eras" (Schön 1974: 45). These demands stretch across the whole gamut of rapidly changing modern societies exposed to the globalising forces of a post-Cold War era. Economically one has seen ever rising levels of commercial involvement in the game, be it in the form of sponsorship, merchandising, television advertising, and generally the corporate branding of top clubs. Progressively rising players' salaries have led to an ever more accelerating social velocity of individuals (such as Beckham) from a working class milieu, outwards and upwards into a new elite of super-wealthy high achievers drawn from the world of pop music, show business, film, the creative arts, fashion, and latterly sport. In fact, sport has come to occupy a central and expanding space in the domain of leisure and recreation thus providing the entertainment and pleasure we seek. And, as we, the people, are expected to pay for these valuable wares of our lifestyle, so we demand in return gratification from 'our' sporting actors, especially from the 'charismatic playing personalities'.

Whilst Helmut Schön evidently still felt comfortable using terms such as 'player', 'personality' and 'charisma', the language in which and with which football is now discussed and debated has changed along with the trends adumbrated in the previous paragraph. The former West German manager spoke about technique, tactics, body strength, character and attitude when he was assessing sporting prowess and potential. Here was a factual and traditional register of human qualities and athletic talents at his disposal with which to characterise the charismatic playing personality. Since Schön's era, however, this register of still recognisably human qualities has been supplanted by an inflationary and hyperbolic diction culled increasingly from the world of mythology, religion (or at least pseudo-religion), astronomy and show business. One speaks of a player's 'image', glorifies his status as a 'hero' or more likely as a 'star', and embellishes this stratospheric status even further with the superlatives 'mega-star' and 'super-star'. This status is of course also expressed through the Spanish 'galactico', a term synonymous with the galaxy of stars from around the world assembled by Real Madrid from the early fifties onwards, and in 2003 David Beckham himself joined this illustrious team of galactic stars.[4] The accolade though which places the 'charismatic playing personalities' completely outside the framework of ordinary human experience and firmly into the sphere of religious idolatry, is 'icon', not infrequently accompanied by the epithet 'global'. The popular soccer players who appear regularly in the public gaze are also deemed 'celebrities', or 'media stars' or 'media superstars'. The lexis of German language reporting is qualitatively the same with their terminology strongly impregnated by Anglo-Americanisms. In German press reports on David Beckham one invariably comes across 'Fußball-Star', 'Fußball-Ikone', 'Weltklasse-Fußballer', 'Englands Fußball-Idol', 'Trendsetter', and 'Glamourboy'.

This chapter's authors too have not felt able to escape these changing linguistic values and have consciously chosen to integrate the word 'phenomenon' into the title. Firstly, for the purposes of this essay it is used in the everyday sense of something or somebody embodying such significant meaning for a large number of observers that it may be considered representative of the *Zeitgeist* or spirit of the age, and is therefore worthy of public interest. Secondly, we are following Günter

---

4   And, of course, he moved on from Real Madrid's galaxy of stars to join Los Angeles Galaxy.

Netzer's perfectly sensible advice, which we have quoted as a preface for the chapter, "to throw light on individual phenomena and try and see what's behind them" in order to understand a little better the aesthetic effect of football, and sport in general, on our senses and thus on the collective imagination of us, the masses. For this reason we have introduced the subject of outstanding individual players through the expert critical reflections of Helmut Schön. Using his more temperate terminology and relying on his impressive footballing wisdom and experience we are trying from the outset to grasp the 'Spielerpersönlichkeit' and 'Meisterspieler' David Beckham as an integrated, corporeal and psychological-spiritual reality not in isolation but through his play-ful, complex interactions with the other 21 players around him on the pitch and through the equally play-ful game he has learned to contest with the media and popular culture in general off the pitch.

In adopting this approach we are attempting to sidestep the pitfalls of the perspective found, for example, in Ellis Cashmore's biography of the footballer. His book portrays Beckham far less as an integrated human personality or as an extraordinary player with both on-field and off-field charisma, but as a rather vacuous product of the post-modern nexus of culture industry, modern media, and of pure naked marketing and self-marketing. Manchester United (the only English team for which Beckham ever played apart from a brief spell for Preston North End on loan) is, in Cashmore's analysis, the crucible in which this nexus is initially forged: "Beckham's inauguration in football was through a club that was in the process of building one of the world's leading sports brands [...] Almost by default, Beckham became part of a brand. He acquired the cachet associated with United. Playing for a global brand was vital for Beckham: it drew him media attention in a way that would have been impossible if he had played for a lesser club" (Cashmore 2004: 16). Moving on in a later chapter to consider the circumstances surrounding his transfer from Manchester United to Real Madrid, Cashmore opines: "With the likes of Zidane, Figo, Ronaldo and Raul on its roster, Real already had a surplus of talent. Beckham may not have had the technical proficiency of these players, but he had something they lacked: global renown. At the time of his transfer, he was the supreme celebrity athlete. Real was buying a commodity as much as a player" (ibid: 54). The author quite openly concedes that he is interested "less in Beckham the man, more in the extensive changes that have affected contemporary popular culture, a culture that has created Beckham the phenomenon" (ibid: 56). And the phenomenon is the result of "the emergence of a special kind of culture that reveres and pays homage to celebrities" (ibid).

These examples selected from Cashmore's arguments paint a picture of a sportsman who is an object, and a willing one at that, of contemporary global forces. He does not actually function as a sovereign individual subject, an agent of his own destiny, but rather as a "brand", even "a global brand", a "commodity", and a mass-manufactured "celebrity". One of our objectives in this essay, on the other hand, is to argue that David Beckham's odyssey from Leytonstone in East London via Manchester United, Real Madrid, Los Angeles Galaxy, AC Milan, and finally at the age of 37, to Paris Saint-Germain, has given him the "maturity" that Helmut Schön regards so highly in his holistic assessment of any player. And crucially it has also endowed him with a sense of autonomy vis-à-vis his native country which is a precondition for developing that "intellectual and aesthetic stance of openness toward divergent cultural experiences" which is the essence of "genuine cosmopolitanism" in the eyes of the anthropologist Ulf Hannerz (1990: 47).

3 Britain's Ambivalent Relationship with Other National Football Cultures

Whilst one cannot deny the existence and power of brands or commodities or celebrities in the age of advanced capitalism, the position taken by Cashmore is, as we have implied, a somewhat one-sided and cynical one. Regarding our own further aims we are not intending to offer a fully rounded biographical portrait nor a chronological narrative of Beckham's sporting (or commercial) achievements. We will look more closely at two facets of Beckham's personality in particular which have helped secure him a prominent role not only in his native British culture, but also in twenty first century world culture. We will firstly consider Beckham as an example of a migrant English footballer, leaving behind his national roots and playing in the Spanish, North American, Italian and French leagues, and we will briefly compare his experiences with those of other British players since the end of the Second World War. Secondly, and inter-linked with the evident agility of Beckham on the field of contemporary culture, we will be addressing the undeniable fact that Beckham has metamorphosed fairly effortlessly into a citizen of the world whilst still preaching and practising a fierce allegiance to his homeland and retaining a strong English identity. In 2012, this dual identity equipped him to be the almost perfect ambassador at the London Olympic Games personifying both Britishness and cosmopolitanism in one.

Returning now to the aforementioned issue of migration and football in the context of British social history, one is struck by a true British paradox. On the one hand, our massive missionary influence in popularising the sport world-wide is self-evident. On the other hand, in comparison with other nationalities our own home-bred players have such a poor record, historically, of adapting to other cultures and playing styles. Regarding the first part of the enigma, one of Germany's best known football writers, Dietrich Schulze-Marmeling, whom Günter Netzer referred to by name in the preface's quotation, has written an authoritative history of the sport entitled *Fußball: Zur Geschichte eines globalen Sports*. It is fair to claim that a good half of the work is actually about the English game, its pioneers and its continuing influence on the creation of its landmarks and legends. In a chapter symptomatically entitled 'Ein Ball geht um die Welt: Britanniens erfolgreichstes Exportprodukt' ('A Ball Goes Round The World: Britannia's Most Successful Export') he looks at continental Europe's football origins and claims: "The first teams on the continent were founded either by Britons already living abroad or by anglophile citizens of these countries. Frequently it was in the seaport towns where lots of foreigners had been 'stranded', including especially Englishmen, that kicking a ball around began. That applies especially to the Mediterranean region, but also to France (Le Havre), Germany (Bremen and Hamburg) or Sweden (Gothenburg)" (Schulze-Marmeling 2000: 47).

Britain did not just export the packaged game's concept complete with rules, or individuals such as Jimmy Hogan (the inspirational figure for Helmut Schön) and thousands like him, or the passionate emotions, in the wake of the game's emergence from the morass of Victorian society's class conflicts. Stephen Wagg reminds us of how an "exodus" of British players had begun soon after the ending of warfare half way through the last century. For example, several headed for Colombia in 1950, and "by the end of the 1950s some very prominent players had left, or were preparing to leave, England" (Wagg 1984: 108). He cites the names of some genuinely impressive players, especially those who were recruited to play in Italy: Joe Baker, Gerry Hitchens and Jimmy Greaves of England, Denis Law of Scotland, John Charles of Wales. What is striking though is that of these five players only one, John Charles, adjusted to styles of play in the Italian league (and in fact went on to create a place in Italian football folklore too as "Il Gigante Buono").[5] Also critically comparing international player mobility after the war,

---

5   In his novel *Striker*, the writer Hunter Davies gives an authentic account, full of irony, of the problems of British players in adapting to foreign countries and their different ways of life. Joe Swift, his anti-hero, progresses from the English First Division to European Club Football and eventually lands in Serie A in Italy. In one of his many internal monologues he reflects: "It's noticeable that the footballers who didn't learn the language, like Jimmy Greaves, Ian Rush and Luther Blisset, did poorly in Italy. [...] While people like Liam Brady, Trevor Francis, Ray Wilkins learned the language and played well. On the whole though, British players have not really succeeded in Italy, none of them becoming mega, not since John Charles, and I don't want to hear about him again, thank you very much. Three Italian Championships, two Italian cups, a hundred goals, *grazie*, I know, I get reminded of that, everywhere I go" (Davies 1992: 221).

the sociologists Giulianotti and Robertson observed: "British players seeking fortunes abroad ran into legal trouble when joining the breakaway Di Mayor league in Colombia, or commonly found their new environment too alien to settle in (e.g. Baker, Law, and Greaves in Italy in the early 1960s)" (Giulianotti and Robertson 2009: 16).

The conspicuous failure of several generations of British star players to acclimatise to the "alien" way of life in the society in which they have chosen to live and work attracted the ironic attention of serious German press coverage, especially at the time of Beckham's move from Manchester United to Madrid in 2003. *Der Spiegel* reported in its customary laconic fashion: "It doesn't make the English happy when their players prove a success abroad; after all, the belief that they are celebrating the one and only version of the game that creates true bliss in their stadia is indestructible in the motherland of football. One of the 'lads' playing abroad – that's still like being handed paella instead of cucumber sandwiches for tea at five. Uncivilised, somehow. Memories are awoken of other players before Beckham's exodus who went off seeking fame and fortune on the playing fields of the continent and failed. Men like Paul Gascoigne who is said to have gone knocking in despair on his team mates' hotel room doors when playing in Rome to cry his heart out. Or Ian Rush, a pale faced man of a simple disposition who, after a barren year playing in Turin, on the return flight bound for England shared the following insight: 'It felt as if I was playing in a different country'".[6] The reference by *Der Spiegel* to 'lads' and the examples of these lads' behaviour abroad is an indictment of the deeply entrenched working class and rigidly insular values with which these and many other British players over the years have travelled abroad to work. But whilst their athletic mobility on the field may have been indisputable, their cultural mobility, or to quote Hannerz, a "personal ability to make one's way with other cultures, through listening, looking, intuiting and reflecting" (1990: 239), has been sorely lacking.

With some justification one could claim that only five players over the past half century, including David Beckham, have moved abroad and made a success of it: John Charles (Juventus), Gary Lineker (to Barcelona), Chris Waddle (to Marseille), and most notably, Kevin Keegan (to Hamburg SV). Keegan, who was affectionately dubbed 'Mighty Mouse' by the Germans, not only became a household name throughout Germany, quite literally so by inspiring many new German parents to choose his first name for their sons, but his exploits on the pitch raised his own game and status to the very pinnacle of European football. Twice he was

6   Thomas Hüetlin: Zehn Männer und eine Marke. Der Spiegel 35, 15.09.2003, http://www.spiegel.de/spiegel/print/d-28591014.html. Access: 27th April 2013.

voted European Player of the year (in 1978 and 1979). The case of Keegan in particular provided Chas Critcher with evidence for what he had to say about 'style'
in football, the changing social contours of the game and the emergence of a newer, more post-modern mentality in certain players: "From the mid-1960s onwards,
the status of top-level professional footballers changed dramatically. Previously
they had been retained within the economic and cultural confines of the everyday
working-class world [...] What they expected, and what was expected of them
was that they would express the virtues and vices of the world of the working-
class male. From that they drew their style: of playing, bearing and appearance"
(Critcher 1991: 74). Critcher looked at the new type of "superstar / dislocated from
any cultural milieu", who finally in a series of life transformations becomes the
"superstar / relocated in the world of show business" (ibid: 75). Kevin Keegan per-
sonifies several if not all of these moves towards the apex of the social pyramid:
"Keegan may have been one of the first to show that the status of superstar could
be exploited by the player himself as much as by others. But it required determination, a sense of personal stability and the acumen to know when to move on. These
were comparatively rare qualities in professional footballers" (ibid: 76).

4   Beckham, Outward Mobility and a Different Pattern of Adaptation

Beckham certainly shared these qualities of Keegan, qualities which Helmut
Schön would also have understood as belonging to the versatile mindset of the
charismatic playing personality. One could maintain, however, that Keegan's adaptation to the social and cultural world of West Germany was somewhat easier
given how anglophile the region of Hamburg and North Germany has long been,
and how outwardly looking Northern European the way of life is there. We know
full well how much at home the Beatles felt when they played in Hamburg, com-
muting frequently from Liverpool over a three year period in the early sixties.
The Southern European culture that Beckham chose to play and live in when he
moved to Madrid made different demands on a Northern European player[7]. The
conformism to traditional personal values that Alex Ferguson had required of
him at Manchester needed to be replaced by a greater sense of autonomy and

---

7   Aged 11, Beckham had won a ball skills contest and his prize was a two week trip to
    Barcelona where Terry Venables was the coach, and have the opportunity to train at
    the ground. This was a far cry from his working-class family's roots in the East End of
    London. See Beckham's autobiography, *My Side* (Beckham 2004).

individualism. To assert oneself in such a team of outstanding personalities as was assembled at Real Madrid (Zidane, Figo, Ronaldo and Raul) meant knowing who one is and how to express oneself both on and off the pitch. Style and giving pleasure mattered: "Spanish people dress up for football in the way that we might dress up to go to the theatre or to a party [...] What the *socios* – the members – really want is style: to be entertained by Raul and Figo and Roberto Carlos and the rest of us" (Beckham 2004: 432).

In his autobiography Beckham makes very clear how he, together with his family, approached the move to Spain from Manchester, both professionally and culturally: "things that had seemed scary when we'd first thought about them – leaving England, settling in a new country, learning a new language – started to seem more like an opportunity for all of us. I was so excited about the idea of Madrid, the football club, that it was easier for me to get excited about Madrid, the city, and Madrid, the way of life, as well" (ibid: 395-396). The ambience of a city like Madrid and of a country which was part of mainland Mediterranean Europe, yet historically linked with the North African region and intrinsically attuned to South American vibrancy, flamboyance and colour, necessitated a greater sensibility to one's own "bearing and appearance" (Chris Critcher). This was expressed through dress and hair style, as well as via body aesthetics through jewellery and piercing. And Beckham knew well before his move that Real Madrid were strategically targeting the immense and varied Asian market to grow their fan base, and he understood that his personal image was to play a crucial role by appealing to millions of potential new fans to identify with him and his team of globetrotters. That self-image amalgamating physical and social mobility, technical aesthetics (*Bend It Like Beckham*) and metropolitan style, was ideal for transcending the boundaries of colour, creed, nationality, gender and sexual orientation: "Whether young or old, black, yellow or white, everyone worships the blond deliverer of divine crosses from the wings, whom even a Nelson Mandela was determined to meet and wanted to shake hands with".[8] And finally, in a society such as that of contemporary democratic Spain, there is still a powerful conservatism and devotion to religious values at play, with which many a player originating from these more secularised islands and merrily embracing a macho Anglo-Saxon credo of matey drinking, sex, possibly drugs or gambling, may have had little natural affinity. Beckham, on the other hand, was perceived as a clean-living, abstinent family man incorporating a strong work ethic built firmly on self-discipline and fitness.

---

8   Jürgen Krönig: Beckham – Der erste wahrhaft globale Kicker. *Die Zeit* 26, 2003, http://www.zeit.de/leben/beckham. Access: 27th April 2013.

It was not only the four years spent in the Mediterranean yet still metropolitan European world of Madrid that gave proof of Beckham's cultural mobility and cosmopolitan confidence. Already by 2007 the most famous soccer player in the world, the Englishman moved with his family to live in the United States where he had signed a five-year contract to play for Los Angeles Galaxy. In North America he will have encountered some of the familiar 'old' values of the Europe he had spent the first 32 years of his life growing up in, mingled with the cockily 'new' values of the USA. Regarding the influence of European values, the US displays in several respects a similar kind of conservative outlook to that of Southern Europe underpinned by moral and religious principles. Additionally, a more Northern European, Protestant-based work ethic places a premium on effort, duty and achievement, notions which a consummate athlete such as Beckham has had no difficulties accepting. However, in particular the keenness of American society to reward individual effort and materially acknowledge success differs from the somewhat ambivalent social and political climate of opinion in Europe. The individualism and competitiveness fostered by his relocation to Spain combined with his belonging to a team of outstanding talents were more than useful assets when adjusting to life in the socially dynamic world of the United States. One important component of the social dynamics of this non-traditional, non-class-ridden nation of the New World is the fusion of different ethnic groups to whom a by now high-profile, public figure like Beckham has self-evident appeal.

A further influential factor especially found at the interface of sport and broader social groupings in the States are the millions of women who play sport, watch sport, write and report about it in the media, and who of course as mothers actively organise their children's involvement in games and team sports, especially in soccer. Crucially, soccer for them does not carry the associations of the kind of traditional male tribal rituals it has done for a century or more in Europe, and one of Beckham's greatest cultural assets in North America vis-à-vis the female population was his projection of athletic prowess devoid of provocative and alienating male ferocity. He embodies instead a healthy, abstemious and quasi-erotic athleticism which chimes with clean-cut, cross-gender images of the personal value of physical vitality in the United States. This has led German scholars to comment on his remarkable multi-dimensionality, and specifically his capacity for fusing seemingly opposing or irreconcilable modes of being: "In a society divided by a new type of capitalism Beckham is especially important precisely because he is not divisive but brings social distinctions as well as gender differences closer together through the manner in which he projects himself and through his frequent media appearances. It is no coincidence that he is especially attractive to women. He radiates both of the following traits: on the one hand sensitivity and openness towards feminine inclinations and attributes, but on the other hand the masculine side is also tangible as communicated via football and the criterion of 'success' which dominates everything in this society" (Böhnisch / Brandes 2006: 140).

Finally, in considering the cultivation of a charismatic and cosmopolitan personality off the field, one must not overlook how crucial California has been. David Beckham, and of course his wife Victoria too, exposed themselves to the creative amalgam of different yet inter-connected networks of film actors and directors, fashion designers, pop artists, writers and musicians, and show business too, frequently drawn to that region from right across the globe. For his wife Victoria the glamour, style and celebrity ethos of Los Angeles were nothing alien. Far from it. Victoria Beckham had risen to fame in precisely such a world of style, mobility, and entertainment as a member of one of the most successful girl groups in the history of pop music, the Spice Girls, where, as Posh Spice, she had learned how to handle the media, stand confidently in the limelight of global attention, and with the four other group members on world tours move daily in and out of changing cultural milieus. The scope of this essay does not allow us to consider in any detail the role of Victoria or of David Beckham's family life but her own experiences will have taught him certain lessons and helped him to see the world from an even more cosmopolitan perspective. Though this world can be and will be identified with glamour, wealth and popular culture, and thus critically rejected by sections especially of the European intelligentsia for those values, California is undeniably a creatively vibrant focal point for the production of new ideas and for a vital sense of belonging to a world community.

5   A Paradigmatic Fusion of the Local and the Global

David Beckham's odyssey had originally taken him from fairly humble social beginnings in the East End of London to Manchester, and thus to the very heartlands of football rooted in the industrial communities of the North of England. By the time he had become a full professional with Manchester United in 1991 the city was busily dismantling its industrial past and re-building a post-industrial base around the services and hi-tech industries, around a burgeoning youth, pop and club culture, and around an urban leisure sector at the heart of which old established football clubs were actively re-structuring and re-modernising themselves. Manchester United Football Club emerged from this re-urbanising process as a potent brand. Representing this club throughout the 1990s meant that Beckham travelled extensively throughout the continent playing in European club championships. Though the matches abroad were of course not primarily for

sightseeing and educational purposes – any more than his international appearances for England were – the continental fixtures would undoubtedly help this
focused ambitious young man to overcome in particular that sense of insularity,
provincialism and introspectiveness which have characterised earlier generations
of our footballers and made them 'travel badly' in the broader social and cultural
sense. One George Best, a supremely gifted footballer like Beckham and equally
blessed with good looks and charm, had also been the star of a Manchester United side two decades earlier, but never even moved out of the city to another club
in the full-time professional part of his playing career. Best's personal let alone
cultural vision was myopic. In total contrast, Beckham's acculturation process
towards becoming a European sportsman continued apace through the four years
at Real Madrid, whilst the following five years spent playing in the North American League and based in California consolidated the acquisition not only of the
'charismatic playing personality' on and off the field discussed earlier but of a charismatic and cosmopolitan personality as a sportsman bestriding a world stage,
yet always accompanied by a beguiling modesty.

This world stage was symbolised in July and August 2012 when the Olympic
Games took place in London. David Beckham had been personally involved with
the Games for over ten years having been selected by Tony Blair to be part of the
original bid team to bring the Games to London. His global fame coupled with
his reputation as a significant representative of present-day Britain were already
established by the turn of the century so that *The Times*' leading article of 13 August 2012, entitled 'A Great Exhibition', reviewing the remarkable success of The
London Games, could write of his original role in the long bidding process: "David Beckham drove home the message of inclusivity and inspiration".[9] He was also
an official London 2012 ambassador, performing a variety of public duties. One
example of these reminded us why his cultural adaptation to North American
society specifically, which we have just reviewed, has been so successful when he
teamed up with Michelle Obama, the American President's wife, for a kick about
with youngsters at the US ambassador's residence in Regent's Park, London. More
than a thousand American and British children took part in the Let's Move event
to promote the kind of health awareness the so-called soccer moms in the States
support.

Beckham's seemingly natural ability to bridge imaginary national divides and
cultural boundaries is testimony to his cosmopolitan credentials. Yet the notion
of being a cosmopolitan is multi-layered. It certainly implies on one level, such as
this example has shown, that an individual (or a group) is free of national prejudice

---

9   *The Times*, 13th August 2012: 2.

or bigotry. But it also carries connotations of a person being urbane and sophisticated. This was alluded to spectacularly when the film director responsible for the opening ceremony, Danny Boyle, had David Beckham at the helm of a speedboat carrying the Olympic flame on the Thames to deliver it with the proverbial safe pair of hands to its final destination. It was a sequence overtly referencing James Bond films, with the No 7 on the pitch impersonating 007, the legendary figure of Fleming's novels and Hollywood movies. The multi-dimensional phenomenon of David Beckham indeed lends itself both to helping to publicise serious charity and awareness raising work as well as to making ironic cultural allusions to global myths and narratives Made in Britain.

Melvyn Bragg, novelist, cultural critic, and well known media personality, wrote and presented a three part series for television in 2012 entitled *Melvyn Bragg on Class and Culture*. In it he looked at Britain over the past 100 years to consider how different our present-day conception of culture might be from that of 1900. The final part, covering the 30 years from 1980 to 2010, opens with a sequence of brief images, including one where David Beckham and Prince William are seen standing chatting quite leisurely at a garden party. Bragg's comment is: "Today working class heroes consort with royals." In other words, the "working class hero" David Beckham has risen upwardly through the class hierarchy to be at the apex of the modern British class system. Not only does this demonstrate Beckham's social status (and wealth) but also his cultural mobility and significance for present-day Britain. He is a symbol of what Bragg calls Britain's "classless elite".

The 2012 Olympic Games took place a stone's throw from the playing fields of Leytonstone and Chingford, where Beckham was raised. His rise from these modest surroundings to become part of this "classless elite" of contemporary British society along with the likes of Elton John, J. D. Rowling, Damien Hirst, Sebastian Coe, Tracy Emin, Danny Boyle, Irvine Walsh and many others, has become almost as legendary as that of, say, The Beatles in the world of popular culture. Over the past forty years sport in Britain has become as central to popular culture as music, cinema, television and radio, and fashion. Football of course has always actually been at or close to the centre of popular culture, but one which for over a hundred years was based around working class communities and values. It required firstly the technology of the media to place it into the broader, more classless popular consciousness and, secondly, it needed the legitimacy which writers (for example, Nick Hornby and Hunter Davies) and public intellectuals (such as Melvyn Bragg) have bestowed upon it. These individuals have given it that legitimacy by helping to break down the old boundaries erected to keep 'culture' and 'anarchy'[10] safely apart.

Furthermore, popular culture like elite culture needs real human beings with charismatic personalities and performing exceptional deeds of artistry to vitalise and embody it and give us, their fans and followers, the reason to seek vitality from it in the form of thrills, excitement, sensation, debate, controversy, and essentially pleasure. Beckham is one such agent incorporating our national cultural pleasures, yet crucially one who has learned to transcend national boundaries and exert an appeal as a modern everyman figure across cultures and continents. As a German journalist wrote almost ten years ago of David Beckham's legacy: "[...] he is an excellent midfield player possessing great technical ability and enormous tactical sense, and he's also a wonderful crosser of the ball. But his popularity cannot be explained any longer by what he does on the pitch. When he plays again in the European Championships in Portugal, masses of people will be sitting watching their television sets who are not at all interested in football. Many just want to see him and his emotions, how he expresses happiness or how he suffers. We think we actually know him because one sees him daily, even if it's only in the media. Since the mid-nineties though football is no longer just a sport, it is entertainment for everybody, and that is due to Beckham".[11]

6   Conclusion: An Exceptional English Footballer

When one looks at and assesses a nation's economic performance one of the measures used is to compare the value of goods and services exported to other countries with the value of those imported. This is called the trade balance. Some countries have a trade surplus, i.e. they sell more abroad than they buy. Others show a trade deficit. Over the past decades the United Kingdom has rarely re-

---

10 Matthew Arnold, Victorian poet and cultural critic, published his famous book entitled 'Culture and Anarchy' in 1869. His views on what constitutes culture, namely that which cultivated, distinguished members of society judge to represent the very best, in the sense of beauty and perfection, which society has created and used as a yardstick of human progress, were part of an already existing tradition of thinking, and, it could be argued, they remained influential until at least the 1950s and 1960s. Anarchy as culture's antipode was visible for Arnold in the philistine views of the newly created middle classes as well as in the ugliness of the industrialisation and urbanisation processes of his time.

11 Ronald Reng: Die Marke Beckham. *Zeit Online*, 09.06.2004 (*Die Zeit* 25, 2004), http://www.zeit.de/2004/25/Tabloid_EM_2fReng. Access: 27th April 2013.

corded trade surpluses. The parallel with English soccer (as a consumer product) is self-evident. When one looks at the make-up of teams in the English Premier League one is struck by a surfeit of imported players vis-à-vis home grown talent. We import hundreds, possibly thousands of players from all over the world. The majority appear to acclimatise speedily, learning to adapt to our customs and traditions and acquiring knowledge of our language, often with startling proficiency. Yet, conversely, few of our genuinely gifted players ever seek to leave these shores. Of course, there is one very obvious immediate explanation for this reluctance to play abroad, namely pay. Our players earn such good money at home that they need not go abroad to be better remunerated. Or at least they feel they need not look beyond the borders of their native country. David Beckham is the exception to what appears to be the rule, at least in the present time. Not only has he played abroad for almost as many years as he played in domestic football here, but he has played for some of the world's best club sides. He perfectly exemplifies Helmut Schön's dictum quoted in the preface that "a player's personality will only ever reach the highest degree of maturity if he [...] has learned how to adapt to the manifold realities on the field of play and outside the stadium".

David Beckham is also exceptional in having manifestly succeeded in retaining his own identity as well as acquiring an identity as a citizen of the world. Whilst he, like most English footballers over the past century and a half, originates from a working class background, he has never sought to shed his working class way of speaking which instantly betrays these origins, nor has he ever allowed his social background to be a handicap in moving upwards through his own class-ridden and class-obsessed society, nor in moving outwards through different cultures to becoming idolised and emulated especially by young people right across the globe. Beckham is exceptionally un-blinkered, just as he has always been on the pitch where he has instinctively spotted opportunities for passes and crosses to other players over very considerable distances and invariably executed them to perfection.

In respect of his behaviour off the field there is a solidity of character and personality which we have alluded to through the word 'incorporating' used in the title of our chapter. The good looks, the easy, natural charm, the slim athletic figure, not to mention the narcissistic trappings of real wealth on his person, could so easily have become his sole trademark for the media's delectation and exploitation. But his itinerant lifestyle, especially after leaving Manchester United and his native country, has tested his mettle. Like the technically astute, thinking and opportunistic midfield player he was, Beckham has woven his way into the divergent cultural systems of the countries he has resided in, and kept his sights fixed firmly on the goal of success on and off the field of play. His sense of balance too and spatial awareness generally, which is part of the secret of his free kicks and of his control of the ball when under pressure from opponents, have helped him to stake out and control his environment once outside the foreign stadia and of course control his own self and self-image as a charismatic personality in face of the massed ranks of the international media and of stardom *per se*. He never became the sad caricature of the English soccer player abroad; forlorn, disorientated and, culturally speaking, constantly caught offside. Instead his legacy at least in part will have been to demonstrate, like Kevin Keegan over three decades ago, that it is perfectly possible for an English player to move abroad, to integrate himself into continental styles of playing, but also crucially to grow as an individual personality in harmony with the supposed 'alien' culture.

In short, the unconventional, multi-faceted and cosmopolitan personality, combined with global popularity, are integral to the explanation of the phenomenon of David Beckham.

Bibliography

Beckham, D.: 2004. My Side. London: Harper Collins Publishers.

Biermann, C. (2012): Die Missionare des Heiligen Britischen Fußballs. 11 Freunde Spezial. Sonderausgabe: Football's Coming Home. Die Geschichte des britischen Fußballs. September 2012, 48-51.

Böhnisch, L. / Brandes, H. (2006): „Titan" und „Queen von Madrid" – Fußball zwischen Männlichkeitspraxis und Kommerz. In: Brandes, H. / Christa, H. / Evers, R. (eds): Hauptsache Fußball. Sozialwissenschaftliche Einwürfe. Gießen: Psychosozial-Verlag, 133-145.

Cashmore, E. (2004): Beckham. Cambridge: Blackwell Publishers.

Critcher, C. (1991): Putting on the style: aspects of recent English football. In: Williams, J. / Wagg, S. (eds): British Football and Social Change: Getting into Europe. Leicester: Continuum International Publishing, 67-84.

Davies, H. (1992): Striker. London: Bloomsbury Publishing

Fanizadeh, M. / Hödl, G. / Manzenreiter, W. (eds) (2005): Global Players – Kultur, Ökonomie und Politik des Fußballs. Frankfurt am Main: Brandes & Apsel.

Featherstone, M. (ed) (1990): Global Culture. Nationalism, Globalization and Modernity. London: Sage Publications.

Giulianotti, R. (1999): Football: A Sociology of the Global Game. Cambridge: Polity Press.

Giulianotti, R. / Robertson, R. (eds) (2009): Globalization & Football. London: Sage Publications.

Harig, L. / Kühn, D. (eds) (1974): Netzer kam aus der Tiefe des Raumes. München: Hanser.

Hannerz, U. (1990): Cosmopolitans and Locals in World Culture. In: Featherstone, M. (1990), 237-251.

Klein, G. / Meuser, M. (eds) 2008: Ernste Spiele. Zur Soziologie des Fußballs. Bielefeld: transcript.

Schön, H. (1974): Spielerpersönlichkeiten und Wasserträger. In: Harig, L. / Kühn, D. (eds) (1974), 44-46.

Schulze-Marmeling, D. (2000): Fußball. Zur Geschichte eines globalen Sports. Göttingen: Die Werkstatt.

Schulze-Marmeling, D. (ed) (2005): Strategen des Spiels. Göttingen: Die Werkstatt.

Sugden, J. / Tomlinson, A. (1998): FIFA and the Contest for World Football. Who Rules the Peoples' Game? Cambridge: Blackwell Publishers.

Wagg, S. (1984): The Football World. A Contemporary Social History. Brighton: Branch Line.

Williams, J. / Wagg, S. (eds) (1991): British Football and Social Change: Getting into Europe. Leicester: Continuum International Publishing.

Acknowledgements We would like to thank the following for giving their time and stimulation to our early thinking about the subject: Daphne Heid, David Machin, Kristian Naglo, Annik Taylor, Peter Thompson, Scott Thompson (a true ManU fan with vivid memories of Beckham at Old Trafford).

And we also express our appreciation to the following who looked at and gave us useful feedback on the early manuscript draft: Carol Bean, Sue and Tony Heward, Markus Waine.

Over the Line?
England, Germany and Wembley 1966

Hinter der Linie?
England, Deutschland und Wembley 1966

Dilwyn Porter & Christoph Wagner

Abstract

Memories of the World Cup final of 1966 – England's controversial third goal in particular – are deeply embedded in popular culture, though probably more so in England than in Germany. For the 'fifty years of hurt' since 1966, English football has lived in its shadow, not least because of the failure of any England team since that date to equal the achievements of Bobby Moore and his colleagues and the determination of the tabloid press to ensure that the event is not forgotten. In contrast, German response to the disappointment of defeat and the injustice of *Das Wembleytor* has generally been more restrained, though there was some excitement in the 1990s when Oxford University scientists 'proved' that Hurst's shot had not crossed the line. This chapter explores reactions to the match at the time and seeks to explain how this key moment in Anglo-German cultural relations has been remembered over the following decades.

Zusammenfassung

Erinnerungen an das Endspiel der Weltmeisterschaft von 1966 – und insbesondere an das umstrittene dritte Tor der Engländer – sind in der populären Kulturgeschichte tief verankert, jedoch eher in England als in Deutschland. In den 'fifty years of hurt' seit 1966 existierte der englische Fußball im Schatten dieses Ereignisses, da seitdem keine englische Mannschaft mehr mit dem Erfolg von Bobby Moore und seinen Mannschaftskollegen gleichziehen konnte. Die englischen Boulevardmedien etwa erinnern bis heute mit großem Nachdruck an die Unvergänglichkeit dieses Spiels. Im Gegensatz dazu waren die deutschen Reaktionen auf die Enttäuschung der Niederlage und die Ungerechtigkeit des *Wembleytors* insgesamt zurückhaltender. Erst als in den 1990ern Wissenschaftler der Universität Oxford 'bewiesen', dass Hursts Schuss die Linie nicht überquert hatte, gab es begeisterte Zustimmung. Vor diesem Hintergrund untersucht der Beitrag damalige Reaktionen auf das Spiel und versucht zu erklären, wie dieser Schlüsselmoment der englisch-deutschen kulturellen Beziehungen in den folgenden Jahrzehnten erinnert wurde.

Tony Mason, later to become Professor of Social History at the University of Warwick and England's most distinguished football historian, was there on 30 July 1966, when England played West Germany at Wembley in the final of the World Cup. As he left the stadium, excited by the drama that had unfolded and elated by an England victory, he commented: „Well, we did it ... but only just". This was overheard and misunderstood by a Frenchman who turned to him and said: „Yes, you won, but it was not just"[1]. The French had reason to complain, having lost to England earlier in the competition when their team had effectively been reduced to ten men after a wild tackle by Nobby Stiles on Robert Herbin; substitutes were not allowed in 1966. However, it was clear that he was referring to England's third goal in the final, scored by Geoff Hurst in the eleventh minute of extra time, with a shot that rebounded off the underside of the crossbar. For a goal to be given the ball has to be completely over the goal-line; it was not at all clear that this had actually happened. As players from both sides appealed, the Swiss referee Gottfried Dienst consulted Tofik Bakhramov, known ever since in England simply as 'the Russian linesman', though he was in fact from Azerbaijan. A goal was given, a decision that initiated forty years of soccer controversy.

This goal, *Das Wembleytor*, as it is known in Germany, gave England a 3-2 lead. They added to it in the very last minute of the match, also in controversial cir-

---

1   Tony Mason interviewed by Dilwyn Porter, 15 October 2012.

cumstances. The words used by television commentator Kenneth Wolstenholme to describe the closing passage of play have become as famous in England as those used by Herbert Zimmerman in describing Helmut Rahn's goal in the 1954 final for radio listeners in Germany. Heard by 26 million BBC viewers on the day and millions more since, they are now deeply embedded in English popular culture. "Some people are on the pitch; they think it's all over ... [then as Hurst scores] It is now!" Hurst has claimed that he is often approached by Scotsmen keen to let him know that England's third goal should not have been allowed. Some Scots even like to joke that England are the only team that has won the World Cup by drawing 2-2, arguing that the fourth goal should also have been ruled out because, as Wolstenholme's commentary indicated, some over-excited fans encroached onto the field of play just before Hurst scored (see Ramsden 2006: 353). It is important to remember that not everyone in the United Kingdom celebrated England's victory in 1966 (Porter 2009: 520-21)[2].

Jake Arnott's powerful crime novel *He Kills Coppers*, published in 2001 but set in 1966, supplies characterisations of Dienst and Bakhramov as seen from an English viewpoint. For the English, Dienst's Swiss homeland was "a faraway country of which we know nothing", as Neville Chamberlain famously said of Czechoslavakia in 1938. If it was known at all it was for its mountains, its chocolate, its cuckoo-clocks, and for its "supposed neutrality". As for Bakhramov "... he had served in the Red Army in the Great Patriotic War against the Third Reich' and shouts from the crowd urged him to 'Remember Stalingrad!" (Arnott 2001: 96-97). This seems a little fanciful though historian Richard Weight, in his account of the match, thought it necessary to explain that the linesman was "a former Red Army private" who had fought on the Eastern front. "The Germans", he added, "claimed this influenced his decision but only he knows" (Weight 2002: 460). Interviewed years later Bakhramov was an unimpressive witness. Stefan Keber's film, *Der Fluch von Wembley* (2006), made for a German television audience, repeated the claim that the linesman had been "crucially influenced, if not biased"[3].

"A goal for England", noted a correspondent for the *New Yorker*, who had been at the match, "– and yet none of us were entirely happy with its inconclusive aura"[4].

---

2   For those who were indifferent or hostile see Dominic Sandbrook 2007: 322.

3   Der Fluch von Wembley. Geschichte eines Jahrhunderttores (2006). www.donotmentionthewar.wordpress.com/2012/09/05/the-curse-of-wembley. Accessed 15 October 2012.

4   Alastair Reid, 'The World Cup', *The New Yorker*, 10 September 1966. www.newyorker.com/archive/1966/09/10/1966_09_10-152-TNY_CARDS_0002866584?currentPage=all. Accessed 29 April 2013.

It is not our purpose here to dwell at length on whether the match officials were right or wrong. Research undertaken in the mid 1990s by two Oxford University scientists, Ian Reid and Andrew Zisserman, using computerised images to retrace the path of the ball after it hit the crossbar seems to have resolved that particular dispute in Germany's favour (Reid / Zisserman 1996: 647-58). Our intention instead is to reflect on the 1966 final and the controversy that it generated; to ask what the match meant at the time in both England and Germany; and also to ask how it has been remembered across the half-century that followed. International sport, with the assistance of the media, has the capacity to deliver high drama to mass audiences. It supplies occasions or moments - experienced communally and remembered collectively – that shape the way nations see themselves and others. What happened on that distant sunny afternoon at Wembley was experienced at the time and has been remembered since in very different ways in England and Germany.

1   1966: English football's 'finest hour'

There are many reasons – apart from *Das Wembleytor* - why interest in the 1966 final has lasted for so long. In terms of football history the match occurred at a point at which the balance of power between England and Germany was delicately poised. Ulrich Hesse-Lichtenberger in his history of German football has argued that the foundations for the success that West Germany enjoyed after 1966 were in place even before they arrived for the tournament. Against Sweden in 1965 Franz Beckenbauer had burst at speed from midfield in a way that would become his trademark. It was his explosive run that resulted in the equaliser that secured qualification: "West Germany were on their way to England – and to becoming a footballing superpower" (Hesse-Lichtenberger 2002: 181). Dettmar Cramer, West Germany's assistant manager, believed that his team were at least as good as England by the start of 1966.[5] In a friendly match played in February, five months before the tournament began, England gained a 1-0 win but "the Wembley crowd had its first sight of how slick Beckenbauer and Netzer could look in combination" (Downing 2001: 103). England's performance that evening disappointed the home fans and only a referee's decision which mystified even the patriotic *Daily Express* denied Germany the equalizer they deserved[6].

---

5   Cramer interviewed in *Der Fluch von Wembley.*
6   *Daily Express*, 24 February 1966: 18.

It was to take one or two more matches but the scales were gradually tipping in Germany's favour and the 1966 final has to be viewed in this context. "What the statistics show", as John Ramsden pointed out in his study of Anglo-German relations, "is that the 1966 World Cup final was the fulcrum between two very different periods: England dominant until 1966 but Germany afterwards" (Ramsden 2006: 357). In reality, the subsequent change in the relative positions of England and Germany in international football's world order was even more decisive. While 1966 remains England's only victory in a major international tournament, West Germany/Germany went on to win the World Cup in 1974 and 1990 and to reach the final in 1982, 1986 and 2002; they also won the European championship in 1972, 1980 and 1996. Significant victories over England, achieved in a 1970 World Cup quarter-final, when Germany came from 2-0 down to win 3-2 in extra time, and in a 1972 European Championship quarter-final at Wembley when England were outclassed, probably helped Germans to come to terms with any injustice they might have suffered in 1966. "By the time England and Germany met again in Turin for the 1990 World Cup semi-final", observes Raphael Honigstein, a German journalist based in England, "Germans were mostly unaware that their opponents saw this as a very special occasion" (Honigstein 2009: 204).

In the immediate aftermath of victory it would have seemed unpatriotic for Englishmen to express serious doubts about their team's third goal, and also rather pointless. In the *Sunday Express*, Alan Hoby admitted that the goal "had its doubters" but argued that it was "fair compensation" for the referee's controversial decision to award the free kick which had led to Germany's equalizer in the last minute of normal time[7]. Peter Wilson in the *Daily Mirror* admitted that he had been in no position to make a judgement before adding, "But merciful heavens ... the decision was in our favour"[8]. Brian Glanville, chief football writer for the *Sunday Times*, who later supplied the English commentary for FIFA's official cinematic record of the tournament, found himself in a better position to judge than most. He recalled in his memoirs (Glanville 1999: 204):

"Was it a goal? Did the ball cross the line? Time and again I looked at the incident on the moviola while we were finishing the film ... I couldn't tell. I never have been able to, on any other evidence, though a few years ago a German laboratory produced 'evidence' that it was not a goal".

While English soccer basked in the sunshine of success – and for many years after - agnosticism was in the ascendancy. It was probably best not to know, and

---

7   *Sunday Express*, 31 July 1966: 16.
8   *Daily Mirror*, 1 August 1966: 23.

not knowing meant that responsibility for the decision remained with the match officials, the Swiss referee and 'the Russian linesman'.

Der Spiegel later suggested that there had been much "alcoholically enhanced discussion" over the years of the decision which had robbed Germany of the chance of victory[9]. Psychological closure may not quite have been achieved but later successes made it possible for Germans – if they were so inclined - to take a relaxed view. Perhaps what had happened back in 1966 was really not so important after all. When, in 1996, Reid and Zisserman supplied scientific proof that Dienst and Bakhramov had made the wrong decision (Reid / Zisserman 1996: 657), at least one German who had every reason to feel aggrieved, simply shrugged his shoulders. "It's almost thirty years ago", reflected Wolfgang Weber, whose goal had dramatically levelled the scores at 2-2. "Today', he explained, 'I don't think it is important to say yes or no ... but England deserved to win"[10]. By this time, most English football fans would have conceded that their team's third goal was at the very least doubtful, not least because Bobby Moore, England's captain in 1966, before his death in 1993, was on record as saying: "At the time I was in no doubt but on reflection I've got to say that I wouldn't have liked a goal like that to be given against England" (see Powell 2002: 106-7). However, they were less likely than their German counterparts to consign the 1966 final to the historical past simply because England's solitary victory had come to mean so much. This may also explain why Wembley 1966 has received more attention from historians in England than in Germany.

Of course, it was not clear in 1966 that this was how it would turn out. The 'thirty years of hurt' referred to in the hypnotic 'Three Lions', the anthem composed by Ian Broudie of the Lightning Seeds for Euro 96, lay in the unknown future. England's international team had been defeated by the USA when they first entered the World Cup in 1950; they had been also-rans in 1954 and defeated quarter-finalists in 1958 and 1962. Victory in 1966, therefore, however controversial the circumstances, was gratefully received, especially by those seeking reassurance regarding their country's position in the world. A conversation between Arnott's three criminals as they watch the match on television neatly encapsulates the full range of British responses as the drama surrounding England's third goal unfolds (Arnott 2001: 97).

> "Stan has risen from the settee, a beer bottle held aloft, cheering.
> 'That was never in', Jimmy [a Scot] mutters.

---

9   „Kein Tor. Nie. Niemals!", *Der Spiegel*, 31/1995: 18.
10 Weber quoted in the *Sunday Times*, 23 July 1995: 20.

'It does look a bit dodgy', agrees Billy.
'Yeah, but it doesn't matter now, does it?' Stan with a stupid grin on his face. 'The ref's given it, hasn't he?'"

And, it could be argued, that was all that mattered. "We were not of a mind to subject to detailed analysis whether Hurst's shot had really ricocheted from the bar and down over the German goal-line", recalled one young England supporter (Chapman 1999: 183). Why should they have been?

This idea is picked up and developed by film historian David Thomson in his book *4-2* as he views a video-recording of the match while seeking to recall how it felt over thirty years earlier as he had watched on television. He knows that some Englishmen, eager to validate their team's victory, point to Roger Hunt, the English forward nearest the ball as it bounced on or near the line, who raised his arms to claim the goal rather than applying the finishing touch. As Thomson sees it, however, Hunt "hesitates, as if in uncertainty", and allows Weber to clear. While arguing that it was impossible to determine what actually happened – "one would need a camera in the goal or on the line, or one of those electronic lines that spy movies love" – he senses that the whole of the ball has not crossed the line. And then, he continues, "there is the fact that the referee decided it was a goal". Such errors, he notes, "are very hard to bear like the goal against England that Maradona punched in for Argentina in the Mexico World Cup of 1986" (Thomson 1996: 181-82). It is as if the injustice suffered by England on that occasion somehow cancels out that suffered by Germany twenty years earlier. Significantly, Frank Lampard's disallowed goal against Germany at the South Africa World Cup in 2010, when the ball had clearly crossed the line, could be – and often was – viewed in the same light. "As regards the ball over the line thing", wrote 'John Bull' of Wolverhampton to *Mail Online*, "the Germans will remember Geoff Hurst's goal in 1966 and smile". "It is called Karma", another correspondent added helpfully[11].

But we should not look too far ahead. One of the reasons why Wembley 1966 has left such a powerful legacy is that it was so immensely reassuring at the time. "If Germany beat us at Wembley this afternoon at our national sport" wrote Vincent Mulchrone in the *Daily Mail* on the morning of the match, "we can always point out to them that we have recently beaten them twice at theirs" (cited in Ramsden 2006: 353-54; see also Weight 2002: 459-60). This may not have been in the best

---

11 See the online comments in *Mail Online*, 27 June 2010. www.dailymail.co.uk/sport/worldcup2010/article-1290040/WORLD-CUP-2010-The-goal-Frank-Lampard-strike-Germany-denied-referee-Jorge-Larrionda-html#comments. Accessed 15th October 2012.

possible taste but one did not have to agree with the *Mail's* right-of-centre politics to see the point. Two wars against Germany were experiences that had been endured by the English people as a whole and had helped to shape their collective sense of identity. Given the predilection of sports writers for military metaphors it was hardly surprising that past Anglo-German conflicts cast a shadow over Wembley in 1966. At a time when the English public were becoming increasingly aware of West Germany's 'economic miracle', its higher levels of productivity and its faster rate of growth, it was comforting to have an excuse to turn the clock back to 1945 when the English had last beaten the Germans at 'their national sport' – and away from home too. It seems significant that so many descriptions of the post-match celebrations in London, both at the time and since, compare them to the 'Victory' celebrations at the end of the Second World War. "Older people", recalled Peter Chapman, a teenager in 1966, "compared the celebrations to those on VE Day, the difference being that there may not have been so many Germans in the crowd then" (Chapman 1999: 183; see also McIlvanney 1966: 164). In reality, of course, the economic fundamentals did not change when Bobby Moore lifted the Jules Rimet Trophy and Britain's retreat from Empire and Great Power status continued uninterrupted.

In considering how Wembley 1966 is remembered in England it is important to realise what it has come to represent. Memory, as one historian has observed, "is a process by which people shape the past into a set of meanings that makes sense to them in the present" (Giles 2004: 25). It might be argued that this process operates especially powerfully when individuals are able to connect personal memories to the stories they tell themselves about how it was then and how it is now. In *The Last Game*, journalist Jason Cowley recalls that he had grown up in a household in which Bobby Moore had been revered. When Moore died in 1993, Cowley was in mourning for his own father, like Moore from working-class East London. Perhaps inevitably, he made a connection between the two deaths (Cowley 2009: 226):

> "... the end of two East End lives, yes, but something more besides, something to do with the end of a certain way of life, with the loss of a certain sense of old-fashioned duty and decorum. As young boys both men had been told by their mothers the same thing: to stand tall, speak well, to be polite, to make the best of themselves".

Wembley 1966, as remembered by many English people in the 1980s and 1990s and beyond, belonged to a world that they had lost, a more innocent world before hooliganism, Heysel and Hillsborough, when rival fans exchanged banter rather than kicks, punches and verbal abuse. It also represented sport in an illusory age of pre-commercial innocence before it was twisted out of shape by money and the media.

The English players of 1966 are routinely portrayed and routinely portray themselves as authentic working-class heroes, world champions who were happy to eat modest meals in motorway service stations as they made their way home after winning the trophy. In his autobiography, published in 2004, Jimmy Armfield, an England squad member in 1966, explains how they decided to share the £22,000 win bonus equally at a meeting on the Sunday after the final (Armfield 2004: 153-54).

> "Incredible as it may seem today, it was the first time anyone had mentioned money since the start of the competition. Now, agents ensure that bonuses and all the other perks are worked out well in advance. All we got was a suit and tie, a tracksuit that never quite fitted and, of all things, a briefcase".

Armfield's references to how it was then and how it is now are significant. There are more ways than one in which the current generation of English soccer stars – often criticised for being self-centred, pampered and overpaid, as well as for persistently underperforming – stand in the shadow of the 'boys of 66' (Porter 2009: 525-29; see also Hattenstone 2006: 120).

2   1966: German perspectives

In the immediate aftermath of the final it was clear that many Germans believed their team had been unfairly treated and they did not need the Scots to make the point for them. England's fourth goal could be discounted; it came so late that it could not have changed the outcome. But England's third goal had been decisive; it was the moment when the match had turned in favour of the home team. Thus, when the German squad landed at Frankfurt, they were greeted by banners proclaiming that they were the real world champions. "Inevitably, perhaps", *The Times* reported from Bonn, "there are sad and bitter feelings about Britain's *(sic)* third goal". Much press comment in Germany focused on the way in which the decision had been made; it was regarded as significant "that the referee gave the goal only after consulting a Russian linesman". It quoted *Bild am Sonntag's* claim that most eye-witnesses were convinced that the ball had not crossed the line and its view that the match had been lost on account of "the most discussed, and most universally contested goal in the history of football"[12]. Despite West Germany's outstanding record in international football after 1966 *Das Wembleytor* was a disappointment that was hard to forget completely and controversy resurfaced from time to time thereafter. The press comments collected by Henschel and Willen for their book *Drin oder Linie? Alles übers dritte Tor*, published in 1996, makes this clear. Writing in 1974, the year of West Germany's second World Cup triumph, Ulfert Schröder, deputy editor of *Sports Bild*, reminded readers of the injustice that their team had suffered in 1966. Dienst had been cowardly in refusing to make a decision and for pressurizing Bakhramov, a hapless Russian distracted by "all the nice things in England", who had allowed "the atmosphere of Wembley" to influence his judgement. When the controversy resurfaced in the mid-1990s Ludger Schulze of *Süddeutsche Zeitung* returned to the attack describing Dienst as a gutless postman from Basel and Bakhramov as an equally gutless teacher from Baku. Three years later, football journalist Roland Eitel, argued that Dienst had "shied away from taking responsibility" when he had walked over to Bahramov (cited in Henschel / Willen 1996: 23-4).

English perspectives have predominated to date in the published literature on the 1966 World Cup final. It is important to redress this imbalance as far as possible, though there are some difficulties in assessing exactly how Germans felt at the time. The context is important. International matches between the two countries had resumed only in December 1954 and West Germany had visited England only twice before the start of the tournament. Playing in England – and especially staying in England for a period of a month or so as in 1966 – was not an experience with which German players and officials were especially familiar. Burdened with the legacy of recent history, they were anxious to make a good impression and to avoid situations in which their actions and words might be misinterpreted. Answering critics of Franz Beckenbauer, who had twice been cautioned by referees during Germany's progress to the final, *Deutscher Fussball-Bund* (DFB) spokesman Dr Wilfried Gebhart explained that the young star had not protested even though one of his bookings had been a case of mistaken identity; "he did not protest because we do not encourage our players to do so"[13].

In 1966, though English people would have been unlikely to mention the war directly if they had encountered any Germans, a degree of ill-feeling persisted. This was understandable given the suffering so many had experienced between 1914 and 1918 and again between 1939 and 1945. As the competition reached its climax, however, the awkward silence surrounding this sensitive area was broken.

---

12 *The Times*, 1 August 1966: 5.
13 *Daily Express*, 28 July 1966: 16.

Britain's popular press has never been noted for its reticence and the fact that four of the five players sent off during the tournament had been playing against Germany supplied a convenient pretext. Reports such as those appearing in the *Daily Express* after the West Germany-Soviet Union semi-final, would have left Germans in England – players, officials, supporters – in no doubt that the war had not been forgotten and that German aggression was to blame.

> "Helmut Schoen, West German team manager, *advanced on London* yesterday 'angry, upset and disillusioned'.
> Why? Because of suggestions that his *well-drilled soccer troops* had 'provoked' opponents and 'overacted' on their *march* to Saturday's Wembley final"[14].

This was the kind of reporting that led German television presenter Werner Schneider to complain about Fleet Street's "tin soldiers". Coming a few days before the final, it made the point that Germany was still on probation and that the team still had to prove that they were 'good' rather than 'bad' Germans (see Porter 1999: 530-31; Ramsden 2006: 353-54).

Surveying Germany in the mid 1990s for a mainly British audience, John Ardagh observed (Ardagh 1995: 224):

> "In any country, sport provides a focus for national feeling, sometimes hysterical and excessive but at least better than making war; and in Germany today it offers a fairly harmless channel for the tentative rediscovery of a national spirit and a sense of identity".

By the end of the century this may have been so, though Ardagh also notes that the celebrations following West Germany's World Cup win in 1990 "were probably less fervent than they would have been in many countries, such as Britain" (ibid.: 577). In the 1950s and 1960s, as Germany struggled to shake off its Nazi past, unrestrained expressions of national identity were often seen as problematic, not least because they might re-open old wounds and raise new doubts regarding the two Germanies that had emerged from the ruins of war, the Federal Republic in particular (see Goldblatt 2006: 331; Hesse-Lichtenberger 2002: 129-31).

When Germany had won the World Cup for the first time in 1954 the celebrations were cut short lest they should rekindle the flame of nationalism. Reports that German supporters at the final in Berne and elsewhere had spontaneously broken into the first verse of *Deutschland über alles* rather than the less provoca-

---

14 *Daily Express*, 27 July 1966: 14; authors' italics.

tive third verse had caused Konrad Adenauer's government some anxiety. An ill-judged speech by Peco Bauwens, the DFB's president, which explained the German victory in terms that would have been acceptable in the 1930s but were now frowned upon, was another cause for concern (Goldblatt 2006: 354-55). It was as if readmission to the community of nations after 1945 had been offered only on condition that the Germans behaved themselves.

In Keber's film Rudi Michel, the match commentator for German television in 1966, is asked why, after Helmut Haller had opened the scoring in the twelfth minute of the match, he had exclaimed "Goal!" and then said nothing at all for 32 seconds. Michel explained: "We were the first post-war generation. We knew about radio in the Third Reich. It frightened us". In these circumstances – and especially when the implications of commentating on a match against England and in England are taken into account – it is clear that Michel had good reason to believe that the right thing to do at the time was to show restraint. To have behaved otherwise, to have followed his natural instincts and celebrated Haller's goal might have appeared arrogant and, in 1966, any hint of *Goebbelsschnauze*, the name many Germans gave to the state radio broadcasting in the Nazi era, was to be avoided, whatever the cost. Later, at the decisive point in the match, Michel's immediate reaction suggests that he doubts that the ball has crossed the line: "Hurst! Not in goal, no goal! Maybe a goal?" But by the time that the referee reaches his decision he has recovered his composure. *"Das wird wieder Diskussionen geben"*, he observes mildly. "There will be discussions about this"; an understatement as it transpired[15].

Arguably, in 1966, the main concern of the West German squad was to leave a good impression on and off the pitch and this they largely achieved. Helmut Schön seems to have been acutely sensitive in this respect. Perhaps because of what had happened to his home city of Dresden during the war he realized that some English people would find it difficult to forgive and forget. As Ulrich Hess-Lichtenberger has observed (2002: 181):

> "[Schön] was very well aware that his team represented a country which only 26 years previously had reduced London to rubble. Again and again he drummed the idea into the players that the most important thing, more important than winning, was to behave like gentlemen and sportsmen. So impressive were Schön's lectures that even 30 years later, Hans Tilkowski would say: 'The main thing was that we left a good impression".

---

15 For Michel's commentary see WM 1966 Finale: Duetschland-England 2-4 n.V. "Wembleytor" (German TV). youtube.com/watch?v=WatTYsOocrI. Accessed 29th April 2013.

In this Schön's team was successful and the German press responded accordingly. *Bild am Sonntag* praised the players for their sporting behaviour and for resisting the temptation to claim a moral victory; *Welt am Sonntag* reported that the goal was "the only discord in an otherwise splendid final"[16]. This was very much in line with what British newspapers were happy to say about the German team *after* England had won. The *Daily Express*, having described the Germans as "brutish" after their semi-final win over the Soviet Union, now took a different view, observing two days after the final that England were "the greatest" but "the Germans were pretty good too". Desmond Hackett's match report continued: "Their behaviour on the field and on the terraces made this game an example to the rest of the world"[17].

Thirty years later, the German players interviewed by Hesse-Lichtenberger were still inclined to take a generous view and he was keen to put the record straight on their behalf. "What is perhaps not so well understood", he explained, "is that Germany did not hold a particular grudge about the outcome, and the controversial third goal in particular". Only one player, goalkeeper Hans Tilkowski, "couldn't get the third goal out of his system", but he had experienced three controversial decisions given in favour of English sides in the space of a few months – the first at Wembley in February 1966, the second while playing for Borussia Dortmund against Liverpool in May, and then the disputed goal in the final. Wolfgang Overath's view was more typical: "England had a great side. We accepted this defeat, and I hope our conduct brought credit to the German team" (Hesse-Lichtenberger 2002: 183). This suggests that much English reporting since 1966 has been wide of the mark. Despite Overath and his colleagues telling Hesse-Lichtenberger how it really was, a leading article in the *Sunday Times* a few years later vehemently criticized Helmut Haller, who seemed reluctant to hand over the ball that he had taken away at the end of the match. "Germany's reluctance to declare an armistice on the 1966 World Cup final by repatriating the ball" was deemed unsporting. Helmut Kohl, apparently, should have "told his recalcitrant fellow countrymen that holding Mr Hurst's ball to ransom simply was not cricket"[18]. An *armistice*? Arguably, for an English newspaper, recourse to the military metaphor was instinctive, even when striving to achieve a jokey effect. The cultural gap separating England and Germany was as wide as ever.

One other factor which helped to ensure that West German teams behaved with propriety in 1966 was that they were being watched by their neighbours in

---

16 *Bild am Sonntag*, 31 July 1966; *Welt am Sonntag*, 31 July 1966.

17 *Daily Express*, 1 August 1966: 14.

18 *Sunday Times*, 28 April 1996: 4.

the East. There had been no sterner critics of the outpouring of nationalist sentiment prompted by the 'miracle of Berne' in 1954 than the East German press which claimed that West Germany's victory would encourage fascists and aggressive nationalists of all kinds to come out of the closets in which they had been hiding since 1945 (Goldblatt 2006: 354). After 1966 the East German authorities were anxious to ensure that any interest that the tournament had aroused should be kept in check. One curious outcome of this policy was a detective story, *Der Mörder sitzt im Wembley Stadion* by Hans Walldorf, a pseudonym that hid the identity of Erich Loest, a writer whose early works had attracted unfavourable attention in official circles leading to his imprisonment in 1957. Now released, Loest was encouraged by the Stasi to write a work of detective fiction that would exploit current interest in the World Cup while simultaneously conveying anti-capitalist propaganda to East German readers. His book, published in 1967 and adapted for television, sold well though Loest, who had never been to London, was later embarrassed to discover that his depiction of Wembley and of life in England generally had been woefully inaccurate (Walldorf 1967: 197-199). Though there was probably little to be gained by returning to the 1966 theme it seems likely that the East German government were aware that *Das Wembleytor* was a sensitive subject that its counterpart in Bonn would rather avoid. In 1987 another East German writer, Günter Simon, re-opened the case. He praised the players for their sporting behaviour in defeat but criticized politically-motivated journalists who still claimed that West Germany had been the victims of a conspiracy in 1966 and denied a victory that they deserved. Referring to the banners which had greeted Schön's team as the "real world champions", he asked mischievously if this implied that England were "false world champions" (cited in Henschel / Willen 1996: 21).

3   Some conclusions

"Finally, we know the truth, ladies and gentlemen. The ball did not cross the line. Football history has to be re-written" (cited in Henschel / Willen 1996: 12-13). Ulrich Wickert, anchor-man for the late news on German television opened his broadcast with these words and went on to give details of Reid and Zisserman's research. What made the story especially newsworthy from a German viewpoint – even thirty years after the event – was that the findings carried the imprimatur of one of England's most prestigious and well-known academic institutions. The *Frankfurter Rundschau* (1995) demanded that the two researchers should be awarded professorships because they had not allowed their feelings for their country to interfere with the search for the "truth" (Henschel / Willen 1996: 13). Back in England, there were some who remained unimpressed. Gordon Banks, England's goalkeeper in 1966, was adamant that the ball had crossed the line and criticized "boffins from the Academy of Rear-End Speech" who had "wasted countless hours of computer time". "What's the point?", he asked, before adding significantly, "Where's their patriotism?" (Banks 2002: 138). By the turn of the century, however, few in England, even among Banks's former teammates, were inclined to challenge the verdict of science. "The relatively infant TV technology wasn't really conclusive", observed George Cohen, "but when all the emotions had drained away I had to concede that the most beautiful goal I have ever seen was also the most dubious" (Cohen 2005: 251; see also Porter 2009: 534-35). Perhaps the main contribution of the Oxford University researchers has been to take any heat that was left out of the debate.

Confronted with Reid and Zisserman's conclusions the referee at the centre of the controversy had responded wearily. "These people must have plenty of time", said Dienst. "Why are they doing this? No computer could convince me. My decision will stand forever" (cited in Henschel / Willen 1996: 14). He was right to point out that the hours which Reid and Zisserman had spent in resolving the mystery had actually changed nothing. "Every so often", Roger Hunt observed forty years after the event, "someone analyses the film and 'conclusively' proves that it was or wasn't over the line". The only thing that mattered, he added, "was that the linesman gave it" (Hunt interviewed in Massarella / Moynihan 2006: 73). Moreover, by then, apart from tabloid journalists and soccer 'anoraks', very few people – Hans Tilkowski and Gordon Banks aside – cared passionately about the details. Over the period since the 1966 final football relations between England and Germany had been normalized, and Germany normally won. This meant that there was no pressing imperative for German fans to rake over the ashes of an old controversy, though there was no doubt some satisfaction in being proved right at the end of the day. The publication in 1996 of Henschel and Willen's collection *Drin oder Linie? Alles übers dritte Tor* might be seen as an attempt to put the topic to bed.

To later generations who did not have to carry the burden of war guilt that still lay heavily on German shoulders in 1966, the equanimity with which Schön's players accepted defeat may have seemed a little strange. As Honigstein observes, only after a few glasses of champagne at the official banquet did anyone seriously challenge Dienst's decision. Yet he also observes that subsequent wins over England and success in the World and European championships "quickly tempered" any lingering sense of injustice (Honigstein 2009: 204-5). In Jochen Schimmang's *Der schöne Vogel Phoenix*, first published in 1979, the author focuses on Murnau, a representative figure of his generation, whose teenage fixation on England in the

1960s settles at first on the unlikely figure of Nobby Stiles before shifting to Mick Jagger after he advised the audience at the Rolling Stones' famous Hyde Park concert in 1969 to "keep it cool". Murnau reaches maturity when he is able to put football, Nobby Stiles and 1966 behind him and thus becomes "cool", an interesting and significant metaphorical transformation (Waine 1989: 69; Schimmang 1979).

It was much more difficult for the English to be cool about 1966 because the story of England's victory was recycled by the media whenever a major tournament or a match against Germany approached. The received wisdom was that England had won on merit in 1966, thus the question of whether the ball had crossed the line was largely irrelevant, except when it could be used by tabloid journalists in their protracted pantomime war against the Germans (Young 2007: 10-14). In Kleber's film, Thomas Keilinger, a former journalist who has specialised in Anglo-German relations, compared England's World Cup victory in 1966 with Germany's in 1954. Both had a positive impact on national morale. However, whereas 'the miracle of Berne' helped to initiate West Germany's 'economic miracle', England's victory simply provided a welcome distraction from the economic problems that it was experiencing at the time and a happy memory which provided some comfort when these worsened in the 1970s[19]. Thus, though the difficulties which the English had in coming to terms with relative economic decline and the end of empire are sometimes overstated, Wembley 1966 may have played some part in helping to sustain a sense of national well-being. Ironically, the myth of 1966 seemed to become more powerful as later generations of English footballers failed to build on what Moore, Hurst, Charlton and their colleagues had achieved. Perhaps, as the title of Kleber's film implies, Wembley was cursed. Perhaps, as Downing and others have argued, it was simply that the 'fatal victory' made English football complacent and reluctant to change its ways (Downing 2001: 118; see also Porter 2004: 43-45).

Though the story of the final has been rehashed so many times that it has acquired the status of a national myth few English people have any idea of how other countries viewed their team's one and only world championship victory. Professor Chris Young, a football fan as well as a distinguished historian of Germany, has related that he first encountered photographic evidence of spectators on the pitch as Hurst scored England's fourth goal only when he was shown it years after the event by a professor at the University of Bochum (Young 2007: 14-15). The English press, especially the tabloids, have played a major part in ensuring that their readers remain in blissful ignorance but there are signs that even they are at last recognizing the ball-over-the line saga for the tired cliché that it has become. On 1 April

---

19 Keilinger interviewed in *Der Fluch von Wembley*.

2010, the *Sun* newspaper's webpage ran a story that Sir Geoff Hurst had finally admitted that "the Russian linesman got it wrong". After 44 years he thought it only right that people "should know the truth".[20] This was, of course, an elaborate 'April Fool's Day' hoax which was plausible only because the *Sun* was parodying itself. More recently, an article in the *Daily Mirror* marking Helmut Haller's death in a respectful fashion seemed to establish a new tone. He was pictured with Hurst holding the match ball which he had returned to England in 1996. Both were wearing T-shirts carrying the message "IT'S ALL OVER NOW"[21]. We shall see.

Bibliography

Ardagh, J. (1995): Germany and the Germans: the United Germany in the mid-1950s. London: Penguin Books.

Armfield, J. (with Andrew Collomosse) (2004): Right Back to the Beginning: the Autobiography. London: Headline.

Arnott, J. (2001): He Kills Coppers. London: Sceptre.

Banks, G. (2002): Banksy: My Autobiography. London: Michael Joseph.

Chapman, P. (1999): The Goalkeeper's History of Britain. London: Fourth Estate.

Cohen, G. (2005): My Autobiography. London: Headline.

Cowley, J. (2009): The Last Game: Love, Death and Football. London: Simon & Schuster.

Downing, D. (2001): The Best of Enemies: England v Germany. London: Bloomsbury.

Giles, J. (2004): The Parlour and the Suburb: Domestic Identities, Class, Femininity and Modernity. Oxford: Berg.

Glanville, B. (1999): Football Memories. London: Virgin Publishing.

Goldblatt, D. (2006): The Ball is Round: a Global History of Football. London: Viking.

Hattenstone, S. (2006): The Best of Times: What Became of the Heroes of '66'. London: Guardian Books.

Henschel, G. / Willen, G. (eds) (1996): Drin oder Linie? Alles übers dritte Tor. Leipzig: Reclam.

Hesse-Lichtenberger, U. (2002): Tor! The Story of German Football. London: WSC Books.

Honigstein, R. (2009): Englischer Fussball: A German's View of Our Beautiful Game. London: Yellow Jersey Press.

Massarella, L. / Moynihan, L. (eds) (2006): Match of My Life: England World Cup. Studley: Know the Score Books.

McIlvanney, H. (1966): The Final: England v West Germany. In: McIlvanney, H. (ed): World Cup '66. London: Eyre & Spottiswoode.

Porter, D. (2009): Egg and Chips with the Connellys: Remembering 1966. In: Sport in History, 29 (3), 519-39.

---

20 www.thesun.co.uk/sol/homepage/sport/football/2915942/Sir-Geoff-Hurst-it-didn't-cross-the-line.html. Accessed 20 October 2012.

21 *Daily Mirror*, 12 October 2012 at www.mirror.co.uk/news/world-news-rip-helmut-haller-german-nicked-1375592. Accessed 20 October 2012.

Porter, D. (2004): "Your Boys Took One Hell of a Beating": English football and British Decline, c1950-80. In: Porter, D. / Smith, A. (eds.): Sport and National Identity in the Post-War World. London: Routledge, 31-51.

Powell, J. (2002): Bobby Moore: the Life and Times of a Sporting Hero. London: Robson Books, first published in 1993.

Ramsden, J. (2006): Don't Mention the War: The British and the Germans since 1890. London: Little, Brown.

Reid, I. / Zisserman, A. (1996): Goal-directed Video Metrology. Proceedings of the Fourth European Conference on Computer Vision. Cambridge UK, vol. II.

Sandbrook, D. (2007): White Heat: A History of Britain in the Swinging Sixties. London: Abacus.

Schimmang, J. (1979): Der schöne Vogel Phönix: Erinnerungen eines Dreißigjähren. Frankfurt am Main: Suhrkamp.

Thomson, D. (1996): 4-2. London: Bloomsbury Publications.

Waine, A. (1989): Recent German Writing and the Influence of Popular Culture. In: Bullivant, K. (ed): After the "Death of Literature": West German Writing of the 1970s. Oxford: Berg, 69-87.

Walldorf, H. (Erich Loest) (1967): Der Mörder saß im Wembley-Stadion. Halle: Volk und Welt.

Weight, R. (2002): Patriots: National Identity in Britain 1940-2000.Basingstoke: Macmillan.

Young, C. (2007): Two World Wars and One World Cup: Humour, Trauma and the Asymmetric Relationship in Anglo-German Football. In: Sport in History, 27 (1), 2007, 10-14.

„Ich dusch nur mit dem Arsch zur Wand": Verletzungsmacht und Verletzungs- offenheit als simultane Konstruktion von Heteronormativität

"I only take a shower standing with my arse to the wall": Power to Inflict Hurt and Vulnerability to Sustain Hurt as Simultaneously Constructing Heteronormativity

Nina Degele

Zusammenfassung

Männer können sich über unterschiedliche Strategien ihrer Verletzungsmacht als Signum von Männlichkeit versichern. Zum einen eignen sich dafür hierarchische Geschlechterdifferenzierungen, zum anderen die Konstruktion eines verletzungsoffenen homosozialen Gegenübers, was unter dem Titel hegemoniale Männlichkeit verhandelt wird. Relevant ist aber auch – das ist die These des Beitrags – eine dritte Option, nämlich die Herstellung von Verletzungsmacht über Verletzungsoffenheit. Gemeint ist damit ihre simultane diskursive Konstitution: Sehen sich Akteure durch Gewalt von Männern gefährdet, schlagen sie prophylaktisch zu (und nicht lediglich als Reaktion zurück). Wie eine solche

Gewaltrelation – auch wenn sie nicht real existiert, sondern kontrafaktisch anti-
zipiert wird – für identitäre Positionierungen genutzt wird, will ich am Beispiel
von Homophobie im Fußball darlegen: Fans, Spieler und Fußballinteressierte
konstruieren mit dem ominösen Ort der Dusche ein exklusives homosoziales
Schlachtfeld für die Herstellung und Bewahrung von Mannsein, das außerhalb
dieses Raums und sonst in der Gesellschaft vermutlich kein Pendant hat.
Grundlage meiner Ausführungen sind 24 Gruppendiskussionen mit
Fußballinteressierten, SpielerInnen und Fans unterschiedlicher Geschlechter,
sexueller Orientierungen, Nationalitäten und Ethnizitäten, Alter, Schichten
und (Nicht)Behinderungen.

Abstract

Men are able to reassure themselves of their power to inflict hurt as a sign
of masculinity by using different strategies. One type of strategy available for
achieving this is creating hierarchical gender differentiations, whilst another
lies in the construction of an opposing homosocial other who is open to being
hurt. This strategy is dealt with under the heading of hegemonic masculinity.
The argument being put forward in this essay is the relevance of a third option
which is how men generate power to inflict pain over those who are vulner-
able to it. By this we are referring to its simultaneous discursive constitution.
If social actors see themselves threatened by male violence they hit out pro-
phylactically (and not merely as a reaction). I intend to show how such power
relations – even when they do not actually exist but are being counterfactually
anticipated – are being employed for positioning one's identity, by using the
example of homophobia in football. Fans, players and those interested in football construct via the dubious sphere of the showers an exclusive homosocial
battle ground where manliness is created and maintained and which presum-
ably has no equivalent outside this sphere nor found anywhere else in society.
Forming the basis of my analytical observations are 24 group discussions with
people interested in football, women footballers and fans of both sexes, of different sexual orientations, ethnic backgrounds and nationalities, and from different social classes and with (non) disabilities.

1   Einleitung

Um sich ihres Mannseins zu versichern, können sich Männer beispielsweise für
Fußball interessieren. Denn Fußball ist noch immer ein „Reservat scheinbar ungebremster Maskulinität" (Sülzle 2005: 39), und Homophobie ist unhinterfragter

Teil einer solchen Fußballkultur (vgl. Leibfried u. a. 2011: 14-28). Vor mehr als zwei Jahrzehnten hat dies der britische Stürmer Justin Fashanu schmerzhaft erfahren: Er war 1990 der erste Profispieler, der sich als schwul outete. Acht Jahre später erhängte er sich in seiner Garage, nachdem er der Vergewaltigung an einem Siebzehnjährigen bezichtigt wurde, was sich als nicht haltbar erwies (Krennhuber 2006). Ein Outing im Profifußball hat es seitdem nicht mehr gegeben, auch wenn Bundeskanzlerin Angela Merkel im September 2012 im Zusammenhang mit der DFB-Aktion „Gehe deinen Weg", die gegen Rassismus und Ausgrenzung gerichtet war, schwule Fußballer zu einem öffentlichen Bekenntnis ermutigte: „Ich bin der Meinung, dass jeder, der die Kraft aufbringt und den Mut hat – wir haben in der Politik einen längeren Prozess hinter uns – wissen sollte, dass er in einem Land lebt, wo er sich eigentlich davor nicht fürchten sollte" (http://bundesliga.t-online.de/homosexualitaet-im-fussball-merkel-ermutigt-spieler/id_59526858/index. Zugriff am 15.1.2013). Genau im beiläufigen ‚eigentlich' steckt das Problem. Denn ‚eigentlich' sollte etwas nicht mehr benannt werden müssen, weil es nicht mehr relevant sein soll, faktisch muss es überhaupt erst einmal benannt werden, um überhaupt erst relevant zu werden. Das gilt nicht nur für den Profifußball, sondern auch – wenngleich hinsichtlich der massenmedialen Wirkung anders akzentuiert – für den Amateur- und Freizeitfußball, auf den ich mich in diesem Beitrag konzentriere.

Die Abwertung von Schwulen (im Hinblick auf Sexualität) und Frauen (in Bezug auf Geschlecht) ist hierzulande nicht mehr unbedingt politisch korrekt. Entsprechend fassen TeilnehmerInnen einer Studie zu Sexismus, Rassismus und Homophobie im Fußball kein anderes Thema so vorsichtig an wie Homosexualität[1]. Gleichwohl entwischt einer Dorfmannschaft zu Beginn ihrer Diskussion beim Anblick eines Plakats, bei dem unter anderem zwei sich (offensichtlich nach einem Tor) umarmende und auf dem Boden liegende Fußballer die Bezeichnung ‚Schwuchtel'. Ohne Trikots sähe die Szene schwul aus, „aber schwul zu sein gibt es ja im Fußball nicht". In dieser Logik darf es im Fußball keine Schwulen geben, weil man bei solchen Umarmungen sonst immer den Hintergedanken haben müsste, dass die Mitspieler Hintergedanken haben. Das klingt verquast und wird

---

1 Bei der Untersuchung haben 24 Gruppen von SpielerInnen, Fans und anderen Fußball-interessierten unterschiedlicher Geschlechter, sexueller Orientierungen, Nationalitäten und Ethnizitäten, Alter, Schichten und (Nicht)Behinderungen zum Thema Fußball diskutiert. Um Tabuthemen wie Homophobie, Sexismus und Rassismus im Fußball sichtbar zu machen, ohne Diskutierende zu verschrecken und ohne zu reifizieren, haben wir als Diskussionsanreiz ein Plakat mit acht Bildern auf einem Fußballfeld als Hintergrund verwendet (vgl. Degele/Janz 2011). Die folgenden Zitate sind den Gruppendiskussionen entnommen.

es noch mehr, denn der paradigmatische Ort, an dem sich solche Hintergedanken bündeln, ist nicht das Spielfeld, sondern – diese These möchte ich entwickeln – die Dusche. So ist für einen Dorfverein klar: „Man duscht ja nicht mit einem Schwulen".

Um die Umkleide und Dusche als Ort der Konstruktion von Heteronormativität zu rekonstruieren, beziehe ich mich auf Befunde einer explorativen Studie zur Umkleide[2]. Dort findet ein Wechsel sozialer Kontexte (und nicht nur der Kleidung) statt, ich stelle dabei die Ordnung der Blicke in den Vordergrund (3). Dann spüre ich anhand der Befunde einer abgeschlossenen Studie zu Fußball als Arena von Ein- und Ausschlüssen (Degele 2013) dem Zusammenhang von Verletzungsmacht und -offenheit nach (4). Abschließend entwickle ich die These verängstigter Körper, die in Ermangelung habitualisierten Umgangs mit Unsicherheit ihre Ängste vor Kontrollverlust in Schwule projizieren (4). Zunächst aber skizziere ich Duschen und Umkleiden als Forschungsfeld, in dem ich die Konstruktion von Heteronormativität zunächst theoretisch verorte (2).

2 Beim Duschen und Umkleiden: Heteronormativität konstruieren

Hinter der Abneigung, gemeinsam mit einem Schwulen unter der Dusche zu stehen, verbirgt sich das Unbehagen bis hin zur Angst, objektiviert, verführt oder gar vergewaltigt zu werden. Um das zu zeigen, erweitere ich Heinrich Popitz' (1992: 43) Konzeption von Verletzungsoffenheit und Verletzungsmacht hetero-

---

2   Diese Untersuchung haben Stephanie Bethmann, Karolin Heckemeyer und ich im Rahmen eines Methodenprojekts 2010 am Institut für Soziologie der Universität Freiburg durchgeführt. Die Untersuchung umfasst 101 Beobachtungsprotokolle von Menschen in Umkleiden, die durch Protokolle durch Skizzen und Fotos der Räumlichkeiten ergänzt wurden. Diese befanden sich in Sportstätten (Schwimmbäder, Sporthallen, Fitnessstudios, Kampfsportstudios), Intensivstationen von Krankenhäusern, Praxen von Frauenärzten und Bekleidungsabteilungen von Kaufhäusern. An der Untersuchung beteiligt waren Anne-Kerrin Gomer, Magdalena Jaglo, Gregor Kühnrich, Marina Sawazki, Victoria Stark, Martin Teske und Petr Vasek, dafür herzlichen Dank. Die untersuchten Umkleiden werden von Gemeinschaften (von Sportteams), von Bekannten und FreundInnen, Familien, ArbeitskollegInnen oder Einzelnen genutzt, relevante Kontexte sind Freizeit und Beruf. Alle Umkleiden waren nach Geschlechtern segregiert, ein knappes Drittel der Beobachtungen erfolgte in Männerumkleiden, gut zwei Drittel in Umkleiden von Frauen. Mein Dank für die intensiven Diskussionen wie auch die Verwendung der gemeinsamen Ergebnisse geht an Stephanie Bethmann und Karolin Heckemeyer.

normativitätstheoretisch. Einer etablierten Figur traditioneller Geschlechterord-
nung zufolge ‚sind' Männer ihrer Sexualität ausgeliefert und damit verletzungsoffen, Frauen dagegen mit verführerischer Körperlichkeit ausgestattet und damit
verletzungsmächtig. Männer gelten als verführbar, triebhaft, haben (wie etwa
Dominique Strauss-Kahn) ihre sexuellen Bedürfnisse nicht unter Kontrolle und
sind deshalb permanent in Versuchung, über Frauen herzufallen. Um nun eine
Vergewaltigung zu vermeiden, sind Frauen dafür verantwortlich, solchermaßen
triebgesteuerte Wesen nicht zu provozieren. Das kann über eine Verhüllung körperlicher Reize (z.b. weiter und langer Kleidung, Kopftuch oder noch wirkungs-
voller Burka) oder Ausschluss (z.B. aus Herrenclubs) bewerkstelligt werden.

Nach diesem Muster funktioniert auch die Konstruktion von Heteronormativität in der Dusche: Schwulen wird Verletzungsmacht unterstellt, egal ob aufgrund
verführerischen Charmes (das wäre der feminisierte Schwule) oder ungebremster
Triebhaftigkeit (das entspricht dem Bild des hypermaskulinen Schwulen). Diese
beiden Formen schwuler Versuchung oder Gewalt sind als Idealtypen eines Kon-
tinuums zu verstehen, nicht einer Dichotomie. In jedem Fall sind duschende Heterosexuelle einer doppelten Bedrohung ausgeliefert: Im Fall der schwulen Verführung geschieht eine Feminisierung des Mitduschenden, entsprechend besteht
die Herausforderung darin, kein eigenes schwules Begehren zuzulassen. Beim
Gegenpart des aktiven Schwulen dagegen findet eine nicht minder bedrohliche
Umkehrung statt, nämlich eine Eigenfeminisierung: Der mitduschende Schwule
ist mit dem Privileg der physischen Verletzungsmacht ausgestattet. Was sich in
gemischtgeschlechtlichen Konstellationen in der Gefahr des Vergewaltigtwerdens
von Frauen durch Männer niederschlägt, wird nun zur Möglichkeit unter Männern.

Hinter diesem doppelten Bedrohungsszenario steckt eine heteronormative
Logik der Geschlechterkonstruktion (vgl. Degele 2005): Mannsein ist konstitu-
tiv an Heterosexualität und Nicht-Frausein geknüpft. Der Sport allgemein und
die Dusche und Umkleide im Besonderen sind dabei ein homosozialer Raum der
Mannwerdung in Abgrenzung zu Frauen und nicht-heterosexuellen Männern.
Weil im Männersport (außer als Zuschauerinnen) und in der Umkleide üblicherweise keine Frauen anzutreffen sind, stellen dort nicht-heterosexuell begehren-
de Männer die einzig mögliche ‚Gefahr' und damit die Bedrohung schlechthin
dar und müssen deshalb ausgeschlossen werden. Dass die Umkleide und Dusche
diese Gefahr verschärfen, liegt neben der Exklusion von Frauen zum einen daran, dass dort nackte Körper aufeinandertreffen, was außerhalb dieser Räume im
homosozialen Umfeld kaum der Fall ist. Zum anderen verfügen nur wenige über
regelmäßige eigene Erfahrungen in (halb)öffentlichen Umkleiden, weshalb sich

diese als Projektionsfläche für Vorstellungen, Wünsche und Ängste eignen und zu Ikonen entsprechender Szenarien werden. Vor diesem Hintergrund frage ich danach, was die Umkleide als einen die Dusche einbettenden Interaktionsraum auszeichnet. Es erstaunt nämlich, dass dieser Ort der Bündelung physischen und sozialen Wandels so wenig wissenschaftliche Aufmerksamkeit erfährt: „There are no definitive studies that document the effects of participating in locker room culture" (Curry 1991: 133). Das stellte Timothy Curry vor zwei Jahrzehnten fest, und 2006 beklagte Caroline Fusco, dass über die Umkleide als Mix von „cleanliness, hygiene, and disgust" (Fusco 2006: 7) immer noch zu wenig bekannt sei. Für Hans Peter Duerr (1988: 92-116, 145-165) liefern Beobachtungen zum Umkleiden im Kontext von Baden in der Neuzeit wie auch zum indiskreten und nudistischen Blick den Beweis, dass die traditionellen Menschen viel enger miteinander verflochten waren und über deutlich höhere Scham- und Peinlichkeitsschwellen verfügten als Norbert Elias dies in seiner Zivilisationstheorie behauptete. Ken Plummer (2006) sieht in Umkleiden und Duschen Orte der Mannwerdung, in die Homophobie eingeschrieben ist. Damit gerät der Aspekt der Sexualität in den Vordergrund, was Rob Cover mit der These der Unmöglichkeit nicht-sexueller Nacktheit verbindet: „nakedness, as the exposure of the genitals, cannot be disconnected from sexuality" (Cover 2003: 55), Nacktheit sei in der jüdisch-christlichen Tradition ein Euphemismus und ein verbotener Code für Sexualität. Im Anschluss an Elizabeth Grosz unterscheidet er vier Kontexte legitimer Nacktheit, nämlich erstens innerhalb von Machtbeziehungen (z.B. Eltern/Kind), zweitens intimer (Liebes)Beziehungen, drittens medialisierter Repräsentationen/Kunst und viertens explizit nicht-sexualisierte Orte mit praktischen und vergnüglichen Zwecken wie Duschen in Umkleiden, Straßenkunst oder FKK, die durch Verhaltensregeln genau strukturiert seien (Cover 2003: 56f.). Dieser letzte Aspekt ist im Folgenden relevant, genauer: Techniken der Legitimierung des Wechsels von bekleidet zu nackt und umgekehrt, wie es etwa Jean-Claude Kaufmanns (1996) in seinen Beobachtungen zum Phänomen des Oben-ohne von Frauen am Strand unternommen hat.

3   Geregelte Umkleide: kontrolliert blicken

Umkleiden als „places where people are half naked or completely naked" (Fusco 2006: 7) sind ebenso gefährdete wie auch durch Interaktionsstrategien gesicherte „Räume, Gelegenheiten und Zusammenkünfte, in denen die Individuen [...] einen Arbeitskonsens über die Beschaffenheit ihrer Wirklichkeit herstellen" (Hettlage 2003: 190). Die Wirklichkeit von Umkleiden ist dadurch gekennzeichnet, dass dort nackte, und das heißt geschlechtlich markierte Körper den Blicken anderer, meist ausschließlich des eigenen Geschlechts ausgesetzt sind. Dabei lassen sich in erster Annäherung Kontakte zwischen Bekannten und Unbekannten unterscheiden: „Als allgemeine Regel könnte man sagen, dass miteinander bekannte Personen in einer sozialen Situation einen Grund haben müssen, Blickkontakt zu vermeiden, während einander nicht Bekannte eines Grundes bedürfen, um miteinander in Kontakt zu treten" (Goffman 2009: 136). So dominiert in Umkleiden bei Unbekannten eine durch Beiläufigkeit charakterisierte nicht-zentrierte Interaktion: Mindestens zwei AkteurInnen nehmen einander wahr und richten das eigene Verhalten daran aus (Goffman 2009: 40). Zwischen Unbekannten stellt damit eine höfliche Gleichgültigkeit den Originalmodus der Interaktion(svermeidung) dar. Dieser geschieht allerdings nicht einfach, sondern muss aktiv hergestellt werden. Dazu dienen die drei Techniken des Nicht-Schauens, des Abwendens/Schließens des Körpers sowie der Abstandsmaximierung:

Was Kaufmann hinsichtlich der Ordnung des Blicks (Goffman 2009: 102-117) für halbnackte (Frauen)Körper am Strand beschreibt, gilt auch für die Umkleide: „[e]s gibt kaum einen Ort, an dem das, was offensichtlich den Blicken ausgeliefert wird, so privat wäre, an dem sich das Private so intensiv in der Öffentlichkeit ausliefern würde, ohne sich preiszugeben" (Kaufmann 1996: 134). So gilt in der Umkleide die Norm des Nicht-Schauens, das heißt das Vermeiden eines direkten Blickkontakts. Kaufmann bezeichnet das Sehen, ohne zu sehen, als visuelles Dahingleiten (Kaufmann 1996: 164). Blicke auf Körper werden vermieden, statt dessen dominiert der Blick in die Augen. Blicke und Kommentare sind nur zu unverfänglichen Körperteilen erlaubt, „die Normalisierung hat es geschafft, Unsichtbarkeit zu konstruieren" (Kaufmann 1996: 160)[3]. Weiter wenden sich Menschen in der Umkleide zumeist mit der Körpervorderseite dem Spind oder der Wand zu und das heißt mit der Rückenseite zu den anderen. Durch diese Position wie auch durch eine geschlossene Körperhaltung (Senken des Kopfs und Bücken des Oberkörpers) verbergen sie ihre primären und sekundären Geschlechtsmerkmale und machen ihre aktive Körperhälfte weitgehend unsichtbar. Schließlich gilt neben den Geboten des Nicht-Schauens und des Abwendens des Körpers die Norm der Abstandsmaximierung bei der Platzwahl. Danach suchen sich die hinzu Kommenden eine möglichst weit von den bereits belegten Plätzen entfernte Stelle. Eine solche Abstandsmaximierung darf allerdings nicht offen-

---

3 Die Praxis des Oben-ohne am Strand beispielsweise ist normalisiert, wenn die Blicke es nicht mehr sehen, wenn sich das Auge auf etwas anderes konzentriert: „Weil es normal wird, sehen es die Blicke nicht mehr und weil es die Blicke nicht mehr sehen, wird es normal, Oben-Ohne zu praktizieren" (Kaufmann 1996: 156).

sichtlich erfolgen, um nicht den Anschein unfreundlicher Distanzierung zu erwecken. Kaufmann (1996: 120f) bezeichnet das als Banalisierungscode: Implizite Regeln dürfen zum Beweis ihrer Normalität nicht expliziert werden. Vielmehr ist die Platzwahl mit Zielstrebigkeit verbunden, es interessiert in diesem Moment nichts anderes. Gleichwohl kann es zu Phasen erhöhter Zugänglichkeit kommen, die ebenfalls über Blicke eingeleitet werden. Sie entstehen beispielsweise durch das Zusammenrücken und damit verbundene Gewähren von Platz vor einer Spindreihe, durch Hilfestellung bei der Spindbenutzung (wenn er sich nicht verschließen oder öffnen lässt), durch Bekundung von Solidarität wie etwa dem mitfühlenden Blick auf das sich als technisch schwierig entpuppenden Schließen des BHs, oder auch durch ein zustimmungsheischendes Lächeln angesichts eines in der Umkleide störenden Kindes.

Etwas anders gestaltet sich die Interaktionsordnung in Umkleiden bei Gruppen. Dort definieren Blicke nicht nur höfliche Gleichgültigkeit, sondern auch Zugehörigkeiten: Legitime und illegitime Blicke unterscheiden zuverlässig nach dem Bekanntheitsgrad der Beteiligten. So schauen sich Kampfsportlerinnen einer Trainingsgruppe direkt an, im Schwimmbad sind es nur diejenigen, die sich kennen. Besonders deutlich wird dies beim Vergleich zweier Frauenumkleiden in einem Freibad. Eine der beiden Umkleiden gehört zum einzigen Damenbad in Deutschland exklusiv für Frauen – dort kennen sich die meisten Frauen untereinander und treffen sich regelmäßig –, sie nehmen sich in der Umkleide Zeit, und viele zeigen sich auch über den technischen Teil des An- und Ausziehens hinaus nackt. Die andere Umkleide führt zum geschlechtergemischten Teil des Bads, dort bewerkstelligten die beteiligten Frauen das Umkleiden zielgerichteter und hastiger. Bei Gruppen lässt sich auch beobachten, dass das Gebot der größtmöglichen Entfernung nur bei Bekannten aufgehoben wird, körperliche Nacktheit wird offen gezeigt. Auch sind die Gesprächsthemen intimer als es der öffentliche Charakter des Ortes nahe legen würde. In der Männerumkleide eines Schwimmbads kam es im Beobachtungszeitraum zweimal zu der Situation, dass sich innerhalb einer Gruppe untereinander bekannter junger Männer ein Halbkreis bildete, der die noch nicht fertig umgezogenen Männer wie eine Mauer vor Blicken anderer abschirmte. Gruppen schaffen also ihrerseits Räume, die Einzelne draußen halten[4].

---

4 Eine Zwischenform bilden Arbeitsbeziehungen, wie sie etwa bei Krankenschwestern einer Intensivstation zu beobachten sind: Zwar kennen sich die Frauen mitunter schon über Jahre, sie wenden sich beim Umziehen aber wie unter Unbekannten dem Spind zu, bringen die nie ganz nackten Körper (die Frauen behalten Unterhosen, BH und Socken meist an) in eine Schutzposition, sichern das eigene Territorium gegenüber der Nachbarin mit Gegenständen wie Taschen, Kleidungsstücken oder auch Bildern von Männern

Muss in der Umkleide und beim Duschen der Blick kontrolliert werden (Cover 2003: 59), interessiert doch, um welche Art von Blick es sich dabei handelt. Dazu folgende Szene aus der Umkleide eine Hallenbads[5]: An einem Sonntagnachmittag ist die größere von zwei Umkleiden rappelvoll mit Frauen und kleinen Kindern. Eine etwa 50jährige Frau (C) steht dort gerade nackt mit der Unterhose in der Hand, als eine ältere Dame (A) mit einem etwa 8-jährigen Jungen (B) herein kommt. Dieser schaut einmal rundherum und setzt sich dann auf einen Rest freier Umkleidebank. Darauf entspinnt sich folgendes Gespräch:

A: Los jetzt, trockne dich ab!

B: Die Umkleidekabine ist nicht frei.

A: Dann fang wenigstens oben rum schon mal an.

C (noch nackt, zieht sich weiter an und fragt den Jungen): Sag mal, wie alt bist du eigentlich?

B (artig): Acht.

A: Du musst der Frau nicht antworten, [Name]!

C: Nein, aber es ist doch interessant, dass Jungs mit acht noch hier reindürfen. Ich dachte, sechs ist die Grenze.

A: Der kuckt Ihnen schon nix weg!

C: Darum geht's nicht. Es geht darum, dass der Kleine augenscheinlich schon groß genug ist, sich für seinen Pimmel zu schämen, also hat er sehr wohl ein Bewusstsein für Geschlechtlichkeit.

A: Das kann Ihnen ja wohl egal sein!

C: Ist es nicht, immerhin guckt uns der Junge offenbar als Frauen an, in einem geschützten Raum, in dem Frauen sich eben nicht begaffen lassen müssen.

A: Ach, Quatsch...

---

in Boxershorts im Spind. Zum Dienstbeginn führen sie dienstliche Gespräche, danach schalten sie unmittelbar auf Freizeit um und wünschen sich einen guten Feierabend. Mit Kaufman lässt sich das so interpretieren, dass die Zugehörigkeit zu einer Gruppe den Zustand der Nacktheit nicht einfacher macht; Unbekanntheit operiert vielmehr als positive Voraussetzung für das Nackt-Sein. In seiner Studie zum Oben-ohne am Strand berichtet er von peinlichen Situationen, wenn Oben-ohne-Frauen etwa bekannten Personen wie BerufskollegInnen begegnen. Er erklärt dies mit der Entstehung von Rollenkonflikten, die durch die Gefahr einer Erotisierung hervorgerufen werden (Kaufmann 1996: 105). Im Umkleide-Sample war sich eine Gruppe von Kampfsportlerinnen anfangs fremd, sie haben sich erst beim Sport kennen gelernt, entwickeln dann aber eine Interaktionsform mit direktem Blickkontakt und unverhüllter Nacktheit, hier dominiert das vertraute und als Freizeitvergnügen gemeinsame Sporttreiben.

5   Für das Protokoll danke ich Julia Littmann.

C: Nein, kein Quatsch: Denn so lernt der ja von klein auf, dass er sich bedeckt halten kann und zugleich Frauen anglotzen. Das heißt, der lernt doch von klein auf den pornografischen Blick. Stört Sie das nicht, dass Ihr Enkel so was lernt?

A: Also, jetzt reicht's aber!

C: Okay, dann klären wir das doch gleich einfach noch mit dem Bademeister, bis wann Jungs mit in die Frauenumkleide dürfen.

Die Frauen fragen den Bademeister und bekommen die Auskunft: bis sechs.

A: Ja, dann kann ich eben nicht mehr mit meinem Enkel ins Bad kommen.

C: Warum nicht den Kleinen einem Badbesucher bis in die Halle in die Hand drücken?

A: Also, sechs, das ist ja völlig unsinnig.

C: Stimmt! Sinniger wäre es, Jungs, die groß genug sind, sich unter Frauen zu schämen, nicht mehr in die Frauenumkleide reinzulassen, egal, wie alt die sind.

A: Also, jetzt reicht's aber wirklich! (A und B gehen).

In dieser Szene ist die Umkleide eine Arena zur Einübung eines Blicks, der zu sehen in Anspruch nimmt, was er selbst nicht preiszugeben bereit ist, nämlich Nacktheit. Entscheidend ist dabei, dass es sich um einen Blick von Männern (oder hier eines Jungen) auf Frauen handelt und nicht umgekehrt. Er konstruiert weibliche Körpererfahrung als allgemeine Erfahrung des Körper-für-andere-seins, „der unablässig der Objektivierung durch den Blick und die Reden der anderen ausgesetzt ist" (Bourdieu 2005: 112). Das macht den Blickenden unverletzbar (das Gegenteil von verletzungsoffen) und gleichzeitig verletzungsmächtig: Er ist in der exklusiven Lage, Frauen zu taxieren und zu bewerten, ohne sich der umgekehrten Konstellation auszusetzen. Ob dieser Blick am sinnvollsten mit ‚pornografisch', ‚männlich' oder ‚heteronormativ' zu bezeichnen ist, lasse ich hier offen. Auch interessiert nicht, ob der Blick des Achtjährigen sexuell konnotiert *ist*. Gleichwohl handelt es sich hier mitnichten um eine naive kindliche Szenerie. Vielmehr konstruiert die Großmutter eine soziale Situation, in der der Junge einiges über das Zusammenspiel von Verletzungsmacht und -offenheit am eigenen Körper lernt: Er kompensiert seine (verletzungsoffene) Scham durch eine (verletzungsmächtige) Überlegenheit des Blicks.

Auch Ken Plummer rekonstruiert Umkleide und Dusche als Orte, die Normen richtigen Mannseins zum Ausdruck bringen, indem dort falsche sanktioniert werden: „homophobia appears to mark an intragender divide between appropriate peer-endorsed masculine behavior and a lack of masculinity (a failure to measure up)" (Plummer 2006: 135). Er analysiert ungleiche Machtverhältnisse nicht entlang geschlechtlicher, sondern sexueller Differenzen (der Mechanismus ist allerdings der gleiche). ,Schwuchtel' und ,schwul' sind in diesem Zusammenhang die Marke für alles, was ein heranwachsender Junge nicht sein sollte. Homophobie ist in Form von Graffitis und Unterhaltungen präsent und in Umkleiden und Duschen eingeschrieben. Entsprechend sind Umkleiden für Jungen, die sich anders fühlen, oft ein Ort der Angst. Wenn sie dort nicht lernen, uninteressiert herumzulungern oder einen prestigeträchtigen Blick in die Mädchenumkleide zu erhaschen, setzen sie sich Schwulenverdacht aus[6]. Ein richtiger Mann werden heißt also, sowohl keine Frau wie auch heterosexuell sein, und genau dieser Zusammenhang kommt in der simultanen Konstruktion von Verletzungsmacht und Verletzungsoffenheit zum Ausdruck. Die Umkleide ist also nicht nur – wie es die Studien von Goffman und Kaufmann nahe legen könnten – ein Ort der Verletzungsoffenheit, sondern gleichzeitig auch der Verletzungsmacht: Die eigene potentielle Schwäche (Verletzungsoffenheit) wird in eine Stärke (Verletzungsmacht) umgemünzt, indem sie auf andere projiziert wird. Solche Projektionen bedürfen nicht zwingend eines eigenen Erfahrungshintergrunds, vielmehr wird die Dusche zum paradigmatischen Ort und zu einer Ikone von Homophobie im Fußball: „Duschen mit dem Arsch zur Wand" (taz, 14.12. 2002).

4   Duschende Fußballer: Verletzungsoffenheit und -macht wechselseitig konstituieren

Den Diskutanten zweier schwuler Fangruppen zufolge könnte das Bild mit den sich umarmenden Spielern ebenso in einer Schwulenzeitung abgedruckt sein. Gleichwohl darf es im Stadion um Sexualität gerade *nicht* gehen. Deshalb sind Schwule im Stadion so lange kein Problem, wie sie als Schwule unsichtbar bleiben. Tun sie das nicht – diese Furcht lässt sich rekonstruieren –, können sich auch Heteros nicht mehr ,gefahrlos' umarmen. Schwule im Stadion konfrontieren die

---

6   Plummer unterscheidet dabei drei mögliche Bloßstellungen (Plummer 2006: 130-133): Weil erstens die körperliche sportliche Entwicklung zählt, ist derjenige ein Verlierer, der lange in der Pubertät bleibt. Zweitens sind diejenigen Jungen mit geringem Status besonders gefährdet, die in der Umkleide/Dusche eine Erektion bekommen, sie werden der homosexuellen Erregung bezichtigt. Drittens können illegitime Blicke eine homophobe Dynamik in Gang setzen, weshalb eine permanente Kontrolle erforderlich ist: Einerseits sind die Jungen neugierig und wollen wissen, wie weit die anderen in ihrer körperlichen Entwicklung sind, andererseits ist das Blicken mit Tabus behaftet: „I would have had to have been inquisitive to see ... what other blokes had ... but at the same time, you would be conscious all the time of not trying to look" (Plummer 2006: 132).

sich vor Freude in den Armen liegenden Geschlechtsgenossen nämlich mit der Frage, was möglicherweise Schwules an ihnen selbst sein könnte. Brisanter stellt sich die Situation für einige aktive Spieler dar. Ihnen gelingt es nicht immer, das Thema Freude und Torjubel aktiv zu desexualisieren. So interpretiert eine Altherrengruppe das Bild mit den zwei sich umarmenden Spielern zunächst als Freude nach einem Torschuss:

A: Jubel, des gibt's bei uns AU.
B: Schwuchtel
C: oder die MEGAT sich oifach (alle lachen laut)

Mit einem dreifachen Kontextwechsel, nämlich von Freude („Jubel") zu Sexualität („Schwuchtel"), von Sexualität zu Verkameradschaftung („die MEGAT sich") und von Verkameradschaftung zum Lachen bewältigt die Gruppe ihre Unsicherheit bei der Thematisierung des Tabuthemas Homosexualität, das abschließende Lachen löst die Verlegenheit. ‚Schwuchtel' soll dabei nicht unter der Flagge der Beleidigung segeln, sondern gehört zur kulturellen Logik des Fußballs (vgl. Walther-Ahrens 2011: 85) – von einer Diskriminierung kann/soll im Kontext der Gruppe also keine Rede sein.

So ist Ironie ein probates Mittel, um die eigene Unsicherheit zu kaschieren und sich der geteilten Wahrnehmung und Deutung des Bilds zu versichern: „Spaß im Gras", die „haben sich vermisst", „die täte davON laufe (Lachen) un täte sage ‚Halt emol, was bisch du für einer'", die ironische Feststellung des Kuscheln, des sich Liebhabens und Zusammengehörens, „do muss schu (.) viel Liebe drin si (Lachen), wenn der, wenn die zwei des machet", all dies entschärft das Bedrohungsszenario sexualisierter Umarmungen unter Männern. Witzig soll auch eine Feminisierung männlicher Umarmungen sein („sie gibt ihm ä... Kuss"). Der Anstrich von Toleranz wird in Scherzhaftigkeit gekleidet, gleichwohl operieren Aussagen wie „jetzt wird's vertraulich" und „jetzt wird's interessant" mit einer Konspirativität, die auf Tabuisiertes, Verbotenes und Schlüpfriges schließen lassen. Eine Altherrengruppe reagiert auf die heraufbeschworene Möglichkeit von schwulen Fußballern mit der lustig gemeinten Feststellung, man kenne schließlich keinen.

Ein Freizeitteam dagegen kennt sehr wohl eine Fußballmannschaft mit einem Schwulen. Das sei kein Problem, ab und zu gebe es mal Witzchen unter der Dusche, „aber damit kommt der völlig klar". Der projektive Charakter der Dusche als Ort vermeintlich schwuler Umtriebe wird beim Bezug auf Frauen deutlich: Der Leiter eines katholischen Kirchenchors zeigt sich konsterniert über die Vorstellung eines gemeinsamen Duschens von Frauen, womit er vor einigen Jahren konfrontiert war: „Ich erinnere mich noch damals an ne Skifreizeit, da äh musst man, wenn man ins Bad wollte, musst man durch des Zimmer durch, in dem ich mit nem andern Freund war. Und dann kamen plötzlich zwei Mädels rein, die gingen durch unser Zimmer und sagen: ‚Alla wir gehen dusche': Und dann sagte der [Name] zu mir: ‚Gehn die jetzt zu zweit duschen'. Sagte ich: ‚Ja scheinbar.' (vereinzeltes Lachen) (flüsternd den Freund imitierend): ‚Das würd ich ja nie machen, stell dir mal vor, wir würden zusammen duschen gehen (lautes Lachen), das gäb ein Gerede, ja.'" Das gemeinsame Duschen sei nicht weit entfernt von einem gemeinsamen Gang aufs Klo. Das stelle ein völliges Tabu dar (bei Männern noch mehr als bei Frauen), im Fußball dagegen sei das – so die Auffassung der Gruppe – möglich. Entscheidend ist hier, dass die Dusche gar keinen realen Erfahrungshintergrund bildet, sondern einen Ort darstellt, in den Peinlichkeiten und Normüberschreitung projiziert und in dem Bedrohungen und Gefahren weniger über Worte als über Blicke organisiert werden.

Die Dusche ist aber auch ein Gradmesser erfolgreicher Outings, zumindest wenn man die Berichterstattung von Massenmedien zu Homosexualität im Fußball in den letzten Jahren beobachtet (vgl. Degele/Janz 2011: 35-45): „Alle haben das sofort akzeptiert, keiner verhält sich seitdem anders zu mir, auch in der Dusche guckt keiner betreten weg" (ZEIT.online 2012). In diesem, sich auf den Amateurfußball beziehenden Medienbericht dient die Dusche als Chiffre für etwas Bedrohliches, das mit Homosexualität in Verbindung steht[7]. Sie liefert Bilder für Verständigung und Offenheit („Man duscht ja schließlich, schließlich auch miteinander ne" (lacht)), für die Anerkennung von Leistung („Und man, man sieht

---

7 Das ist nicht auf Männer beschränkt. In einer Untersuchung über Fußball spielende Frauen berichtet eine Ligaspielerin über die Konfrontation mit Homosexualität in Form eines traumatischen Duscherlebnisses: „One day I saw it in the shower. I was almost grabbed, not actually grabbed but I had propositions that shocked me" (Mennesson/Clément 2003: 327). Was sie dabei Schockierendes gesehen hat, bleibt offen. Ebenfalls sollten solche Befunde nicht darüber weg täuschen, dass dieser für die sportliche Nachsorge so bedeutende Ort in den Gruppendiskussionen auch in anderen Zusammenhängen auftaucht. Dazu zählt die Kritik eines Kirchenchors an den Medien, die nicht davor zurückschreckten, mit der Kamera bis in die Dusche vorzudringen. Ein Team von wohnungslosen Kickern debattiert darüber, ob das erste Bier nach dem Spiel noch vor dem Duschen erlaubt sein soll („aber des fand ich PRINZIPIELL immer total assig, kann ja sein Bierchen auch unter der Dusche trinken, wenn's denn sein muss"). Für eine Altherrenmannschaft steht die Dusche für strukturelle Grenzen der Integration von Fußballerinnen („wir haben nur zwei Kabinen und eine gemeinsame Dusche zwischen der Kabine."). An Frauen – dessen ist sich eine junge Dorfmannschaft gewiss – sollten sich die Männer allerdings kein Beispiel nehmen: „Ich weiß bei einem Frauenfußballverein Richtung [Ort]. Da gibt es ein paar, die falsch gepolt sind (.) und die duschen auch alle zusammen." Bei den in der Studie beteiligten Frauen-/Lesbenteams dagegen war die Dusche in keiner Diskussion ein Thema.

ja auch sehr oft, dass wenn der Spieler ausgewechselt wird und dass der Trainer
dann beim Vorbeilaufen ihm noch einen Klaps gibt, entweder auf die Schulter
manchmal auch auf den Arsch, wenn es sein muss. Das ist dann eher so was vom,
vom Vater an den Sohn so: ‚dusch' (Schlag auf den Hintern) ((Lachen)) ‚gut gemacht!'") wie auch für Skandale. Eine Altherrenmannschaft etwa berichtet von
einer homosexuellen Affäre zwischen zwei Schiedsrichtern, bei der es laut Me-
dienberichten auch zu Erpressung gekommen sei:

> F: und die haben anscheinend sich immer (.) nette SMS ausgetauscht. Und
> wenn sie mal unter sich waren ein bisschen gestreichelt oder so anschei-
> nend! Man weiß es ja nicht so genau.
> C: Oder haben geduscht
> F: Oder haben miteinander geduscht.

Über die Dusche lässt sich witzeln und auch gleich die Lösung des Problems präsentieren:

> Desch heut nemme so schlimm, weil's heut koina Soifa meh gibt. (alle lachen) heut
> gibt's äh (.) Flascha. ((gleichzeitig P: Duschgel) Friher war des no schlimmer, wo
> die Soife nunder gfalla isch, do hot mer bigga missa, aber heut got des. (alle
> lachen laut)

Das kommt recht spaßig daher: Flaschen oder an der Wand angebrachte Seifen-
spender verhindern ein Herunterfallen glitschiger Waschutensilien und damit die
Notwendigkeit, durch ein Bücken dem Mitduscher den nackten Hintern entgegen
strecken zu müssen und sich damit verletzungsoffen zu präsentieren. In solchen
ironisch inszenierten Bemerkungen[8] kommt die Angst vor objektivierenden Blicken, Körpernähe und Verletzbarkeit am deutlichsten zum Ausdruck. Ihre explizite Benennung tauchte in keiner Diskussion auf. Möglicherweise käme das in
den Augen der Diskutanten einem Eingeständnis von Schwäche gleich, weshalb
sie sich lieber hinter Witzeleien verstecken. Ein anderer Altherrenverein bemüht
ebenfalls das Bild der Seife:

---

8   Daneben lassen sich noch weitere Strategien der ‚Wegdefinition' von Homosexualität
    aus dem Fußball unterscheiden. Sie reichen über Problemverschiebung auf Medien,
    Fans und andere Ethnizitäten, Umdeuten über Totschweigen und Ausweichen bis hin
    zu Beleidigung (vgl. Degele/Janz 2011: 19f.). Ob dabei die Fans die größte Drohkulisse
    für ein Outing im Profifußball darstellen (vgl. http://www.guardian.co.uk/football/
    blog/2011/mar/12/the-secret-footballer-gay-players. Zugriff am 15.1.2013), lasse ich
    hier offen.

A: Wobei ich sag jetzt mal, wenn es ein guter Kollege jetzt wäre oder so, hätte ich wahrscheinlich beim Fußball spielen auch kein Problem, ja ...

D: Nee

A: ... auch nicht beim Duschen auch nicht oder so ja (leises Lachen)

C: (??) Seife (??)

A: nein ist jetzt doch scheiß egal (leises Lachen)

Egal ist es für viele Fußballer indes nicht, denn als es tatsächlich einmal einen Schwulen im Team gab, hat eine andere Dorfmannschaft die entsprechenden Vorkehrungen getroffen: „Bei uns, aber da hat man auch glaub ich gebührenden Abstand in der Dusche gehalten." Den Hintergrund und die Vorbereitung dafür liefert diese Aussage:

C: Man duscht ja nicht mit einem Schwulen. (Lachen)

E: Ja, da ist es dann wiederum anders egal, welche Sachen (Lachen) man wirklich macht, sei es auf dem Platz bis in die Dusche rein, aber sobald glaub ich einer schwul ist, dann ... ändert sich die Blickweise total.

D: Ja.

(Lachen)

Y: Du würdest mit keinem duschen, der schwul ist?

(Lachen)

D: Nein. (kurzes Lachen)

Diese Äußerung bleibt so stehen und wird nicht zurück genommen oder korrigiert, sondern auf Nachfrage konkretisiert:

Y: Wenn du wüsstest, du hast eine Mannschaft, du spielst mit denen schon ewig, und dann stellst du irgendwann fest, einer von denen ist schwul. Würdest du dann mit dem nicht mehr zusammen spielen wollen?

D: Das kann ich jetzt so nicht sagen, weil das was anderes ist. Aber wenn ich jetzt von vornerein weiß ..., der ist schwul und ich kenne ihn noch nicht lang, dann tät ich ganz be.. gewiss nicht mit dem in die Dusche rein gehen.

Ein offener Schwuler stellt also nicht notwendigerweise auf dem Spielfeld eine Bedrohung dar, sondern erst in der Dusche. Für die meisten Spieler einer anderen Dorfmannschaft scheint ein Schwuler im Team zunächst unproblematisch zu sein bzw. haben eine entsprechende Strategie der Gefahrenabwehr parat: „Im Notfall wenn er dir zu nah auf die Pelle rückt, Seife nehmen in ein Handtuch einwickeln und ihm mal sagen, was du davon hältst". G dagegen sähe beim gemeinsamen Duschen das Gebot der Abstandsmaximierung verletzt, das er für Schwule anders definiert als für Heterosexuelle. Er will auch keinen geouteten Schwulen im Verein haben („Ja und wenn er dann so auf dir liegt nach dem Torjubel, was willst du machen?"). Offen bleibt in diesem Szenario, ob die eigentliche, von einer Umarmung mit einem Schwulen ausgehende Gefahr in einem gewalttätigen Übergriff oder einer Verführung lauert. Im Anschluss daran konfrontiert die Gruppe G mit dem Gedankenexperiment, in G's favorisiertem Bundesligaclubs gebe es einen Schwulen:

> G: Das wird nicht passieren
> Lachen
> G: Ja nee (.) äh oh... Aber es gibt ja auch Spieler von meinem Verein, die ich am liebsten totschlagen würd' ((leises Lachen)) aber (.) ich also mit Liebe zum Verein hat es nichts=würde es nichts ausmachen, gar nicht. Aber ich find das halt ...
> E: Lass mal acht Sp=lass mal acht Sp=Spieler schwul sein.
> (Lachen)
> G: Nein ich ...
> B: Na und dann würde er halt acht sch... totschlagen, aber der Verein ist trotzdem noch klasse.

Die Wortwahl kippt nun ins Brachiale, die übrigen Teilnehmer versuchen, die Situation mit Ironie zu retten. Dabei verlieren sie zunehmend die Kontrolle über den Diskussionsverlauf (und die Inhalte) – und lassen G's Thesen zunehmend unwidersprochen stehen[9].

5   Ängstliche Körper: schamhaft projizieren

Im weiteren Verlauf behauptet G, ihm würde man seine Heterosexualität anmerken, H dagegen hat ihn am Anfang für schwul gehalten – in der Folge scheint die Gruppe selbst nicht mehr zu wissen, was Spaß und was Ernst ist.

---

9   Diskursorganisatorisch fällt in dieser Diskussion auf, dass G die Rolle des Meinungsführers innehat und die übrigen Teilnehmer zu Mitläufern macht. Diese äußern sich zunächst nicht manifest homophob, können sich gar einen Schwulen im Team vorstellen. G's immer wieder apodiktisches „das geht nicht" bringt die Gruppe jedoch sukzessiv auf Linie – wozu G's in Anschlag gebrachte, auf Abitur und Fußballwissen gründende Autorität beiträgt, die die Gruppe auch anerkennt.

H: Ich weiß nicht ((gleichzeitig) warum (??) schwul. (lacht) Ich hab echt gedacht du bist schwul am Anfang so.) (lachend)

B: ((gleichzeitig) Aber wenn der Fall} halt nicht ist und dich frägt trotzdem
  keiner dann würdest du es trotzdem nicht erzählen)

F: Ich?

H: Spaß Mann du Ekel

F: Du meinst es doch ernst.

H: Awa

F: (??) Schläge Mann.

C: Ja aber...

E: Du hättest doch gern was mit ihm.

G: (lacht) Gell? Wollt ich grad sagen. (lachend)

B: Der H mit dem Vollbart.

((2′ Gelächter))

G: Terrorist (lachend)

((1′ Lachen))

C: Mit dem Vollbart.

Das Tabuthema Homosexualität geht die Gruppe offensichtlich mehr an als sie
wahrhaben will: Stakkatohaft und in schnellem Wechsel gesteht ein Sprecher (H)
eine falsche Vermutung ein (dass G schwul wäre), setzt sich gegen einen unterstellten Homosexualitätsvorwurf F gegenüber zur Wehr, F wiederum gerät nun
erst recht unter Schwulenverdacht, in den E, G und H einstimmen. Zu einer
Eskalation indes kommt es nicht. Einerseits bleibt das Diskussionstempo durch
Schlagabtausche in Form sofortigen Parierens und Weiterführens reduzierter
Satzbrocken („Spaß Mann du Ekel") stabil. Andererseits halten die Teilnehmer
die Stimmung durch häufiges spannungslösendes Lachen hoch – was möglicherweise auch auf den stattfindenden Bierkonsum zurückzuführen ist.

Dennoch kann die Gruppe die entstandene Unsicherheit rund um das Thema Schwule im Fußball nur schwer auffangen. Zum einen mahnt der politische
Korrektheitsdiskurs zunehmend zur Vorsicht: Acht schwule Spieler totschlagen
kommt auch in einer traditionell geprägten Dorfmannschaft als Witz nicht gut
an. Zum anderen zeigen die dargestellten Diskussionsausschnitte, dass die Männer über kaum habitualisierte Scripts beim Umgang mit Situationen verfügen,
die für sie mit körperlichem Kontrollverlust verbunden sind. So spricht Eve Ko-
sovsky Sedgwick (1990: 22) von Homosexualität als „the open secret"[10] und zeigt
darin, „in welchem Ausmaß die Epistemologie der modernen westlichen Gesell-

---

10 Für diesen Hinweis danke ich Karolin Heckemeyer.

schaft vom offenen Geheimnis der Homosexualität mit seinen widersprüchlichen Regeln der Geheimhaltung und Enthüllung, der Privatheit und Öffentlichkeit, des Wissens und der Ignoranz regiert wird. Das schwule und lesbische Versteck (closet) ist ein Problem nicht nur desjenigen, der es fortwährend neu betritt und verlässt [...], sondern auch der widersprüchlichen, zwischen minorisierenden und universalisierenden Vorstellungen von Homosexualität schillernden Denkordnung der heterosexuellen Gesellschaft" (Kraß 2003: 25).

Alle wissen um Schwule im Fußball, aber niemand will es aussprechen und das Geheimnis lüften. Die Dusche wird vielmehr zum imaginierten Raum, der ,optimale' Bedingungen für homosexuelle Wünsche und Praktiken bietet, und genau das macht sie so bedrohlich. Denn mit der körperlichen Nähe geht eine (physische und noch mehr psychische) Nacktheit einher, die es für viele offenbar schwierig macht, eine implizite Homoerotik auch tatsächlich implizit zu halten (Dembowski 2002; Pronger 2000: 237). Gleichzeitig schafft sie eine Umgebung für Verletzungsoffenheit, die es erlaubt, sexuelle Demütigungsrituale bei Männern auszuleben (Engelfried 2008: 62; Plummer 2006: 130-135). Das wiederum ist mit dem immer noch gepflegten Bild unvereinbar, Männer könnten nicht vergewaltigt werden. Der Begriff des männlichen Opfers stellt vielmehr ein kulturelles Paradox dar: „Entweder gilt jemand als Opfer, oder er ist ein Mann" (Lenz 2007: 109). Deshalb ist die Dusche auch ein so ambivalenter Raum: Die Angst vor einer Grenzübertretung in welche Richtung auch immer existiert (was in der herunter fallenden Seife zum Ausdruck kommt), darf aber nicht explizit gemacht werden. Das wiederum macht Homophobie aus: die Ablehnung von Schwulen, weil sie – mit Sigmund Freud und Judith Butler gesprochen – für die Angst vor einem abgespaltenen schwulen Anteil stehen könnten, der dann umso heftiger bekämpft wird. Schwul im Fußball bedeutet also nicht nur Tabuisierung von Sexualität, sondern auch Angst vor einem Kontrollverlust. Auch dafür stehen Mauerbildungen in Umkleiden, die noch nicht fertig umgezogene Männer vor den Blicken Außenstehender abschirmen (siehe Abschnitt 3). An einen solchen Kontrollverlust könnten die spontanen Freudenausbrüche auf dem Rasen und das hemmungslose Weinen der Fans erinnern. Zwar bleibt für ein Mitglied eines schwulen Fanclubs die Hoffnung, „dass es einfach ganz normal wird, dass der mit DEM auch unter (.) äh,t dass dieser Spieler mit den andern unter eine... unter der Dusche geht". Noch aber ist körperliche Nähe zwischen Männern im Fußball so wenig verselbstverständlich, dass sich Justin Fashanus Suizid noch immer erschreckend schlüssig erklären und nachvollziehen lässt.

Literatur

Bourdieu, P. (2005): Die männliche Herrschaft. Ffm: Suhrkamp.

Cover, R. (2003): The naked subject: Nudity, context and sexualization in contemporary culture. In: Body & Society 9, 53-72.

Curry, T. J. (1991): Fraternal Bonding in the Locker Room: A Profeminist Analysis of Talk about Competition and Women. In: Sociology of Sport Journal 8, 119-135.

Degele, N. (2005): Heteronormativität entselbstverständlichen: Zum verunsichernden Potenzial von Queer Studies. In: Freiburger Frauen Studien, Ausgabe 17, 15-40.

Degele, N. (2013): Fußball verbindet – durch Ausgrenzung. Wiesbaden: Springer/VS-Verlag.

Degele, N./Janz, C. (2011): Hetero, weiß und männlich? Fußball ist viel mehr! Eine Studie der Friedrich-Ebert-Stiftung zu Homophobie, Rassismus und Sexismus im Fußball. Berlin: Friedrich-Ebert-Stiftung. http://library.fes.de/pdf-files/do/08165.pdf.

Dembowski, G. (2002): Von Schwabenschwuchteln und nackten Schalkern. Schwulenfeindlichkeit im Fußballmilieu. In: Dembowski, G./Scheidle, J. (Hg): Tatort Stadion. Rassismus, Antisemitismus und Sexismus im Fußball. Köln: Papy Rossa, 140-146.

Duerr, H. P. (1988): Der Mythos vom Zivilisationsprozeß. Band 1: Nacktheit und Scham. Ffm: Suhrkamp.

Engelfried, C. (2008): Konstruktionen von Männlichkeiten im Sport – Bedeutung und Funktion von Jungen- und Männergruppen. In: Beiträge zur feministischen Theorie und Praxis 31, 59-68.

Fusco, C. (2006): Spatializing the (Im)Proper Subject. The Geographies of Abjection in Sport and Physical Activity Space. In: Journal of Sport & Social Issues 30, 5-28

Goffman, E. (2009): Interaktion im öffentlichen Raum. Die Interaktionsordnung. Ffm: Campus. Orig. 1963.

Hettlage, R. (2003): Erving Goffman (1922-1982). In: Kaesler, D. (Hg.): Von Talcott Parsons bis Pierre Bourdieu. 4. Aufl., München: Beck, 188-205.

Kaufmann, J.-C. (1996): Frauenkörper – Männerblicke. Konstanz: UVK.

Kraß, Andreas (2003): Queer Studies – eine Einführung. In: Kraß, A. (Hg.): Queer Denken. Ffm: Suhrkamp, 7-28.

Krennhuber, R. (2006): Dieser Bericht ist schwul! In: http://derstandard.at/2618068/Dieser-Bericht-ist-schwul. Zugriff am 15.1.2013.

Leibfried, D./Erb, A. (2011): Das Schweigen der Männer. Homosexualität im deutschen Fußball. Göttingen: Verlag Die Werkstatt.

Lenz, H.-J. (2007): Mann oder Opfer? Jungen und Männer als Opfer von Gewalt und die kulturelle Verleugnung der männlichen Verletzbarkeit. In: Kawamura-Reindl, G./Halbhuber-Gassner, L./Wichmann, C. (Hg.): Gender Mainstreaming – ein Konzept für die Straffälligenhilfe? Freiburg: Lambertus, 108-128.

Mennesson, C./Clément, J.-P. (2003): Homosociability and Homosexuality. The Case of Soccer Played by Women. In: International Review For The Sociology of Sport 38, 311-330.

Plummer, K. (2006): Sportophobia. Why do some men avoid sport? In: Journal of Sport and Social Issues 30, 122-137.

Popitz, H. (1992): Phänomene der Macht. Tübingen: Mohr.

Pronger, B. (2000): Homosexuality and Sport. In: McKay, J./Messner, M./Sabo, D. F. (Hg.): Masculinities, Gender Relations, and Sport. Thousand Oaks: Sage, 222-244.

Sedgwick, E. K. (1990): Epistemology of the Closet. Berkeley: UCP.

Sülzle, A. (2005): Fußball als Schutzraum für Männlichkeit? Ethnographische Anmerkungen zum Spielraum für Geschlechter im Stadion. In: Hagel, A./Selmer, N./Sülzle, A. (Hg.): Gender Kicks: Texte zu Fußball und Geschlecht. (Herausgegeben von der Koordinationsstelle Fanprojekte bei der Deutschen Sportjugend, Bd. 10). Ffm: KOS, 37-52.

Walther-Ahrens, T. (2011): Seitenwechsel. Coming-Out im Fußball. Gütersloh: Gütersloher Verlagshaus.

ZEIT.online (2010): Schwul, geoutet und Kapitän, 8.12.10, http://www.zeit.de/sport/2010-12/homosexualitaet-amateurfussball-kreisliga-zwanziger. Zugriff am 15.1.2013.

Ist die postmoderne Frau eine Fußballerin?

Is the Postmodern Woman a Footballer?

Eva Gros

Zusammenfassung

Durch den Erfolg der Frauenfußball-Nationalmannschaft hat der Frauenfuß-ball in Deutschland an Medienpräsenz und Relevanz deutlich gewonnen. Die Spielerinnen bewegen sich als Fußballerinnen innerhalb eines Feldes, das als Schauplatz hegemonialer Männlichkeit gelten kann. Damit befinden sie sich im Kontext des Frauenfußballs in einer durch den Widerspruch zwischen Fußball und Weiblichkeit geprägten Situation.

In der vorliegenden Analyse bildet dieser vermeintliche Widerspruch den zen-tralen Fokus. Leitend ist die Frage, ob die Spielerinnen in der Überwindung des genannten Widerspruchs eine postmoderne Geschlechtsidentität entwickeln, die sich von klassisch weiblichen Geschlechterrollenstereotypen zu lösen be-ginnt. Anhand der Aussagen der Spielerinnen der Frauenfußball-Weltmeister-schaft im Jahr 2007 im Rahmen des Dokumentarfilms ‚Die besten Frauen der Welt' und aufgrund der Inszenierung von Weiblichkeit und (Frauen)Fußball im Film zeige ich, dass die Spielerinnen sowohl an klassischen weiblichen Ge-schlechterstereotypen festhalten als auch Eigenschaften und Verhaltensweisen für sich reklamieren, die als klassisch männlich gelten mögen.

Abstract

Thanks to the success of the German women's international football team, women's football has made considerable progress in terms of media coverage and relevance. The players occupy a domain as female soccer players which may be regarded as the site of hegemonic masculinity. They consequently find themselves in the context of women's football in a situation marked by the incongruity of football and femininity.

In the following analysis this supposed contradiction forms the principal focus. The issue being addressed is whether, in the process of overcoming this contradiction, the female players are developing a postmodern gender identity which is starting to break free from classic female gender role stereotypes. On the basis of statements made by the players in the context of the documentary film 'The Best Women in the World', who took part in the 2007 women's World Cup, and looking at the portrayal of femininity and (women's) football in the film, I will be showing that the players are bound to classic female gender stereotypes as well as reclaiming for themselves character traits and modes of behaviour which may be seen as classic male ones.

Die Spielerinnen der Frauenfußball-Nationalmannschaft Annika Doppler, Kristina Gessat, Ivana Rudelic, Julia Simic und Selina Wagner posierten im Kontext der Frauen-Fußball-Weltmeisterschaft 2011 für das Magazin ‚Playboy'. Die Photographien zeigen die Spielerinnen nicht als Sportlerinnen, sondern dem Stil der Zeitschrift entsprechend in leichter Bekleidung und dekorativen Posen. In einem zugehörigen Interview nennen die Spielerinnen als Motiv: „Wir wollen mit unseren Playboy-Bildern ja auch genau dieses Mannweiber-Klischee widerlegen" (Playboy 2011). Spielerinnen der höheren Ligen seien zwar gut trainiert, sähen aber dennoch „weiblich […] und oft auch sehr gut" aus (ebd.). Zudem gäbe es unter den Fußballerinnen „immer mehr süße, hübsche Mädels […], die auch shoppen gehen und Wert auf ihr Äußeres legen." (ebd.). Angesichts des Befunds, dass Fußball als Schauplatz hegemonialer Männlichkeit gelten kann (vgl. Müller 2009: 13), fällt die Inszenierung weiblicher Attraktivität auf, die einem vermeintlichen „Mannweiber-Klischee" entgegengestellt wird[1].

Nimmt man die Geschichte des Fußballs in den Blick, so wird deutlich, dass dieser nicht immer als in erster Linie männlicher Sport wahrgenommen wurde: Gegen Ende des 19. Jahrhunderts wurde scheinbar nicht zwischen Männer- und Frauenfußball differenziert (vgl. ebd.: 71), doch mit der Entstehung der Idee der Geschlechtscharaktere (Hausen 1978) gegen Ende des 19. Jahrhunderts erfolgte

---

1   Erotische Inszenierungen von Sportlerinnen in den Medien sind kein Einzelfall: so ließen z.B. auch die erfolgreichen Sportlerinnen Katharina Witt, Annika Walter und Anke Feller erotische Photographien von sich anfertigen und veröffentlichen (vgl. Hartmann-Tews/Rulofs 2003: 29)

eine Trennung des Fußballs in eine weibliche und eine männliche Variante mit jeweils unterschiedlichen Regeln für Männer- und Frauenteams. Den sogenannten Geschlechtscharakteren zufolge erforderten die Wesenseigenschaften beider Geschlechter eine Trennung und komplementäre Ergänzung von Männern und Frauen; Natur und Wesenseigenschaften als Bezugspunkte verlagerten geschlechtliche Identität als „Wesensmerkmal in das Innere der Menschen" (ebd.: 162). Als gegensätzlich, komplementär und naturhaft sowie durch Medizin, Anthropologie und Psychologie wissenschaftlich bestätigt (ebd.), etablierte sich die Idee der Geschlechtscharaktere.

Beide Geschlechter konnten dem Diskurs über die Geschlechtscharaktere zufolge darüber hinaus nur zu vollendeter Menschlichkeit finden, wenn sie eine Ergänzung durch das jeweils als gegensätzlich konstruierte Geschlecht erfuhren (ebd.: 166, 169). Langfristig führten die genannten Differenzierungen beispielsweise zu geschlechtsspezifischen Bildungsprogrammen, die letztlich dazu führten, dass Unterschiede der Geschlechter als gesellschaftliche Realität empirisch nachweisbar wurden (ebd.: 176, 178). Zentrale Annahmen der Diskurse zu den Geschlechtscharakteren begannen erst nach Beginn der Zweiten Frauenbewegung nach 1968 langsam an Bedeutung zu verlieren; teils bestimmen sie bis in die Gegenwart hinein mediale Diskurse über Männer und Frauen (ebd.: 161). Einer der Bestseller des Ehepaares Allan und Barbara Pease mit dem Titel *Warum Männer nicht zuhören und Frauen schlecht einparken* (Ullstein 2010) verweist auf die Bedeutung kontrastierender Geschlechterbilder in der Gegenwart.

In der Erforschung des Geschlechterverhältnisses durch Frauen- und Geschlechterforschung sowie die Gender Studies setzte sich früh die Erkenntnis der sozialen Konstruktion des Geschlechts durch. In westlichen Gesellschaften sei die Bedeutung der Geschlechtszugehörigkeit in Anlehnung an Harold Garfinkel zudem als „omnirelevant" zu bezeichnen (Treibel 2006: 108; Kleindienst-Cachay/ Kunzendorf 2003: 114f.) und die Entwicklung von Identität sei ohne geschlechtliche Überformung in westlichen Gesellschaften grundsätzlich nicht möglich (Treibel 2006: 116). Die Entwicklung von Identität ist darüber hinaus nicht ohne grundlegenden Bezug auf den Körper möglich (vgl. Kleindienst-Cachay/Kunzendorf 2003: 113). Judith Butler ergänzte die Befunde der Geschlechterforschung durch die Diagnose eines Ideals der Geschlechtsidentität und des Geschlechterverhältnisses; dieses sei durch Heteronormativität bzw. hegemoniale Heterosexualität (vgl. Butler 1991, 2003) geprägt, der zufolge es nicht nur klare Vorstellungen der jeweiligen Geschlechterrolle gibt, sondern auch eine klar definierte Vorstellung legitimer Beziehungen zwischen Männern und Frauen in Form einer heterosexuellen Zweierbeziehung. Im Bereich des Sports bewirkte die soziale Konstruktion der Geschlechtscharaktere vielfach den Ausschluss von Frauen, der sich bis in das 21. Jahrhundert hinein in Form von unterschiedlichen Regeln der Zulassung von Männern und Frauen zu Wettkämpfen zeigt, so z.B. beim Boxen oder im Zehnkampf (vgl. Hartmann-Tews 2003: 13f.). Frauen, die zu Beginn des 20. Jahrhunderts Fußball spielten, sahen sich der Annahme ausgesetzt, ihre Physis sei nicht für das Fußballspielen geschaffen und gefährde ihre Gebärfähigkeit und Eignung für die Mutterschaft; zudem sei es Frauen nicht möglich, unter Ausübung des Sports angemessen attraktiv auszusehen (Müller 2009: 75). Argumente der physischen Ungeeignetheit von Frauen für Fußball bildeten noch 1955 die Grundlage eines expliziten Verbotes der Einführung des Frauenfußballs (vgl. ebd.: 83). Eine Lockerung geschah erst in den 1970er Jahren – jedoch nur unter Bedingungen einer Abgrenzung des Frauenfußballs von Männerfußball, beispielsweise durch das Verbot des Tragens von mit Stollen ausgestatteten Schuhen durch Frauen, eines kleineren Feldes, der Verwendung leichterer Bälle und kürzerer Spielzeiten für Frauenspiele (ebd.: 77). Die Marathonläuferin Katherine Switzer berichtet für die 1960er Jahre von der verbreiteten Annahme, sie sei als Frau nicht des Laufens einer Langstrecke fähig – für Frauen war Mitte der 1960er Jahre eine maximale Distanz von ca. 800m erlaubt (Switzer 2011: 37). Switzer trat den Gegenbeweis an, als sie 1967 als erste Frau den Marathon in Boston erfolgreich bestritt (ebd.: 85). Während des Laufes versuchte einer der Leiter des Rennens, Jock Sample, sie von der Strecke zu ziehen – ein Begleiter Switzers verhinderte dies (ebd.: 97ff.). Frauen, die längere Strecken als die maximal vorgesehenen 800m liefen, sahen sich mit der Annahme konfrontiert, in der Folge niemals ein Kind austragen zu können (ebd.: 194). Auch im Basketball galten für Frauen Regeln, die einen Schutz vor zu hoher Belastung gewährleisten sollten: durch das viele Springen könne die Gebärmutter der Frauen verrutschen (ebd.: 27).

Vor dem Hintergrund des eingangs geschilderten Beispiels der Playboy-Photographien und der Konnotation des Fußballs als Männersport gehe ich davon aus, dass sich besonders im Bereich des Frauenfußballs die Widersprüche zwischen modernen und herkömmlichen Vorstellungen der weiblichen Geschlechterrolle zeigen. Die Fußballerinnen bewegen sich in einem Feld, das als männlich gilt und befinden sich mutmaßlich in einem Konflikt zwischen der Aneignung eines männlich geprägten Feldes und weiblicher Geschlechtsidentität (vgl. hierzu Kleindienst-Cachay/Kunzendorf 2003: 114f., 116). Im Bereich des Sports, insbesondere des Spitzensports kommen gesellschaftliche verankerte Geschlechterstereotype und Vorstellungen der Hierarchie des Geschlechterverhältnisses verstärkt zum Tragen (vgl. Kleindienst-Cachay/Kunzendorf 2003: 116).

Betrachtet man die Erfordernisse des professionellen Fußballspiels, so stehen mit Kampfbereitschaft, Körpereinsatz und Wettkampforientierung als männlich erachtete Eigenschaften im Vordergrund des Spiels. In diesem Beitrag gehe ich der Frage nach, welche Repräsentationen der weiblichen Geschlechterrolle sich unter diesen Bedingungen etablieren: entsteht gegenwärtig an der Schnittstelle zwischen Fußball und Weiblichkeit ein postmodernes Konzept von Weiblichkeit, das sich von der herkömmlichen weiblichen Geschlechterrolle zu lösen beginnt? Oder ist vielmehr eine Verfestigung des weiblichen Geschlechterrollenstereotyps zu beobachten, die aus Konflikten innerhalb des durch Weiblichkeit und Fußball bestimmten Feldes resultiert (vgl. ebd.: 110)? Im Zuge der folgenden Analyse wird sich zeigen, dass die Fußballerinnen einerseits vermeintlich männliche Eigenschaften und Verhaltensweisen für sich reklamieren, andererseits jedoch ebenso an klassische weibliche Geschlechterbilder gebunden bleiben. Im Mittelpunkt der Fragestellung steht als Kristallisationspunkt sowohl der geschlechtlichen Identität als auch sportlicher Betätigung der Körper der Spielerinnen. Im Rahmen soziologischer Theorie sind Zusammenhänge zwischen gesellschaftlichen Strukturen und gesellschaftlich verankerten Bezugnahmen auf den menschlichen Körper aus unterschiedlichen Perspektiven aufgegriffen worden – einige davon werden im Folgenden kurz dargestellt. Der Zusammenhang zwischen Körper und Gesellschaft bildet den Hintergrund meiner Ausführungen.

Die hier verfolgte Fragestellung lässt sich ebenso gut an die Bedingungen des englischen wie des deutschen Frauenfußballs herantragen; der Forschungsstand im deutschsprachigen wie im anglo-amerikanischen Raum verweist auf deren Gemeinsamkeiten hinsichtlich eines strukturellen Konflikts zwischen der sozialen Konstruktion der weiblichen Geschlechterrolle und den Praktiken des Fußballs sowie einer medialen Repräsentation von Frauen- und Männersport, die sich an herkömmlichen Geschlechterrollenstereotypen orientiert (vgl. Hartmann-Tews/Rulofs 2003: 29-34). Ich beziehe mich zur Bearbeitung der Fragestellung auf den deutschen Frauenfußball, da dieser in Folge des Gewinns der Frauenfußball-Weltmeisterschaft im Jahr 2007 durch die deutsche Mannschaft und in Folge der Erwartungen eines erneuten Gewinns im Jahr 2011 einen starken Bedeutungszuwachs und eine erhöhte Medienpräsenz erfuhr. Die Spielerinnen gerieten so verstärkt in den Fokus öffentlicher Aufmerksamkeit, die dazu beigetragen haben dürfte, den o.g. möglichen Konflikt zwischen Fußball als Schauplatz hegemonialer Männlichkeit und Weiblichkeit potenziell zu verschärfen.

1 Theoretische Perspektiven auf den Zusammenhang zwischen Körper und Gesellschaft

Der Zusammenhang zwischen menschlichen Körpern und gesellschaftlichen Verhältnissen ist bereits bei den Klassikern der Soziologie erforscht worden. Norbert Elias untersuchte Zusammenhänge zwischen dem Prozess der Zivilisation und der Überformung des Affekts sowie einer damit einhergehenden Kontrolle des Körpers im Zuge des Übergangs von Fremdzwängen zu Selbstzwängen als Regulativ des Zusammenlebens und im Kontext des staatlichen Gewaltmonopols der Moderne (Elias 1997). Einen expliziten Zusammenhang zwischen gesellschaftlichen Machtverhältnissen und Zugriffen auf den Körper hat Michel Foucault in seinem Werk Überwachen und Strafen hergestellt (Foucault 1977). Foucault nimmt die Entstehung der Disziplinarmacht und die sich daran anschließenden Folgen für gesellschaftliche Zugriffe auf den Körper in den Blick. Der Entstehung der Humanwissenschaften kommt in diesem Zusammenhang eine spezifische Funktion der Generierung von Wissen durch neue Zugriffe auf den Körper zu, das wiederum auf den Körper angewendet wird. Die Formen des Strafens und der jeweils zugehörige Umgang mit menschlichen Körpern im Zuge des Strafens bilden den roten Faden seiner Darstellung. Menschliche Körper geraten im Laufe der Entwicklung der Moderne zunehmend in die feingliedrigen Strukturen, die Foucault als Mikrophysik der Macht gekennzeichnet hat.

Der französische Soziologe Pierre Bourdieu hat mit dem Konzept des Habitus ebenfalls den Zusammenhang zwischen gesellschaftlichen Machtstrukturen und dem menschlichen Körper beschrieben. Im französischen Original erschien 1998 Bourdieus Analyse des Geschlechterverhältnisses, in der deutschen Übersetzung: *Die männliche Herrschaft* (2005). Seine Ausgangsfrage richtet sich auf die seines Erachtens erstaunliche Stabilität der männlichen Herrschaft; zu deren Erklärung bezieht er sich auf das Konzept der symbolischen Gewalt, die im Habitus wirksam wird. In ihm schlagen sich gesellschaftliche Machtstrukturen als persönliche Empfindungen nieder, so dass diese erscheinen, als seien sie „wie Triebfedern in die Tiefe der Körper eingelassen" (Bourdieu 2005: 71). Sie bestimmen von dort aus das alltägliche Handeln der Menschen und strukturieren es u.a. gemäß gesellschaftlich etablierten Vorstellungen von Männlichkeit und Weiblichkeit.

In Ansätzen der Gender Studies bildete der Körper von Beginn an einen Zugang zur Analyse gesellschaftlicher Machtverhältnisse zwischen den Geschlechtern. Im Zuge der Zweiten Frauenbewegung in Deutschland setzten die Protagonistinnen sich mittels körperpolitischer „Selbstverständigung" (Holland-Cunz 2003: 143) mit zentralen frauenpolitischen Themen auseinander. Hierzu gehörten Themen, die einen direkten Zusammenhang zwischen gesellschaftlichen Lebensbedingungen von Frauen und Körperlichkeit herstellten, wie etwa die Forderung, den Abtreibungsparagraphen 218 zu reformulieren, sexualisierte Gewalt zwischen Männern und Frauen in den Blick zu nehmen und die Freiheit der sexuellen Orientierung (ebd.: 144). Theoretisch entstanden unterschiedliche Konzepte, die den Körper analytisch mit gesellschaftlichen Machtverhältnissen verbanden. Die Idee der sozialen Konstruktion des Geschlechts mit der Unterscheidung in ein soziales Geschlecht, *gender*, und ein biologisches Geschlecht, *sex* (vgl. Dietzen 1993; Knapp/Wetterer 1995), stellte den Versuch dar, biologische Gegebenheiten der Körper der Menschen in theoretischen Zugriffen auf das Geschlechterverhältnis sowie seine konkrete Gestaltung von sozialen Zwängen zu entbinden. Die Gebärfähigkeit von Frauen sollte beispielsweise nicht in direkter Linie zur alleinigen Verantwortung der Frauen für private Reproduktionsarbeit führen. Der Ansatz des *doing gender* (West/Zimmerman 1991) betonte die interaktive Herstellung des Geschlechts: zur sozialen Konstruktion von Geschlecht gehören nicht nur Vorstellungen, die unsere Wahrnehmung strukturierten, sondern auch Interaktionspartner, die eine konkrete Inszenierung von Geschlecht bestätigen, indem sie sie interpretieren und als ‚richtig‘ anerkennen. Judith Butler radikalisierte zu Beginn der 1990er Jahre bis dahin existierende Ansätze der sozialen Konstruktion von Geschlecht, indem sie nicht nur die soziale Geschlechterrolle als konstruiert beschrieb, sondern darüber hinaus auch die biologischen Körper von Männern und Frauen als Ergebnis gesellschaftlicher Konstruktionen auffasste (Butler 1991). Den Ausgangspunkt bildete dabei Foucault, auf den Butler sich insofern berief, als sie die vermeintliche Existenz männlicher und weiblicher Körper der Einschreibung gesellschaftlicher, dem Individuum vorgängige, Diskurse in diese Körper zuschrieb und die Unterscheidung in *sex* und *gender* grundsätzlich anzweifelte (ebd.: 24).

Im Rahmen neuer Konzepte der Gender Studies und der Queer Theory zeichnen sich Zugänge zur Konstruktion von Geschlecht ab, die vermehrt eine dichotome Trennung der Geschlechter sowie der Geschlechtsidentität in Frage stellen. Stattdessen gehen diese davon aus, dass es ein Kontinuum als weiblich und als männlich geltender Eigenschaften, Identifizierungen und Empfindungen gäbe, das Individuen sich sozusagen kleinteilig aneignen könnten, ohne sich im ganzen auf eine Identität als eindeutig männlich oder weiblich festzulegen (vgl. Jagose 2001; Kraß 2003). In dem Dokumentarfilm *Gendernauts* aus dem Jahre 1999 hat Monika Treut (1999) Menschen interviewt, die sich hinsichtlich ihrer geschlechtlichen Identität nicht für eine der beiden eindeutigen Kategorien entscheiden wollten: sie spielten mit Attributen beider Geschlechterrollen und entzogen sich einer eindeutigen Zuschreibung. So sagt eine/r der Protagonist/inn/en im Film: "Ich habe mich nie weiblich oder männlich gefühlt. Gender ist mir egal. Ich lasse die Leute selbst entscheiden und wenn sie verwirrt sind, dann ist das in Ordnung. »Bist Du ein Mann oder eine Frau?« - »Ja.«" (Treut 1999: TC 01:11:38).

2   „Die besten Frauen der Welt"

Der Film *Die besten Frauen der Welt* von Britta Becker stammt aus dem Jahr 2008
(Becker 2008). Dem Cover ist zu entnehmen, dass es sich um einen Dokumentarfilm handelt, der aus der Begleitung der deutschen Frauenfußball-Nationalmannschaft während der Weltmeisterschaft in China hervorgeht. Der Hauptfilm
besteht aus 14 Kapiteln, die sich auf eine Laufzeit von 91 Minuten erstrecken. Auf
einer zweiten DVD („Extras") finden sich Ausschnitte aus dem Hauptfilm, die hier
offenbar unter inhaltlichen Aspekten neu zusammengefügt wurden. Die Inhalte
des Films bestehen aus Aufnahmen des Trainings und Alltags der Fußballerinnen
in China, ihren Spielen und Reisen zwischen den Spielen sowie Besuchen im Rahmen des Aufenthaltes in China, beispielsweise der Deutschen Schule in Shang-
hai. Den roten Faden des Films bilden die Spiele, die im Rahmen der Frauen-
fußball-Weltmeisterschaft 2007 gespielt wurden und Interviewsequenzen mit den
Spielerinnen, die sich über den gesamten Film hinweg zwischen den genannten
Szenen finden. Die Gestaltung des Films setzt über die Aussagen der Spielerinnen
und über die Bilder des Films hinaus selbst Schwerpunkte und gibt Perspektiven
vor, die zwar in den Handlungen und Aussagen der Spielerinnen zum Ausdruck
kommen, aber auch über die Platzierung innerhalb des Films, die Länge der Szenen und den filminternen Kontext gestaltet sind. So werte ich es beispielsweise
als maßgebliche Gestaltung, dass Aussagen der Spielerinnen zu Unterschieden
zwischen Männerfußball und Frauenfußball noch vor dem Vorspann des Films
– nach 12 Sekunden Laufzeit – den Einstieg in die Dokumentation bilden und sie
ebenso beenden. Entsprechend lässt sich der Film als Repräsentation der Fußballerinnen als Frauen lesen, die sich in der Männerdomäne Fußball verorten.

Die Methode der Analyse orientiert sich an der *Inhaltsanalyse* (Mayring 2003).
Mit dieser ist eine Verfahrensweise gegeben, die sich gleichermaßen auf Bilder
und „fixierte Kommunikation" (ebd.: 13) anwenden lässt. Die genannten Erzähl-
sequenzen der Spielerinnen wurden im Rahmen des Gesamtfilms betrachtet
und im Hinblick auf die wichtigsten Inhalte zur Fragestellung strukturiert, um
schließlich die zentralen Aussagen der Sequenzen zu den Hauptthemen zu ana-
lysieren. Die Erzählungen der Spielerinnen werden ergänzt durch Aussagen, die
drei Spielerinnen der Frauennationalmannschaft im Rahmen eines von ihnen
selbst publizierten Büchleins zu im Film aufgegriffenen Themen getätigt haben
(Künzer/Huth/Smisek 2011). Die Gestaltung des Films kommt in allen Bereichen
der Analyse nach den o.g. Aspekten als zusätzliche Information zum Tragen.

3 Repräsentationen von Weiblichkeit im Feld des Fußballs

In der nun folgenden Analyse stelle ich anhand der thematischen Schwerpunkte des Films *Die besten Frauen der Welt* die jeweils im Film enthaltenen Repräsentationen des Verhältnisses zwischen Weiblichkeit und Fußball als männlich konnotiertem Sport dar.

Wo ich mich auf Passagen des Films beziehe, gebe ich in Klammern den jeweiligen Beginn der betreffenden Szene in Form eines Timecodes (Becker 2008: TC) an, der die bis dahin vergangene Laufzeit des Films in Stunden, Minuten und Sekunden wiedergibt.

3.1 Wege zum Fußball – Fußballspielen als Mädchen

Im Film finden sich Aussagen mehrerer Spielerinnen zu ihrem Einstieg in das Fußballspielen. Nimmt man die Aussagen der Spielerinnen zu diesem Thema in den Blick, so zeigt sich, dass dieser direkt mit dem Thema des Fußballspielens *als Mädchen* verbunden ist. Diese Verknüpfung zeigt sich in den Selbstbeschreibungen der Spielerinnen, wenn sie von ihren Erinnerungen an ihre Zeit als Mädchen erzählen. Hier kann eine Abgrenzung von als typisch weiblich geltenden Eigenschaften und Verhaltenswiesen im Mittelpunkt stehen oder auch die Schwierigkeit benannt werden, das Mädchensein und Fußballspielen miteinander zu vereinbaren. Dies taucht bei mehreren Spielerinnen in der Beschreibung des altersbedingten Wechsels aus gemischtgeschlechtlichen Mannschaften in reine Mädchenmannschaften auf, der in allen Fällen zunächst nachteilig erscheint und ungewollt ist.

Drei der Spielerinnen, unter ihnen Torfrau Nadine Angerer, benennen als Vorbilder für das eigene Fußballspiel Familienmitglieder: ihre Fußball spielende Mutter (Nadine Angerer, ebd.: TC 00:04:21) und große Brüder, die ebenfalls als Vorbilder fungiert haben (ebd.: TC 00:04:31). Während die Fußball spielende Mutter Nadine Angerers mögliche Brüche zwischen Fußballspiel und Weiblichkeit bereits entkräftet haben mag, beziehen sich weitere Spielerinnen auf männliche Vorbilder. Sie beschreiben sich als Mädchen fern von vermeintlich typischen Mädchenspielen oder -verhaltensweisen. So wird beispielsweise betont: „Seilchenspringen oder Fangenspielen war nicht so mein Ding, ich wollte mit den Jungs Fußball spielen" (ebd.: TC 00:03:57) oder: „Ich habe nie so wirklich mit Puppen gespielt". Die betreffende Spielerin hat in den großen Pausen stattdessen ebenfalls „mit den Jungs Fußball gespielt" (ebd.: TC 00:04:03). Die Orientierung am Fußball scheint begleitet zu sein von einer Selbstbeschreibung, die Distanz zu vermeintlichen Mädchenspielen beinhaltet, wie etwa das Spielen mit Puppen oder „Seilchenspringen" (s.o.).

Angesichts des Wechsels in eine reine Mädchenmannschaft im Alter von 12 Jahren berichtet Torfrau Silke Rottenberg, dieser sei „der Horror" (ebd.: TC 00:06:25) gewesen, da sie gedacht habe, Mädchen könnten kein Fußball spielen – „dabei war ich selbst eins" (ebd.). Es habe dann jedoch eine Mädchenmannschaft gegeben, mit der das Spielen ebenso Spaß gemacht habe (ebd.). Die Vermutung, Mädchen könnten nicht Fußball spielen, erscheint hier aufgrund der Tatsache paradox, dass sie von einem Mädchen getätigt wurde, das selbst Fußball spielte. Zum Ausdruck kommt darin jedoch der bei allen Spielerinnen unwidersprochene Gegensatz zwischen Weiblichkeit und Fußballspiel. Eine weitere Spielerin berichtet, sie habe die Jungenmannschaft nicht verlassen wollen, so dass sie ein Jahr lang weiterhin in der Jungenmannschaft unter falschem Namen gespielt habe. „Ich hatte ganz kurze Haare, das fiel nicht so auf" (ebd.: TC 00:05:51).

Svenja Huth berichtet, ihr Vater habe gewollt, dass sie Tennis spielt. Sie habe ihn jedoch überredet, Fußball spielen zu dürfen; in der Mannschaft der Jungen erfuhr sie jedoch die Konfrontation mit der Annahme, Mädchen könnten kein Fußball spielen (Künzer/Huth/Smisek 2011: 12f).

Schärfer und konflikthafter als bei allen anderen Spielerinnen zeigt sich der Gegensatz zwischen Weiblichkeit und Fußball bei Sandra Smisek, die mit dem altersbedingten Wechsel in eine Mädchenmannschaft den Fußball zunächst aufgibt – sie wünscht sich jedoch, ein Junge zu sein, um weiterhin Fußball spielen zu können. Als Mädchen erscheint es ihr nicht möglich, beim Fußball zu bleiben, „vielleicht, weil das der bequemere Weg war" (ebd.: 22f). Der Wiedereinstieg in den Fußball erfolgt als Einsatz für eine verlorene Wette. Den bevorstehenden Einstieg in das Training mit einer Mädchenmannschaft nimmt Sandra Smisek zunächst als unliebsame Verpflichtung wahr; nach der erneuten Aufnahme des Trainings jedoch empfindet sie den Wiedereinstieg als Rettung (ebd.: 24). Sie schreibt: „Ich habe geackert, gefightet, gelächelt, geweint, gehüpft, geschwitzt, gegrätscht und bin von Tor zu Tor gerannt" (ebd.). In dieser Beschreibung zeigt sich der Spaß am Fußballspiel, der offenbar nun im Vordergrund steht. Die als männlich aufgefassten Eigenschaften – ackern, fighten, schwitzen, grätschen – sind nun offenbar Teil des Spielspaßes.

Alle Beschreibungen zeigen, dass der Widerspruch zwischen Weiblichkeit und Fußballspiel wahrgenommen und – auf unterschiedliche Weise – gelöst werden muss. Keine der Spielerinnen geht als typisches Mädchen in die Fußballmannschaft. Ein Weg zum Fußball besteht darin, sich selbst als Mädchen zu beschreiben, das eher männliche Eigenschaften auf sich vereinen kann: man habe schon immer lieber mit den Jungs Fußball gespielt und sich nicht für das Spiel mit Puppen interessiert. Ein weiterer Ausdruck des Widerspruchs besteht in der Unmöglichkeit, Mädchensein und Fußballspiel als miteinander vereinbar zu denken: man kann als Mädchen nicht Fußball spielen und man kann nicht als Mädchen mit anderen Mädchen (gut) Fußball spielen.

Der Widerspruch löst sich jeweils auf, indem auf unterschiedliche Weise die Mitgliedschaft in einer Mädchenmannschaft zustande kommt – und die Spielerinnen erfahren, dass das Spielen in einer Mädchenmannschaft sogar Spaß macht.

Dennoch wird nicht nur aus dem eigenen Empfinden heraus spürbar, dass Weiblichkeit und Fußballspiel nicht bruchlos zusammenpassen, sondern auch aus dem Umfeld wird dies an die Spielerinnen herangetragen. So beschreibt eine der Spielerinnen die an sie herangetragene Annahme, dass sie als Mädchen nicht Fußball spielen könne, während eine weitere Spielerin erzählt, es sei den Jungen der Mannschaft peinlich gewesen, wenn eine Frau „ein Tor hat" (Becker: TC 00:04:41).

Aus Sicht der Spielerinnen wird das Verhältnis zwischen Weiblichkeit und Fußball erstmals anhand des Einstiegs in den Fußball und darauf folgend beim altersbedingt anstehenden Wechsel in eine Mädchenmannschaft deutlich. Können die Spielerinnen sich problemlos als Mädchen fühlen, die eben nicht gerne „Seilchen springen", sondern mit den „Jungs Fußball spielen", ist der Übergang in die Mädchenmannschaft ein mitunter krisenhafter Umbruch. Die Annahme, Mädchen könnten nicht Fußball spielen oder der Wunsch, ein Junge zu sein, um weiter Fußball spielen zu können, bringen dies zum Ausdruck.

3.2   Männerfußball – Frauenfußball

Ein Hauptthema des Films bildet die Beschreibung der Unterschiede zwischen Frauenfußball und Männerfußball. Eines der Kernthemen sind dabei die physiologischen Unterschiede der Geschlechter, aufgrund deren das Spiel von Männern und Frauen nicht miteinander vergleichbar sei.

Vergleichbar sind die Leistungen von Männern und Frauen im Fußball tatsächlich nicht, da sie in der Regel nicht gegeneinander oder miteinander spielen – Frauenfußball und Männerfußball sind ab einem Alter von 15 Jahren der Spieler/innen institutionell getrennt voneinander organisiert (vgl. Müller 2009: 296f)[2].

---

2   Kleindienst-Cachay und Kunzendorf (2003: 138) verweisen auf Berichte von Fußballerinnen, die – offenbar zu Trainingszwecken – an Spielen zwischen Männer- und Frauenteams teilgenommen hatten.

Die Vergleiche der Spielerinnen beziehen sich also mit großer Wahrscheinlichkeit auf Beobachtungen und Bewertungen, die ohne direkte Leistungsvergleiche zustande kommen. Die physische Überlegenheit der Männer kommt hier
insofern zum Tragen, als die Spielerinnen der Meinung sind, Frauenfußball sei
langsamer (Becker 2008: TC 01:08:18) und Männer seien den Frauen athletisch
voraus (Melanie Behringer, ebd.: TC 01:08:43). Zudem spielten Männer aggressiver: „Denen ist es ja egal, wenn sie einen mit beiden Beinen umhauen" (ebd.: TC
01:08:25). Frauen- und Männerfußball seien verschiedene Sportarten, die man
nicht miteinander vergleichen könne: „Dafür sind wir halt Mann und Frau" (ebd.:
TC 01:08:39).

In einigen Aussagen der Spielerinnen finden sich auf der Grundlage der zunächst unbewerteten Differenz des Männer- und Frauenfußballs Aussagen über
qualitative Differenzen. Diese beziehen sich auf die Art und Weise des Spielens,
etwa wenn davon die Rede ist, dass Frauenfußball auf hohem Niveau ansehn-
licher sei (ebd.: TC 00:00:12). Damit übereinstimmend findet sich die Aussage
„Frauenfußball ist zwar weniger schnell als Männerfußball, dafür aber vielleicht
auch schöner!" (Künzer/Huth/Smisek 2011: 45).

Eine weitere Differenzierung gründet in den institutionellen Bedingungen des
Frauen- im Vergleich zu denjenigen des Männerfußballs: die unterschiedliche
finanzielle Ausstattung, die sich aus dem weniger starken Interesse für den Frauenfußball ergibt (vgl. Müller 2009: 12). Eine Spielerin zieht den Vergleich zur Profimannschaft der Männer in Köln. Sie sei Fan der Mannschaft und besuche deren
Spiele im Stadion. Das Spiel der Männer sei jedoch „echt schlecht" und sie spielten
ohne Einsatz. Die Spielerin führt dies darauf zurück, dass die Spieler der Mannschaft nicht wertschätzten, was sie tun, während Frauenmannschaften um des
Spielens willen spielten und nicht „überbezahlt" seien (Becker 2008: TC 00:02:06).
Diese Differenz zeige sich auch im Kontakt mit den Medien: Fußballerinnen seien
vergleichsweise besser erreichbar, „authentischer und dadurch auch vor dem Mi-
krofon etwas frischer, da sie eben nicht Tag für Tag im Mittelpunkt des Medien-
interesses stehen" (Künzer/Huth/Smisek 2011: 43).

Die geringere finanzielle Ausstattung und Anerkennung des Frauenfußballs
bringt Konsequenzen für die Lebensplanung der Spielerinnen mit sich. Aufgrund
der geringeren Bezahlung sind sie nicht nur darauf angewiesen, neben dem zeit-
intensiven Training sowie Turnieren einen bezahlten Beruf auszuüben. Darüber
hinaus ermöglicht auch eine Karriere als Fußballspielerin der Nationalmannschaft keine umfassende Altersvorsorge, so dass die Berufsbiographie während
und nach der Zeit als aktive Spielerin einer Ergänzung durch bezahlte Erwerbsarbeit bedarf. Die zusätzliche Belastung, die hierdurch entsteht, und die Ein-
schränkung, die dies für das Fußballspiel bedeutet, schlagen vermutlich im Ver-

gleich mit dem professionellen Männerfußball doppelt zu Buche. Eine Spielerin resümiert: "Irgendwann ist man 33, 34, 35 und da ist noch ein Leben zu leben – die andere Hälfte. Und da muss dann halt auch ein anderes Standbein vorhanden sein. Wenn das nicht gegeben ist, kann das halt auch nach hinten losgehen" (Becker 2008: TC 01:05:46)[3].

Zugleich ist aus Sicht der Spielerinnen jedoch erkennbar, dass es eine erhebliche Verbesserung der Bedingungen des Frauenfußballs gibt. So sei das Begleitteam der Weltmeisterschaft sehr groß und bestehe aus der Cheftrainerin, zwei Assistenztrainerinnen, einem Torwarttrainer, einem Fitnesscoach, einem Equipmentmanager, zwei Physiotherapeuten, einem Arzt, einer Person für die Spielanalyse sowie einem Koch (ebd., DVD 2: Extras: TC 00:32:40). Mit der qualitativen Verbesserung des Spiels der Frauen gehe auch eine Verbesserung der Rahmenbedingungen einher: es seien höhere Zuschauerzahlen zu verzeichnen und während „früher alles auf Männer abgestimmt" gewesen sei, hätten die Trikots nun sogar einen Frauenschnitt (ebd.: TC 00:33:54) – der Fußball bewegt sich auf die Frauen zu.

Aus den Schilderungen der Spielerinnen geht hervor, dass sie zwischen Männer- und Frauenfußball differenzieren und dies auf physiologische Geschlechterunterschiede zurückführen. Hierin ist die Fortsetzung des Widerspruchs zwischen Fußball und Weiblichkeit zu erkennen, den die Spielerinnen nun angesichts ihrer Teilhabe am (Frauen)Fußball aus der Innensicht beschreiben.

Aus der konstatierten Differenz ergeben sich in der Folge mitunter Vorteile für die Spielerinnen, die aufgrund einer Leistungssteigerung über ein höheres Maß finanzieller Ressourcen verfügen können, was zu einer weiteren Verbesserung führt. Der Anstieg der Leistung entsteht aus der Sicht einer Spielerin gerade aus der zuvor geringeren Anerkennung des Frauenfußballs: Frauen verfügten über eine intrinsische Motivation, so dass sie letztlich besser spielten als z.B. die männliche Kölner Profimannschaft.

3.3   Kämpfernaturen

Die Spielerinnen sprechen an mehreren Stellen im Film über Aspekte ihres Spiels, in deren Kontext sie sich selbst unter Bezugnahme auf zunächst als männlich verstandene Attribute beschreiben.

---

3   Siehe hierzu Abschnitt 3.4 ‚Frauenfußball als Beruf?'

Im Mittelpunkt einer Aussage von Linda Bresonik steht der Spaß am Spiel: „Das ist schon ein geiles Gefühl, wenn Du aus 16 m abziehst und Du haust das Ding ins Netz" (Becker 2008: TC 00:01:43).

Einige Spielerinnen erzählen vom Umgang mit Verletzungen, die sie sich beim Spielen zugezogen haben. Sie stellen sich selbst dabei als unbeeindruckt von Schmerz dar und nehmen eine Relativierung der Verletzung zugunsten des Spielens vor. Eine der Spielerinnen ist im Film zu sehen, während sie eine ärztliche Behandlung erhält. Diese ist in Folge einer mehrfachen Stauchung am Vortag während eines Spiels notwendig geworden. Ihr Knöchel erscheint im Bild und sie zeigt auf eine deutlich sichtbare Schwellung. Unbeeindruckt sagt sie, nach der Erzählung über die Entstehung der Verletzung: "Das ist 'ne WM, da wird nicht rumgememmt" (ebd.: TC 00:57:36). Sie wird im nächsten Spiel mit der Verletzung teilnehmen und eine Bandage in Form eines Tapes tragen.

Eine weitere Spielerin befindet, Verletzungen würden außerhalb des Fußballs häufig überbewertet: „Wenn Du mit andern Mädels mal sprichst, die sich das Bein stoßen und einen blauen Fleck haben, dann ist das eine riesen Verletzung und ja, Gott… Ist ja eigentlich gar nix, ein Kratzerchen" (ebd.: TC 00:56:36). Des Weiteren müsse man einen Bänderriss keinesfalls eingipsen, wie sie es bereits im privaten Umfeld erlebt habe. „Da kommt bei uns ein Tape drauf und dann wird weitergespielt, ist halt so" (ebd.: TC 00:57:12).

Während im ersten Fall die Bereitschaft, trotz einer Verletzung aktiv am kommenden Spiel teilzunehmen, im Vordergrund steht, kann man aus der Aussage der zweiten Spielerin darüber hinaus auch eine Abgrenzung gegenüber Personen lesen, die weniger unbeeindruckt im Umgang mit Verletzungen sind. Bezieht man sich hier auf die von Karin Hausen beschriebenen Geschlechtscharaktere und bekannte Stereotype der Geschlechter, so ist eine Abgrenzung gegenüber einem als weiblich bewerteten Attribut zu erkennen: Die Spielerin ist nicht auf vermeintlich weibliche Weise empfindlich oder gar wehleidig. Daran anschließend wiederum kann auf eine Aufwertung der eigenen Person oder der eigenen Praxis geschlossen werden, die sich aus der Aneignung einer als männlich konnotierten Eigenschaft ergibt, die weiblichen Eigenschaften gegenüber per se als höherwertig erscheint (vgl. Hartmann-Tews 2003: 25). Der vermeintliche Gegensatz zwischen Weiblichkeit und Fußball wird hier durch Abgrenzung zum Trittbrett der Aneignung einer – gemäß der Logik der Geschlechterstereotype vergleichsweise höherwertigen – Aneignung von Männlichkeit durch eine weibliche Spielerin. Grundlage einer solchen Wahrnehmung ist die binär codierte Teilung der meisten Sportarten in weibliche und männliche Disziplinen, die in ihren Ausprägungen den Bildern der männlichen und weiblichen Geschlechtsidentität entsprechen. Gymnastik und Reiten gelten demnach als weibliche, Fußball und

Rugby beispielsweise als männliche Sportarten. Durch die ergänzende Hierarchisierung von als männlich und als weiblich wahrgenommenen Attributen und Eigenschaften zuungunsten der Frauen bzw. Weiblichkeit, erfahren Männer, die sich in einer Frauensportart engagieren tendenziell eine Abwertung, Frauen aber, die sich in einer Männersportart etablieren, tendenziell Anerkennung und die Steigerung ihres Status (vgl. ebd.).

Die deutlichsten Selbstbeschreibungen als starke Person finden sich beinahe gleichlautend bei den beiden Torfrauen der Mannschaft: Nadine Angerer sagt von sich selbst: „Ich bin eine Kämpfernatur" (Becker 2008: TC 00:43:44); Silke Rottenberg sagt: "Ich bin ein Kämpfertyp" (ebd.: TC 00:44:16).

Nadine Angerer positioniert sich in einem Interview am Rande eines Trainings durch Journalist/inn/en, die nicht an der Produktion des Films beteiligt zu sein scheinen, als entschlossene Kämpferin für den Gewinn der eigenen Mannschaft. Der Interviewer fragt sie: „Wie sehr brennt man jetzt auf so ein Spiel?" Nadine Angerer antwortet: „Jetzt is alles oder nix, jetzt wollen wir natürlich alle ins Finale. Jetzt haben wir Blut geleckt und jetzt wollen wir natürlich unser großes Ziel, das Finale, erreichen" (ebd.: TC: 01:02:38). Ihre Bezugnahme auf das explizit kämpferische Bild des Blutleckens erfüllt möglicherweise eine ähnliche Funktion wie die zuvor angenommene Aufwertung im Kontext der Bereitschaft des Hinnehmens und Aushaltens von Verletzungen: erschließt sich doch im Kontext des Fußballs die Teilhabe an männlich geprägten Kulturtechniken des Betonens der eigenen Lust am Gewinnen.

Ein ähnlicher Eindruck ergibt sich aus einer Szene, die im Kampfsportcenter Frechen aufgenommen wurde und ein Training der Spielerinnen zeigt. Sie boxen gegen Boxsäcke und Bratzen. Eine der Spielerinnen boxt gegen einen Trainingspartner, der seine Hände in Boxhandschuhen vor sein Gesicht hält. Die Trainerin der Mannschaft, Silvia Neid, feuert die Spielerinnen in beiden Situationen an (ebd.: TC: 00:04:57). Auf der Ebene der filmischen Gestaltung entsteht der Eindruck kämpferischer Frauen, die sich auf als männlich wahrgenommene Weise zeigen. Aus Sicht der Beteiligten mag dies ebenfalls als eine Aufwertung verstanden werden; möglicherweise ist dies jedoch nicht das Motiv der beteiligten Spielerinnen, sondern das Motiv der kämpferisch inszenierten Frauen bildet ein ideales Kondensat eines der Grundthemen des Films: der Differenz zwischen Frauenfußball und Männerfußball, die hier konterkariert wird.

3.4   Frauenfußball als Beruf?

Die Spielerinnen thematisieren im Film die Tatsache, dass das Fußballspielen sie nicht als Hauptberuf finanzieren kann: „Wir können zwar ´ne gewisse Zeit davon leben, aber wir können da nich so viel sparen, dass wir, wenn wir mit 30 aufhören, oder mit 32 oder mit 34, dass wir dann davon leben können" (Linda Bresonik, ebd.: TC 01:04:49). Zum selben Thema sagt Torfrau Nadine Angerer, man könne nicht so viel Geld ansparen, dass man sich „eine Villa in Afrika" kaufen könne – „und dann ist alles tutti" (ebd.: TC 00:01:05). Eine weitere Spielerin sagt: „Weil, wenn ich dann wirklich mit'm Fußball mal aufhör', dann steh' ich da und hab' keine Ausbildung, hab' keinen Job und nix. Ich glaub', das wär' mir zu gefährlich. Ich meine, ich verdien' ja keine Millionen" (ebd.: TC 01:04:58). So kommt auch der Wunsch zum Ausdruck, dass Frauen vom Fußball leben können, ohne sich Gedanken darüber machen zu müssen, „was danach kommt" (ebd.: TC 01:28:38).

Aus dieser Situation ergibt sich die Notwendigkeit, neben dem Fußball einen Beruf zu erlernen und dort tätig zu sein, um über den Lebenslauf hinweg auf eine ergänzende Finanzierung zugreifen zu können. So sind Sandra Smisek und Nia Künzer sich beide darüber bewusst, dass Frauenfußball im Gegensatz zu Männerfußball nicht die Möglichkeit eines Hauptberufs bietet (Künzer/Huth/Smisek 2011: 27, 35f.), so dass Fußball und Beruf für die Spielerinnen stets zweierlei bleiben. Dies bringt nicht nur eine doppelte Belastung mit sich, die potenziell sowohl den Beruf als auch das Fußballspiel beeinträchtigen kann, sondern dies bedeutet auch, dass Frauenfußball und Männerfußball sich hinsichtlich der unter gegebenen Umständen möglichen Professionalisierung nur begrenzt vergleichen lassen.

Eine der Nationalspielerinnen der Weltmeisterschaft 2007 beschreibt, wie sie ihren Hauptberuf mit dem „zweiten Beruf" des Fußballs überein bringt: „Der normale Ablauf ist einfach so, ich mach' morgens meinen Beruf und fahr' vom Beruf ins Training und mach' dann meinen zweiten Beruf. So seh' ich das" (Becker 2008: TC 01:04:27). An einer anderen Stelle im Film äußert sich dieselbe Spielerin zum Thema und bringt den Aspekt der doppelten Belastung durch Fußball einerseits und Erwerbsarbeit andererseits stärker zum Ausdruck: „Das nervt manchmal total. Also manchmal pack' ich meine Tasche für's Training und bin grad zehn Minuten vorher von der Arbeit nach Hause gekommen … Echt kein Bock. Aber es ist ja auch meine Arbeit, das ist halt so, den Schweinehund überwinden und dann doch nochmal zwei Stunden durchziehen. Und dann bist Du zu Hause und dann kannst Du die Füße hochlegen. Aber das jeden Tag machen zu müssen, das ist schon Horror" (ebd.: TC 00:07:08).

Ariane Hingst sagt: „Ich würde sicher ein Gehalt von einem Männerprofi nicht abschlagen" (ebd.: TC 01:05:11); sie distanziert sich jedoch zugleich davon, ein

Leben zu führen, in dem das Fußballspielen die einzige berufliche Tätigkeit wäre. Birgit Prinz stimmt Ariane Hingst zu, wenn es darum geht, den Fußball alleine in den Mittelpunkt des (Berufs)lebens zu stellen: Man sei dann auf Fußball fixiert, so dass die eigene Laune nur noch vom Fußball abhänge. Alle Leute, die man kenne, kenne man aus dem Fußball – „das ist auf die Dauer auch langweilig" (ebd.: TC 01:05:26). Linda Bresonik weist auf eine weitere Bedeutung beruflicher Alternativen hin, indem sie ins Feld führt, dass Fußball allein intellektuell nicht anregend genug sei: „Ich werde auch wieder in den Beruf gehen, weil irgendwann verblödest Du ja" (ebd.: TC 01:05:43).

Zwei Spielerinnen sprechen über die Ungewissheit des Erfolgs des Fußballs und somit auch über die unsichere finanzielle Basis, die er perspektivisch bedeutet: „Mir war's einfach wichtig, dass ich auch irgendwo wieder, ich mein', ich bin 27, wieder in den Beruf reinkomme, weil der Fußball kann halt schneller vorbei sein als man denkt" (ebd.: TC 01:04:40).

Einen direkten Vergleich mit den Bedingungen des Männerfußballs stellt eine der Spielerinnen an: „Wenn wir nicht erfolgreich sind, ist es ganz schnell auch wieder vorbei, im Gegensatz zu den Männern (ebd.: TC 01:28:05).

In den zitierten Aussagen zeigt sich, dass die Spielerinnen sich der vergleichsweise unsicheren Bedingungen bewusst sind, die mit dem Frauenfußball einhergehen. Aus ihren Aussagen wird jedoch neben der Thematisierung der Differenzen zu den Bedingungen des Männerfußballs deutlich, dass gerade auf deren Grundlage Freiräume rechts und links des Fußballs entstehen, die die Spielerinnen wertschätzen und nutzen.

Die Spielerinnen ziehen aus den gegebenen Umständen die Konsequenz, sich um ein „zweites Standbein" (s.o.) zu bemühen und für die Zeit nach dem aktiven Fußballspiel vorzusorgen. Bei einigen der Spielerinnen erscheinen jedoch auch Vorstellungen eines Lebenskonzeptes, das sich nicht damit vereinbaren lässt, sich beruflich zu 100% auf das Fußballspielen zu konzentrieren. Hier werden unterschiedliche Gründe angeführt, wie etwa die mangelnde intellektuelle Anregung oder der Wunsch nach der Beschäftigung mit Tätigkeiten, die über den Fußball hinausgehen – um nicht alleine auf Fußball festgelegt zu sein.

3.5   Klischees

Im Verlauf des Films kommen Szenen zum Tragen, die die Spielerinnen bei Handlungen der Körperpflege zeigen, die man als typisch weiblich betrachten und Nina

Degele (2004) zufolge als „Schönheitshandeln" bezeichnen kann[4]. Betrachtet man diese Szenen als Teile eines Films, dessen Beginn und Ende auf einen Vergleich zwischen Männer- und Frauenfußball zugespitzt ist, so verweisen sie auf einen Aspekt von Weiblichkeit, der im Film als Widerspruch zum Fußball erscheint. In einer Szene, die länger als eine ganze Minute dauert, sind die Spielerinnen dabei zu sehen, wie sie sich vor einem Spiel in einem Umkleideraum frisieren. Sie stecken ihre Haare fest, besprühen sie mit Haarspray, bürsten sie, befestigen Gummibänder darin und zupfen Strähnen zu recht (Becker 2008: TC 00:34:08 bis 00:35:14). Die Spielerinnen prüfen dabei ihr Aussehen im Spiegel und beziehen sich auf die Handlungen der anderen Spielerinnen. Die Anknüpfung an Geschlechterstereotype macht deutlich, dass hier Handlungen gezeigt werden, die Weiblichkeit symbolisieren.

Eine weitere Szene mit Bezügen zum Schönheitshandeln dreht sich um das notwendige Schneiden der langen Fingernägel vor einem Spiel. Eine Dame in Uniform, die offenbar seitens der Veranstalter für derlei Fragen Sorge trägt, weist eine der Spielerinnen darauf hin, sie müsse sich vor dem Spiel die Fingernägel schneiden. Als die angesprochene Spielerin sich wortlos von ihr abwendet und geht, ergänzt die Dame: „Falls nicht, werden Sie nicht spielen" (ebd.: TC 00:24:43). In der Folge sind mehrere Spielerinnen zu sehen, die sich selbst und anderen Spielerinnen die Fingernägeln schneiden und feilen. Einige von ihnen sind dabei offensichtlich alles andere als erfreut.

Ein indirekter Bezug zum Schönheitshandeln kommt in einer Interviewpassage mit Fatmire Bajramaj zum Ausdruck. Sie sagt zunächst: „Wenn ich in die Stadt gehe und komm' zurück und hab' nix gekauft, dann fühl' ich mich einfach schlecht!" (ebd.: TC 01:00:05). Kurz darauf ergänzt sie: „Was ich natürlich auch liebe, ist Schuhe. Schuhe ist ALLES für mich. […] Ohne die Fußballschuhe mitzuzählen, habe ich bestimmt über 30. Ist das viel oder wenig?" (ebd.: TC 01:00:45). Der Bezug zu Geschlechterrollenklischees liegt hier in der vermeintlichen Leidenschaft für das Einkaufen – besonders von Kleidung und insbesondere von Schuhen.

Die Torhüterin Nadine Angerer erzählt von einer Vereinbarung mit Ariane Hingst: „Wir rasieren uns, also die Beine, erst wieder, wenn wir ein Spiel verloren haben. Jetzt haben wir ja seit vier Wochen kein Spiel verloren […] Ich kann nur so viel dazu sagen, ich muss meine Augen zumachen beim Duschen, weil ich das so

---

4 Als Schönheitshandeln sind dabei Maßnahmen zu verstehen, die auf das Ziel hin ausgerichtet sind, einen Zustand zu erreichen, der sich möglichst nahe an geltenden Idealen von Schönheit orientiert, wie etwa Körperpflege, sportliches Training oder andere Gestaltungen des Aussehens bzw. des Körpers (vgl. Degele 2004).

eklig finde. Aber jetzt kann ich's nicht mehr rasieren, das ging jetzt so gut, also es darf sich keiner wundern, wenn ich bald soo durch's Tor laufe [macht eine Geste, die Breite zum Ausdruck bringt, EG] oder bald keine Schienbeinschoner mehr brauch', weil es einfach soo eklig ist" (ebd.: TC 01:13:20 – 01:13:57).

Auch hier kommt eine Bezugnahme auf Schönheitsideale und der Wunsch, ihnen zu entsprechen zum Ausdruck. Auf der Ebene der Erzählung Angerers wird deutlich, dass diese sich von einem Zustand ihres Körpers distanziert, der aus einem gegebenen Anlass nicht ihren Wünschen entspricht.

Die zweite Torfrau, Silke Rottenberg, ist in einer weiteren Szene in einem Umkleideraum inmitten des Teams dabei zu beobachten, wie sie gemeinsam mit einer Mitspielerin die Innenhose aus einer Sportshorts heraustrennt. Dabei sagt sie: „Ich hab' ein Problem, aber ich find's eigentlich schön. Ich bin kein Mann, deswegen fülle ich die Innenhose nicht aus" (ebd.: TC 00:24:31). Die Bezugnahme auf Weiblichkeit erfolgt hier explizit und durch die Spielerin selbst. Silke Rottenberg erscheint in dieser Szene nicht als Frau, die Stereotypen von Weiblichkeit entspricht, sondern sie ergreift eine Maßnahme der Umgestaltung eines für Männer ausgelegten Kleidungsstücks, um dieses für sich selbst als Frau passend zu gestalten.

4   Zusammenfassung der Ergebnisse, Resümee und Ausblick

In der Gesamtheit der Aussagen der Spielerinnen zeigt sich, dass die Frage nach dem Verhältnis von Fußballspiel und Weiblichkeit an mehreren Punkten zum Thema wird. Teils zeigt sich, dass die Spielerinnen bereits früh wahrnehmen, dass ihr Umfeld das Fußballspiel nicht als für ein Mädchen geeignet erachtet. Der Vater von Svenja Huth wünscht sich ihrer Erinnerung zufolge, dass sie Tennis und nicht Fußball spielt; eine weitere Spielerin berichtet, es sei den Jungen peinlich gewesen, wenn ein Mädchen gegen sie ein Tor erzielt habe. Hier kommt nicht nur eine Gegensatz zwischen Weiblichkeit und Fußball(spiel) zum Ausdruck, den die Spielerinnen selbst wahrgenommen haben, sondern ihr Umfeld reagiert auf sie als fußballspielende Mädchen in einer Weise, aus der sich schließen lässt, dass die Spielerinnen nicht den allgemeinen Erwartungen an ein Mädchen/eine Frau entsprechen – daraus entsteht scheinbar eine peinliche Situation für die beteiligten Jungen.

Die möglichen Schwierigkeiten bei der Aneignung eines Sportes, der als männlich gilt und mit Bewegungen und Verhaltensweisen einher geht, die im Widerspruch zur weiblichen Geschlechterrolle stehen, kommen hierin klar zum

Ausdruck (vgl. Hartmann-Tews 2003: 15). Die eingangs dargelegten und bereits bei den Klassikern der Soziologie erforschten Wechselwirkungen zwischen gesellschaftlicher Ordnung und Überformung des menschlichen Körpers, bzw. der etablierten Sichtweisen auf ihn, kommen im Schnittfeld zwischen (männlichem) Fußball und Weiblichkeit zum Tragen. Die Spielerinnen begegnen der Herausforderung, gesellschaftliche Vorstellungen von Weiblichkeit mit dazu als konträr aufgefassten Eigenschaften in Einklang zu bringen (vgl. ebd.: 17). Hierzu überwinden sie Hindernisse, die sich ihnen als Mädchen in der Aneignung des Fußballs stellen.

Biographisch erlangt ein potenzieller Konflikt zwischen weiblicher Geschlechterrolle und Fußball erstmals beim Einstieg in das Fußballspielen Bedeutung. Die widersprüchliche Anlage der weiblichen Geschlechterrolle einerseits und als männlich erachteter Erfordernisse des Fußballspiels andererseits treffen hier aufeinander (vgl. Kleindienst-Cachay/Kunzendorf 2003: 118). Die Fortsetzung des Themas findet sich in leicht veränderter Form bei der altersbedingten Geschlechtertrennung der Fußballteams in reine Jungen- und Mädchenmannschaften. Die Annahme, Mädchen könnten nicht Fußball spielen, bringt die Befürchtung mit sich, keinen Spaß beim Fußballspiel mehr zu haben. Silke Rottenberg bringt im Film ihr eigenes Erstaunen darüber zum Ausdruck, als fußballspielendes Mädchen selbst geglaubt zu haben, Mädchen könnten nicht Fußball spielen (Becker 2008: TC 00:06:25). Offenbar ist in diesem Fall bereits die Aneignung einer als männlich erachteten Fähigkeit – Fußball spielen – geschehen, ohne dass damit bereits Geschlechterstereotype entkräftet worden sind. Die Spielerinnen reklamieren über den Film hinweg an mehreren Stellen Eigenschaften für sich, die als männlich konnotiert gelten können: etwa, wenn sie sich als Kämpfernaturen beschreiben, den Spaß am Spielen hervorheben oder den Willen, zu gewinnen, zum Ausdruck bringen. Ebenso werden jedoch sowohl in den Aussagen der Spielerinnen als auch auf der Ebene der Gestaltung des Films Klischees weiblicher Geschlechtsidentität sichtbar: Ob es um das Frisieren oder die Freude an vermeintlich weiblichen Tätigkeiten, wie etwa Einkaufen, geht.

Weitere Kontexte eines Widerspruchs zwischen Fußball und Weiblichkeit zeigen sich in Abgrenzungen vom Männerfußball. Die Spielerinnen im Film sind sich darüber einig, dass Männer- und Frauenfußball aus verschiedenen Gründen keine vergleichbaren Sportarten sind. Auch im Hinblick auf das jeweils eigene Verhältnis zum Fußball kommt diese Abgrenzung insofern zum Ausdruck, als die vergleichsweise geringeren Möglichkeiten des Frauenfußballs zusätzlich zu diesem Freiräume ermöglichen, sich mit anderen Dingen zu befassen und eine intrinsische Motivation für das Spielen zu erhalten. Diese Differenzierung mag über Männer- vs. Frauenfußball hinaus für Unterschiede zwischen mehr und weniger professionellem Fußball gelten; im Film und von den Spielerinnen wird sie jedoch in erster Linie vor dem Hintergrund der Geschlechtszugehörigkeit der Spielerinnen und Spieler sowie den sich daraus ergebenden Folgen gedeutet.

Die institutionellen Aspekte des Frauenfußballs geraten auch im Kontext notwendiger Doppelbelastungen in den Blick, die sich daraus ergeben, dass eine berufliche Existenz allein mit Hilfe des Fußballspiels für die Spielerinnen nicht möglich ist. Nicht zum Tragen kommen Hindernisse, die sich möglicherweise aus Widerständen ergeben, die seitens der Organisationen des Fußballs an die Spielerinnen herangetragen werden könnten – hier ist beispielsweise an Konfliktlagen im Kontext der Öffnung des Fußballs für Frauen zu denken (vgl. Kleindienst-Cachay 2003: 110).

Befasst man sich mit der Analyse von Geschlechterstereotypen, so ist man stets in der Lage, mit der doppelten Bedeutung umgehen zu müssen, die Geschlechterstereotypen zukommt. Einerseits ist deren soziale Konstruiertheit die Grundlage jeglichen Nachdenkens über die Kategorie Geschlecht jenseits essenzialistischer Vorstellungen. Andererseits gestaltet sich soziale Realität aufgrund normativer Erwartungen, geschlechtsspezifischer Aneignungen des Körpers durch die Akteure, durch gesellschaftlich gebahnte Perspektiven auf den Körper und vieles mehr durchaus gemäß geltenden Geschlechterstereotypen – hier sind sie ein nicht zu leugnender Bestandteil gesellschaftlicher Realität. Hier schlagen sich gesellschaftliche Strukturen bis auf die Ebene persönlicher Empfindungen nieder. Bei Pierre Bourdieu findet sich dies im Habituskonzept gefasst, Foucault betrachtet das Verhältnis zwischen Körper und Gesellschaft machttheoretisch und Norbert Elias stellt einen Zusammenhang zwischen Überformung der Affekte und gesellschaftlicher Entwicklung her, der letztlich auch körperlich zum Tragen kommt. Untersucht man die konkrete Gestalt eines Verhältnisses der Geschlechter und die dazugehörigen Ausprägungen geschlechtsspezifischer Identität, sitzt man also stets zwischen den beiden Stühlen der sozialen Konstruktion der Geschlechterrollen und der gesellschaftlichen Realität, die ihnen dennoch zukommt.

Kommt man vor diesem Hintergrund auf die Frage zurück, ob und wie Fußballerinnen einen potenziellen Konflikt zwischen männlich geprägtem Fußball und Weiblichkeit auflösen – ob die postmoderne Frau eine Fußballerin ist – so ist diese Frage nicht ganz eindeutig zu beantworten.

Die im Film vorgestellten Fußballerinnen reklamieren für sich Eigenschaften, die den gesellschaftlich etablierten Normen zufolge als männliche Eigenschaften betrachtet werden: Sie wollen gewinnen, sie haben Spaß am Fußballspielen, das unter Kraft- und Körpereinsatz geschieht, sie halten Schmerzen aus und spielen trotz Verletzungen. Dies erzeugt offenbar keinerlei Widersprüche zu ihrer Rolle als Frauen, nachdem sie sich den Fußball als Mädchen angeeignet haben. An anderen Stellen des Films kommen, ebenfalls sowohl auf der Ebene der Erzählungen als auch auf der Ebene der Gestaltung des Films, Bilder der Spielerinnen zum Tragen, die auf weibliche Geschlechterstereotype rekurrieren; hier handelt es sich um das Frisieren und Fingernägel schneiden der Spielerinnen, ihr Vergnügen am Einkaufen und die Abgrenzung von Männerfußball als aggressiver und schneller aufgrund der athletischen Überlegenheit der Männer.

Beides, die Bezugnahme auf als männlich erachtete Eigenschaften durch die Spielerinnen und ihre (durch den Film unterstützte) Selbstdarstellung als typische Frauen, bleibt auf der Ebene der Darstellung im Film und der Aussagen der Spielerinnen unverbunden.

Postmoderne Frauen mögen die Spielerinnen dort nicht sein, wo sie sich auf das sichere Feld weiblicher Geschlechterrollen zurückziehen. Ganz sicher sind sie es jedoch dort, wo sie Kämpfernaturen sind, gegen Bratzen boxen und auf den Gewinn eines Spiels brennen.

Literatur

Bourdieu, P. (2005): Die männliche Herrschaft. Frankfurt am Main: Suhrkamp.
Butler, J. (3003): Imitation und die Aufsässigkeit der Geschlechtsidentität. In: Kraß, Andreas (Hg.): Queer Studies. Frankfurt am Main: Suhrkamp, 144-168.
Butler, J. (1991): Das Unbehagen der Geschlechter. Frankfurt am Main: Suhrkamp.
Degele, N. (2004): Sich schön machen. Zur Soziologie von Geschlecht und Schönheitshandeln. Wiesbaden: VS/GWV.
Dietzen, A. (1993): Soziales Geschlecht. Soziale, kulturelle und symbolische Dimensionen des Gender-Konzepts. Opladen: Westdeutscher Verlag.
Elias, N. (1997): Über den Prozeß der Zivilisation. Soziogenetische und psychogenetische Untersuchungen, Bd. 1 u. 2. Frankfurt am Main: Suhrkamp.
Foucault, M. (1977): Überwachen und Strafen. Die Geburt des Gefängnisses. Frankfurt am Main: Suhrkamp.
Hartmann-Tews, I. (2003): Soziale Konstruktion von Geschlecht im Sport: Neue Perspektiven der Geschlechterforschung in der Sportwissenschaft. In: dies./Gieß-Stüber, P./ Klein, M.-L./Kleindienst-Cachay, C./Petry, K.: Soziale Konstruktion von Geschlecht im Sport. Opladen: Leske + Budrich, 13-27.
Hartmann-Tews, I./Rulofs, B. (2003): Sport in den Medien – ein Feld von semiotischer Markierung von Geschlecht?. In: Hartmann-Tews, I./Gieß-Stüber, P./Klein, M.-L./ Kleindienst-Cachay, Christa/Petry, Karen: Soziale Konstruktion von Geschlecht im Sport. Opladen: Leske + Budrich, 29-68.
Holland-Cunz, B. (2003): Die alte neue Frauenfrage, Frankfurt am Main: Suhrkamp.
Hausen, K. (1978): Die Polarisierung der >>Geschlechtscharaktere<<. Eine Spiegelung der Dissoziation von Erwerbs- und Familienleben. In: Rosenbaum, H. (Hg.): Seminar: Familie und Gesellschaftsstruktur. Frankfurt am Main: Suhrkamp 1978, 161-191.
Jagose, Annamarie (2001): Queer Theory. Eine Einführung. Berlin: Querverlag.

Kleindienst-Cachay, C./Kunzendorf, A. (2003): ‚Männlicher' Sport - ‚weibliche' Identität? Hochleistungssportlerinnen in männlich dominierten Sportarten. In: Hartmann-Tews, I./Gieß-Stüber, P./Klein, M.-L./Kleindienst-Cachay, C./Petry, K.: Soziale Konstruktion von Geschlecht im Sport. Opladen: Leske + Budrich, 109-150.

Knapp, G.-A./Wetterer, A. (Hg.) (1995): Traditionen Brüche. Entwicklungen feministischer Theorie. Freiburg i.Br.: Kore.

Kraß, A. (Hg.) (2003): Queer Studies. Frankfurt am Main: Suhrkamp.

Künzer, N./Huth, S./Smisek, S. (2011): Wie ich wurde, was ich bin. Drei Weltmeisterinnen erzählen. Frankfurt am Main: weissbooks.

Mayring, P. (2003): Qualitative Inhaltsanalyse. Grundlagen und Techniken. Weinheim: Beltz.

Müller, M. (2009): Fußball als Paradoxon der Moderne. Zur Bedeutung ethnischer, nationaler und geschlechtlicher Differenzen im Profifußball. Wiesbaden: VS/GWV.

Switzer, K. (2011): Marathon Woman. Hamburg: spomedis.

Treibel, A. (2006): Geschlecht als soziale Konstruktion und Dekonstruktion. In: dies.: Einführung in soziologische Theorien der Gegenwart. Wiesbaden: VS/GWV, 101-127.

West, C./Zimmerman, D. H. (1991): Doing Gender. In: Lorber, J./Farrell, S. A.: The Social Construction of Gender. Newbury Park/London/New Delhi: Sage, 13-37.

Filme

Becker, B. (2008): Die besten Frauen der Welt. Shark TV/WDR.

Treut, M. (1999): Gendernauts . Hyena Films/WDR/arte.

Fußballfans und sozialer Wandel – Die Verbürgerlichungsthese im historischen Ländervergleich zwischen England und Deutschland

Football Fans and Social Change: The Subject of Embourgeoisement in Historical Comparisons between England and Germany

Oliver Fürtjes

Zusammenfassung

Sowohl in England als auch in Deutschland gilt der Fußball in der Vergangenheit als klassischer Proletariersport. Vor diesem Hintergrund wird der als *Verbürgerlichung* bezeichnete Wandel zum gegenwärtigen klassenlosen Fußballpublikum vornehmlich auf die voranschreitende Kommerzialisierung und Mediatisierung des Fußballs in der Postmoderne, wie sie vor allem in den 1990er Jahren eine enorme Dynamik erfuhren, zurückgeführt. Auf der Grundlage empirischer Daten kann jene Verbürgerlichungsthese jedoch nicht nachgewiesen werden. Die Überprüfung der Berufsstrukturen in den Stadien der höchsten Fußballliga in England (1983 bis 2008) und Deutschland (1977 bis 2009) verdeutlicht vielmehr, dass der Fußball kulturübergreifend sowohl in England als auch in Deutschland auch schon in der Zeit vor 1990 ein klassenloses Massenvergnügen war. Dies kann empirisch gesichert auf der Basis repräsentativer Daten zum Sozialprofil der regelmäßigen Leser von deutschen Fußballfachmagazinen auch für die 1950er Jahre nachgewiesen werden, die länderübergreifend als Hochphase des Arbeiterklasse-Fußballs gelten. Daraus lässt sich schlussfolgern, dass die Verbürgerlichung des Fußballpublikums allein aus der inter- und intragenerationellen Aufstiegsmobilität infolge des sozialstrukturellen Wandels erklärbar wird und die Kennzeichnung des Fußballs als Proletariersport aus einer undifferenzierten Wahrnehmung der Gesellschaftsstruktur im Industriezeitalter resultiert.

Abstract

Football is regarded, historically speaking, as a classic proletarian sport in England and Germany. The supposition that this has changed and that football spectators have become classless has been described as *embourgeoisement*. In specialist debates in recent years this process has been attributed to the increasing commercialization and mediatisation of football in a postmodern context principally since the 1990s. However, by examining the professional backgrounds of people attending football matches in the stadia of the top league clubs in England and Germany between 1983 and 2008, one sees instead that football was already a form of classless mass entertainment both in England and Germany prior to the 1990s. As far as Germany is concerned, this can be proven empirically even for the 1950s on the basis of representative data pertaining to the social class profile of regular readers of specialist football magazines. And the 1950s are generally considered to be *the* era of working class football. The analysis demonstrates that the partisan characterisation of football as a proletarian sport in both countries is the result of an undifferentiated perception of social structures in the industrial age.

1 Der Fußball in der Postmoderne und seine Verbürgerlichung

Die Gesellschaften Englands und Deutschlands unterlagen in den vergangenen Jahrzehnten dem grundlegenden sozialen Wandel vom Industriezeitalter zur Postmoderne. Kennzeichnete die taylorisierte Arbeitsorganisation und industrielle Produktionsstruktur die Knappheitsgesellschaften im Industriezeitalter, kann die postmoderne Gesellschaft im Gegensatz dazu als hoch technisierte verwissenschaftlichte Dienstleistungsgesellschaft, Konsum-, Freizeit- oder Mediengesellschaft beschrieben werden. Handlungsleitend für den Großteil der Bevölkerung ist nicht mehr die noch in der Industriegesellschaft prägende Überlebensorientierung, sondern infolge der kollektiv verbesserten objektiven Lebensbedingungen eine zunehmende individualisierte Konsum-, Freizeit- und Unterhaltungsorientierung der postmodernen Akteure, die in Anlehnung an Schulze (1992) passend als subjektbezogene Erlebnisorientierung umschrieben werden kann. Im Kontext der marktorientierten Gesellschaftsformen Englands und Deutschlands hat sich als Reaktion darauf eine weitverzweigte und umfangreiche Freizeit-, Unterhaltungs- und Kulturindustrie entwickelt, die vermarktungsstrategisch hoch professionell und technisiert entsprechende erlebnisorientierte Dienstleistungsprodukte anbietet.

Dieser gesellschaftliche Wandlungsprozess hat nicht zuletzt und insbesondere auch die Rahmenbedingungen im Fußballsport grundlegend verändert. Die massiv gestiegene Medienpräsenz, die exorbitant gestiegenen TV-Gelder-Zahlungen, das zunehmend lukrative Sportsponsoring, die Kapitalisierung und kommerzielle Neuausrichtung der Vereins- bzw. Unternehmensstrategien vornehmlich der Großklubs, das wachsende Merchandising, die Modernisierung der Fußballstadien zu Erlebnisarenen, die zunehmende Eventkultur und nicht zuletzt der Popstarkult der Starspieler veranschaulichen beispielhaft die Vermarktung des Fußballs zu einem der bedeutsamsten Wirtschaftszweige und Kristallisationspunkte der postmodernen Freizeit-, Unterhaltungs- und Kulturindustrie in England und Deutschland.

Dass sich im Kontext der zunehmenden und sich vor allem seit den 1990er Jahren dynamisierenden Vermarktung des Fußballs nicht nur die Rahmenbedingungen im Fußball grundlegend gewandelt haben, sondern auch das Fußballpublikum, bestimmt dabei sowohl die englische als auch die deutsche Forschungsliteratur gleichermaßen. Vor dem Hintergrund der kulturübergreifenden Kennzeichnung des Fußballs als weitestgehend exklusives Kulturphänomen der Arbeiterklasse[1] in der Vergangenheit und der gegenwärtigen klassenlosen Fuß-

---

1 Im Folgenden werden die Begriffe Klasse und Schicht synonym verwendet. Grundsätzlich kann gesagt werden, dass die englische Forschungsliteratur traditionell den Klassenbegriff in Anlehnung an Marx und die deutsche Forschungsliteratur zumeist den Schichtenbegriff in Anlehnung an Geiger verwendet. Auch wenn damit unterschiedliche Konzepte verbunden sind und kulturbedingt in England das Klassenkonzept und in Deutschland das Schichtkonzept die vertikale Gesellschaftsstruktur möglicherweise adäquater abzubilden vermag, lassen sich aus einer Vergleichsperspektive doch grundsätzliche Ähnlichkeiten feststellen, die eine synonyme Verwendung rechtfertigen. Dies betrifft vor allem die analytische Trennung in Arbeiterklasse und bürgerliche Mittel-

ballbegeisterung in beiden Ländern bestimmt vor allem die Verbürgerlichungsthese die fußballsoziologische Analyse. Gemeint ist damit die Verlagerung des
sozialen Schwerpunkts des Fußballpublikums von unten in die Mitte, von der
proletarischen zur bürgerlichen Zentriertheit. Zurückgeführt wird dieser grundlegende Klassenwandel darauf, dass der Fußball infolge seiner strukturellen
Transformation zum professionalisierten, kommerzialisierten und mediatisierten
Showsport vor allem in den bürgerlichen Mittel- und Oberschichten eine bisher
nicht gekannte Popularität erfahren hat und nicht zuletzt der Besuch eines Fußballspiels zu einem beliebten Event in diesen Kreisen geworden ist. Bezogen auf
das Stadionpublikum wird auch der in der Stadtsoziologie gebräuchliche Begriff
der Gentrifizierung verwendet, womit die bauliche und soziale Aufwertung von
Stadtteilen bezeichnet wird (vgl. Friedrichs 2000) und im Fußballkontext seine
Übertragung auf das Stadion findet.

Die Verbürgerlichungsthese als Resultat der veränderten Rahmenbedingungen im Fußball zu betrachten, hat dabei sowohl in England als auch in Deutschland eine lange Forschungstradition. Bereits in den 1970er Jahren und frühen
1980er Jahren war sie Gegenstand substantieller und kritischer Analysen unter
Soziologen. Besondere Relevanz erfährt sie indes in der gegenwärtigen Debatte
um die Wirkungen der Vermarktungsdynamik in der ‚postmodernen Fußballära‘
(Giulianotti 1999: 168f.) seit den 1990er Jahren.

Im historischen Kulturvergleich können daher auffällige Gemeinsamkeiten
hinsichtlich der Verbürgerlichungsthese festgemacht werden. Gleichwohl zeigen
sich auch zeitgeschichtliche und kulturspezifische Unterschiede, die unterschiedliche Publikumsstrukturen im Ländervergleich vermuten lassen. In welcher Hinsicht dies zutrifft und ob sich die vermutete Verbürgerlichungsthese als kultur-
übergreifender Prozess empirisch nachweisen lässt, wird im Folgenden vertiefend
betrachtet.

---

klasse, respektive Arbeiterschicht und bürgerliche Mittelschicht, die hier im Fokus
steht. Dasselbe gilt für die analytische Dreiteilung in Unterklasse/Arbeiterklasse –
Mittelklasse – Oberklasse, respektive Unterschicht/Arbeiterschicht – Mittelschicht –
Oberschicht.

2 Die Verbürgerlichungsthese im historischen Ländervergleich

2.1 Die Entwicklung des Fußballs zur Showbranche in den 1960er und 1970er Jahren

Die Grundannahme der Verbürgerlichungsthese ist die Sichtweise des Fußballs als exklusiver Sport für die unteren proletarischen Schichten in der Vergangenheit. Neben der Präferenzannahme jener unteren Arbeiterschichten für den Fußball ist damit zugleich die Distinktionsannahme gehobener bürgerlicher Statusgruppen zu plausibilisieren. Dies vor allem vor dem Hintergrund, dass der Fußballsport zu Beginn seiner Verbreitung in beiden Ländern zunächst ein Reservat und Privileg bürgerlicher Eliten war (vgl. z.B. Mason 1980; Eisenberg 1997). Dies änderte sich jedoch mit der vertikalen Verbreitung des Fußballs in die unteren Schichten, wofür verschiedene gesellschaftliche Entwicklungen die Grundvoraussetzung schufen. Als wichtigste kann diesbezüglich die sich entwickelnde Freizeitkultur im Industriezeitalter genannt werden, die in England bereits im letzten Viertel des 19. Jahrhunderts (vgl. Vampley 1988) und in Deutschland während der Weimarer Zeit in den 1920er Jahren entstand (vgl. Fürtjes 2012). Maßgeblich dafür waren jeweils die wachsenden Freizeitressourcen aufgrund gesetzlicher Regelungen zur Arbeitszeitverkürzung und verbesserter Lebensbedingungen für die arbeitende Bevölkerung sowie die infrastrukturelle Versorgung mit Freizeitanlagen und die Schaffung entsprechender umfassender privatwirtschaftlicher und öffentlicher Freizeitangebote.

Dass speziell der Fußballsport in der Folgezeit ein Massenphänomen vornehmlich in der Arbeiterschaft wurde und seinen Höhepunkt als klassischer Arbeiter- und Proletariersport in den 1950er Jahren erreichte, kennzeichnet sowohl die deutsche als auch englische Forschungsliteratur zur Sozial- und Kulturgeschichte des Fußballs gleichermaßen (vgl. Bausenwein 2006; Fishwick 1989; Gehrmann 1988; Hering 2002; Mason 1980; Russell 1997; Schulze-Marmeling 1992 u. 2000; Wagg 1984; Walvin 1994). Auch das Erklärungsmuster für die besondere Präferenz der Arbeiter für den Fußball unterscheidet sich nicht. Diese wird kulturübergreifend zumeist in der Flucht vor dem entfremdenden harten Arbeitsalltag der Fabrikarbeiter und in der Passung spielcharakteristischer und berufsalltäglicher Anforderungen in sowohl physischer, psychischer als auch sozialer Hinsicht gesehen. So verlangt das Fußballspiel das aus dem industriellen Arbeitsalltag vertraute Maß an körperlicher Kraft, Härte, Robustheit, Gewandtheit, physischen Mut und sozialer Angewiesenheit.

Die Distinktion von den ursprünglichen gehobenen Trägerschichten des Fußballsports plausibilisiert sich der Forschungsliteratur folgend wesentlich durch
den klassenspezifischen proletarischen Habitus, der in der Zeit, als die Arbeiter-
massen in die Stadien strömten, die Verhaltensweisen der damals entstandenen
Fußballkultur kennzeichnete. Die gemeinsam geteilte proletarische Arbeits-
und Lebenssituation in Kombination mit der gemeinsam geteilten Fußballlei-
denschaft der Arbeiter evozierte demnach eine starke Identifikation mit dem
örtlichen Fußballverein, der als Repräsentant des eigenen Viertels und damit
auch der eigenen wahrgenommenen Arbeiterkultur zumeist in subkulturellen
Fangemeinschaften intensiv, vor allem aber lautstark und verrohend unterstützt
wurde, weshalb bürgerliche Kreise ihn als „Proletensport" abstempelten und entsprechend mieden.

Diese homogene proletarische Publikumsstruktur im Fußballstadion sollte sich jedoch in den 1960er und 1970er Jahren verändern. Kulturübergreifend
werden in beiden Nationen die voranschreitende Kommodifizierung, Kommerzialisierung und Professionalisierung im Fußball dafür verantwortlich gemacht.
Gewandelt hat sich seit dieser Zeit vor allem die Finanzierungsbasis der Fußballvereine (Eisenberg 2004: 56f.). Dies freilich in jeweils anders gelagerten Kontexten.

In Deutschland war diesbezüglich die Einführung der Fußball Bundesliga im
Jahre 1963 fundamental. Erstmals waren offiziell Gehaltszahlungen an die Spieler erlaubt. Zur Professionalisierung der Spieler in der Hinsicht, dass die Spieler
das Fußballspielen als Hauptberuf ausüben konnten, kam es aber erst 1972. Der
Grund dafür war die Aufhebung aller Gehaltsschranken infolge des Bundesliga-
Skandals. Einschneidend für den deutschen Fußball war indes die Konzentration
der Spitzenvereine in einer nationalen Liga und die seitens des Deutschen Fußball Bundes (DFB) vorangetriebene Vermarktung der neu geschaffenen Bundesliga. Die damit einhergehenden gestiegenen Werbe- und Sponsoreneinnahmen
und erstmals auch Fernseheinnahmen trugen maßgeblich zur finanziellen Kon-
solidierung der Spitzenvereine in Deutschland bei (vgl. Eisenberg 1997). Diese
waren zwar weiterhin juristische Idealvereine im Vereinsregister, konnten aber
dank der Gemeinnützigkeitsregelung gewinnorientiert wirtschaften (Gehrmann
1992). Zudem erfolgten seinerzeit umfassende Modernisierungsmaßnahmen von
Stadien bzw. Stadion-Neubauten, die in den ausgewählten Städten für die Weltmeisterschaft 1974 durch Mittel der öffentlichen Hand subventioniert wurden.

In England hatte sich im Gegensatz zu Deutschland bereits im Jahre 1888 eine
nationale Profi-Liga etabliert. Auch die Vereine fungierten anders als in Deutschland schon seit frühester Zeit als Kapital- bzw. Aktiengesellschaften, wobei Vereinsdirektoren kein Gehalt bezogen und Dividendenauszahlungen restringiert

waren. Dennoch veränderte sich auch in England die Finanzierungsbasis der Vereine grundlegend. Einnahmen aus Sponsoren- und Werbegeldern wurden immer bedeutsamer, die auch dank der Weltmeisterschaft 1966 im eigenen Land zunehmend die Vereinskassen auffüllten. Notwendig wurden diese zusätzlichen Einnahmequellen zum einen durch die gestiegenen Ausgaben infolge der Aufhebung der Gehaltsgrenze für die Spieler und die Abschaffung des Transfer- und Rückhaltesystems zu Beginn der 1960er Jahre. Zum anderen sanken die Zuschauerzahlen in den Stadien und damit auch die dadurch generierten Einnahmen (vgl. z.B. Wagg 1984).

Ähnlich wie in Deutschland wurden auch in England viele Stadionanlagen in dieser Zeit modernisiert und die Spiele durch zusätzliche Showaspekte, „such as pre-match displays" (Guilianotti 1999: 40), angereichert. Dies vor allem auch deshalb, um den rückläufigen Zuschauerzahlen entgegen zu wirken und den Stadionbesuch für ein größeres Publikum attraktiv zu machen. Dass die Vereinsdirektoren dabei vor allem Familien aus gehobenen bürgerlichen Schichten im Blick hatten, nimmt Taylor (1971a u. 1971b) zum Anlass seiner Theorie von der Verbürgerlichung der Fußballkultur. Demnach richten sich die auf Show und Unterhaltung setzenden Vermarktungs- und Inszenierungsstrategien seitens der Vereinsdirektoren gezielt an die Interessen eines wohlhabenden bürgerlichen Mittelschichtenpublikums. Dabei wurde die Absicht verfolgt, das einstige exklusive Arbeiterklassenphänomen Fußball für das Bürgertum zu legitimieren, um zusätzlichen Profit zu erwirtschaften. Dazu trug auch die bauliche Aufwertung der Stadien bei. Die Konsequenz war, dass die lokalverwurzelte arbeiterzentrierte Vereinsanhängerschaft mehr und mehr zugunsten jener bürgerlichen Zuschauer aus den Stadien verdrängt wurde. Verstärkt wurde dieser Prozess noch durch die voranschreitende Internationalisierung des Fußballs und Professionalisierung der Spieler, die als gefeierte Stars vermeintlich nicht mehr viel gemeinsam haben mit der traditionellen Arbeiterkultur. Der dadurch entstandene Bruch der Arbeiterklasse mit dem kommodifizierten Fußball vor allem unter den jungen Arbeitern, verleitet Taylor zu seiner scharf kritisierten und später von ihm selbst revidierten Erklärung des in den 1960er Jahren entstandenen Hooligan-Phänomens in England.

Eine kulturalistische Ausarbeitung des Ansatzes von Taylor liefert Critcher (1979). Bezugnehmend auf Williams' (1961) Modell der dreigliedrigen historischen Entwicklung in den kulturellen Beziehungen zwischen Individuen oder sozialen Gruppen zu Institutionen in ‚members', ‚customers' und ‚consumers' theorisiert er den bei Taylor inhärenten historischen Wandel der veränderten Beziehung der Zuschauer zum Fußball. Seiner These folgend werden die sich stark mit ihrem Verein identifizierenden traditionellen Vereinsanhänger – die members – im Zuge der voranschreitenden Ökonomisierung des Fußballs zunehmend durch die Kunden bzw. Konsumenten verdrängt. Letztere sehen den Verein nicht mehr als lokales Identifikationsobjekt, wie dies noch für die traditionellen *Supporter* aus der Arbeiterklasse galt, sondern betrachten den Besuch eines Fußballspiels als eines von vielen möglichen Freizeitalternativen und das Spiel selbst als Konsumprodukt, das entsprechend der eigenen Präferenzstruktur konsumiert wird oder eben nicht. Der Logik des Marktes entsprechend gilt es folglich für die Anbieter, jene neuen Kunden und Konsumenten durch gezielte Maßnahmen zu werben.

In Deutschland formulierten erstmals Lindner und Breuer (1978) die hier als Verbürgerlichungsthese bezeichnete Annahme, dass die kulturelle Anpassung des Fußballs als Element proletarischer Kultur an die bürgerliche Gesellschaft auf den zunehmenden Showcharakter des professionalisierten und kommerzialisierten Fußballsports zurückzuführen ist. So hat der Showfußball einen Imagewandel weg vom Proletariersport bewirkt und dadurch zur sozialen Akzeptanz in höheren Schichten geführt, ihn aber auch andererseits der traditionellen Wurzeln beraubt. So wie die lokalen Helden der Arbeiterklasse zu gefeierten und von den Medien geformten Stars geworden sind, sind auch die Vereine der lokalen Arbeiterkultur entrückt und zum Bestandteil der Unterhaltungsbranche geworden.

In komparativer Perspektive zeigen die Ansätze zur Erklärung der Verbürgerlichung des Fußballpublikums trotz kulturspezifischer Besonderheiten deutliche Gemeinsamkeiten im theoretischen Zugang. Erstens werden die veränderten Angebotsstrukturen der Unterhaltungsbranche und dabei speziell die strategischen Vereinsstrategien zur Bewerbung neuer bürgerlicher Publikumsschichten in den Blick genommen. Und zweitens wird das neu gewonnene Interesse seitens des Bürgertums auf eine dem bürgerlichen Habitus entsprechende distanzierte und genussorientierte Haltung zum Fußball infolge der veränderten Angebotsstrukturen zurückgeführt. In der sozialwissenschaftlichen Sportforschung spricht man auch von den ‚soccer interested consumers‘, die seit dieser Zeit die Fanbasis im Fußball zunehmend dominieren und sich von jenen traditionellen, sich stark mit ihrem Verein identifizierenden ‚local club supporters‘ abgrenzen lassen (Eisenberg 2004: 56f.).

Gemeinsam ist allen vorgestellten Ansätzen zudem ihr kritischer, marxistisch geprägter, vor allem aber spekulativer Gehalt: Allen Theorien zur Verbürgerlichungsthese fehlt es an fundierten, geschweige denn empirischen Nachweisen. Im Ländervergleich erfährt die für Deutschland formulierte Verbürgerlichungsthese freilich größere Plausibilität, was die Annahme der Entlokalisierung und Entfremdung der Vereine von der traditionellen Fankultur betrifft. Jedenfalls waren die Veränderungen in den 1960er Jahren in Deutschland wesentlich einschneidender. Während sich in England der Spitzenfußball auf nationaler Ebene schon lange bewährt hatte und die Vereine wesentlich professioneller geführt wurden, trifft dies auf die Amateurstrukturen der regionalen Oberligen vor der Einführung der Bundesliga weit weniger zu.

Angesichts der noch für die 1980er Jahre identifizierten Dominanz der traditionellen fußballzentrierten proletarischen Fankultur in den Stadien in gegenwärtigen Ansätzen zur Verbürgerlichung des Fußballpublikums scheint aber weder für Deutschland noch für England der angenommene Klassenwandel im Fußballpublikum in dieser Zeit eingetreten zu sein. Allenfalls punktuell, z.B. bei hoch frequentierten Spitzenbegegnungen, kann angenommen werden, dass der Besuch eines Fußballspiels auch für Teile jener konsumorientierten bürgerlichen Fußballfans einen angemessenen Unterhaltungswert bot. Vom allumfassenden grundlegenden Gentrifizierungsprozess des Fußballpublikums ist deshalb erst infolge der Entwicklung des Fußballs zum Showbusiness in den 1990er Jahren auszugehen, wie die folgenden Ausführungen nahe legen.

2.2   Die 1990er Jahre

Sowohl in England als auch in Deutschland galt der Fußballsport noch in den 1980er Jahren als Proletariersport. Begründet wird die weiterhin bestehende proletarische Zentriertheit des Fußballs anhand der kulturübergreifenden Krise des Fußballsports in dieser Zeit, wie sie im historischen Rekordtief der Besucherzahlen in den Stadien sichtbar wird. Daraus kann geschlossen werden, dass das Produkt Fußball für die konsumorientierten bürgerlichen Schichten offensichtlich nicht attraktiv genug war. Vor dem Hintergrund der umfassenden Hooligan-Problematik, die sich in den 1980er Jahren noch verschärfte, erscheint dies auch plausibel. Sein Proletarierimage konnte der Fußball bis in die 1990er Jahre jedenfalls nicht ablegen. Unter der Annahme der Fortexistenz des Fußballs als Freizeitvergnügen vorwiegend bildungsschwacher proletarischer Unterschichtenangehöriger noch in den 1980er Jahren plausibilisiert sich daher der grundlegende Klassenwandel des Fußballpublikums als Resultat der in England und Deutschland ähnlich verlaufenden Vermarktungsdynamik des Fußballs zum mediatisierten Showbusiness in der postmodernen Fußballära. Zumal auch in beiden Ländern das Besucheraufkommen in den Stadien seither rapide anstieg. Es ist daher naheliegend, eine kulturübergreifende gestiegene Popularität des Fußballs in den bürgerlichen Mittel- und Oberschichten anzunehmen. Gleichwohl lassen sich aber erneut länderspezifische Besonderheiten ausmachen.

In Deutschland war für die Entwicklung des Fußballs zu einem der bedeutsamsten Wirtschaftsmärkte der postmodernen Unterhaltungsindustrie die Pri-
vatisierung des Fernsehens Mitte der 1980er Jahre und die damit einhergehende
Einführung des Satellitenfernsehens und später des Pay-TVs fundamental. Zum
einen verschärfte sich dadurch die Konkurrenzsituation um die Vergabe der TV-
Rechte mit der Konsequenz exponentiell gestiegener Einnahmeerlöse aus Fern-
sehgeldern für die Spitzenvereine. Zum anderen ist die Medienpräsenz des Fußballs im deutschen Fernsehen immens gestiegen und damit folgerichtig auch sein
Vermarktungswert. Zugleich änderte sich aber auch die Darstellung des Fußballs
im Fernsehen. Zusätzlich zur traditionellen Spielberichterstattung finden seither vermehrt auf Show- und Unterhaltungsaspekte setzende Präsentations- und
Inszenierungsformen Eingang in die Fußballberichterstattung (vgl. Digel/Burk
1999; Großhans 1997; Leder 2004). Nicht weniger trifft dies auch auf die Inszenierung und Präsentation der Fußballspiele als Event in den modernen Arenen
zu. Fußballspiele werden seither zunehmend medial vermarktet, aufwändig inszeniert und mit kommerzialisierter Unterhaltung und Erlebnisprogrammen
angereichert (Bleeker-Dohmen 2007 et al.: 506f.). Verantwortlich dafür zeichnet
eine neue Generation professioneller Manager in den Fußballabteilungen der Vereine, welche nun auch formal juristisch als Kapitalgesellschaften geführt werden.
Hinzu kommen seit Ende der 1980er Jahre umfassende Modernisierungs- und
Sicherheitsmaßnahmen in den deutschen Stadien (vgl. Merkel 2012). Nicht zuletzt
die im Zuge der Weltmeisterschaft 2006 in Deutschland umgestalteten und zum
Teil neu errichteten Stadien setzen diesbezüglich neue Maßstäbe.

Auch in England kam es in den 1990er Jahren zu einer einschneidenden strukturellen Veränderung der Fußballwelt (Giulianotti 2002). In gleicher Weise wie in
Deutschland mutierte der englische Fußball zu einem der bedeutsamsten Wirtschaftsmärkte der postmodernen Unterhaltungsindustrie. Dies zeigt sich parallel
zu den deutschen Verhältnissen in den explosionsartig gestiegenen (trans-)na-
tionalen Kapitaltransfers aus Übertragungsrechten, Sponsoring und Merchandising, im immensen Professionalisierungsschub auf allen Ebenen des Fußball-
geschäfts und nicht zuletzt in der intensivierten Kopplung des Fußballs mit den
Massenmedien. Auch in England setzte das Satellitenfernsehen und Pay-TV in
der Fußballberichterstattung in den 1990er Jahren neue Maßstäbe in Bezug auf
Inszenierungs- und Präsentationsstrategien (vgl. Boyle/Haynes 2004).

Die fundamentale Restrukturierung des englischen Fußballs in den 1990er
Jahren wird aber vor allem auf die Hillsborough-Katastrophe 1989 in Sheffield
und den daraus resultierenden politisch erzwungenen Modernisierungs- und
Sicherheitsmaßnahmen in den englischen Stadien zurückgeführt (vgl. Crabbe/
Brown 2004). Die Empfehlungen des Taylor-Reports (1990), der die Ursachen der

Katastrophe untersuchte, zwangen die Politik zum Handeln und als Konsequenz daraus die Vereine zu umfassenden Restrukturierungsmaßnahmen. Maßgebend waren dabei die aktuell auch in Deutschland diskutierte Abschaffung der Stehplatztribünen in den Stadien der beiden höchsten Divisionen im Jahre 1994 mit der Konsequenz einer Erhöhung der Eintrittspreise sowie der Implementierung verbesserter Videoüberwachungssysteme.

Dass mit dieser baulichen Aufwertung auch eine soziale Aufwertung einhergeht und sich das Stadionpublikum entsprechend gentrifiziert hat, bestimmt seitdem die Forschungsliteratur. Dabei hat sich das Erklärungsmuster im Vergleich zu den früheren Ansätzen zur Verbürgerlichungsthese nicht grundlegend verändert. In den Fokus zur Erklärung des Klassenwandels geraten erneut die exponierten Marketingstrategien der freilich wesentlich professionelleren neueren Generation von Clubmanagern und Fußballfunktionären. Diese bewerben gezielt besser Verdienende und Familien durch die aufwändige Inszenierung der Fußballspiele als unterhaltsames und erlebnisorientiertes Stadionevent und durch die Einrichtung entsprechender Komfortzonen wie VIP-Lounges und Familienbereiche (vgl. King 1997a u. 1997b). Die auffällige Konformität zu den früheren Ansätzen zeigt sich aber nicht nur in der gezielten Kundenorientierung jener Vereinsstrategien, sondern auch in der Annahme der damit verbundenen Transformation der Fußballkultur. Erneut sind es die sich stark mit ihrem Verein identifizierenden, aus der Arbeiterkultur stammenden fußballzentrierten traditionellen Fans, die zunehmend von den konsumorientierten, distanzierten und nicht-authentischen neuen Fans der bürgerlichen Mittelklasse aus den Stadien verdrängt werden (vgl. Crabbe/Brown 2004; Giulianotti 2002; Nash 2000).

Zusätzlich zu den Business-orientierten kommerziellen Vermarktungsstrategien der Vereins- und Verbandsfunktionäre und den umgreifenden Modernisierungs- und Sicherheitsmaßnahmen in den Stadien wird das gestiegene Fußballinteresse in den gehobenen bürgerlichen Schichten verstärkt auf die Breitenwirkung und Ästhetisierung des Fernsehfußballs infolge der Mediatisierungsstrategien, und hier speziell des Satellitenfernsehens zurückgeführt (Holt/Mason 2000: 4). Ähnlich wie dies für die auf Show und Unterhaltung setzenden Vereinsstrategien diskutiert wurde, spiegelt sich hierin ein *kulturelles Image*, das ein Interesse am Fußball für die bürgerlichen Schichten sozial akzeptabel erscheinen lässt. Als besonders einschneidend in dieser Hinsicht wird die Weltmeisterschaft 1990 in Italien betrachtet. Die Präsentation dieses Turniers als klassenloses Ereignis, was in der Regel auf die allzeitige Klassenlosigkeit des Fußballs in Italien zurückgeführt wird, und die nachgewiesene Verträglichkeit und Passung des Fußballs mit Elementen der Hochkultur sorgten demnach für eine zuvor nicht angenommene Akzeptanz des Fußballs in den gehobenen bürgerlichen Kreisen (Giulianotti 1999:

35; King 1998: 103ff.; Taylor 2008: 363f.). In Kombination mit den veränderten Stadionstrukturen wird entsprechend ein zunehmendes Interesse des wohlhabenderen Bürgertums am Besuch eines Fußballspiels seit den 1990er Jahren auch aus dieser Perspektive verständlich.

Wie in England wird die Verbürgerlichung der Fußballfanbasis auch in Deutschland einerseits auf die Breitenwirkung und Inszenierung des Fußballs als Show- und Unterhaltungsevent im Fernsehen zurückgeführt (vgl. Großhans 1997; König 2002; Schulze-Marmeling 2000) und andererseits durch die bauliche Aufwertung der Stadionstrukturen und Vermarktungsstrategien der Clubmanager erklärt (vgl. Aschenbeck 1998; Bleecker-Dohmen et al. 2007; Lenhard 2002; Merkel 2012). Im Vordergrund steht dabei auch in Deutschland die eventkulturelle Vermarktung der Fußballspiele und gezielte Bewerbung von ,besser Verdienenden' und Familien (vgl. Pfaff 2004). Nach Aschenbeck (1998: 18) führt dies dazu, dass der Fußball mehr und mehr aus seinem proletarischen Zusammenhang gerissen und von einer Domäne der unteren Klassen zu einem ausschließlichen Vergnügen der bürgerlichen Mittel- und Oberschicht werden wird. Diese Sorge kennzeichnet auch die sich der Tradition verschriebenen verschiedenen Fangruppierungen und –Organisationen in Deutschland (vgl. Gabler 2012; Merkel 2012). Die Kommerzialisierung des Fußballs seitens der Vereins- und Verbandsfunktionäre wird scharf kritisiert und ist wesentlicher Bestandteil des gegenwärtigen Fanaufbegehrens. Diese kritisch reflexive Sichtweise bezogen auf die kommerzialisierte und mediatisierte Entwicklung des Fußballs zum Showbusiness kennzeichnet vor allem auch den von Giulianotti (1999: 148f.) und Redhead (1997: 29ff.) für den englischen Kulturraum beschriebenen postmodernen Fan. Dabei handelt es sich um jene Fans, die sich aktiv in den Fanorganisationen einbinden und vor allem die kulturübergreifende neu entstandene hochwertige Fußballliteratur und Fanzines-Entwicklung maßgeblich vorantreiben. Aschenbeck (1998) kennzeichnet diesen Typus als kritischen fußballzentrierten Fan. Ein Merkmal dieser Ausprägung des postmodernen Fans ist die berufliche Tätigkeit im hochprofessionellen verwissenschaftlichten Dienstleistungssektor. Folglich indiziert auch dieser neue Fantypus die Statushebung des Fußballpublikums sowohl in Deutschland als auch in England.

In komparativer Perspektive zeigen sich hinsichtlich der dargestellten Verbürgerlichungsthese erneut deutliche Parallelitäten. In beiden Ländern kann sie als Hauptbestandteil der Vermarktungs- und Mediatisierungsdynamik in der postmodernen Fußballära betrachtet werden. Auffällig ist dabei die Konformität der Erklärungsmuster zu den früheren Ansätzen zur Verbürgerlichung der Fußballkultur (vgl. Abschnitt 2.1). Wieder werden erstens die gewandelten Angebotsstrukturen in den Blick genommen, und zweitens eine daraus abgeleitete veränderte Fußballkultur identifiziert. Dies freilich vor dem Hintergrund wesentlich elementarer gesellschaftlicher und fußballimmanenter Entwicklungsdynamiken im Vergleich zur Fußballwelt in den 1960er und 1970er Jahren.

Bezogen auf das Stadionpublikum ist gleichwohl angesichts der Abschaffung der Stehplatztribünen und der damit einhergehenden Verteuerung der Ticketpreise eine deutlichere Publikumstransformation in englischen Stadien zu erwarten. Zwar stiegen auch in Deutschland die Ticketpreise in den 1990er Jahren, im Vergleich zu England jedoch wesentlich moderater (vgl. Merkel 2012).

Parallelitäten zeigen sich auch hinsichtlich der fehlenden empirischen Gültigkeit der Verbürgerlichungsthese. Der Grund dafür ist simpel: Es fehlt an entsprechenden Daten, was sich am Taylor-Report 1990 illustrieren lässt, der von keinen Daten zur Sozialstruktur des Fußballpublikum in der Zeit vor der Hillsborough-Katastrophe berichten konnte (vgl. Duke 1991). Diese überraschende Erkenntnis wiederum ist der einseitigen Forschungsstrategie in der Zuschauerforschung geschuldet, die sich fast ausschließlich auf die gewaltbereiten Fußballfans bzw. Hooligans konzentrierte. Ähnliches lässt sich für den deutschen Fall sagen (vgl. Stollenwerk 1996). Dennoch lassen sich einzelne fragmentarische Erhebungen zum Stadionpublikum in der Zeit vor 1990 sowohl in England als auch in Deutschland auffinden, die im Folgenden in komparativer Perspektive analysiert werden.

3 Gentrifizierung des englischen und deutschen Stadionpublikums? Ein empirischer Vergleich

3.1 Datenquellen

Die in Tab. 1 präsentierten Stadionerhebungen aus England bis 1997 sind der Studie von Malcom et al. (2000) entnommen. Das Autorenteam verweist angesichts der spärlichen Datenlage auf die grundsätzlich schwierige Vergleichbarkeit ihrer präsentierten Erhebungen, da unterschiedliche Forschungsdesigns und Erhebungsmethoden verwendet wurden. Der Carling Survey 1993/94 bezieht sich beispielsweise auf ‚programme buyers', während der Carling Survey 1996/97 ‚season ticket holders' befragte. Für die Befragungen der Fans von Arsenal und Aston Villa wurde ein Methodenmix angewendet: Zum Teil wurden die Besucher vor Ort befragt und zum Teil wurden die Fragebögen an Dauerkarteninhaber gemailt. Aufgrund spezifischer Forschungsfragen ist zudem die Repräsentativität der Erhebungen in Coventry und Watford äußerst fraglich. Gleichwohl handelt es sich bei den von Malcom et al. zusammengetragenen Erhebungen um die einzigen auffindbaren empirischen Datenquellen, die es ermöglichen, den Verbürgerlichungsprozess in England zu untersuchen. Für den Zeitraum nach 1997 wurden zusätzlich die FA Fan Surveys von 2001/2002[2], 2005/2006[3] und 2007/2008[4] herangezogen. Das Problem der Methodenvielfalt und fraglichen Repräsentativität trifft auf die in Tab. 1 präsentierten deutschen Erhebungen nicht zu. Die im Rahmen des Langzeitprojekts „Publikumsforschung" am Institut für Sportsoziologie an der Deutschen Sporthochschule Köln unter der Leitung von Dr. Hans Stollenwerk durchgeführten Erhebungen zeichnen sich durch ein einheitliches Forschungsdesign aus[5]. Das jeweils angewendete kombinierte Verfahren aus Quoten- und Zufallsauswahl der Vor-Ort-Befragungen kann darüber hinaus Repräsentativität beanspruchen. Gleichwohl handelt es sich aufgrund der Einmaligkeit der Befragung nur um einzelne aufs Jahr zu beziehende Stichproben, weshalb weitere veranstaltungsbezogene Rahmenbedingungen zu beachten sind. So war das Besucheraufkommen mit 13.000 Zuschauern bei der Erhebung 1977 äußerst gering, da das Spiel am letzten Spieltag stattfand und für den Ausgang der Meisterschaft unbedeutend war. Es handelt sich hierbei also tendenziell um ein spezifisch fußballzentriertes Stammpublikum, während 1985 das besuchte Fußballspiel gegen Bayern München das Spitzenspiel des 7. Spieltags der Saison war und ca. 42.000 Zuschauer anlockte. Dass sich diese unterschiedlichen Konstellationen auch auf die Publikumsstrukturen auswirken können, ist zwar nicht auszuschließen. Auf die Überprüfung der Verbürgerlichungsthese haben sie jedoch insofern keine gravierenden Auswirkungen, da es sich dabei um eine allgemeingültige Trendaussage handelt. Den theoretischen Erörterungen zufolge ist unabhängig davon in der Zeit vor 1990 ein deutlicher ‚proletarischer' Einschlag zu vermuten.

---

2   http://www.premierleague.com/content/dam/premierleague/site-content/News/publications/fan-surveys/national-fan-survey-2001-02.pdf

3   http://www.premierleague.com/content/dam/premierleague/site-content/News/publications/fan-surveys/national-fan-survey-2005-06.pdf

4   http://www.premierleague.com/content/dam/premierleague/site-content/News/publications/fan-surveys/national-fan-survey-2007-08.pdf

5   Größter Dank gilt Dr. Hans Stollenwerk, der mir die Erhebungen ab 1997 zur Verfügung stellte. Die früheren Erhebungen sind in Stollenwerk (1996) publiziert. Zusätzliche Angaben sind der Tab. 1 zu entnehmen.

Tabelle 1 Berufsprofile von Stadionbesuchern in England und Deutschland im historischen Kulturvergleich (in %)

England	Coventry City	Watford	Arsenal	Aston Villa	Carling Survey	Carling Survey	Luton	FA Survey	FA Fan Survey	Fan Survey
1983 - 2008	1983	1987	1992	1992	1993/1994	1996/1997	1997	2001/2002	2005/2006	2007/2008
Arbeiter	49	33	33	48	32,7	33,6	35,8	34	28	25
bürgerliche Berufe	51	67	67	52	67,3	66,4	64,2	66	72	75

Deutschland	Köln	Köln	Leverkusen	M' Glad-bach	Duisburg	Stuttgart	Stuttgart	Bremen	Köln
1977 - 2009	1977	1985	1997	1997	1998	1998	2005	2008	2009
Arbeiter	29,9	39,7	29,8	35,5	28,9	28,8	33,4	22,3	17,9
bürgerliche Berufe	70,1	60,3	70,2	64,5	71,1	71,2	66,6	77,7	82,1

Hintergrundinformationen zu den deutschen Publikumsbefragungen:

Jahr	Ort	Liga	Gegner	ZA	RQ	N	N (BP)
1977	Köln	1. Liga	Bremen	13000	48,0%	480	476 (234)
1985	Köln	1. Liga	Bayern München	42000	55,8%	558	548 (264)
1985	Leverkusen	1. Liga	Bremen	20000	17,8%	180	180 (106)
1997	Leverkusen	1. Liga	Bochum	22000	82,4%	742	719 (321)
1997	M'gladbach	1. Liga	Hamburg	21000	69,0%	621	599 (383)

Jahr	Ort	Liga	Gegner	ZA	RQ	N	N (BP)
1998	Duisburg	1. Liga	K'lautern	19941	74,3%	743	732 (415)
1998	Stuttgart	1. Liga	Köln	33000	91,0%	910	883 (420)
2005	Stuttgart	1. Liga	Bayern München	47000	80,6%	967	948 (581)
2008	Bremen	1. Liga	Nürnberg	37073	92,2%	1106	1089 (585)
2009	Köln	1. Liga	Bochum	50000	78,2%	782	768 (497)

Erläuterungen: ZA=Zuschaueranzahl; RQ=Rücklaufquote; N=Anzahl Befragte N (BP)=Anzahl Befragte, die eine Berufszugehörigkeit angegeben haben (in Klammern Anzahl Befragte, die einer Berufstätigkeit nachgehen)

Zeigen sich also bereits Schwierigkeiten in der Vergleichbarkeit der Stadionerhebungen in den einzelnen Ländern, trifft dies erst recht auf den Ländervergleich zu. Bezogen auf die Berufsstruktur kommt zusätzlich noch erschwerend hinzu, dass diese kulturspezifische Besonderheiten aufweist und entsprechend divergent erhoben wird. Um diese dennoch vergleichen zu können wurde eine einfache Dichotomisierung in Arbeiter[6] und bürgerliche Berufe[7] vorgenommen.

3.2 Ergebnisse

Die empirischen Daten der Erhebungen in englischen Stadien verdeutlichen, dass die Verbürgerlichungsthese für den englischen Fußball nicht bestätigt werden kann. Ein Trend derart, dass in den 1990er Jahren infolge der Vermarktungsdynamik vermehrt bürgerliche Schichten in den Stadien vorzufinden sind, kann nicht festgestellt werden. Das Stadionpublikum 1987 in Watford setzte sich ebenso zu zwei Dritteln aus bürgerlichen Berufsgruppen zusammen wie die Stadionpublika von Arsenal 1992 und Luton Town 1997. Dasselbe Ergebnis zeigt sich auch im englischen Querschnitt der Saisons 1993/94 und 1996/97. Der höchste Arbeiteranteil beziffert sich auf 49 % in Coventry 1983 und 48 % in Aston Villa 1992. Von einem Arbeiterpublikum kann freilich nicht gesprochen werden. Gehrmann (1988: 57) folgend sollte der Arbeiteranteil zumindest 70 % betragen, um von einem „beträchtlichen proletarischen Einschlag" sprechen zu können. Dies trifft aber offensichtlich auf das englische Stadionpublikum in den 1980er Jahren nicht zu. Die für die Verbürgerlichungsthese vorauszusetzende proletarische Publikumskomposition kann daher nicht bestätigt werden. Auch in den 1980er Jahren war der Stadionbesuch für bürgerliche Klassen offensichtlich sehr beliebt. Gleichwohl zeigen die Daten zum Berufsprofil der FA Fan Surveys seit 2000 einen marginalen Anstieg der bürgerlichen Berufsgruppen an. Von einem Gentrifizierungsprozess kann dabei freilich nicht die Rede sein.

Die Erhebungen in deutschen Stadien können die Verbürgerlichungsthese ebenso wenig bestätigen. Der Anteil bürgerlicher Berufsgruppen am Stadionpublikum bewegt sich zwischen 60% und 70 %. Selbst 1977 betrug der Anteil von Arbeitern im Stadion nur 30 % und war damit sogar niedriger als 1985, was aufgrund der in Abschnitt 3.1 dargestellten besonderen Konstellationen sogar konträr zur Verbürgerlichungsthese verläuft. Jedenfalls kann angesichts des attraktiven Gegners und der besonderen Spielkonstellation vermutet werden, dass im

---

6   „Skilled manual", „semi skilled manual" und „unskilled" in den englischen Erhebungen, „Arbeiter" und „Facharbeiter" in den deutschen Erhebungen
7   Darunter fallen dann alle anderen erhobenen Berufsgruppen: „Professional", „Intermediate", „Skilled non-manual" in den englischen Erhebungen; „Selbständige", „Freiberufler", „Angestellte", „Beamte" in den deutschen Erhebungen

Vergleich zur Erhebung 1977 wesentlich mehr der sogenannten „soccer interested consumers" im Stadion zugegen waren. Interessant ist ferner, dass selbst in Duisburg 1998 der Arbeiteranteil nur 29 % betrug. Immerhin gilt das Ruhrgebiet als Arbeiterhochburg.

Ein Vergleich der Erhebungen in Leverkusen 1985 und 1997 veranschaulicht, dass sich das Berufsprofil in den 1990er Jahren nicht grundlegend verändert hat, sondern in etwa gleich geblieben ist. Die Stuttgarter Erhebungen indizieren sogar einen leichten Proletarisierungsprozess, wohingegen die aktuellen Erhebungen in Bremen 2008 und Köln 2009, ähnlich wie dies für England zutrifft, Verbürgerlichungstendenzen anzeigen. Von einem Gentrifizierungsprozess kann aber auch in Köln angesichts der bürgerlich bestimmten Stadionstruktur selbst 1977 nicht die Rede sein.

Die Verbürgerlichungsthese kann daher weder für den englischen noch für den deutschen Fall bestätigt werden. Denn sowohl in England als auch in Deutschland zeigt sich, dass der Besuch eines Fußballspiels im Stadion in den 1980er Jahren entgegen der weitläufigen Kennzeichnung des Fußballs als Proletariersport in dieser Zeit kein exklusives Freizeitvergnügen der Arbeiterklasse war. Im Gegenteil: In allen betrachteten Erhebungen dominierten bürgerliche Berufsgruppen das Sozialprofil. Ein Vergleich des Arbeiteranteils in englischen und deutschen Stadien lässt sogar vermuten, dass sich in dieser Hinsicht die Stadionpublika grundsätzlich sehr ähnlich sind. Im Schnitt beträgt der Arbeiteranteil übergreifend etwa ein Drittel. Dass etwa ein Drittel der berufstätigen Stadionbesucher der Arbeiterklasse entstammen, bestätigt auch eine komparative Studie zur Sozialstruktur verschiedener Stadionerhebungen in West-Europa in den 1990er Jahren (Waddington et al. 1998).

Angesichts der kulturübergreifenden Ablehnung der Verbürgerlichungsthese in den 1990er Jahren und der Feststellung, dass vom Fußball als Sport der Arbeiterklasse in den 1980er Jahren weder in England noch in Deutschland die Rede sein kann, stellt sich nun die Frage, ob Taylor und Critcher für England sowie Lindner und Breuer für Deutschland Recht hatten mit ihrer Vermutung, dass es bereits in den 1960er und 1970er Jahren zur Verbürgerlichung des Fußballpublikums gekommen ist.

4 Die Verbürgerlichung des Fußballpublikums als Folge des sozialstrukturellen Wandels

Die Verbürgerlichungsthese setzt voraus, dass der Fußballsport ein weitestgehend exklusives Kulturphänomen der Arbeiterklasse in der Vergangenheit war. Wie gezeigt werden konnte, trifft dies auf die 1980er Jahre nicht zu, weshalb die Verbürgerlichung des Fußballpublikums als Resultat der Vermarktungsdynamik seit den 1990er Jahren nicht bestätigt werden konnte. Die Forschungsliteratur ist sich indes darüber einig, dass dies zumindest auf die 1950er Jahre zutrifft. Allgemein gilt diese Zeit als Hochphase des Arbeiter- und Proletariersports Fußball (vgl. Abschnitt 2.1). Folgerichtig müsste sich zeigen, dass der Fußball in den bürgerlichen Schichten insbesondere in den 1950er Jahren ein distinktives Freizeitvergnügen darstellte und entsprechend gemieden wurde. Dass diese Annahme zumindest für Deutschland nicht zutrifft, fundiert die rekrutierungsperspektivische Analyse des Sozialprofils der Kernleserschaft von Fußballfachmagazinen in dieser Zeit (vgl. Tab. 2).

4.1 Datenquelle

Als Datenquelle fungiert die von der Arbeitsgemeinschaft Leseranalyse zur quantitativen Erfassung der Lesegewohnheiten durchgeführte repräsentative Bevölkerungsbefragung im April bzw. Mai 1954[8], in der sich die Befragten zur Frage äußerten, ob sie die Fußballzeitschriften *Sportmagazin* und *Kicker* regelmäßig lesen. Es handelt sich dabei um die einzige auffindbare Quelle, die empirisch abgesicherte, repräsentative Daten zur sozialen Zusammensetzung des Fußballs in der Zeit vor der Entwicklung des Fußballs zur Showbranche (vgl. Abschnitt 2.1) liefern kann.

Grundsätzlich ist zu konstatieren, dass sowohl der regelmäßige *Kicker*-Leser als auch der regelmäßige *Sportmagazin*-Leser aufgrund seiner erworbenen Sachkenntnis, Urteilsfähigkeit und Objektivität in einer Fantypologie als hochgradig am Fußballgeschehen beteiligt und besonders fußballinteressiert angesehen werden kann (Fürtjes 2012: 65). Folglich kann die Kernleserschaft der beiden Fußball-Zeitschriften als Teilmenge der Fußballanhängerschaft betrachtet werden. Diese umfasst annähernd 1,13 Millionen Fußballinteressierte[9] und ermöglicht die Betrachtung eines bundesdeutschen repräsentativen Querschnitts, so dass stichhaltige Schlussfolgerungen auf die soziale Zusammensetzung der Fußballanhängerschaft insgesamt erlaubt sind.

---

8   Größter Dank gilt dem Leiter des Medienwissenschaftlichen Lehr- und Forschungszentrum der Universität zu Köln, Dr. Jörg Hagenah, der mir den Datensatz zur Verfügung gestellt hat.

9   Dies ergab die Berechnung der Reichweite auf Basis des vorliegenden Datensatzes der Leseranalyse 1954.

Tabelle 2 Sozialprofile der Kernleserschaft von Fußballfachmagazinen (Sportmagazin & Kicker) und der bundesdeutschen Bevölkerung 1954 in % (Quelle: Leseranalyse 1954).

	Kernleserschaft von Fußballzeitschriften	Gesellschaftsstruktur der bundesdeutschen Bevölkerung
Berufsprofil		
selbständige Geschäftsleute und Großunternehmer	1,1	0,9
mittlere und kleine Geschäftsleute	10,1	10,1
leitende Angestellte	3,7	3,3
übrige Angestellte	18,3	15,2
leitende Beamte	1,6	1,5
übrige Beamte	9,0	7,1
Inhaber forstwirtschaftlicher Betriebe	2,9	11,1
landwirtschaftliche Arbeiter	2,4	3,5
Arbeiter und nicht-selbständige Handwerker	47,5	43,4
freie Berufe	2,1	2,6
Studenten	1,1	0,4
k.A.	0,3	0,9
Bildung		
Volksschule	79,3	84,9
mittlere Reife	14,3	11,2
Abitur	4,8	2,8
Universitätsabschluss	1,6	1,1
soziale Schicht		
obere Schicht	20,7	16,6
mittlere Schicht	58,1	51,1
untere Schicht	21,2	32,2

n=13.258

4.2   Ergebnisse

Betrachtet man das Berufsprofil[10] der fußballinteressierten Kernleser von Fußballfachmagazinen, kann festgehalten werden, dass die Arbeiter und die nicht-
selbständigen Handwerker mit 47,5% den größten Anteil am Sozialprofil der fußballinteressierten Leser ausmachen und damit die wichtigste Trägerschicht des
Fußballs in der damaligen Zeit darstellten. Allerdings erscheint es nicht gerechtfertigt, in dieser Hinsicht vom Arbeiter- und Proletariersport zu sprechen. Von
einem beträchtlichen proletarischen Einschlag kann jedenfalls nicht die Rede
sein. Berücksichtigt man zusätzlich die damalige Erwerbsstruktur, dann zeigt
sich vielmehr, dass der Arbeiteranteil unter den Fußballinteressierten in etwa
dem der Gesamtgesellschaft (43,4%) entspricht. Vor allem aber wird deutlich, dass
auch die anderen bürgerlichen Berufsgruppen ein ausgeprägtes Fußballinteresse
zeigen. Ein der damaligen Erwerbsstruktur entsprechendes, teilweise sogar über-
repräsentativ großes Fußballinteresse zeigen nämlich auch Geschäftsleute, Freiberufler, Beamte, Angestellte und Studenten.

Selbst in den bildungsbürgerlichen Zirkeln erfreute sich das Lesen von Fußballzeitschriften offensichtlich auch damals größter Beliebtheit. So ist der Anteil
der Leser mit einem Universitätsabschluss gar um 0,5 Prozentpunkte höher als
in der bundesdeutschen Gesellschaft insgesamt. Zählt man auch die Abiturien-
ten der damaligen Zeit zur Bildungselite, dann zählten immerhin 6,4% der Leser
dazu. Insgesamt betrug der Anteil der so definierten Bildungselite nur 3,9%.

Auch die Analyse der Schichtzugehörigkeit, wie sie seitens der Leseranalyse
1954 vorgenommen wurde[11], kann die Kennzeichnung des Fußballs als Proletariersport oder Freizeitvergnügen der unteren Schichten nicht bestätigen. Vielmehr ist zu konstatieren, dass fast 80% der Leser demnach aus der Mittel- bzw.
Oberschicht entstammt, was die Bezeichnung des Fußballs als Proletariersport
geradezu konterkariert. Gleichwohl sollten diese Zahlen aufgrund der theoretisch

---

10 Das Berufsprofil erfasst nahezu alle Befragte, da bei nicht Vollberufstätigen der Beruf
    des Haushaltsvorstandes und bei Rentnern die ehemalige Berufsstellung eingetragen
    wurde.

11 Bei diesem Schichtindex handelt es sich um eine ganzheitliche Betrachtungsweise im
    Sinne der Gestaltpsychologie, bei der bildungsmäßige, niveaumäßige und wirtschaft-
    liche Faktoren ineinander verwoben sind. Die Aufteilung erfolgte in A-, B-, C- und
    D-Schichten, wobei die A- und B-Schichten der „oberen Schicht", die C-Schicht der
    „mittleren Schicht" und die D-Schicht der „unteren Schicht" zuzuordnen sind. Die
    jeweilige Zuordnung erfolgte durch die Interviewer. Das Dokument „Die Zeitschrif-
    tenleser 1954" von der Arbeitsgemeinschaft Leseranalyse kann beim Autor angefragt
    werden.

und methodisch fragwürdigen Schichteinteilung nicht überinterpretiert werden. Im Gesellschaftsvergleich zeigt aber auch die Schichtzugehörigkeit ein leicht statushöheres Profil der fußballinteressierten Leserschaften an.

Die Analyse der Kernleserschaft von Fußballfachmagazinen bestätigt abschließend, dass der Fußball im Frühjahr 1954 kein exklusives Arbeiterphänomen war. Bedenkt man zusätzlich, dass sich bei der Analyse der Kernleserschaft von Fußballfachmagazinen „insbesondere hier der Proletariersport hätte zeigen müssen" (Fürtjes/Hagenah 2011: 296), dann ist die Grundvoraussetzung für die Verbürgerlichungsthese der 1960er und 1970er Jahre, nämlich die Annahme vom Fußball als klassischen Arbeiter- und Proletariersport, nicht erfüllt. Vielmehr zeigt sich, dass der Fußballsport in Deutschland in den 1950er Jahren in allen Schichten sehr beliebt war und daher als ein schichtenübergreifendes Massenphänomen gekennzeichnet werden kann. Die Kennzeichnung des Fußballs als Arbeiter- und Proletariersport ist vielmehr einer undifferenzierten Wahrnehmung der Gesellschaftsstruktur im Industriezeitalter geschuldet. Diese war bekanntlich durch proletarische Verhältnisse gekennzeichnet, so dass folgerichtig auch das massenhafte Fußballpublikum proletarische Züge annahm. Die von Lindner und Breuer (1978) beobachtete Verbürgerlichung des Fußballpublikums ist deshalb einzig auf die inter- und intragenerationelle Aufstiegsmobilität der deutschen Bevölkerung im Zuge des sozialstrukturellen Wandels in der Nachkriegszeit zurückzuführen. In gleicherweise wie die bundesdeutsche Gesellschaft einen kollektiven sozialen Aufstieg infolge der Tertiärisierung, Bildungsexpansion und Wohlstandssteigerung erfuhr, hob sich auch der allgemeine Status des massenhaften Fußballpublikums. Dies konnten Fürtjes und Hagenah (2011) auf der Grundlage der Kernleser des *Kicker-Sportmagazins* auch empirisch nachweisen.

Die Frage, die sich abschließend stellt, ist, inwiefern der erbrachte Nachweis für Deutschland, dass der Fußball selbst in den 1950er Jahren ein schichtenübergreifendes Massenphänomen war und die Verbürgerlichung des Fußballpublikums folglich allein auf die Verbürgerlichung der Gesellschaft zurückzuführen ist, auch auf das Beispiel England übertragen werden kann.

5   Der Fußball und seine Kontinuität als klassenloses Massenphänomen auch in England

Zunächst kann festgehalten werden, dass die englische Gesellschaft einem vergleichbaren sozialstrukturellen Wandel von der Industriegesellschaft zur Postmoderne unterlegen war wie die deutsche und sich in den 1970er Jahren im Zuge der Tertiärisierung zur Dienstleistungsgesellschaft verbürgerlicht hat (vgl. Lash/

Urry 1987). Dass sich dieser Wandel auf die Publikumsstrukturen im Fußball auswirkte, wird in der Forschungsliteratur auch nicht bestritten. Angesichts der Exklusivität des Fußballs in der Arbeiterklasse wird er jedoch nicht als maßgebend betrachtet. Fraglich ist indes, inwiefern die Zuweisung des Fußball als exklusives Arbeiterklassenphänomen in der Vergangenheit in England tatsächlich gerechtfertigt ist.

Bei näherer Betrachtung der englischen Sozial- und Kulturgeschichte lassen sich Indizien und Plausibilitätsbetrachtungen auffinden, die dafür sprechen, den englischen Fußball ähnlich dem deutschen als „kontinuierliches schichtenübergreifendes Massenphänomen" (Fürtjes 2012: 68) zu bezeichnen. Unzweifelhaft ist, dass der Fußball sich in der Arbeiterschaft großer Beliebtheit erfreute. Allein die Entstehung des Massenphänomens Fußball im letzten Viertel des 19. Jahrhundert in England, zu einer Zeit als fast 80 % der Bevölkerung aus Arbeitern bestand, bestätigt dies. Vom Proletariersport kann aber nur dann die Rede sein, wenn sich die bürgerlichen Schichten kollektiv vom Fußball distinguierten. Dies erscheint vor dem Hintergrund der bürgerlichen Ursprünge des Fußballs in England jedoch wenig plausibel. Im Zuge der Professionalisierung des Fußballs mag dies zwar auf die dem Amateurethos verschriebenen Gentlemen zutreffen. Von einem kollektiven Rückzug kann aber auch bei diesen ursprünglichen Trägerschichten nicht die Rede sein, wie die Analysen zum Sozialprofil der Clubdirektoren in der Anfangszeit des Massenphänomens Fußball nachweisen[12] (Mason 1980: 42f.; Tischler 1981: 71ff.; Vampley 1988: 161ff.). Vor allem aber zeigt sich dort, dass sich die Vereinsdirektoren fast ausnahmslos aus bürgerlichen Schichten rekrutierten. Dasselbe trifft auch und insbesondere auf die soziale Basis der Verbandsfunktionäre in der Football Association (FA) zu (Mason 1980: 44f.). Ferner zeigen Analysen der Shareholder von Clubanteilen, dass diese vornehmlich der Mittelschicht entstammten (Fishwick 1989: 29; Vampley 1988: 161). Überdies rekrutierten sich die Fußballjournalisten und Redakteure aus Presse und Rundfunk in der Regel aus der Mittelklasse (Mason 1980: 151), was genauso auf die Schiedsrichter zutrifft (Fishwick 1989: 62). Ähnliches gilt für die in den 1920er Jahren entstandenen Fanclubs, die ein „substantial element of middle-class influence and leadership" (Fishwick 1989: 56f.) kennzeichnet. Dass die verschiedenen bürgerlichen fußballinteressierten Personengruppen auch dem Live-Erlebnis Fußball in den Stadien beiwohnen wollten, ist angesichts der damaligen Alternativlosigkeit – Fußball im Fernsehen hatte sich ja noch nicht etabliert – keine allzu gewagte These. Die

---

12 Immerhin beträgt der Anteil der Gentlemen am Sozialprofil der Clubdirektoren 4 bis 4,7 % und ist damit vermutlich deutlich höher als der am Sozialprofil der damaligen englischen Gesellschaft.

unterschiedlichen Komfortbereiche in den Stadien und die seitens der Clubver-
antwortlichen vorgenommenen Preisdifferenzierungen fundieren schlussendlich
die soziale Strukturierung in den englischen Stadien in der Zeit vor 1960. Zu diesem Schluss kommt auch Mellor (1999). Auf der Basis von lokalen Zeitungen und
mündlichen Interviews indiziert er die „diversity of football crowds in the North-
West of England in the immediate post-war period" (25).

Reflektiert man abschließend noch die Begründung der Verbürgerlichungsthese aus der Vermarktung des professionellen und kommerziellen Fußballs,
dann stellt sich insbesondere für die englische Fußballkultur die Frage, wieso die
bürgerlichen Schichten ihr Konsuminteresse am Fußball erst ab den 1960er Jahren entdeckt haben sollten. Anders als in Deutschland kann der englische Fußball schon in seiner Frühphase als „commercial-professional football" (Tischler
1981) bezeichnet werden. Vermarktungsstrategien seitens der Clubverantwortli-
chen kennzeichnen den englischen Fußball seit seiner Professionalisierung (vgl.
Taylor 2008; Tischler 1981; Vampley 1988). Dass sich in den Stadien in der damaligen Zeit nicht nur die „local club supporters" einfanden, verdeutlichen allein
die unterschiedlich hohen Zuschauerzahlen bei unterschiedlich attraktiven Be-
gegnungen. Offensichtlich gab es auch damals schon Zuschauer, die sich weniger
stark mit dem Verein identifizierten und in erster Linie aus Motiven des besonderen Unterhaltungs- und Erlebniswertes mancher Spitzenbegegnungen in die
Stadien pilgerten (vgl. Taylor 2008: 118ff.). Topzuschläge für solche Partien zeigen
zudem an, dass profitorientiertes Handeln keine Erfindung der neuen Generation
von Fußballmanagern ist.

Selbst wenn sich die Annahme klassenbezogener Beziehungsstrukturen im
Fußball bestätigen sollte, nämlich dass sich die Supporter aus der Arbeiterklasse und die Konsumenten aus der Mittelschicht rekrutieren, spricht wenig dafür,
dies erst seit den 1960er Jahren zu unterstellen. Grundsätzlich erscheint eine solche klassenbasierte Dichotomie aber weder für die Vergangenheit noch für die
Gegenwart angebracht (vgl. Malcom 2000).

Verwiesen sei hierbei einerseits auf den lukrativen Markt der ‚working-class
consumers' (Wagg 1984: 35) und andererseits auf die Unternehmensleiter in der
Vergangenheit, die ihren Posten als Clubdirektoren in erster Linie aufgrund ihrer
lokalen Verbundenheit und starken Identifikation mit dem Verein ausfüllten (vgl.
Mason 1980).

Es spricht daher vieles dafür, auch den englischen Fußball als allzeitiges klassenloses Massenphänomen zu bezeichnen und den Verbürgerlichungsprozess des
Fußballpublikums als Resultat des sozialstrukturellen Wandels in der Gesellschaft zu beschreiben. Die ähnliche Berufsstruktur in den englischen und deutschen Stadien seit den 1980er Jahren unterstreicht diese Annahme zusätzlich.

6   Fazit

Aus sozialhistorischer und struktursoziologischer Perspektive kann gezeigt werden, dass der Fußball sowohl in Deutschland als auch in England als kontinuierliches schichtenübergreifendes Massenphänomen verstanden werden muss, der Fußball mithin schon immer in den bürgerlichen Schichten ein beliebtes und keineswegs kollektiv distinktives Freizeitvergnügen darstellte.

Dies plausibilisiert sich sozialhistorisch durch die frühzeitige Verankerung des Fußballs in den bürgerlichen Kreisen in beiden Nationen. Mit der vertikalen Verbreitung des Fußballs in die unteren Schichten, dies freilich in länderspezifisch unterschiedlichen Zeiträumen, wofür verschiedene begünstigende gesellschaftliche Prozesse die Grundvoraussetzungen schufen, wurde er dann zum schichtenübergreifenden Massenphänomen und blieb es bis heute.

Die Besonderheit des Fußballspiels ist es ja geradezu, dass er die Partizipation unabhängig von der Klassenzugehörigkeit ermöglicht und damit auch zum beliebten Freizeitvergnügen in den proletarischen Unterschichten werden konnte. Daraus jedoch abzuleiten, dass er zu einem exklusiven Freizeitvergnügen des Proletariats wurde, ist ein Fehlschluss, der auf einer undifferenzierten Wahrnehmung der Gesellschaftsstruktur im Industriezeitalter beruht.

Besonders deutlich wird dies bei Betrachtung der Publikumsstrukturen in den Arbeitervorortvereinen der Industrieregionen. So verwundert es nicht, wenn bei einer Erwerbsstruktur, in der die Arbeiter mit bis zu 73% dominierten (vgl. Gehrmann 1988), auch die Publikumsstrukturen proletarisch geprägt waren. An Orten mit überwiegend bürgerlicher Einwohnerstruktur, wo der Fußball sich ähnlich großer Beliebtheit erfreute, wie allein der immer wieder bemühte Klassenkampf zwischen Arbeitervereinen und Vereinen der bürgerlichen Mittelklasse indiziert (vgl. Schulze-Marmeling 1992), ist wiederum entsprechend von einem bürgerlichen Einschlag im Publikum auszugehen.

Die in der Öffentlichkeit, unter Fußballfans und in den verschiedenen Forschungstraditionen vertretene Verbürgerlichungsthese kann daher angesichts der fehleingeschätzten Ausgangssituation nicht aufrecht erhalten werden.

Die gleichwohl zu beobachtenden Verbürgerlichungstendenzen im Fußball und speziell im Fußballstadion erklären sich, wie gezeigt werden konnte, aus dem sich vollziehenden sozialstrukturellen Wandel zur gegenwärtigen postmodernen Gesellschaftsstruktur. Dieser äußert sich in der seit der Nachkriegszeit voranschreitenden inter- und intragenerationellen Aufstiegsmobilität in postindustriellen Gegenwartsgesellschaften. Daraus lässt sich ableiten, dass die von Giulianotti (1999) und Redhead (1997) beschriebenen postmodernen Fans der neuen Mittelklasse, die nicht zuletzt in den Dienstleistungsbranchen der postmodernen

Freizeit-, Medien- und Kulturindustrie beschäftigt sind, in großen Teilen noch in Arbeiterhaushalten fußballspezifisch sozialisiert wurden. In Kombination mit den in Mittel- und Oberschichten sozialisierten Fußballfans erklärt sich dadurch das Mehr an bürgerlichen und gleichzeitig das Weniger an proletarischen Fußballinteressierten. Eben dieses Verständnis gesellschaftlicher Veränderungsprozesse verkennen die Vertreter der Verbürgerlichungsthese aufgrund ihrer einseitigen kausalen Fokussierung auf die Verbürgerlichungseffekte ausgehend von den Vermarktungs- und Mediatisierungsentwicklungen. So wird auch die Eventkultur in den modernisierten Stadien der Gegenwart nicht durch den Einfluss der exponierten Marketingstrategien der Manager in den Vereinen verständlich, sondern erklärt sich besser als erfolgreiche Umsetzung veränderter klassenübergreifender Bedürfnisse in der Gesellschaft, wie sie mit der generellen Erlebnisorientierung passend beschrieben werden kann. Abgesehen von den besonders prekär lebenden Bevölkerungsgruppen, die sich ein Ticket nicht leisten können, was im Übrigen auch für die Vergangenheit gilt, resultiert die gestiegene Popularität des Stadionbesuchs daher durch ein Mehr aus allen Bevölkerungsschichten. Überdies scheint die einseitige kausale Fokussierung der Vertreter der Verbürgerlichungsthese auch deshalb problematisch und wenig plausibel, da es fraglich ist, wie es denn überhaupt zu der intensiven Kommodifizierung, Kommerzialisierung und Professionalisierung des Fußballsports kommen konnte, wenn er zuvor ausschließlich in den wenig zahlungskräftigen Bevölkerungsschichten verankert war. Derselben fragwürdigen und bisweilen einseitigen kausalen Fokussierung unterliegt auch die Perspektive, die Verbürgerlichung des Fußballpublikums als Folge veränderter Medienpräsentation der Privatsender und des Pay-TVs in den 1990er Jahren anzunehmen. Die Medienunternehmen haben die TV-Rechte nicht erworben, um den Fußballsport in allen Schichten gesellschaftsfähig zu machen, sondern weil sie davon ausgehen konnten, dass der Fußball bereits auf eine breite gesellschaftliche Akzeptanz stieß und insofern mit entsprechend hohen Einschaltquoten zu rechnen war. Vor allem die Pay-TV-Sender in England und Deutschland stießen zu Beginn der 1990er Jahre auf den Fußballmarkt im Wissen um ein vorhandenes zahlungskräftiges Klientel.

Allein diese skizzenhaften Anmerkungen machen deutlich, dass von einem umgekehrten Kausalitätszusammenhang in der Ausgangslage ausgegangen werden muss. Da der Fußball schon immer auch in den wohlhabenden Schichten auf großes Interesse stieß, konnte sich die Vermarktungsdynamik und Mediatisierung des Fußballs überhaupt erst vollziehen.

Die interpretatorische Bedeutsamkeit gesellschaftlicher Prozesse zur Erklärung fußballimmanenter Entwicklungen, wie sie die struktursoziologische Perspektive einnimmt, entlarvt zusammengefasst die Kennzeichnung des Fußballs als

Proletariersport als Mythos und veranschaulicht den falschen Kausalzusammenhang der Verbürgerlichungsthese. Damit ist freilich nicht gesagt, dass Vermarktungs- und Mediatisierungstendenzen nicht auch Wirkungen auf die Gewinnung neuer Fußballfans in den Mittel- und Oberklassen zeitigen. Dasselbe trifft dann aber auch auf die Gewinnung neuer Fußballfans in den unteren Schichten zu. Vor allem aber hat sich das Fußballpublikum des Massenphänomens Fußball aufgrund seiner allzeitigen klassenlosen Beliebtheit durch die beschriebenen Entwicklungen im Fußball nicht grundlegend gewandelt.

Literatur

Aschenbeck, A. (1998): Fußballfans im Abseits. Kassel: Agon.

Bausenwein, C. (2006): Geheimnis Fußball. Auf den Spuren eines Phänomens. Göttingen: Die Werkstatt.

Bleeker-Dohmen, R./Stammen, K.-H./Strasser, H./Weber, G. (2007): „Sind wir so wichtig?" Fußballfans zwischen Tradition und Kommerz. In: Mittag, J./Nieland, J.-U. (Hrsg.): Das Spiel mit dem Fußball. Interessen, Projektionen und Vereinnahmungen. Essen: Klartext, 499-519.

Boyle, R./Haynes, R. (2004): Football in the New Media Age. London, New York: Routledge.

Crabbe, T. & Brown, A. (2004): You're not welcome anymore: the football crowd, class and social exclusion. In: Wagg, S. (Hrsg.): British Football and Social Exclusion. London, New York: Routledge.

Critcher, C. (1979): Football since the war. In: Clarke, J./Critcher, C./Johnson, R. (Hrsg.): Working class culture: Studies in history and theory. London: Routledge, 161-184.

Digel, H./Burk, V. (1999): Zur Entwicklung des Fernsehsports in Deutschland. In: Sportwissenschaft 29, 22-41.

Duke, V. (1991): The Sociology of Football: A Research Agenda for the 1990s. In: Sociological Review 39, 627-645.

Eisenberg, C. (1997): Fußball, soccer, calcio. Ein englischer Sport auf seinem Weg um die Welt. München: Deutscher Taschenbuchverlag.

Eisenberg, C. (2004): Der Weg des Fußballs um die Welt 1863-2004. In: Jütting, D.H. (Hrsg.): Die lokal-globale Fußballkultur. Münster: Waxmann Verlag, 45-59.

Fishwick, N. (1989): English football and society, 1910-1950. Manchester, New York: Manchester University Press.

Friedrichs, J. (2000): Gentrification. In: Häußermann, H. (Hrsg.): Großstadt. Soziologische Stichworte. Opladen: Leske + Budrich Verlag.

Fürtjes, O. (2012): Der Fußball und seine Kontinuität als schichtenübergreifendes Massenphänomen. In: SportZeiten 12, 55-72.

Fürtjes, O./Hagenah, J. (2011). Der Fußball und seine Entproletarisierung. Eine empirische Analyse zur Erklärung der Veränderung des Sozialprofils des Fußballsports in Deutschland, exemplifiziert an der Leserschaft des Kicker-Sportmagazins von 1954 bis 2005. In: Kölner Zeitschrift für Soziologie und Sozialpsychologie 63, 279-300.

Gabler, J. (2012): Die Ultras. Fußballfans und Fußballkulturen in Deutschland. Köln: PapyRossa Verlag.

Gehrmann, S. (1988): Fußball - Vereine - Politik. Zur Sportgeschichte des Reviers 1900-1940. Essen: Hobbing.

Gehrmann, S. (1992): Ein Schritt nach Europa: Zur Gründungsgeschichte der Fußballbundesliga. In: Sozial- und Zeitgeschichte des Sports, 6, 7-37.

Großhans, G.-T. (1997): Fußball im deutschen Fernsehen. Frankfurt am Main: Lang.

Giulianotti, R. (1999): Football. A Sociology of the Global Game. Cambridge: Polity.

Giulianotti, R. (2002): Supporters, Followers, Fans and Flaneurs: A Taxonomy of Spectator Identities in Football. In: Journal of Sport and Social Issues, 26, 25-46.

Hering, H. (2002): Im Land der 1000 Derbys. Die Fußballgeschichte des Ruhrgebiets. Göttingen: Die Werkstatt.

Holt, R./Mason, T. (2000): Sport in Britain. 1945-2000. Oxford: Wiley.

King, A. (1997a): New Directors, Customers, and Fans: The Transformation of English Football in the 1990s. In: Sociology of Sport Journal 14, 224-240.

King, A. (1997b): The Lads: Masculinity and the New Consumption of Football. In: Sociology 31, 329-346.

King, A. (1998): The End of the Terrace. London: Leicester University Press.

König, T. (2002): Fankultur. Eine soziologische Studie am Beispiel des Fußballfans. Münster: Lit.

Lash, S./Urry, J. (1987): The End of Organised Capitalism. Cambridge: Polity.

Leder, D. (2004): Vom Verlust der Distanz. Die Geschichte der Fußballübertragungen im deutschen Fernsehen. In: Schierl, T. (Hrsg.): Die Visualisierung des Sports in den Medien. Köln: von Halem, 40-81.

Lenhard, M. (2002): Vereinsfußball und Identifikation in Deutschland: Phänomene zwischen Tradition und Postmoderne. Hamburg: Kovac.

Lindner, R./Breuer, H.T. (1978): „Sind doch nicht alles Beckenbauers". Zur Sozialgeschichte des Fußballs im Ruhrgebiet. Frankfurt am Main: Lang.

Malcom, D. (2000): Football business and football communities in the twenty-first century. In: Soccer & Society 1, 102-113.

Malcom, D./Jones, I./Waddington, I. (2000): The people's game? Football spectatorship and demographic change. In: Soccer & Society 1, 129-143.

Mason, T. (1980): Association Football & English Society 1863-1915. Sussex: Harvester.

Mellor, G. (1999): The Social and Geographical Make-Up of Football Crowds in the North-West of England, 1946-1962. In: The Sports Historian 19, 25-42.

Merkel, U. (2012): Football fans and clubs in Germany: conflicts, crises and compromises. In: Soccer & Society 13, 359-376.

Nash, R. (2000): Contestation in modern English professional football. In: International Review for the Sociology of Sport 35, 465-486.

Pfaff, S.M. (2004): Erlebniswelt Fußball-Arena. In: Krüger, A./A. Dreyer, A. (Hrsg.): Sportmanagement. München, Wien: Oldenbourg, 212-245.

Redhead, S. (1997): Post-Fandom and the Millenial Blues: The Transformation of Soccer Culture. London: Routledge.

Russell, D. (1997): Football and the English. A Social History of Association Football in England, 1863-1995. Preston: Carnegie.

Schulze, G. (1992): Die Erlebnisgesellschaft. Kultursoziologie der Gegenwart. Frankfurt/New York: Campus.

Schulze-Marmeling, D. (1992): Der gezähmte Fußball. Zur Geschichte eines subversiven Sports. Göttingen: Die Werkstatt.

Schulze-Marmeling, D. (2000): Fußball. Zur Geschichte eines globalen Sports. Göttingen: Die Werkstatt.

Stollenwerk, H. J. (1996): Sport-Zuschauer-Medien. Aachen: Meyer & Meyer.

Taylor, I. (1971a): „Football mad“: A speculative sociology of football hooliganism. In: Dunning, E. (Hrsg.): The sociology of sport: A selection of readings. London: Cass & Co., 352-377.

Taylor, I. (1971b): Soccer consciousness and soccer hooliganism. In: Cohen, S. (Hrsg.): Images of deviance. Harmondsworth: Penguin, 134-163.

Taylor, Lord Justice (1990): The Hillsborough Stadium Disaster 15 April 1989: Final Report. London: HMSO.

Taylor, M. (2008): The Association Game. A History of British Football. Harlow: Pearson.

Tischler, S. (1981): Footballers and Businessmen. New York/London: Holmes & Meier.

Vampley, W. (1988): Pay up and play the game. Professional Sport in Britain 1875-1914. Cambridge: Cambridge University Press.

Waddington, I./Malcom, D./Horak, R. (1998): The social composition of football crowds in Western Europe: A comparative study. In: International Review for the Sociology of Sport 33, 155-169.

Wagg, S. (1984): The Football World. A Contemporary Social History. Brighton: Harvester.

Walvin, J. (1994): The People's Game. The History of Football Revisited. Edinburgh: Mainstream.

Williams, R. (1961): The long revolution. Hamondsworth: Penguin.

Reinventing the Past: Youth and National Team Development in England and Germany

Die Neu-Erfindung der Vergangenheit: Entwicklungen des Jugendfußballs und der Nationalmannschaften in England und Deutschland

Richard Elliott

Abstract

English and German football had, until recently, shared a number of notable characteristics at both domestic and international level. The similarities observable were, arguably, based largely on the increasingly penetrative commercialisation of the game that occurred in both countries, altering the core values of professional football at similar points in time. The intention of this chapter is to examine these similarities and to provide a comparative analysis of professional football in England and Germany by focusing specifically on aspects of foreign player involvement, youth and national team development. The chapter shows that whilst the English and German systems were affected by a range of similar market forces for much of the 1990s and 2000s, the responses to issues relating to domestic league development, foreign player involvement, youth and national team success have been very different in the last 10 years. Therefore, the chapter concludes by showing how, as the result of

a number of structural changes, the German model is now held up as a model
of best practice, whilst the future of English football, at international level at
least, is less certain.

Zusammenfassung

Der englische und deutsche Fußball teilten kürzlich noch eine Reihe bedeutsamer Charakteristika auf nationaler und internationaler Ebene. Die erkenn-
baren Gemeinsamkeiten bezogen sich vor allem auf die in beiden Ländern
zunehmende, weitgreifende Kommerzialisierung, welche in beiden Fällen
die bis dahin zentralen Werte des Spiels zu einem ähnlichen Zeitpunkt veränderte. Ziel des Beitrags ist es, diese Gemeinsamkeiten zu untersuchen, um
darauf aufbauend eine komparative Analyse des professionellen Fußballs in
Deutschland und England anzubieten. Dabei fokussiert der Beitrag insbesondere die Frage nach der Rolle ausländischer Spieler und die der Entwicklung
der Jugendarbeit bzw. der Nationalmannschaften. Es wird gezeigt, dass das
englische und deutsche System zwar einer Reihe vergleichbarer Marktkräf-
te in den 1990er und 2000er Jahren ausgesetzt waren, diese in den letzten 10
Jahren jedoch zu sehr unterschiedlichen Antworten auf Fragen nach dem
Ausbau der nationalen Ligen, der Einbeziehung ausländischer Spieler und der
Entwicklung der Jugendarbeit bzw. der Nationalmannschaften geführt haben.
Der Artikel zeigt schließlich, warum der deutsche Fußball auf der Grundlage
verschiedener struktureller Veränderungen gegenwärtig als modellhaft angesehen wird, während die Zukunft des englischen Fußballs, zumindest auf
internationaler Ebene, als eher unsicher gilt.

1   Introduction

In the last fifty years, it can be argued that English and German football has become metaphorically entwined. The 1966 World Cup final, the semi-final at Ita-
lia '90, the semi-final at Euro '96, Manchester United versus Bayern Munich in
the 1999 Champions League final, England's victories at Euro 2000 and the 2002
World Cup qualifier in Munich, Germany's victory at World Cup 2010, Chelsea
versus Bayern Munich in the 2012 Champions League final – these are the major
defining moments that have helped to embed the relationship that has developed
in the history of the two nations' football cultures. Whilst it might not seem immediately obvious, the recent histories of the professional game in England and
Germany have also represented a certain sort of enmeshment. For example, the

development of the game in the two countries has resulted in English and German club sides winning European football's showpiece events, the UEFA Champions League and Europa League (UEFA Cup), on a number of occasions. Moreover, the two nations have had highs and lows at international level. Whilst it is Germany who has triumphed on more occasions, the period since the 1966 World Cup final has been one that is punctuated by (relative, in England's case) success and more recent failures for both nations. Indeed, the approach taken to the development of the domestic league and the national team in England and Germany provides a number of comparisons.

The similarities in the development of professional football in England and Germany exist largely as a result of both nations being exposed to similar market forces. In the last twenty years particularly, a rapid and increasingly penetrative commercialisation of the game, driven, in large part, by growing media revenues, has altered the core values of professional football in both countries. During the 1990s, football in both England and Germany rapidly developed into an industry where clubs were increasingly viewed as 'brands', fans as 'customers' and players, often foreign, 'commodities' to be bought and sold.

The involvement of foreign players in English and German football is one of the most ubiquitous markers of the commercialisation of the game in both countries. It is also a signifier of the broader processes of globalisation that influenced the development of professional football at the end of the twentieth century (Elliott/ Weedon 2010). The growing sums of money that media companies were willing to pay to broadcast matches in England and Germany during the 1990s provided new revenue streams for clubs that allowed them to lure foreign imports with the promise of higher salaries and greater levels of exposure. In England and Germany, during the 1990s and into the early 2000s, the number of foreign imports playing in the leagues increased exponentially, reaching a point where foreign players eventually outnumbered their indigenous counterparts in both the English Premier League and the German Bundesliga (Poli/Ravenel/Besson, 2009, 2010). For youth and national team development, the increases in foreign player involvement were argued to be disastrous (Brand/Niemann 2006; Merkel 2007; Elliott/Weedon 2010).

Whilst Germany's national team performance has been vastly superior to England's in the last fifty years, both teams have observed fluctuations in their performances at major tournaments. England has failed to emulate their World Cup success of 1966, coming close again only in 1990 (World Cup) and 1996 (European Championships) losing on both occasions to Germany at the semi-final stage. Germany, on the other hand, after losing the 1966 World Cup final to England, subsequently went on to win the tournament in 1974 and 1990 and European

Championship titles in 1972, 1980 and 1996. Whilst dominating international football for many years, since 1996 however, Germany, like England, has failed to secure any major title at senior level.

In the last ten years the similarities that existed in the structure of English and German football have disappeared and where national team failures have largely been ignored by those responsible for the development of the game in England, the German response to more than a decade of underperformance has been to completely restructure the sport in that country. The results have spoken for themselves and with the Bundesliga now held up as the model for other leagues to follow, this chapter analyses the differences that exist in the two systems with specific reference to foreign players, youth and national team development. To begin to do this, the next part of the chapter provides a brief retrospective of the development of the English Premier League and the German Bundesliga.

2   The Premier League and Bundesliga – a brief retrospective

Sergio Aguero's 93rd minute winner for Manchester City against Queens Park Rangers which robbed their nearest rivals, Manchester United, of the title on the final day of the English Premier League's 20th season reflected the kind of finale that even Hollywood scriptwriters wouldn't dream of positing as reality. The season capped what has been a remarkable turnaround in the fortunes of English football representing a commercial transformation from the 'dark days' of the 1980s where hooliganism was common, many stadia were old and in a state of decay, a poor safety culture existed and fans were largely treated with contempt (Walvin 1994).

The 1980s were a particularly difficult decade for professional football in England. The decade will largely be remembered for the three disasters that resulted in a significant loss of life both in England and abroad. In 1985 a fire at Bradford City's Valley Parade ground killed 56 people and injured a further 265. In the same year, shortly before the start of the European Cup final being played at the Heysel Stadium in Brussels, 33 Juventus and 6 Liverpool fans were killed when a wall collapsed as hooligans breached a fence. In 1989, 96 Liverpool fans were killed as a result of crushing at the Hillsborough Stadium in Sheffield when police controls on stadium entry failed. The disasters at Bradford, Heysel and Hillsborough provide the starkest reminders of the poor infrastructural conditions that existed in professional football in England during this period. It is no surprise, therefore, that the game had little or no appeal to television.

At the end of the 1980s English football found itself in a general malaise. The disasters that had occurred during the decade were reflective of the problems that existed within the game both socially and structurally. However, problems were also evident in the relationship between some of the clubs and the Football League – the organisation responsible for running the four professional divisions in England at the time. The top clubs were discontent with what they saw as an unfair distribution of television money. Under the current regime all 92 professional football clubs in England shared television revenues with only marginal differences in distribution between the top and bottom clubs. Those responsible for a number of the top clubs including Manchester United, Liverpool, Arsenal, Tottenham Hotspur and Everton, thought this unfair, wanting to retain a greater proportion of television money for themselves. To do this, the country's 22 first division teams, in conjunction with The Football Association, broke away from the Football League and formed the Premier League in 1992, negotiating their own television rights with commercial satellite broadcaster BSkyB (Conn 1997) and the BBC. The new TV deal was worth £214million over 5 years. This new figure eclipsed terrestrial broadcaster ITV's previous £48million contract and was, arguably, the catalyst to the transformation of professional football that was about to occur in England.

In 20 years, the increase in media revenues and subsequent commercial transformation of the Premier League has been remarkable. Following the initial £214million BSkyB and BBC contract, domestic Premier League television revenues have increased to £670million in 1997, £1.024billion in 2001, £1.7billion in 2006 and £3.018billion in 2012. When coupled with overseas rights that, in the last sale, generated £1.4billion, the Premier League is now one of the richest sports competitions in the world; it has become a global spectacle of accumulation.

The new wealth that entered football in the 1990s and early 2000s was spent in almost entirely rebranding the sport in England. Indeed, BSkyB's positioning for the first season of the new Premier League was: "It's a whole new ball game" – seemingly emphasising the change in approach that was being taken in the post-1980s period. Clubs spent millions on new stadium development, some clubs choosing to reinvigorate their existing facilities, while others built from scratch. Even more was spent on salaries to entice the world's best players to the league – the result was a considerable increase in the numbers of foreign players recruited. Whereas only 11 foreign players had started games at the beginning of the Premier League's inaugural season (Elliott/Weedon 2010), the number of appearances by foreign players already outnumbered those of their indigenous counterparts by 2001 (Elliott 2009).

By the conclusion of its 20th season, the Premier League was broadcast in 212 territories where 650 million homes received match coverage. Some 36 million fans attended matches and professional football clubs contributed more than £1 billion to the British government in tax. Since the league's first season more than £3 billion had been spent on stadium development with 25 stadia in England and Wales having a capacity greater than 30,000. Foreign investment had increased with a number of Premier League clubs being owned in full or part by overseas investors. The combined revenues of the 20 Premier League clubs equated to £2.3 billion, the clubs posted a combined wage bill of almost £1.6 billion, and spent a total of £364 million on foreign players (Deloitte 2012).

Unlike England, however, where football had been organised around a national league structure since before the turn of the twentieth century, in Germany, no national league existed until 1963. Before this time, football had been organised around and played within specific regions, with nation-wide competition only occurring at the end of each season during a period of league finals (Merkel 2006). The largely regionalised structure of competition meant that support for the German national team and a broader modernisation of the game was resisted for many years (Merkel 2012). However, a challenge to this resistance occurred in 1954 when the German national team won the World Cup in a match that was reinvented as the 'miracle of Berne'. This match would mark the point at which football's transformation began in Germany (Merkel 2007).

The German World Cup victory at the Wankdorf Stadium in Berne on the 4th of July 1954, when the German national team defeated the heavily favoured Hungarian's 3-2, represents the point at which football stopped being viewed as an English import that should be treated with suspicion and began to enter into the German people's social and cultural consciousness (Pyta 2006). After 1945, Germany had been a country that was struggling to come to terms with its own sense of national identity. Indeed, Hitler had pushed nationalism to a point that it had left the country (literally) in ruins. At this time, nationalism was problematic as a force for community development. Football, on the other hand, provided a much more suitable signifier of the German people – post 1945. The miracle of Berne, and football more broadly, filled the symbolic void that existed.

From 1954, football developed quickly in Germany. The previously associated regional ties that had marked the amateur game that was played before 1963 were replaced when the Bundesliga was formed in that year. Now teams competed on a national level throughout the season, rather than at the end of it, which had been the case in previous league structures administered by the Deutscher Fußball Bund (DFB), the national governing body for the sport in Germany. In the 1970s, Bayern Munich epitomised the new German affinity for football. Bayern Munich could be described as the game's first 'football brand' in Germany and whilst often criticised on the basis of their economic power, could count on a supporter base that extended well beyond Bavaria and all across the country. Bayern's economic development is reflective of the broader commercial transformation that occurred in German football from the 1970s, and which intensified during the 1980s and 1990s.

The commercial development of football in Germany bears a resemblance to the processes that were underway in England at the same time. That is to say that both England and Germany were exposed to similar market forces and processes of mediatisation that were reflective of specific forms of modernisation in this period. It was the national broadcasters that initially bought the rights to show Bundesliga football paying just 130,000 DM to broadcast games and highlights from the 1966/67 season. The rights to broadcast Bundesliga football remained relatively stable, growing gradually until commercial broadcasters entered the marketplace to exploit the opportunities that satellite transmission presented (King 2003) and a deregulation of broadcasting occurred at the end of the 1980s (Mikos 2006). Once these processes were underway, the sums paid to broadcast Bundesliga football increased, as they had for the English Premier League, exponentially, rising from 40 million DM in 1988 to €519 million in 2012 (Deloitte 2011).

Similarly to the English Premier League, the new media money that had suddenly entered Germany's top football division resulted in a considerable increase in salaries that subsequently enticed foreign players to the Bundesliga teams. During the 1990s and into the early 2000s the Bundesliga, like the Premier League, saw a significant growth in the numbers of foreign players selecting the league in which to ply their trade (Brand/Niemann 2006). Indeed, like the Premier League, the Bundesliga, at its peak, reported that the number of foreign players making appearances in the league was greater than that of their indigenous counterparts (Poli/Ravenel/Besson 2009).

For a period during the early 2000s, German football bore a significant resemblance to the system in operation in England and vice-versa. In both countries, for example; the national league was administered by a separate organisation to the national governing body who had responsibility for the national team; the top league was largely funded by a highly lucrative television-broadcasting contract worth billions of Euros, player salaries had increased exponentially year-on-year for more than a decade; and the numbers of foreign players had increased considerably, eventually outnumbering the number of home-grown players. This final similarity is worth exploring in greater detail as the involvement of foreign players has been directly related to failures in youth and national team development in both countries.

3   Overpaid and over here: Foreign players in the Premier League and Bundesliga

The commercial transformations that took place during the 1990s and which intensified throughout the early twenty first century period resulted in the Premier League and the Bundesliga becoming positioned in what is commonly referred to as European football's 'big-five'. This is the term that is used in reference to European football's core economies and includes the English Premier League, German Bundesliga, Spanish La Liga, Italian Serie A and French Ligue 1. These leagues, and a number of the teams within them, generally command the greatest media interest, the broadest (sometimes global) fan bases and the highest revenues (Elliott 2012).

A cursory analysis of the changing financial structure of professional football in the Premier League and Bundesliga highlights the growth in club and league revenues, media rights sales, player valuations and salary costs (see, for example, the annually produced Deloitte Review of Football Finance and Football Money League). The rise in salary costs is particularly significant given that both leagues have witnessed enormous salary growth in the last twenty years. The increase in salaries has led some scholars to argue that the major influencing factor in determining a player's decision to migrate is the mercenary desire to secure the greatest financial reward that can be offered by a club (Andreff 2009). Outside of professional sport, such contentions would seem sensible, given that migration often occurs to take advantage of positive wage disparities (Fischer/Reiner/Straubhaar 1997).

Whilst research has shown that the desire to secure the best possible salary must be tempered by a more nuanced interpretation of migrant motivations (see, for example, Maguire 1996; Magee/Sugden, 2002), in both the Premier League and the Bundesliga, it is clear that the numbers of foreign players increased significantly in line with the commercial expansion of both leagues. For example, data show that by the 2008/09 season the number of foreign players playing in the Bundesliga had reached a high of 54%, whilst the number of foreign players peaked in the English Premier League during the 2009/10 season when 59% of players were foreign (Poli/Ravenel/Besson 2009, 2010).

In England the rising number of foreign players has become the source of considerable debate in recent years, perennially within the English media, but also from some of the game's most prominent figures including FIFA President Sepp Blatter, UEFA President Michel Platini, and English Professional Footballers' Association Chief Executive, Gordon Taylor. Indeed, in the 2007 PFA commissioned report entitled 'Meltdown: The nationality of Premier League players and the future of English football', Gordon Taylor concluded that English football was in 'crisis' as a consequence of the numbers of foreign players recruited to ply their trade in the English Premier League (Elliott/Weedon 2010).

These ongoing commentaries, led by the game's senior figures, have predominantly centred on the perceived negative effects of foreign player involvement, and surface when, for example, specific incidents such as the England national team's failure to qualify for the 2008 European Championships, occur. It is argued that the apparent 'feet-drain' (Elliott/Weedon 2010) that is occurring in English football exists where the involvement of foreign players in Premier League teams stifles the development of indigenous talent, taking its place or squeezing it out to the margins of the professional game.

Similar claims have been made in respect of German football where the influx of foreign-born players has been argued to dilute the base of German talent from which the national team could be selected (Merkel 2007). For example, in 2004, Gerhard Mayer-Vorfelder, the then President of the DFB commented: "How can we expect young German forwards to develop in the Bundesliga, if seventy per cent of all forwards are foreign-born" (Brand/Neimann 2006: 131). Mayer-Vorfelder's comments were made with specific reference to the 1995 Bosman Ruling which, along with the commercial transformations that were beginning to gain momentum in England and German football at this time, was instrumental in facilitating the increasing numbers of foreign players that relocated to Europe's core leagues to ply their trade.

The Bosman Ruling resulted in a legal shift that permitted the movement of European footballers as a right and judged that quotas covering EU citizens were "illegal and constituted a restraint of trade" (Maguire 1999: 117). Prior to the Bosman judgement, transfers could only occur if both the selling and purchasing club were in agreement and had set a transfer fee, irrespective of whether the player in question was out-of-contract (Blanpain/Inston 1996). Bosman's case came about as a consequence of his prevented transfer between Belgian club R.C. Liege and French club US Dunkerque. It collapsed because the quota of foreign players at the French club was already full. Bosman argued that the transfer rules imposed by the Belgian Football Association, UEFA, and FIFA disabled the free movement of European workers (Blanpain/Inston 1996; Maguire/Stead 1998). Therefore, in order for these rules to be brought into line with other EU policies on migration, the existing system would have to be amended.

The introduction of the Bosman ruling had major implications for football across Europe. The ruling had rendered illegal any restriction that was based on nationality, such as the 3+2 rule whereby European teams could field 3 foreign and 2 'assimilated players' (players that had played for five consecutive years in a relevant country). In Germany, however, the ruling was liberalised even further. Whereas in most EU nations the right to movement was expanded to all EU passport holding professional footballers, in Germany this was extended to all fifty-one UEFA member states, irrespective of EU membership (Brand/Neimann 2006). In essence this meant that many more foreign players were deemed eligible to play in the Bundesliga than in the professional leagues of other European countries.

The implementation of such liberal policies in respect of foreign player involvement, when coupled with increased salaries derived from greater commercial revenues, resulted in a significant increase in the numbers of foreign players being recruited to Bundesliga teams. Between 1992/93 and 2009/10 the number of foreign players increased from 17% to 51%. For the German national team, such increases inevitably reduced the number of indigenous players available and diluted the overall talent pool (Merkel 2007).

The increases in foreign player numbers observable in the Premier League and the Bundesliga have created similar problems and drawn parallel criticisms. These criticisms are largely focussed on the ways in which the involvement of foreign players stifles opportunities for indigenous talent thus blocking the developmental path of local players, subsequently affecting national team development. The response in England and Germany to these problems has been somewhat different. Indeed, the German response was already being developed and is now held up as a model that the English football authorities should follow. The next part of this chapter examines how the German system was redeveloped.

4   How German football reinvented itself

In 1997 German football was experiencing a period of huge success. Borussia Dortmund won the Champions League, Schalke 04 won the then UEFA Cup (now the Europa League) and the German national team were the champions of Europe, having won the title some twelve months earlier in England at Euro '96. However, all was not well beneath the surface of the German football system. The rapid commercialisation of the Bundesliga, driven largely by increases in television revenues and the subsequent Bosman Ruling, had resulted in the number of foreign players in the league rising significantly since 1992. Behind the scenes, the increasing numbers of foreign imports were already beginning to stifle Germany's home-grown players and, by the end of 1997, the German system found itself starved of talent.

Arguably it was Germany's defeat by Croatia in the quarter-final of the 1998 World Cup that marked the lowest point in German football's recent history. It was at this point that the German authorities realised that something had to be done. In May 1999, DFB Vice President Franz Beckenbauer, Germany national team manager Erich Ribbeck, Bayer Leverkusen General Manager Reiner Calmund and DFB Director of Youth Development Dietrich Weise presented a new concept for producing Germany's future professional footballers.

Implemented in 2002, at grassroots level, the new system included the building of 121 national talent centres that would be used to help develop the technical skills of players aged between 10 and 17. Each of these centres would employ two full-time coaches. At the professional level, a new requirement for all 36 professional clubs in the top two Bundesliga divisions to build youth academies was introduced. Crucially, of the intake that were to be trained within each academy, it was stipulated that 12 players must be eligible to play for the German national team, thus addressing part of the problem presented by the recruitment of foreign players to Bundesliga teams (Honigstein 2010).

Interestingly, the involvement of foreign players was also addressed in another way as the DFB and Bundesliga sought to take advantage of a liberalization of citizenship laws. The increasingly cosmopolitan make-up of the German population meant that a growing number of Germans could be described as being of migrant descent. The DFB recognised this growing cosmopolitanism and took a more proactive approach to integrate young players with a migratory background into the national side. Mesut Özil, Sami Khedira, Piotr Trochowski, Dennis Aogo, and Miroslav Klose are all players who have played in the German national team who can be described as being of migrant descent, either born outside of Germany, or of a migrant parent.

Another mechanism also emerged. However, this mechanism occurred somewhat serendipitously when considered alongside the much more deliberate recruiting strategies that had been implemented in the academies. When the new system was launched in 2002 the percentage of foreign players in the Bundesliga had reached just over 50 per cent (Brand/Neimann 2006). However, the collapse of the KirchMedia TV company proved instrumental in the development of the German game. KirchMedia held the rights to broadcast the Bundesliga and it was the money that had flowed into the league from KirchMedia that had bankrolled it since the early 1990s (Mikos 2006). When the company collapsed in 2002, the Bundesliga clubs were left in severe financial difficulty. Faced with huge, and totally unsustainable wage bills, Bundesliga clubs had no choice but to release many of their foreign players, replacing them with younger, and much cheaper, recruits from their own youth teams. This enforced policy not only injected new home-grown talent into the German football system, but, when combined with the infrastructural legacies of hosting the 2006 World Cup, resulted in increased attendances as fans, who had been put off by the lack of local players playing in Bundesliga teams, suddenly returned to support a new generation of German players in new or renovated stadia (Honigstein 2010).

Finally, the financial regulation and ownership structures that Bundesliga clubs must adhere to should also be considered. Before 2000, all Bundesliga clubs operated as a 'Verein' (member association). However, as a result of commercial pressure and in order to compete with other leagues in Europe, from 2000 clubs could choose one of three governance structures; 1) non-profit (Verein); 2) public football corporation; 3) privately owned firm (Franck 2010). Whilst each structure operated differently one crucial stipulation was introduced to ensure better governance. Therefore, the 50+1 rule was introduced to ensure that the members of Bundesliga clubs retain 51% of control. The only exception to this rule exists where the corporation/owner of a club has substantially funded it continuously for a period of at least 20 years and is likely to continue this support in the future. This form of governance ensures that no individual can own more than 49% of a club, thus protecting it from economic exploitation. It also ensures that the controlling stake in a club is owned by a membership that is likely to have an interest in the national team as well. Therefore, the future of Bundesliga clubs and the national team are more likely to be protected.

The various mechanisms, introduced into the German system, when combined with the collapse of KirchMedia, provide the framework from which German football has been developed in the last decade. Following England's defeat by Germany in the second round of the 2010 World Cup, the German model has been held up as one that English football might wish to replicate. The next part of the chapter explores the differences that exist in the two systems.

5   They think it's all over

Germany's 4-1 victory over England in the second round of the 2010 World Cup in Bloemfontein, South Africa, by a relatively young side marked a remarkable turnaround for the German national team. Whilst Germany would ultimately be unsuccessful in the competition, losing to eventual winners Spain in the semi-finals, the 2010 World Cup represented a watershed moment for the programme of changes that had been implemented some ten years earlier. In England, the reaction to what was considered to be another underperformance was to dissect the strengths of the German system. Indeed, shortly after the match just about every major national newspaper in England printed at least one story that compared the systems at work in England and Germany. The picture that was revealed highlighted the differences that existed.

Arguably, one of the most significant identifiers of Germany's new philosophy was a focus on the development of young players who were eligible to play for the German national team (Jackson 2010). Whilst, until recently, the Bundesliga, like the Premier League, favoured the recruitment of foreign imports over the development of indigenous talent, the various mechanisms implemented since 2000 established a clear change in policy for the Bundesliga and DFB. Youth development systems were designed to give German players every opportunity to progress to professional level and beyond. Therefore, rather than implement UEFA's 'home-grown player rule', where players can qualify as 'home-grown' irrespective of nationality, the German system went further, insisting that academies recruit players who were eligible to play for the German national team, thus maintaining the supply of future internationals. It is no coincidence, therefore, that Germany's 2010 World Cup team was the youngest since 1934 and that Joachim Löw, the German national team coach, had more young players to choose from than any other Germany coach in the last two decades (Honigstein 2010). It is also no coincidence that since 2008, Germany has won the European Championship at U-17, U-19 and U-21 level.

In England the response to increasing numbers of foreign players has been far less defined. Within the country's 41 academies there is no stipulation that the players being recruited should be eligible to play for the national team. Instead the Premier League introduced a variant of UEFA's home-grown player rule for the start of the 2010/11 season which dictates that clubs cannot name more than 17 non home-grown players aged over 21 in a squad of 25. As with UEFA's broader principle regarding home-grown players the crucial difference that exists between the English and German system is that whilst a percentage of the players recruited into German academies must be eligible to play for the German national team, no such stipulation exists in England because home-grown players are not, necessarily, English. Home-grown players are defined, irrespective of nationality, as having been trained by a club of the same national association for a period of three years between the ages of 16 and 21. Whilst the home-grown player rule may assist young players in gaining experience in Premier League senior teams, it is less likely to significantly enhance the numbers of players eligible to play for the England national team.

In addition to the measures applied to develop young players that are eligible to play for the national team, significant also is the broader governance of football in Germany. The 50+1 rule is one signifier of the much stricter regulations that exist in the financing and ownership of Bundesliga clubs relative to their Premier League counterparts (Bond 2010). Premier League clubs are much more likely to be owned by an individual or small group of investors. Increasingly these investors are foreign and criticisms have been made as to whether these new billionaire owners are 'fit and proper' custodians of England's national game. The financial collapse of Portsmouth football club can be used as an example of poor governance that stands in stark contrast to the much more measured approach taken to club ownership in Germany.

The 50+1 rule ensures that clubs are run effectively and with less risk of mismanagement. Corporate interests are controlled by a membership that has a genuine interest (and often historical and social connection) in the club. The Bundesliga clubs, unlike their Premier League counterparts, are not subject to the whims and excesses of what are commonly viewed to be uncaring capitalists. They are also not subject to the ownership decisions of individuals that have no interest in the development of the national team, which is often the case in England. The memberships of Bundesliga clubs are likely to have a much greater interest in the development and success of their national team than single investors. In this respect, recruiting decisions and youth development programmes work in tandem with the national team and not in opposition.

Contributory also to the governance of the Bundesliga clubs and the development of indigenous talent is the league's licensing system. The *Lizenzierungsordnung* regulates the finances of clubs, controlling the levels of debt that each club can carry. It also imposes restrictions on the amount of money clubs can spend on a player's wages, a major issue in the English Premier League. Clubs that fail to comply with the various regulations may have their license withdrawn, meaning that they are not permitted to participate in the Bundesliga. By controlling the finances of clubs, both in terms of debt levels and the salary-cap, Bundesliga clubs are unable to fill their squads with expensive foreign players, relying on their own locally developed players as they had to after the collapse of the KirchMedia company in 2002. These measures ensure that local players are provided with opportunities to gain exposure at first team level.

In England, no such licensing system operates. However, in an attempt to refocus attention on the issue of youth development in the Premier League where clubs often have enormous spending power and are able to buy ready-made foreign imports, the league introduced the Elite Player Performance Plan (EPPP) in 2011. The EPPP was designed to increase the number and quality of 'home-grown' players playing first team football. To do this, all academies in England and Wales were categorized from 1 (being the most elite) to 4 (the least). Different rules were introduced for each category, however, the overall principles were; to create more time for players to be coached; increase the number of coaches; implement a system of quality assurance; improve investment; and seek performance gains in every aspect of player development. Alongside the EPPP the Premier League also introduced a new under-21 league to bridge-the-gap between youth and senior football.

Whilst it is too early to say whether or not the EPPP and the under-21 league will improve the chances for home-grown players gaining places in Premier League first teams, arguably it is unlikely that it will make any substantial difference to the number of local players that qualify to play for the England national team. Unlike the German model where stipulations are made to ensure that players recruited to academies are eligible to play for the national team, the EPPP still relies on UEFA's definition of a home-grown player – thus, home-grown players will not necessarily be English. When coupled with an unregulated ownership system that permits individuals to own Premier League clubs in their entirety and a fractious relationship between the Football Association, the national governing body for football in England, and the Premier League, it is unclear if the England national team will benefit from the new youth development strategies.

6   Conclusion

This chapter has shown that professional football in England and Germany has been subjected to comparable processes of modernisation, and that these processes have affected youth and national team development in similar ways. What the chapter has also shown, however, is that the responses to the increasingly penetrative commercialisation of the game in both countries has been different. In the British media the German model has been held up as one that English football should seek to emulate. It would certainly seem, from this chapter at least, that the German model offers much in terms of a guide to regulation, governance and development.

However, this is not to say that the German system implemented since 2000 is not without criticism. Bundesliga clubs, like their Premier League counterparts, are not immune from financial insecurity and a number, including clubs like Borussia Dortmund, have had to learn to live within their means (Merkel 2006). At the other end of the spectrum some club Presidents have criticised the financial regulations that restrict spending, arguing that many Bundesliga clubs are unable to compete in Europe where greater freedoms exist in club spending. However, it is these regulations that support the development of young German players because Bundesliga clubs are unable to fill their squads with foreign imports. Thus, by the end of the 2010/11 season the number of foreign players contracted to Bundesliga clubs had dropped to 42%, in the Premier League, the number of foreign players was 58% (Poli/Ravenel/Besson 2012).

Whilst the number of foreign players plying their trade in the Premier League remains high and, without greater financial scrutiny, many clubs continue to spend well beyond their means, football in England is in a much better place than it was prior to the introduction of the Premier League some 20 years ago. The improvements that have been made across the sport speak volumes about the investment that has been made. In 20 years the Premier League has emerged to become one of the most watched sports leagues in the world. However, this success stands in contrast to the success of the England national team, who have not won a major tournament since 1966.

There may be something to learn from an analysis of the reinvention of German football since 2000: the focus on youth development with specific attention being paid to those players eligible to play for the national team; the rules in respect of club ownership; and the club licensing system. Each of these interventions has helped to develop the Bundesliga into what is widely regarded as an example of best practice. The Bundesliga may not be as exciting as the Premier League; it may not generate the same revenues or attract the same number of superstar players. What it does appear to be doing, however, is producing a new generation of German players who may, soon, help the German national team to recapture the glories of the past. It is unclear if England's national team is headed in the same direction.

Bibliography

Andreff, W. (2009): The economic effect of 'muscle-drain' in sport. In: Labour Market Migration in European Football: Issues and Challenges. London: Birkbeck Sports Business Centre.

Blanpain, R./Inston, R. (1996): The Bosman Case: The end of the transfer system. London: Sweet and Maxwell.

Bond, D. (2010): Germany's rich pedigree casts long shadow. BBC [online]. Accessed: 16th May 2012.

Brand, A./Niemann, A. (2006): The Europeanization of German football. In: Tomlinson, A. & Young, C. (eds): German Football: History, culture, society. London: Routledge, 127-142.

Conn, D. (1997): The football business. Edinburgh: Mainstream sport.

Deloitte (2012): Annual review of football finance. Deloitte: Manchester.

Elliott, R. (2009, June): A game of two halves?: Foreign players in the English Premier League. Paper presented at *Central Council for Physical Recreation European Summit*, London: England.

Elliott, R. (2012): New Europe, new chances?: The migration of professional footballers to Poland's Ekstraklasa. In: *International Review for the Sociology of Sport*. Sage Online First, 1-16.

Elliott, R./Weedon, G. (2010): Foreign players in the Premier Academy League: 'Feet-Drain' or 'Feet-Exchange'? In: *International Review for the Sociology of Sport*. 46(1), 61-75.

Fischer P. A./Reiner M./Straubhaar T. (1997): Interdependencies Between Development and Migration. In: Hammar, T./Brochmann, G./Tamas, K./Faist, T. (eds): International Migration, Immobility and Development: Multidisciplinary Perspectives. Oxford: Berg, 91-132.

Franck, E. (2010): Private firm, public corporation or member's association governance structures in European football. In: International Journal of Sports Finance, 5(2), 108-127.

Honigstein, R. (2010, July 2nd): How Germany reinvented itself. Sports Illustrated [online]. Accessed: 16th May 2012.

Jackson, J. (2010, July 4th): Germany provide the blueprint for England's Academy system. The Guardian [online]. Accessed: 16th May 2012.

King, A. (2003): The European ritual: Football in the new Europe. Aldershot: Ashgate.

Magee, J./Sugden J. (2002): "The world at their feet": Professional football and international labour migration. In: Journal of Sport and Social Issues 26(4), 421-437.

Maguire, J. (1996): Blade Runners: Canadian Migrants, ice hockey and the global sports process. In: Journal of Sport and Social Issues 21(3), 335-360.

Maguire, J. (1999): Global sport. Cambridge: Polity.

Merkel, U. (2012): Football fans and clubs in Germany: conflicts, crises and compromises. In: Soccer and Society, 13(3), 359-376.

Merkel, U. (2006): The 1974 and 2006 World Cups in Germany: Commonalities, continuities and change. In: Soccer and Society, 7(1), 14-28.

Merkel, U. (2007): Milestones in the development of football fandom in Germany: Global impacts on local contests. In: Soccer and Society, 8(2/3), 221-239.

Mikos, L. (2006): German football – A media-economic survey: the impact of the Kirch-Media company on football and television in Germany. In: Tomlinson, A. &

Young, C. (eds): German Football: History, culture, society. London: Routledge, 143-154.

Poli, R./Ravenel, L./Besson, R. (2009): Annual review of the European football players' labour market. CIES Football Observatory: Neuchatel.

Poli, R./Ravenel, L./Besson, R. (2010): Annual review of the European football players' labour market. CIES Football Observatory: Neuchatel.

Pyta, W. (2006): German football: A cultural history. In: Tomlinson, A. & Young, C. (eds): German Football: History, culture, society. London: Routledge, 1-22.

Walvin, J. (1994): The people's game: A history of football revisited. Edinburgh: Mainstream sport.

English Football Goal Celebrations within a Global Context

Der Torjubel des englischen Fußballs im globalen Kontext

Mark Turner

Abstract

The chapter explores the changing face of football goal celebrations from the 1960s to the present day with particular focus on English Football and its relationship to Europe and the World Cup. Drawing on a range of qualitative library and popular literature such as online newspapers, blogs and DVD footage the chapter critically examines the particular social, cultural and political significance of changes in football goal celebration culture through a series of specific trends and genres. The chapter concludes by offering a tentative theorisation of the current state of play whilst posing critical questions of official goal celebration discourse evident within FIFA and the Football Association's 'laws of the game'.

Zusammenfassung

Der Beitrag untersucht den Wandel des Torjubels von den 1960er Jahren bis heute mit einem besonderen Fokus auf dem englischen Fußball in Bezug auf

Europa und auf Fußball-Weltmeisterschaften. Auf der Grundlage von qualitativen Studien und populärer Literatur wie Online-Zeitungen, Blogs und DVDs analysiert der Artikel kritisch die besondere soziale, kulturelle und politische Bedeutung des Wandels der Torjubelkultur durch die Darstellung spezifischer Trends und Genres. Der Beitrag bietet abschließend eine vorläufige Theoretisierung gegenwärtiger Entwicklungen an und formuliert kritische Fragen zum offiziellen Torjubeldiskurs von FIFA bzw. FA und deren ,Spielregeln'.

1   Introduction

Association football is littered with various significant historical, social, cultural and political moments which are often reflected through a famous goal, result, a controversial refereeing decision, the hosting of an international tournament or the transfer of a player to a rival club. The purpose of this chapter is to capture and critically explore the particular social, cultural and political significance of changes in football culture through an innovative and under researched case study; the football goal celebration.

Every goal scorer whether it be Lionel Messi at the Champions League final, a youth player at Bayern Munich's Säbener Straße academy, a youngster on a local Merseyside playing field or the FIFA computer game's simulacra of Mario Balotelli, faces that moment which occurs directly after the goal is scored. That moment – that celebration or non-celebration – has throughout the history of the game, provided football with some of its most iconic images, some of which incidentally have become more iconic than the goal itself. This chapter will document specific trends and developments over a period of time within the context of English football in particular whilst recognising its relationship with Europe and will consider the cultural influences of goal celebrations performed at various World Cup tournaments.

By drawing on a range of qualitative library, popular literature and electronic research such as online newspapers, blogs, YouTube video uploads and DVD footage, the chapter will provide an initial tentative sociological investigation into the phenomenon of the football goal celebration. This will enable in particular the following question to be posed: what is it about the culture of football and society today, which includes celebrations by the 'robotic' Peter Crouch, the 'dummy-sucking' Carlos Tevez, and the 'shirt statement king' Mario Balotelli, which makes it distinct from those more reserved celebrations of the mid to late twentieth century?

The chapter will begin then by documenting a brief social history of the football goal celebration before turning to a tentative sociological theorisation of the current state of play.

2   The traditional goal celebration

The traditional goal celebration witnessed at the birth of the 1960s was by today's standards very reserved, regardless of how significant the goal scored itself was perceived and often included a 'firm handshake', a 'pat on the back', followed by a 'brisk walk back to the centre circle'. Dorfan (2008) has provided a telling example of the 'traditional' goal celebration, describing the celebration of Helmut Rahn's 1954 World Cup-winning goal for Germany. As he notes, whilst many books have been written about the social, cultural and political significance of Rahn's goal for Germany, specifically regarding the way it "brought them back into the central stream of European culture and provid[ed] a crushed nation with a new identity and sense of pride", the celebration itself was largely reserved: initially "two of Rahn's teammates approached him, with one shaking his hand and the other patting him on the shoulder" before other players embraced him. Here this low-key expression of pleasure was politically conditioned to avoid any fanning of the flames of nationalist hysteria in post-second world war German society.

Meanwhile in England, goals whilst echoing proletarian values of teamwork and solidarity were generally left to speak for themselves, with players preferring to modestly congratulate each other through a 'traditional' gesture. This demonstrated that the goal was perhaps more important for the team, rather than the celebration being important for the individual player and audience. Of course, after every goal is scored in football, the game is restarted from the centre circle; thus players from both teams are required to take up their original positions within each half of the pitch.

What is also intriguing about such 'reserved' and controlled celebrations is how they contrasted with the unalloycd and ecstatic joy of the team's supporters who had just watched one of their players score a goal. When you think of maybe 100,000 or more fans at a Wembley cup final of yesteryear, one now sees almost a paradox in the intensity of the crowd's thunderous roar of triumphal joy and the relative detachment and stiff-upper-lipishness of the players on the field at the heart of the passionate affair.

The 'traditional' goal celebration, then, which a conservative estimate would consider popular up to the mid-1960s, was a product of Fordist modernity (Harvey 1989) in which its reserved universal repetitive style and protestant ethic gesture, signified football as industry. This industrial celebration "largely replicated the rationality and norms of wage-labour" (Morgan in Giulianotti 2004: 175) and thus rather than "being an alternative to labour, it turned out to be just another instance of it". As labour was rationalized to serve the social, cultural and political interests of capitalism (Habermas 1984) so too was the traditional football goal celebration, through an industrial Fordist discourse.

3   The televised celebration is born

1964 saw the birth of Match of the Day, an English football television programme which would, throughout the 60s and 70s, become one of the key ingredients of English football culture. Match of the Day is significant here because it captured the changing face of football in the developing media era and set the context for the relationship between football and popular culture to be screened and experienced by millions.

As televised football grew in popularity throughout the decade, the shaking of the hand and pat on the back slowly started to make way for an accepted raising of the arm and hugging of team mates. This would, however, still occur as players returned to the centre circle. In a game between Tottenham Hotspur and Manchester United in 1965, the third goal, scored by Jimmy Greaves – which gave Tottenham a 3-0 lead – was an individually captivating run and strike. In keeping with the celebration climate of the mid-1960s, Greaves celebrated the goal by returning to the centre circle. However, he demonstrated individuality by raising his arms in the air, as if to acknowledge that it was he who had scored, and was almost mobbed by the rest of his team. This celebration represented the birth of a slow increase in intensity in the way players would show emotion after scoring, and perhaps also in team mates' perceptions of the scorer's importance.

The mid-1960s saw a rise in stardom and football's drama began to take centre stage. Acceleration of this change was indicated during the 1966 FA Cup semi-final between Sheffield Wednesday and Chelsea, when Jim McCalliog scored the winning second goal to put Sheffield Wednesday through to the final against Everton.

After scoring, McCalliog chose not to return to the halfway line, instead running towards the supporters at the side of the pitch and executing a forward roll. This gymnastic expression was a significant moment in the decade that saw the birth of the televised goal celebration, and perhaps represented one way in which sport was slowly moving towards a more modern, mediated, expressive and dramatic spectacle. In an era that saw players gaining in confidence as the maximum wage shackles were removed, goal celebrations were starting to become more individual. Jimmy Hill's new 'football entertainer' now had the potential to make the goal celebration part of this dramatic spectacle.

4 The modern 'organic' celebration

The early 1970s saw an increase in cameras, multiple angles and instant action replays and thus players began to understand that they now played a critical role within the sporting theatre. This acceleration of the modern mediated goal celebration was often seen on Match of the Day, with a number of players running towards supporters behind the goal or at the side of the pitch and often waiting to be congratulated by teammates. Football commentator John Motson noted how during the early 1970s in particular, 'Match of the Day's cameras, were often in the right place at the right time' which nicely captured the new relationship between the modern goal-scoring moment and its audience.

During a fifth-round FA Cup tie between Colchester United and Leeds United in 1971, David Simmons, after scoring the third Colchester goal to knock Leeds out of the competition, celebrated the goal by running towards the crowd behind the goal before turning and leaning his back into them, thus allowing the crowd to grab hold of him. Other significant celebrations during the 1970s included Charlie George's 'lying down on the ground and waiting for his teammates to approach and acknowledge him' after scoring for Arsenal against Liverpool in the 1971 FA Cup final, and Francis Lee's 'big grin' at scoring for Derby County against his former club Manchester City at Maine Road in 1975 which led commentator Barry Davies to proclaim, "Just look at his face, just look at his face", as Lee ran towards the camera. Davies was highlighting that the stage had been set for Lee to score, the script indicated that he had scored, and thus the audience should now watch what happened next – in other words, heightening the significance of his goal celebration.

Interestingly, the media also thought it newsworthy that Denis Law did not celebrate after scoring a significant goal for Manchester City against his old club Manchester United, thus imbuing this lack of celebration, or sadness at having scored against a club he dearly loved, with significance through media discourse.

As football was slowly adapting from its industrial roots to more elaborative entertaining spectacle, goals too were involved in this change, particularly through the introduction of Match of the Day's popular 'Goal of the Month' competition. Goals were being scored regularly by football's new superstars and entertainers and thus players were often given heroic names by supporters and the media –

such as 'Super Mac', the moniker bestowed upon Newcastle United's Malcolm McDonald. As a result, celebrations would often represent this with, for example, 'Super Mac' running with both arms aloft as if flying, in order to acknowledge his individual comic hero status, whilst Mick Channon would regularly celebrate scoring a goal for Manchester City by whirling his arm around like the Who guitarist Pete Townshend.

It is important to recognize, however, that although goal celebrations were now becoming more iconic, in many cases – in a similar way to streaking at sporting events – they were produced "by the occasion and the event" (Mcdonald/Carrington 2007: 15) rather than purely by the individual. In a sense, then, there was still something rather 'organic' about the modern goal celebration throughout the 1970s and 1980s, with the celebration often occurring because the developing football drama demanded it.

From Bob Latchford's 1975 celebration in which he ran intensely down the touchline after scoring for Everton against Derby Country to Trevor Francis' falling on his knees with his head in his hands after scoring for Birmingham City against Burnley in the same year, these celebrations, while breaking from the traditional capitalist factory style and slowly becoming more individual would often express the crowd's relationship to the event. Through the increasing Europeanization and influence of Brazilian futebol, football had become more carnivalesque (Bakhtin 1984) and terrace fan culture would, through the scoring of a goal, come to celebrate itself.

5   The post-Fordist celebration

1981 saw the birth of shirt advertisement, which subsequently became an accepted part of football culture in the United Kingdom. At the same time, the introduction of 'live' football represented an opportunity for advertising to be commodified and consumed. As football clubs were becoming commodified through the new economics of signs and space (Lash/Urry in King 1998) the development of post-Fordist 'live' football provided the opportunity for goal-scorers to advertise the latest products on the market through close-up camera angles. Raising the arm or 'running into the crowd' were no longer the only signs witnessed, and thus the audience of the goal celebration became the audience of post-Fordist and Thatcherite ideology.

The populist law agenda particularly with regard to the problem of football hooliganism and terrace culture throughout the 1980s meant that goal celebrations had to be relatively controlled for fear of being interpreted as part of that same culture. This was clearly evident during Clive Allen's 'jogging on the spot' celebration after scoring for QPR against West Bromwich Albion during an FA Cup semi-final at Highbury in 1982. Allen's celebration, which was directed at the crowd behind the goal, was greeted by police officers patrolling the edge of the stand. Whilst police presence itself wasn't anything new at football matches, the agenda of controlling the crowd to prevent supporters running on the pitch to celebrate with the goal scorer accelerated.

Players and supporters were now realizing that the goal celebration was, to a certain extent, subject to the same conditions of social control, in a climate which perceived the lawlessness and hedonism of the crowd as something that needed curtailing and criminalizing (Mcdonald/Carrington 2007: 17). While the relationship between the football goal celebration and the football authorities intensified throughout the late 1980s and early 1990s, there had been previous examples of law and order issues surrounding specific celebrations – those involving 'mooning' – throughout the 1970s; to some extent, these set the tone for the cultural politics of the 1980s and early 1990s.

Steve Curry, a UK sports journalist, provided a brief history of the 'cheeky' goal celebration, which discussed the famous case of Terry Mancini baring his bottom at QPR chairman Jim Gregory in 1974. Curry notes how Gregory's blocking a proposed move which would have seen Mancini move to Arsenal led the footballer to celebrate a goal and victory by running in front of the directors' box before dropping his shorts. Mancini was later transferred and was given a two-match ban and a £150 fine by the FA for what they found to be an obscene act. Curry adds that five years later, Sammy Nelson, Arsenal's left back, had been the subject of taunts from fans at the North Bank end after scoring an own goal in front of the home crowd. After scoring the equalizer in the second half, Nelson bared his Y-fronts to the fans which resulted in a two-week FA suspension and a fine of two weeks' wages by his club (Curry 2007).

These celebrations captured the way in which society was transforming from old to new, with traditional, conservative, reverential values making way for more rebellious and assertive cultural forms. A telling example of this came in an FA Cup semi-final between Wimbledon and Luton in 1988, where after scoring a goal for Wimbledon John Fashanu was approached by Dennis Wise. Fashanu picked up Wise, who then, while wrapping his legs around the goal scorer, kissed him on the lips. The goal celebration was becoming a "laboratory for masculine style and a place for the display of its 'confusions and contradictions' as well as a location for the reinforcement of its 'traditional' forms" (Russell in Armstrong/Giulianotti 1999: 17).

6   Commodifying and commercializing the goal celebration

Harvey (1989) offers a telling discussion of the opposing tendencies of Fordist modernity and flexible postmodernity, noting specifically how, during flexible postmodernity, an increase in individualism has replaced the influence of trade unions and group solidarity. The playfulness and individual artistry of postmodern goal celebration is often placed on centre stage by teammates, who will often stand back and allow the individualism of the star goal scorer to shine through the celebration, before congratulating them. Alternatively, they often become part of the actual celebration themselves, through the choreographing and pre-rehearsed planning of the celebration before the game or during training.

Kane (2006) suggests that the 'new' generation of footballers after 1992, "shaped by MTV and digital culture, will necessarily have a less 'dignified', more fluid approach to the boundaries and regulations of sport". What concerns Kane is the idea that these 'new' players do not submit to "arbitrary authority, as was once expected in the factory, the school or barracks", and "rather are shaped by music, fashion, dance culture and movies". Perhaps the most significant point noted here is that "among the young football fans he knows, the post-goal celebrations, or mid game tricks of their favourite stars, are as significant as their functionality to the team", and thus motivates him to question whether "this is in fact football, or cabaret?"

There is a suggestion, then, that throughout the 1990s a 'new' goal celebration culture developed specifically through the rise of new media technology, such as satellite and interactive television, computer games and the internet. In many current cases, goal celebrations then act as a fashionable accessory and signature of the postmodern goal scorer.

Kellner's Debordian theorization of the spectacle is appropriate here, because it allows us to understand postmodern creative goal celebration as a symbolic reflection of the football spectacle's commodity form (Tomlinson 2002). The creativity and individualism of celebrations during this phase serve to celebrate the "society of the spectacle, and its dominant values, products and corporations through their unholy alliance with sports celebrity, commercialisation and the media spectacle" (Kellner 2001: 39). The postmodern goal celebration in the current phase has then become image conscious and a product ready to be advertised. Carlsberg have realized this market for advertisement, creating an advert that includes a choreographed goal celebration to fit with its own advertisement slogan, whilst Coca Cola used Roger Milla's famous Cameroon 'corner flag dance' as part of its 2010 South Africa World Cup advertisement.

Additionally, the table football game Subbuteo has recently created models of 'famous' footballers signified by their goal celebration, an example of which is Alan Shearer's retro homage to the old fashioned raising of one arm.

Simon Hattenstone (2006) of the British Guardian newspaper has noted how, during creative modernity, the goal celebration – as all stories – has several basic plots. I hereby draw on some of his ideas and categories, which allow me to develop and document a series of cases as a way of offering a tentative theorization.

6.1 The acrobat

During the mid-1990s, Peter Beagrie of Everton and Manchester City would often celebrate a goal by performing a well-executed summersault (Fletcher 2002). Robbie Keane of Tottenham Hotspur regularly celebrated with a cartwheel and forward roll followed by an "invisible arrow fired at an invisible enemy" (Hattenstone 2006). Julius Aghahowa perhaps performed the most impressive acrobatic celebration after scoring a goal for Nigeria against Sweden at the 2002 World Cup in Japan, running on in ecstasy and performing no less than six forward somersaults. Manchester United's Portuguese international Nani regularly executes four or five somersaults after scoring.

6.2 The pole dancer

The original pole-dancing celebration on the global stage which "created several pulsating moments of limbo hip-jiggling" (Fletcher 2002) was "choreographed by Cameroon's Roger Milla at the 1990 World Cup in Italy". Hattenstone (2006) offers an elaborate analysis, noting how Milla's goals in 1990 were "celebrated by dirty dancing the corner flag with supreme lubricity".

Dorfan (2008) has suggested that Milla created a heritage in which the corner flag, during creative modernity, has often become the site for playful and artisan goal celebrations. In the 1990s, former Manchester United winger Lee Sharpe would often "celebrate by making his way towards the nearest corner flag and pretending to use it as a microphone, before treating his adoring public to a quick rendition of an Elvis tune" (Fletcher 2002). Tim Cahill recently of Everton, often celebrated scoring a goal by running towards the corner flag before using it as a punch bag, showing off his boxing skills to the audience.

6.3   The thespian

Football is flooded with "unrequited mime artists" (Hattenstone 2006) and co-
medians, and in creative modernity the goal celebration has often been a site for
dramatic performance. During the USA World Cup in 1994, the Brazilian striker
Bebeto, after being joined by teammates Romario and Rai, performed a 'cradle
rocking movement' towards the audience and cameras, in "honour of Bebeto's
newborn son" (Dorfan 2008). The legacy of this celebration is that it has been cop-
ied by hundreds of players all over the world, from Premiership stars to teenagers
playing in Sunday junior leagues.

Leicester City's Jermaine Beckford regularly celebrates by imitating throwing a
basketball into a hoop, whilst former Palermo player Mark Bresciano would regularly freeze and mimic a statue. Bafetimbi Gomis of Lyon often celebrates scoring
a goal by imitating a panther, whilst Bologna's Alberto Gilardino often pretends
to play a violin on one knee.

6.4   The egotist

Former Brazilian international Ronaldo and French international Robert Pires
would regularly celebrate scoring a goal by jogging towards supporters and the
camera, waving their right index finger in an "I told you so" fashion. In David
Beckham's mid-1990s Manchester United days he was often the butt of abuse
from rival supporters, particularly through taunts about his famous pop star wife.
Once after he scored against Chelsea at Stamford Bridge, which was "particularly
vicious in its taunts" (Dorfan 2008) Beckham "cupped his ear with his hand to
celebrate the silence in the stadium". Beckham was also the creative architect of
other egotistical celebrations, particularly the way he celebrated goals by spread-
ing his arms out wide by his sides as he ran to supporters in a Christ-like pose.

Steven Gerrard of Liverpool has often invoked the self-referential aspect of creative modernity, running towards rival supporters whilst pointing to his name
on the back of his shirt, as if to egotistically point out "don't forget my name".
However, perhaps the strongest example of the egotist was Manchester United's
Eric Cantona, who, after scoring a famous goal against Sunderland at Old Trafford, stood with his "chest puffed out, arms aloft and collar up', as if to say 'adore
me, I am the resurrection" (Hattenstone 2006). After scoring goals for Manchester
United, Cantona would often wait for his teammates to jump on him, and then
"emerge from the celebration, with a simple straightening of his collar" (Dorfan
2008).

6.5   The ecstatic

Perhaps the most poignant ecstatic goal celebration was Marco Tardelli's "running to nowhere" celebration after scoring the World Cup winner for Italy in 1982 (Hattenstone 2006). Murray (2007) notes how the "enormity of what Tardelli had just achieved took a couple of seconds to hit home". He started running with his "arms stretched out, his eyes wide with wonder then as his head shook and the tears began to flow, he broke into a lunatic semi-circular sprint towards the Italian bench".

Former Georgian star Temuri Ketsbaia after coming on as a substitute for Newcastle United against Bolton Wanderers in 1998 and scoring the winning goal, "raced behind the goal, flung his shirt into the crowd, thought better before taking his shorts off, made an abortive attempt to remove his boots, before violently hooting the pitch-side advertisement boards" (Murray 2007). Ryan Giggs celebrated scoring a late important goal for Manchester United against Arsenal during an FA Cup semi-final in 1999 by sprinting wildly and ecstatically "twirling his top around his head" (Hattenstone 2006) while after scoring a goal for Real Madrid, injury-cursed Jonathan Woodgate celebrated by ecstatically jumping into the arms of Madrid's club doctor (Hattenstone 2006).

6.6   The ironic

After scoring a goal for Argentina against Greece at the 1994 World Cup, Diego Maradona ran towards the side of the pitch and, putting his face right in front of a TV cameraman, screamed as if he were on drugs. The ironic aspect of this celebration was that later in the tournament Maradona was banned for failing a drugs test. Craig Bellamy, after finding himself in a media storm before Liverpool's Champions League match with Barcelona at the Nou Camp in 2007 over reports that he had hit teammate John Arne Riise with a golf club, celebrated scoring by mimicking a golf swing (Brown 2008) producing an ironic and humorous response.

After scoring a great individual goal for England against Scotland during Euro '96, Paul Gascoigne reacted to newspaper reports and photographs of him and fellow England players enjoying a drunken night out in the build-up to the tournament by running to the side of the goal and lying down on the floor, ironically recreating the 'dentist chair' photograph by allowing teammates to spray his mouth with water from a bottle. During the 1990s Jürgen Klinsmann would regularly celebrate scoring a goal for Tottenham Hotspur by performing an "ironic dive as a tribute to himself" (Hattenstone 2006) after arriving in England with a "tainted reputation for being a diver and conning referees into giving free kicks" (Smith 2008). Perhaps one of the most striking examples of the ironic creative goal celebration was Robbie Fowler's celebration after scoring for Liverpool against Everton during a Merseyside derby in the late 1990s. In response to rumours around the city and on internet chat rooms suggesting that Fowler was a cocaine addict, he ironically pretended to 'sniff the line' at the side of the goal in front of the Everton supporters.

6.7   The political

After scoring a goal against Real Zaragoza for Barcelona in 2005, Samuel Eto'o, who had been the subject of racial discrimination in the form of 'monkey' chanting, celebrated scoring a goal by "running a few metres in front of the Zaragoza supporters and . . . jumping up and down, grunting like an ape" (Hawkey 2006). Later that year, during a match between Real Madrid and Barcelona at the Bernabeu, Eto'o once again faced racial discrimination, to which he responded with the 1968 Black Power salute (ibid). In Italy, Paolo Di Canio, after returning to Lazio from England, often celebrated goals "the way he loved to – with a fascist salute" (Dorfan 2008), while in an ideological contrast, Christiano Lucarelli once of Parma often used the goal celebration as a site for his 'clenched fist' salute of Communism.

Tim Cahill created controversy when he celebrated scoring a goal for Everton against Portsmouth in 2008 by running towards the corner flag with "one wrist placed over the other as if in handcuffs" (Edwards 2008). This celebration was dedicated to Cahill's brother, who was serving a six-year prison sentence "for an attack on a man which left him partially blinded". In England there has recently been a "trend for players, including Birmingham City's Curtis Davies and Queens Park Rangers' Andrew Johnson, to make the sign of the letter A with their fingers", which is now "widely recognised as an advertisement for a football development school for underprivileged children" (Smith 2008).

6.8   The propped

In recent years the creative modern goal celebration has in some cases included the introduction of props. Former Fulham centre-forward Facundo Sava regularly celebrated scoring a goal by pulling a face mask from his sock and putting it on as he ran towards the supporters. The 'mask of Zorro' celebration was so eagerly received by fans in Sava's home country of Argentina that "they would often send in their own masks for him to use" (Burnton 2002).

One of the more recent goal celebration cases occurred in the English Premier League, with former Manchester United striker Carlos Tevez introducing a child's dummy to the audience. After scoring a goal against Birmingham on New Year's Day in 2008, Tevez "removed an unused baby's pacifier from his shorts before putting it in his mouth and sucking on it" (Smith 2008). Tevez, now of Manchester City, has since taken this propped celebration further by removing his shin pad with his daughters name printed on it as a tribute, after scoring a hat trick against Wigan Athletic in 2010.

6.9   The 'trend'

As a creative industry, Twitter nicely captures the relationship between the acceleration of late modernity and the technological advancement inherent within global capitalism. This stylised platform has inevitably penetrated the world of football and is going to pose new research opportunities and challenges for sports academics across the board. The development of social media networks such as Twitter, contain examples of Virilio's 'city of the instant' space whereby technology and sport are experienced at the 'speed of light'. This instantaneousness then has implications for the way in which goal celebrations are now packaged and discussed by fans across new media platforms. One way in which Twitter represents this instantaneousness is through its 'trending' feature. In other words, the most popular topics being discussed are highlighted as those #'trending' on the web.

After scoring a vital goal for Manchester City FC in the Manchester Derby on the 23rd October 2011, Mario Balotelli celebrated by placing his shirt over his head before revealing a hidden shirt which conveyed the following message; "why always me?" What this celebration then became was a city of the instant 'trend' on Twitter. Other examples of goal celebration 'trends' were Mario Balotelli's shirtless 'macho pose' after scoring for Italy against Germany during the semi-final of Euro 2012. Incidentally, in keeping with sport's hyper commodified nature this celebration is now performed by the virtual Mario Balotelli on the new FIFA 13 simulated football computer game.

7   Towards a tentative theorisation

Against the background of the above-mentioned specific cases and genres, which represent the accelerating creative modern climate, the chapter now turns towards a tentative theorisation of the current cultural state of play. Tentative is appropriate here because it is not the purpose of the chapter to advocate postmodernity in a crude essentialist fashion. Rather the ambiguous problematic nature of the term 'postmodern' perhaps does capture best these particular stylised ironic comments on modernity.

The acceleration of what Redhead (2004) refers to as creative modernity and the particular development of goal celebrations as a site of "individualised self-realisation, through the embracing of anti-authoritarian gestures, iconoclastic habits and the critique of everyday life" (Harvey 1989: 38) have produced those very acrobatic, thespian, pole-dancing, egotistical, ironic and political performances.

Guilianotti (2005: 179) noted that "postmodern culture is marked by eclecticism and pastiche, where barriers between cultural styles and artistic movements, or systems of identity break down". Goal celebrations which best represents this culture break down or blur the boundaries between 'high' and 'low' art. Individual goal scorers have then "shifted their interest from a concern with the ultimate ends of scoring a goal and restarting the game as soon as possible, to a pragmatic concern relating to the optimal performance of celebration" (Rojek 1995: 133). The role of the temporary contract is also appropriate here whereby the accelerated migration of players on short-term contracts in the post-Bosman period acts perhaps as a microcosm of the temporary nature of those celebrations deemed in fashion with football supporters each weekend.

Whilst Peter Crouch's 'robotic' goal celebration for England at the 2006 World Cup was probably more of a "riposte to critics who first jeered and then sneered that he was a stiff, robotic sort of player" (Barkham 2006) it does nicely capture the paradoxical relationship between the modern and late modern mechanical mind and action, and perhaps acts as an example of Baudrillard's vision of the social world being a world in which the real has given way to simulations, codes and hyperreality (Smart 2000).

As football goal celebrations have become more experimental and playful, there has been a modernist authoritarian reaction to them. These choreographed artistic performances are often viewed as a threat to productivity and a form of time wasting. One interesting example was the case of Aylesbury United and their 1995 FA Cup celebration, which included the whole team forming a line before getting down on their knees and waddling along the pitch pretending to be ducks. This particular celebration, it could be argued, set the context for modernist control in other words, as celebrations became more artistic and performative they were deemed to be less productive (in the traditional sense), where the quiet return to the centre circle is now threatened by potential excessive acts of time-wasting.

8   Can we have our 'normal' goal celebrations back please?

In 2004, FIFA's clarification of Law 12 led to the introduction of a yellow card for players who removed their jersey after scoring a goal. Throughout the 1980s, it was often seen as unsportsmanlike behaviour for a player to remove their jersey when celebrating but this clarification now made it punishable. Under the section 'additional instructions for referees and assistant referees', the laws stated: "removing one's shirt after scoring is unnecessary and players should avoid such excessive displays of joy". Thus the implementation of Law 12 acts as a modernist measure by which FIFA and the FA are able to "legitimize their universal power" (Giulianotti 2005: 174).

Additionally in England, the Football Association's Laws of the Game handbook for 2012/2013 dedicate a specific section to goal celebrations in 'Law 12: fouls and misconduct', which states that "whilst it is permissible for a player to demonstrate his joy when a goal has been scored, the celebration must not be excessive". Reasonable celebrations are allowed, but the practice of choreographed celebrations is not to be encouraged when it results in excessive time-wasting and referees are instructed to intervene in such cases. A player must be cautioned if:

1. In the opinion of the referee, he makes gestures which are provocative, derisory or inflammatory
2. He climbs on to a perimeter fence to celebrate a goal being scored
3. He removes his shirt or covers his head with his shirt
4. He covers his head or face with a mask or other similar item

Today's goal celebrations then offer the goal scorer a Derridean opportunity of "decentring authorial control" through the establishment of a "more creative, experimental and autonomous play role". Furthermore, this celebration becomes a performance art "facilitating performer creativity and interaction of difference" with the audience (Giulianotti 2005: 174).

Perhaps what FIFA and the FA really fear from those provocative gestures and the 'running into the crowd' is a return to the 'dramatic' football theatre in which the collective participatory experience of the terraces, through the goal scorer's incitement of the crowd, comes to regularly replace the 'epic' football theatre and often passive experience created by new English football all-seater stadia, particularly at the top end of the game. Furthermore, perhaps the real discourse of Law 12 is a craving for a return to the hyper-masculine and safe heterosexual nature of the mechanically conservative "brisk walk back to the centre circle" and thus a marginalization of today's often contradictory and sometimes homoerotic celebrations.

9   Conclusion

As this global football entertainment spectacle continues to grow, it is not yet clear which direction these celebrations will take. Some observers may crave for a return to the traditional, some to the organic, while others will see such postmodern dummy-sucking as a commitment to the 'decentring' of football (Rojek 1995: 192). Where players continue to become increasingly self conscious an opportunity arises for them to engage more critically with the spectacle and through a Brechtian multilayered process of self reflection (Jameson 1998) to further transform the prescriptive nature of the goal celebration into the performative, whilst 'alienating, interrupting, and making strange' the critical relationship between players and audience.

One thing is for certain. The art of scoring a goal remains the same and perhaps the most critical ingredient of the football spectacle. The celebration of that art, however, is a wonderfully fluid, dynamic and ever changing phenomenon which often responds to various social, cultural and political processes.

Notes

This is an amended updated book chapter of a previous journal paper published in Soccer and Society (Turner 2012).

Bibliography

Bakhtin, M. (1984): Rabelais and his World. Bloomington: Indiana University Press.
Baudrillard, J. (1994): Simulacra and Simulation. Michigan: The University of Michigan Press.

Barkham, P. (2006, June 1st): C'mon everybody . . . Let's do the Crouch!. The Guardian [online]. Accessed: August 1st 2008.

BBC (2004): Match of the Day: The Best of the 60s, 70s and 80s. DVD: BBC Worldwide.

Brown, O. (2008, March 3rd): Top 10 Memorable Goal Celebrations. The Telegraph [online]. Accessed: August 1st 2008.

Burnton, S. (2002, October 7th): Fulham March On, as Charlton Fail to Keep the Wolf from the Door. The Guardian [online]. Accessed: August 1st 2008.

Curry, S. (2007, November 6th): Over the Moon-ing: A Brief History of the Cheeky Goal Celebration. The Daily Mail [online]. Accessed: August 1st 2008.

Debord, G. (1967): The Society of the Spectacle. London: Rebel Press.

Dorfan, R. (2008): The foot that rocks the cradle. Haaretz Daily [online]. Accessed: August 1st 2008.

Edwards, J. (2008): Has Everton's Tim Cahill taken the art of goal celebration too far?. The Daily Mail [online]. Accessed: August 1st 2008.

FIFA (2012): Laws of the Game [online]. Accessed: August 1st 2008.

Fletcher, P. (2002): Celebrating in Style. Funny Old Game, BBC Sport [online]. Accessed: August 1st 2008.

Football Association (2012): Laws of the Game [online]. Accessed: August 1st 2008.

Giulianotti, R. (1999): Football: A Sociology of the Global Game. Cambridge: Polity Press.

Giulianotti, R. (2004): Sport and Modern Social Theorists. Hampshire: Palgrave Macmillan.

Giulianotti, R. (2005): Sport: A Critical Sociology. Cambridge: Polity Press, 2005.

Habermas, J. (1984): The Theory of Communicative Action. Volume one: Reason and the Rationalization of Society. Boston: Beacon Press.

Harvey, D. (1989): The Condition of Postmodernity. Oxford: Basil Blackwell.

Hattenstone, S. (2006, November 22nd): Bravo Bernardo, from Duffer to Dubber. The Guardian [online]. Accessed: August 1st 2008.

Hawkey, I. (2008, May 15th): Eto's kicking out. Times [Online]. Accessed: August 1st 2008.

Horne, J./Tomlinson A./Whannel, G. (1999): Understanding Sport: An Introduction to the Sociological and Cultural Analysis of Sport. London and New York: Spon Press.

Huyssen, A. (1999): Whither Postmodernism. In: Lemert, C. (ed): Social Theory, The Multicultural and Classic Readings. Oxford and Colorado: Westview Press, 505-509.

Jameson, F. (1998): Brecht and Method. London and New York: Verso.

Kane, P. (2006, July 18th): Let football eat itself. The Guardian [online]. Accessed: August 1st 2008.

Kellner, D. (2001): The Sports Spectacle. Michael Jordan and Nike, Unholy Alliance? In: Andrews, D. (ed): Michael Jordan, Inc. Corporate Sport, Media Culture and Late Modern America, Albany: State University of New York Press, 63-64.

Keyes, D. (2007, May 1st): Culture of Soccer: Blog [online]. Accessed: August 1st 2008.

Lash, S./Urry, J. (1994): Economies of Signs and Space. London: Sage.

Lyotard, J. F. (1984): The Postmodern Condition. Manchester: Manchester University Press.

Mcdonald, I./Carrington, B. (2007): The Ontological Impossibility of the Black Streaker: Towards a Sociology of Streaking. Unpublished paper submitted to the American Sociological Association Annual Conference, New York.

Morgan, W. J. (2004): Habermas on Sports: Social Theory from a Moral Perspective. In: Giulianotti, R. (ed): Sport and Modern Social Theorists. Hampshire: Palgrave, 173-186.

Murray, S. (2007, December 14th): The Joy of Six: Goal Celebrations. The Guardian [online]. Accessed: August 1st 2008.

Porter, D. (2004): "Your Boys Took One Hell of a Beating!": English Football and British Decline, c.1950-80. In: Smith, A./Porter, D. (eds): Sport and National Identity in the Post-War World. London: Routledge, 31-51.

Redhead, S. (2004): Creative Modernity: the New Cultural State. In: Media International Australia incorporating Culture and Policy, 112, 9–27.

Rojek, C. (1995): Decentring Leisure: Rethinking Leisure Theory. London: Sage Publications.

Russell, D. (1999): Associating with Football: Social Identity in England 1863-1998. In: Armstrong, G./Giulianotti, R. (eds): Football Cultures and Identities. Hampshire: Macmillan Press, 21-22.

Smart, B. (2000): Postmodern Social Theory. In: Turner, B. (ed): The Blackwell Companion to Social Theory. Oxford: Blackwell, 447-480.

Smith, G. (2008, January 5th): After Carlos Tevez's Dummy, Goal Celebrations may go Potty. The Times [online]. Accessed: August 1st 2008.

Smith, L. (2008, March 7th): Handcuffs, Cocaine and Robots – the Art of the Goal Celebration. Birmingham Post [online]. Accessed: August 1st 2008.

Tomlinson, A. (2002): Theorising Spectacle. In: Sugden, J./Tomlinson, A. (eds): Power Games: A Critical Sociology of Sport, London and New York: Routledge, 44-60.

Whannel, G. (1986): The Unholy Alliance: Notes on Television and the Re-making of British Sport. Leisure Studies, 5, 129–45.

Profifußball und Nationalität im Netz der Bilder – das Beispiel der Europameisterschaft 2012 im Spiegel deutscher und englischer Printmedien

Professional Football and Nationality in the Mesh of Images – The Example of the European Championships 2012 as Mirrored in German and English Print Media

York Kautt

Zusammenfassung

Der Beitrag behandelt die Frage, welche Bedeutung Bildern unter Bedingungen technischer Bildmedien für die Konstruktion nationaler Identitäten im Profifußball zukommt. Ausgangspunkt ist die einführend erörterte Überlegung, dass sozial konstruierte Vorstellungen vom Nationalen in der Gegenwartsgesellschaft als Apriori und sinnhafter Bezugsrahmen transnationaler Wettkämpfe fungieren. Die im Mittelpunkt stehende Analyse der (Bild-)Berichterstattung englischer und deutscher Printmedien zur Europameisterschaft 2012 identifiziert neben und mit bestimmten Zeichen und Symbolen Nähe und Präsenz, Gedächtnis, Emotionalisierungen sowie die Allegorie der

Gemeinschaft als zentrale Dimensionen der visuellen Arbeit am Nationalen. Nicht zuletzt wird ersichtlich gemacht, wie Bilder in die rituelle (achtungskommunikative) Ordnung des Wettkampfs der Nationen eingebunden werden. Im Ergebnis kann dem Medium des Bildlichen ein sehr großes, transnational gegebenes Potential für die Herstellung von Gemeinschaftsvorstellungen zugesprochen werden.

Abstract

This essay will look at the question concerning the importance attributable to images under the conditions determined by technological visual media for the construction of national identities in professional football. The starting point is the idea, which is being addressed in the introductory remarks, that socially constructed notions of national identity in present-day society operate a priori and within a meaningful referential framework of transnational contests. The analysis of the (visual) reporting of English and German print media on the 2012 European Championships which forms the main body of the essay will identify, alongside and together with specific signs and symbols, how proximity and presence, memory, emotionalizations as well as the allegory of community form the central dimensions in the visual construction of national identity. It will also become evident how images are being woven into the ritualistic and recognition-transmitting order of national contests. In conclusion, a very large transnationally available potential for the production of collective ideas can be attributed to the medium of images.

1 Einleitung

Vorliegender Beitrag setzt sich mit der Frage auseinander, inwiefern massenmedial kommunizierte Bilder an den Bedeutungskonstruktionen von Fußball und Nationalität und deren Beziehung zueinander beteiligt sind. Die Bildberichterstattung während der Fußballeuropameisterschaft 2012 zu dem englischen und dem deutschen Team in den Printmedien *The Sun*, *The Guardian*, *Bild* und *Die Süddeutsche* fungiert hierfür als exemplarischer Untersuchungsgegenstand. Zunächst aber soll mit einigen kursorischen Überlegungen zum Zusammenhang von Gesellschaft, Fußball und Nation die spezifische Reichweite dieser Fragestellung deutlich gemacht werden.

Bekanntlich erfreut sich Fußball auch jenseits nationaler Bezüge einer großen Beliebtheit: Allerorten wird gebolzt, in Amateur- und Profiligen Fußball gespielt, ohne dass die Nation ein Thema wäre. Nationalität *kann*, muss aber keine Dimension dieser Sportart sein. Sie wird zu einer solchen, wenn Wettkämpfe entsprechend organisiert werden. Zu dem engeren Spielrahmen des Fußballs mit seinen zahlreichen Regeln gesellt sich dann der Wettkampf der Nationen. Die Beziehungen zwischen Fußball, Sportberichterstattung und Nationalität ergeben sich also nicht aus dem Spiel selbst. Sie sind vielmehr mit historischen Prozessen der Entwicklung von Nationalstaatlichkeit verbunden. Nur dann, wenn Nationalstaaten neben und mit ihren auf Territorien bezogenen politischen Regimens als Angebote der Herstellung kollektiver Identitäten zur Verfügung stehen, kann Sport als kultureller Stellvertreter des Nationalen in Erscheinung treten[1]. Während die Gründe für die Entstehung von Nationalstaaten hier weniger von Belang sind[2], ist es umso wichtiger darauf hinzuweisen, dass Fußball als Teil einer sozialen Imagination von Staatlichkeit und eines darauf bezogenen kollektiven Gedächtnisses angenommen werden kann. Fußball ist ein integraler Bestandteil von ‚imagined communities‘ (Anderson 1983), die auf verschiedenen Mythen, Narrationen und Bildern gründen. Und das heißt auch: Das kollektive ‚Wir‘ der Nation kann im Fußball angerufen werden, weil es als Vorstellung neben anderen Identitäts-Rahmen (z.B. des Fußballvereins) bereits existiert. Bei Großereignissen wie Fußballeuropameisterschaften weiß man bereits im Vorlauf, dass bei dieser Gelegenheit Alltagstheorien, Klischees und Stereotypen bedient werden. Dabei ist kaum zu überhören, dass sich die Anrufung der Nation bei den Spielen sogenannter Nationalmannschaften (national teams) in Fußballstadien, Fanmeilen, Kneipen, Gartenlauben und Wohnzimmern besonders laut ereignet. Von transnationalen Krisen und Konflikten abgesehen (von Finanzkrisen bis hin zu kriegerischen Auseinandersetzungen) tritt Nation als Bezugsrahmen identitärer Zuschreibungen in verschiedenen Weltregionen kaum jemals so stark hervor wie bei Fußballgroßereignissen.

---

1 Dass moderne (funktional differenzierte) Gesellschaften keine repräsentative Kultur (mehr) aufweisen, die symbolisch für das ‚Ganze‘ der Gesellschaft steht, sondern vielmehr vom Prinzip der kulturellen Stellvertretung zu sprechen sei, betont Weiß (1997). Zum Problem wird dieser Sachverhalt wohl auch und gerade im Rahmen von Nationalsemantiken, die ja alle Mitglieder einer Nation inkludieren müssten – was offensichtlich nicht nur die Debatten um nationale „Leitkulturen", sondern auch die niederschwelligeren (nationalen) Fußballkulturen nicht zu leisten vermögen.

2 Zur Rekonstruktion der sich seit dem 18. Jahrhundert als eine spezifisch moderne Ausprägung des Politischen entwickelnden Nationalstaaten im Blick auf verschiedene mediale, soziokulturelle und gesellschaftliche Entwicklungen vgl. z.B. Eisenstadt 1991, Bendix 1991 und Luhmann 1997: 1045-1055.

Folgt man differenzierungstheoretischen Überlegungen, lässt sich die Entwicklung von Nationalsemantiken und das starke Interesse an ihnen als eine Kehrseite von Prozessen funktionaler Differenzierung beschreiben. Indem im Zuge funktionaler Gesellschaftsdifferenzierung Individuen in der „Umwelt" nunmehr entwickelter Systeme (Bildung, Wirtschaft, Recht, u.a.) positioniert werden, während – mit Prozessen funktionaler Differenzierung zusammenhängend – die Bedeutung von Familie und Schicht als Institutionen gesellschaftlicher Platzierung und Gruppenbildung abnimmt, kommt es zu einer „Generalisierung von Fremdheit" (Hahn 1997) als einer Grunderfahrung der Moderne. Unter diesen Bedingungen muss die Gesellschaft neue Identitätsangebote und Modi der Vergemeinschaftung bereitstellen. Die im 18. Jahrhundert entstehenden Nationalstaaten und Nationalsemantiken lassen sich als Formen segmentärer Differenzierung des politischen Systems so gesehen (auch) als geradezu notwendige Begleitprozesse funktionaler Differenzierung verstehen[3]. Fraglos ist auch der Fußball vom Vereins- bis hin zum ‚Nationalsport' mit seinen Sinnofferten (u.a.) auf die Problemlagen moderner Individuen in Sachen Identitäts- und Vergemeinschaftungsarbeit eingestellt[4]. Die Medialisierung und Kommerzialisierung des Sports ist dabei von zentraler Bedeutung: Medienangebote (Zeitungen, Zeitschriften, Fernseh- und Radioformate) und Konsumprodukte (Sammelkarten, Wimpel, T-Shirts, Fahnen uvm.) bieten für Interessierte (z.b. Fans) eine ausdifferenzierte (Bild-)Semantik für die Gestaltung der individuellen und/oder kollektiven Identität[5].

Im Blick auf die Frage, warum gerade der Fußball (zumindest vorübergehend) starke kollektive Bindungskräfte entfalten kann, bilden diese Überlegungen zur Gesellschaftsstruktur ein Argument unter anderen[6]. Mir geht es hier jedoch nicht um eine Diskussion der verschiedenen Argumentationslinien, sondern darum, dass Reflexionen wie die genannten darauf hindeuten, dass die Motivationslagen für die Herstellung nationalidentitärer Bezüge im Fußball tieferliegende Gründe haben und entsprechend nur eingeschränkt über eine Analyse des Sports oder die Untersuchung von Sportereignissen wie der EM 2012 in den Blick genommen werden können. Die folgende Analyse setzt also das Vorhandensein des Willens

---

3 Vgl. zu dieser Argumentation ausführlich Hahn 1997.
4 In ihrer monothematischen Ausrichtung unterscheiden sich die um Fußball gruppierten Vergemeinschaftungsformen etwa von solchen des Lebensstils oder des Milieus und lassen sich so betrachtet eher als Szenen verstehen (vgl. Hitzler/Niederbacher 2010).
5 Vgl. hierzu z.B. Willems 1998; Leggewie 2006; Klein 2008; Schwier/Schauerte 2009.
6 Ein weiteres geht vom Bedeutungsverlust der Religionen aus und diskutiert Fußball als eine moderne (profane) Religion bzw. als funktionales Äquivalent der Sinnstiftung (vgl. exemplarisch Gebauer 2006; Bromberger 1995).

zur Konstruktion nationaler Identitäten voraus und stellt von hier aus die Frage, *welchen Beitrag Bilder und Bild-Text-Kombinationen zur Herstellung nationaler Semantiken leisten.*

Den Materialkorpus der Untersuchung bilden die Ausgaben der Printmedien *The Sun, The Guardian, Bild* und *Süddeutsche Zeitung* im Zeitraum vom 08.06.2012 bis zum 28.06.2012. Die Festlegung des Erhebungszeitraums ergibt sich über den Beginn des Sportereignisses am 08.06. sowie aus dem Ausscheiden der hier thematisierten Mannschaften aus dem Wettbewerb[7]. Die Auswahl der Zeitungsformate macht die Behandlung der Fragestellung im Rahmen deutscher und englischer Printmedien sowohl im Qualitäts- (*The Guardian, Süddeutsche Zeitung)* als auch im Boulevardjournalismus (*The Sun, Bild*) möglich. Obwohl die erhobenen Formate keineswegs als repräsentativ für die massenmediale Berichterstattung in den jeweiligen Ländern angenommen werden können, handelt es sich in allen Fällen um Druckerzeugnisse mit einer hohen Reichweite und einer breiten Leserschaft, wenngleich um ,kulturelle Foren' (Newcomb/Hirsch 1986) für unterschiedliche Publika.

Thematisch wurde die Analyse auf die Untersuchung der Artikel zu den Spielen des deutschen und englischen Teams eingeschränkt, wobei die Analyse der *Bild*berichterstattung in den Mittelpunkt gestellt wurde. Zugleich wurde den Überschriften besondere Beachtung geschenkt. Denn Überschriften dienen nicht nur dazu, die Aufmerksamkeit des Lesers zu binden und Interesse zu wecken, sondern sie bereiten den Leser auch auf eine „bestimmte Lesart des Geschriebenen vor und instruieren ihn, wie er die folgende Geschichte verstehen soll." (Wolff 2011: 260) Die Kombination von Bild und Überschrift kann oftmals als eine dramaturgische Einheit verstanden werden, die die Aussagen des Textes formelhaft auf den Punkt bringt. Dabei sind Medientextanalysen wie die folgende nicht mit der Wirkungs- oder Rezeptionsforschung zu verwechseln. Bei der Medientextanalyse geht es lediglich um die Frage, wie bildliche und schriftliche Kommunikationen so eingestellt werden, dass bestimmte Lesarten wahrscheinlicher und andere unwahrscheinlicher werden. Wie also forcieren Bilder die nationalidentitären Bezüge des Fußballs?

---

7   Die englische Mannschaft schied nach einer Niederlage gegen Italien am 24.06. im Viertelfinale aus, das deutsche Team unterlag ebenfalls Italien am 28.06. im Halbfinale.

2   Agenda-Setting und sprachliche Zuschreibungen

Eine grundlegende Basis der Konstruktion des nationalen ‚Wir' ist der expliziten (Bild-)Thematisierung nationaler Identität vorgelagert. Sie (die Basis) ergibt sich dadurch, dass die untersuchten Formate offenkundig an nationalstaatlichen (Sprach-)Räumen orientiert sind und die Berichterstattung stark auf die Ereignisse rund um die Nationalmannschaft eben jener Region einschränken. Dieser Fokussierung entspricht das deutlich geringere Quantum von Berichten zu anderen Mannschaften[8]. Entscheidend ist also zunächst weniger das Wie, sondern das Ob der Berichterstattung. Die Rezipienten werden über die Auswahl mit Sinnangeboten konfrontiert, die ihnen ein spezifisches Interesse unterstellen. Man könnte auch sagen: Für die Leser wird gleichsam nicht über die EM berichtet, sondern über ein Nationalteam innerhalb der EM. Wir haben es auf der Ebene des Agenda-Settings mit einer drastischen Zuspitzung zu tun, die als solche – vor jeder inhaltlichen und inszenatorischen Rahmung – zu einer starken Polarisierung zwischen dem ‚Wir' und den ‚Anderen' führt. Dies gilt nicht nur für die boulevardjournalistischen Formate, sondern auch für ‚The Guardian' und ‚Süddeutsche Zeitung'.

Im Medium der Sprache wird die Aktivierung des nationalen Kollektivs semantisch hergestellt. Die Handhabung der Sprache indiziert dabei, dass das Wissen um ein kollektives ‚Wir' der Nation *vorausgesetzt* wird. Das ‚Wir' und die darauf hinführenden Formulierungen, etwa entlang des Possessivpronomens „unsere" (Spieler, Trainer, Spielerfrauen, Trainingsplätze usw.) werden in den Texten entsprechend nicht erklärend eingeführt. Häufig sind vielmehr kryptisch-formelhafte Verkürzungen. Überschriften wie „Roy: We have talent to do it well" (*The Sun*, 10.06.12) oder „We are going to show the nation what we can do', says Hodgson" (*The Guardian*, 11.06.12) geben hierfür ein Beispiel. Ihr Sinn ist nur unter Einbezugnahme eines weiteren Bedeutungshorizonts zu entschlüsseln, der neben dem Wissen um den Namen des Trainers des englischen Teams insbesondere eine Vorstellung davon einschließt, welches Gebilde als „We" angesprochen wird und in welchem Zusammenhang sich dieses ‚Wir' zu bewähren hat. Indem das „We" nicht explizit wird, ergibt sich hier wie in vielen anderen Fällen für den Leser ein variabler Assoziationsraum für die (Nicht-)Kopplung bezeichneter kollektiver Identitäten, zu denen sich der Rezipient ggf. selbst zählen kann – denn es bleibt offen, ob das „We" nur das national team oder zugleich auch die Nation meint, für die die Mannschaft im Wettkampf antritt.

---

8   Besonders deutlich wird diese Asymmetrie an den Spieltagen der in den Mittelpunkt gestellten Nationalteams sowie an den Tagen vor und nach den jeweiligen Spielen.

Bemerkenswert ist allerdings, dass sich die Formate der Boulevard- und Qualitätspresse in beiden Ländern sowohl hinsichtlich der Stärke unterscheiden, mit der die Nationalmannschaften als Stellvertreter der Nation identifiziert werden, als auch hinsichtlich des Ausmaßes, mit dem die Publika als integrales Element des nationalen Kollektivs angesprochen werden. So spricht die *Süddeutsche Zeitung* etwa nicht von „unser Neuner" (*Bild*), sondern distanzierter vom „Neuner Deutschlands". In der *SZ* wird auch nicht das „wir", sondern „die deutsche Mannschaft" zum Thema (z.B. *SZ*, 15.06.12). Entsprechend ist nicht „unser Team", sondern die „Löw-Elf" bzw. nicht „unser", sondern „sein schwerstes Spiel" das Thema, wenn der Bundestrainer die Mannschaft auf den „Angstgegner Italien" vorbereitet (z.B. *SZ*, 15.06.12, 16.06.12 und 28.06.12). Vergleichbar distanziert klingt das ‚Wir' im *Guardian* an: Zum einen sind hier ironische Bemerkungen zum ‚eigenen' Team noch häufiger als in der *Süddeutschen*. Vor dem Viertelfinal-Spiel gegen Italien heißt es z.B.: „Wayne Rooney observed that it is nice to be able to understand the manager's tactical instructions." (*The Guardian*, 23.06.12) Zum anderen haben wir es aber auch im Falle des *Guardian* mit einer deutlichen Fokussierung auf die englische Nationalmannschaft zu tun, die (wie in der *SZ*) zwar nicht als ‚Wir' identifiziert wird, wohl aber durch sprachliche Synonyme mit der Bezeichnung der Nation in eins gesetzt wird. Formulierungen wie die folgenden sind auch hier in der Berichterstattung zum national team durchaus häufig: „For England the healing process is almost complete. (…) England have as yet achieved no more here than they did on the high veld …" (*The Guardian*, ebd.).

Demgegenüber wird in *Sun* und *Bild* die Adressierung des ‚Wir' in die Kommunikation so eingestellt, als sei die mediale Konstellation zwischen Medienproduzenten, Medientext (Zeitung) und Rezipienten eine Hinterbühne, auf der sich die ‚Hiesigen' (der Nation) in Abwesenheit der ‚Anderen' begegneten. Die Kommunikation erweckt den Eindruck, an der (parasozialen) Interaktion zwischen Medienformat und Rezipient nähmen keine Leser anderer Nationen teil. Vergleichbar der Klatsch-Kommunikation ist die (hier: imaginierte) Abwesenheit derer, über die geklatscht wird, strukturelles Merkmal[9]. Und wie in der Klatsch-Kommunikation sozialer Situationen ist eine Präferenz für moralische Kommunikation zu beobachten, die sich im Falle transnationaler Wettbewerbe an die Identitäts-Fiktion der Nation heftet: „Die Engländer spielen hässlich wie Chelsea (…) wie der Championsleague-Sieger stehen sie meistens hinten drin" (*Bild*, 12.06.12).

Bemerkenswert ist weiterhin, dass die behandelten Medienformate das Nationale auch jenseits der Spielereignisse zu einem Thema machen. *The Sun* und *Bild* berichten mehr oder weniger ausführlich über die verschiedenen Fangrup-

---

9   Vgl. Bergmann/Luckmann 1999.

pen, *The Guardian* und *Die Süddeutsche* thematisieren zudem wirtschaftliche, kulturelle und politische Gegebenheiten. In den Qualitätszeitungen wird darüber hinaus die Frage nach nationalen Identitäten und ihrer Herstellung behandelt. Aufhänger hierfür sind oftmals transnationale Biographien wie etwa diejenige Miroslav Kloses, der z.b. in einem Interview der *SZ* zu seiner polnischen/oberschlesischen, deutschen und europäischen Identität befragt wird (*SZ*, 04.06.12). Wir haben es diesbezüglich mit Symptomen einer reflexiven Moderne zu tun, in der das Wissen um die soziale, kulturelle und gesellschaftliche Konstruiertheit von (u.a. nationaler) Identität vorausgesetzt wird. Entsprechend wird die Bedeutung der Medien für die (Re-)Konstruktion des Nationalen wiederholt selbst zum Thema. Stereotype Zuschreibungen, Rassismus oder auch die Fokussierung auf die Ereignisse rund um die je ‚eigene' Mannschaft werden kritisch kommentiert (vgl. *SZ*, 27.06.12, *The Guardian*, 11.06.12). Gelegentliche Überzeichnungen von Stereotypen, die weniger als ernste Identifizierungen, sondern als Klischees mit Unterhaltungswert zum Einsatz kommen, kann man ebenfalls in diesen (reflexiven) Zusammenhang stellen. Nach dem Sieg des englischen Teams über die schwedische Mannschaft setzt *The Sun* mit einem Sprachspiel die Popgruppe Abba als Synonym für Schweden und einen Sieg über selbiges ein: „Abba Dabba Done it! Ah-haa! 3 Lions battle back to historic victory" (*The Sun*, 16.06.12). Im Qualitätsjournalismus finden sich analoge Anspielungen. So formuliert die *SZ* im Blick auf das letzte Spiel der portugiesischen Mannschaft und deren prominentesten Star in der Überschrift: „Der Pistolero knallt nicht. Zum Abschied vom Turnier fällt Ronaldo durch skurrile Anlaufszenarien bei ineffektiven Freistößen auf" (*SZ*, 29.09.12).

3   Nähe, Präsenz, Erinnerungskultur und Vergemeinschaftung

Dass Kommunikationsmedien substantiell an der Entwicklung von National-staaten und National-Semantiken beteiligt sind, ist des Öfteren betont worden[10]. Techniken wie der Buchdruck führen nicht nur zu Vereinheitlichungen im Bereich der Sprachen, die dann als identitätsstiftende Gebilde fungieren können. Als Verbreitungsmedien ermöglichen sie zugleich die Erschließung größerer Territorien mit Erzählungen wie denen der Nation: Indem die Thematisierung des Nationalen als eine spezifische Selbstbeschreibung der Gesellschaft mit einer hohen Reichweite kommuniziert wird, kann sich die Narration des Nationalen

---

10 Vgl. z.B. Giesecke 1998 und Luhmann 1997.

zu einem festen und daher anschlussfähigen Bestandteil kollektiven Wissens entwickeln. Unter modernen Medienbedingungen übernehmen dabei Bilder (Fotografien, Film- und Fernsehbilder) eine entscheidende Funktion. Indem sie z.b. Sportereignisse ‚dokumentieren' (und nicht nur von diesen erzählen) führen sie zu einer neuartigen Erinnerungskultur des Fußballs auch im Kontext national-identitärer Bezüge. So zeigt die *Süddeutsche Zeitung* vor der Begegnung Deutschland-Niederlande im Rahmen der EM 2012 eine Szene der WM 1990, in der der am Boden kniende Stürmer Völler von dem niederländischen Torwart de Breukelen von oben herab angeschrien wird und macht in eben diesem Artikel über ein Interview mit de Breukelen den Konflikt der Nationen zum Thema (*SZ*, 13.06.12).

Neben und mit der massenhaften Reproduzierbarkeit bzw. der hohen Reichweite ist die spezifische Darstellungsform technischer Bildmedien von großer Bedeutung. Ihre indexikalischen Zeichenvehikel referieren in ganz anderer Weise als manuelle Bilder (Zeichnungen, Gemälde usw.) auf die ‚Realität' der visuellen Wahrnehmung. Erst mit der Fotografie zeigen Bilder ‚die Sache selbst', so z.B. die in einer jeweiligen Gegenwart existierenden Fußballer bzw. die fußballbezogenen Ereignisse. Wenn *The Guardian* ein Foto auf der Titelseite abbildet, das Terry und Rooney beim Torjubel zeigt („England rock on with Rooney"), ist das ein solcher Fall (*The Guardian*, 20.06.12). Wie in unzähligen anderen Bildern wird der Leser mit dem ‚Abbild' tatsächlicher Ereignisse konfrontiert, die er in vielen Fällen bereits zuvor ‚live' im Fernsehen zu sehen bekam. In seinem scheinbar dokumentierenden Zeigen ist der ‚Realismus' der technischen Bildmedien Voraussetzung verschiedenster Bedeutungskonstruktionen, die den Fußball als Medienereignis kennzeichnen und fundiert auch maßgeblich die Ausbildung von Nationalsemantiken: Man identifiziert auf den Bildern eben jene Menschen aus Fleisch und Blut, die tatsächlich in einem bestimmten Team spielen oder eine Torszene, die sich eben so und nicht anders ereignet hat. Im Medium des audiovisuellen Fernsehens kann die Vergegenwärtigung des ‚Realen' über die stillen Bilder der Fotografie hinaus nochmals erheblich gesteigert werden. Die Einbezugnahme von Bewegungen, Geräuschen, Sprache, Musik usw. und nicht zuletzt die „Liveness" der Echtzeitübertragung führen die Rezipienten über Wahrnehmungen sehr ‚nahe' an das Geschehen heran. Und weil die Bevölkerungen in Echtzeit am Geschehen ‚teilnehmen' und mit Medieninszenierungen „parasozial interagieren" (Horton/Wohl 1956), spricht Vieles für die Annahme, in den Bildmedien einen zentralen Generator nationaler Vergemeinschaftung zu sehen[11]. Indem die Medien die

---

11 Bekanntlich wirken sich die Medienverhältnisse auch auf den Sport selbst aus, so z.B., wenn Regeln zur Steigerung von Telegenität verändert werden oder wenn die Spielzeiten der „prime-time" des TV folgen.

kommunikativen Voraussetzungen schaffen, versetzen sie die Rezipienten zudem
in die Lage, Unterschiede im Verhalten der Akteure (Spielweisen, Umgang mit
Siegen und Niederlagen, (Nicht-)Fair-Play, Reagieren auf die Fans im Stadion
usw.) als ,typisch' für die Bürger einer Nation zu identifizieren.

4   Zeichen und Symbole des (Trans-)Nationalen

Indem technische Bilder die Spieler als Individuen identifizieren, die Rezipienten
im Rahmen ihres Kontextwissens als Staatsbürger eines bestimmten Landes wie-
dererkennen können, tragen bereits die körperlichen Erscheinungen der Sportler
zur nationalen Rahmung eines Sportereignisses bei. Darüber hinaus wird ein national-identitärer Bezugsrahmen in Wettkämpfen wie der EM durch bestimmte
Zeichen und Symbole hergestellt. Insbesondere die Trikots unterscheiden sich
vom Vereinsfußball. Sie weisen im Zeitverlauf eine höhere Formkonstanz als
die variantenreicheren Vereinstrikots auf. Zudem kann durch den weitgehenden
Verzicht auf Werbung (sichtbar ist lediglich das Typologo des Textilherstellers)
die Emblematik des Nationalen (z.b. Three Lions, Bundesadler) umso besser her-
vortreten. Den sprachlichen Zugehörigkeitsetikettierungen von Spielern, Mannschaften, Fangruppen usw. analog, fungiert die Ikonographie des Nationalen
als eine Klammer, die das mit ihm Bezeichnete in das Bezugssystem der Nation
einordnet[12]. Die Landeswappen fungieren dementsprechend als sichtbarer Identitätsaufhänger der Kleidung und ihrer Träger[13].

Zugleich geht die visuelle Markierung des Nationalen eine Verbindung mit
jenen Image-Komplexen ein, die die Werbung für Sportartikelhersteller im The-
menkontext Fußball modelliert[14]. Entsprechende Beziehungen ergeben sich schon
deshalb, weil die Werbung mit denselben Individuen, die in nationalen Wettbewerben wie der EM 2012 als Stellvertreter der Nation erscheinen, jenseits solcher
Wettbewerbe in ganz anderen Bezugssystemen positive Images konstruiert. Ein

---

12 Selbiges gilt für die zahlreichen kommerziellen Produkte, die der Markt im Kontext
    nationaler Fußballwettkämpfe anbietet (T-Shirts, Schals, Trinkflaschen, Sammelkar-
    ten usw.). Auch hier beschränkt sich die Bildsemantik des Nationalen auf grundlegende
    Symboliken (Nationalfiguren und -farben).

13 Eine bemerkenswerte Besonderheit des englischen Nationaltrikots ist der Polokragen,
    der im Bereich der funktionsorientierten Sportkleidung wenig verbreitet ist und in An-
    lehnung an den Hemdkragen ein vergleichsweise business-orientiertes bis ,staatstra-
    gendes' Erscheinungsbild des Distinguierten vermittelt.

14 Zu einem auf massenmediale (Bild-)Identitätskonstruktionen bezogenen Image-Be-
    griff vgl. Kautt 2008.

häufiges Werbe-Sujet ist z.b. der gleichsam übermenschliche Heros, dessen ‚herausragende' Größe durch passende Kameraeinstellungen versinnbildlicht wird. Typisch sind auch dynamische Körperhaltungen, die Dynamik, Kraft, Ausdauer, Flexibilität u.a. zum Ausdruck bringen sollen. Insbesondere die transnational operierenden Sportartikelhersteller kolonisieren mit dieser Bildsprache den öffentlichen Raum[15]. Ein Beispiel gibt eine Reklame des britischen Autoherstellers Vauxhall, die während der EM publiziert wurde. Sie zeigt in einer Untersicht einige Spieler des englischen Nationalteams als entschlossen nach vorne schreitende Helden. Dem Bild-Sinn wird hier nun durch den Slogan eine nationale Rahmung hinzugefügt: „We´re not just supporting a team. We´re supporting a Nation" (*The Sun*, 15.06.12). Ein ähnlicher Fall liegt in einer zweiseitigen (!) Anzeige für die Marke Nike vor, die das überlebensgroße Portrait Wayne Rooneys mit der Aussage „My time is now" kombiniert (*The Sun*, 19.06.12). Im Zeitfenster der EM wird die individuelle Mission als nationales Anliegen lesbar. Die Gestaltung fügt sich dabei ganz in die Image-Logik anderer Werbekampagen des Absenders. Sie soll in ihrem Purismus (schwarzer Hintergrund, ungeschönte Frontalaufnahme des Gesichts im Anschnitt) die authentische Fokussierung auf das Wesentliche und Eigentliche als (Image-)Identitätswert des Sportlers und der beworbenen Marke zum Ausdruck bringen.

In diesen wie in anderen Fällen macht sich ein Verflechtungszusammenhang von werblichen und journalistischen Bildern bemerkbar: Indem der Fußballprofi sein wahres Können auf dem Platz im Rahmen ‚realistischer' Bilder der Sportberichterstattung unter Beweis stellt, fungieren eben jene Bilder als eine Hintergrundfolie, die im Werbungs-Rahmen ihren Glanz entfaltet: Man sieht gleichsam hinter den Werbebildern den echten Sportler in Aktion, insofern man entsprechende Bilder erinnert. In umgekehrter Richtung strahlt der überhöhte Glanz heroischer Werbungsinszenierungen auf die Akteure ab, die man in den Zeitungen und im Fernsehen auf dem Rasen (wieder-)erkennt. Wechselseitige Bezüge werden auch dadurch hergestellt, dass in beiden symbolischen Sphären (des Journalismus, der Werbung) die Zeichensprache der Sportartikelhersteller präsent ist, wobei die Schuhe als deutlich erkennbare Markenprodukte von besonderer Bedeutung sind. Sie sind die symbolischen Vehikel der globalen Image-Kommu-

---

15 Die Unternehmen Nike, Adidas und Puma dominieren weltweit das symbolische Image-Universum des Sports (u.a. des Fußballs), wobei die Image-Semantiken der Unternehmen erstaunliche Parallelen aufweisen. Im Zentrum der Image-Komplexe steht neben der Inszenierung des singulären Helden seit einigen Jahren die positive Beschreibung der sportiven Arbeit am Selbst und das Lob auf den Willen zum Ziel der Selbstoptimierung von Jedermann und jeder Frau, das im Rahmen ‚authentischer' Inszenierungen ‚gewöhnlicher' Individuen umgesetzt wird.

nikation, die die verschiedensten Fußballereignisse von der bunten Off-Szene der
Bolzplätze über die Amateurligen bis hin zum Profifußball transzendieren und
auch im Rahmen von Wettkämpfen wie der EM die Identitätskonstruktion des
Nationalen flankieren. Ob Rooney, Messi oder Müller: Sie alle partizipieren neben
und mit ihren nationalen Identitäten nicht nur an den Gruppen-Identitäten von
Vereinen bzw. Clubs, sondern auch an den Image-Konstruktionen der Werbung,
die sie mit ihrem Schuhwerk bei größeren Spielen einem Millionenpublikum vor
Augen führen. Wir haben es also mit einer engmaschigen Intertextualität berich-
tender und werbender Bilderströme zu tun, die in die Konstruktion des Nationalen hineinwirkt.

5 Individuum, Team, Masse: Allegorien (nationaler) Vergemeinschaftung

Für die Frage, inwiefern Bilder an der Konstitution des ‚Wir' beteiligt sind, ist weiterhin bedeutsam, dass unter modernen Medienbedingungen die *Mannschaft als
solche bildhaft zum Ereignis wird*. Gerade im Bilderrahmen des Fernsehens wird
der netzwerkförmig agierende Kollektivkörper des Teams evident. Die Bilder zeigen von Moment zu Moment, dass einzelne Handlungen im Kollektiv und für das
Kollektiv erfolgen, so dass das Fußballteam zu einer Körper-Metapher der Vielen
werden kann. Dieses Deutungsmuster legen die *Bilder von den Fans* in den Fußballstadien umso näher: Nationalsymbolisch codierte Staffagen vom T-Shirt über
Frisuren und Hautbemalungen bis hin zu Spruchbändern und Nationalflaggen
machen aus dem Bild der Vielen ein „Ornament der Masse" (Kracauer 1963), das
als visuelles pars-pro-toto der nationalen Gemeinschaft fungieren kann und zu
eben diesem Zweck sowohl in die Bildberichterstattung des Fernsehens als auch
in die der Zeitungen wiederholt integriert wird[16].

---

16 Ohnehin ist der Fan ein wichtiges mediendramaturgisches Element zur Konstruktion
der Kollektividentität Nation. Eine Werbeanzeige im Guardian für den Schokoriegel
„Mars" macht eine Strategie der Herstellung nationaler Fangemeinschaften deutlich.
Sie zeigt auf schwarzem Hintergrund das Produkt, darüber den Slogan: „Thanks, to
the best fans in Europe" (The Guardian, 26.06.12). Sprachlich wird der Imagination
einer einheitlichen (nationalen) Fangemeinschaft gleich doppelt Vorschub geleistet:
Die Gruppe ist unter qualitativen Gesichtspunkten homogen („best") und als solche
von anderen („in Europe") unterscheidbar. Indem die Anzeige nach dem Ausscheiden
des englischen Teams gedruckt wird, fügt sich die Botschaft zudem in die rituelle Logik
des Turniers (vgl. Abschnitt 6), nämlich als Dank an die treuen und daher zu achtenden
Fans.

Hinsichtlich der Mannschaftsdarstellung forcieren die *Beziehungen zwischen Individuum und Gemeinschaft* die Vorstellung vom Team als einem Kollektiv. Da ist zunächst der Sachverhalt, dass die Medien ausführlich über die (Star-)Spieler der von ihnen fokussierten Nationalmannschaft berichten. Zahlreiche (Bild-)Geschichten lassen für den Leser ein facettenreiches Bild der Individuen entstehen, die gemeinsam das Team bilden. Wie in anderen Kontexten (z.b. der Unterhaltungskultur) wird dem imaginierten Kollektiv derart ein vertieftes ‚Gesicht' verliehen, das aus dem Gesicht der Vielen besteht. Das Ausbleiben vergleichbarer Berichte zu anderen Mannschaften belässt dieselben tendenziell im Status einer gesichtslosen, anonymen Masse der ‚Anderen'[17]. Weiterhin stützt die Spannung von Individuum und Gemeinschaft im Bereich der Bilder fußballerischer Ereignisse die Bedeutung des Kollektivs. Zwar treten uns die gegenwartskulturell omnipräsenten Stilisierungen und Überhöhungen sichtbarer Individualität auch hier entgegen: Frisuren, Tätowierungen oder individuell ausgeformte Muskeln der Spieler werden z.T. auch dezidiert zum Thema bzw. Bild-Motiv. Schon durch den überindividuellen Dresscode werden die Einzelnen jedoch deutlich als Teil des Ganzen markiert und in ein Kollektiv eingefügt. Mehr noch als das Outfit macht die Anschauung des Handlungsgeschehens die Unterordnung des Einzelnen unter die Mannschaft deutlich. Denn der buchstäbliche ‚Spielraum' des Einzelnen ist an die *Rollendifferenzierung* des Sports gebunden (Torwart, Verteidigung, Mittelfeld, Angriff). Sie passt den Einzelnen erkennbar in ein größeres Ganzes ein, das mehr ist als die Summe seiner Teile. So ist das Ausbrechen des Stürmers aus dem Netzwerk durch sogenannte „Einzelaktionen"[18] an die ‚Moral' des Mannschaftssports gebunden: Egoismus am Ball wird nur geduldet, wenn damit der Mannschaft ein besonderer Dienst (z.B. ein Tor) erwiesen wird. Dass auch von Stürmern ein hohes Laufpensum für die Mannschaft verlangt wird, haben die Debatten um die Spielweise von Mario Gomez während der EM gezeigt.

---

17 Diese Asymmetrie spielt für Prozesse der Stereotypenbildung eine große Rolle, z.B. in der propagandistischen Malerei (z.B. im Kontext von Kriegsschilderungen) oder auch in den (Anti-)Kriegsfilmen der Unterhaltungskultur (zu einigen Beispielen vgl. z.B. Wilhelm 2005: 182 f.).

18 Schon der Begriff ist aufschlussreich, denn schließlich wird der Ball in der Regel immer von einzelnen Spielern getreten. Das Wort „Einzelaktion" verweist also auf eine Zielvorstellung in sequenzieller Hinsicht. Sie besteht in der Erwartung, dass die Spieler zu jedem Zeitpunkt den Ball schnellstmöglich an einen besser positionierten Mannschaftskollegen abspielen. Demgegenüber werden in Einzelaktionen (typischerweise durchgeführt von Stürmern) gerade nicht die Stellungsvorteile und die freien Räume genutzt, sondern Zweikämpfe eingegangen, die das Risiko des Ballverlusts mit sich bringen.

Nun ist die medial hergestellte Evidenz der Teamhaftigkeit des Fußballs keineswegs für eine der beiden gegnerischen Seiten eines Spiels reserviert – denn
beide Mannschaften agieren ja unverkennbar als Team. Für sich selbst genommen
ist die Beobachtbarkeit von Teams also kein sachlich zwingender Ausgangspunkt
für die Konstruktion nationaler Identifizierungen. Auch hier gilt vielmehr, dass
das „Wir" als Imagination vorbereitet sein muss, so z.b. durch Wettkämpfe, die,
wie die EM, Mannschaften als Nationenvertreter gegeneinander positionieren.
Im Blick auf die symbolische Funktion des sichtbaren Teams wird aber verständlich, dass sich das soziale Imaginäre der Nation und dessen mediale Dramatisie-
rung an den Fußball erheblich leichter als etwa an die diesbezüglich defizitären
Individualsportarten (Schwimmen, Leichtathletik u.a.) binden.

6 Emotionalisierung

Dass das gemeinsame Erleben von Emotionen für Prozesse der Gruppenbildung
und -Kohäsion von großer Bedeutung und eben deshalb die Schaffung emotions-
generierender Ereignisse für die (Re-)Produktion von Kollektiven von großer Bedeutung ist, wurde seit Durkheim wiederholt bemerkt[19]. Die am menschlichen
Körper sichtbar werdenden Gefühle (Freude, Wut, Angst, Trauer u.a.) gehören
zu den somatisch fundierten „human-interest"-Themen, deren Betrachtung bei
den Betrachtenden ihrerseits die Entstehung von Gefühlen nahelegt[20]. Bilder des
Emotionalen erwecken Aufmerksamkeit und Interesse, mithin jene Ressourcen,
auf die die Medien existentiell angewiesen sind. Schon aus diesen Gründen ergibt
sich eine gewisse Präferenz für Darstellungen des Emotionalen dies- und jenseits
der Sportberichterstattung. Dramaturgisch folgt die Auswahl, Gestaltung und
Kontextierung der Bilder der Logik des Sports. Typisierend lassen sich die Bilder
der hier analysierten Materialien in drei Sujets einteilen: Da sind zunächst die in
allen untersuchten Formaten quantitativ deutlich überwiegenden Fälle von Darstellungen *kämpferischer Handlungen*. Zu Inszenierungen werden sie über das
selektierte Zeigen von Szenen, in denen Spieler gegnerischer Mannschaften um
den Ballbesitz ringen. Fotos des offenen Stellungsspiels neben den Zweikämpfen
– im Spielverlauf fraglos die häufigste Situation – kommen hingegen kaum vor.
Im Bilderreigen der Zeitungen verdichtet sich Fußball gleichsam zum Kampf von

---

19 Zu Emotionen als Generatoren nationaler Vergemeinschaftung vgl. z.B. Speth 1999
   und Ciompi/Endert 2011.
20 Zu den Zusammenhängen von Visualität und Emotionalität vgl. z.B. Müller/Kappas
   2011.

Mann gegen Mann. Die Momentaufnahmen unterstützen dabei die Dramatik der Situation, denn sie zeigen die Gesichter in ‚Ausnahmezuständen', die der natürlichen menschlichen Wahrnehmung in temporeichen Ereignisfolgen verborgen bleiben. Ohnehin übernehmen die Bilder der Printmedien eine wichtige Funktion in Sachen Emotionalisierung, da sie die „Mikroökologie des Gesichtsrahmen" (Goffman 1969: 198) betonen und als stille Bilder nicht im Ereignisstrom weiterer Bilder untergehen. Weiterhin erfreuen sich die um Siege bzw. Niederlagen gruppierten emotionalen Darstellungen in den Medien einer großen Beliebtheit. In ihrer Anbindung an allgemeinmenschliche Erfahrungszusammenhänge kann man die Bilder der Freude (Sieg) und Trauer (Niederlage) zu jenen „Pathosformeln" zählen, die Aby Warburg als kontinuierende Topoi der Bildgeschichte beschrieben hat[21]. Ein deutliches Beispiel hierfür ist die offensive Triumph-Performance von Mario Balotelli im Halbfinalspiel Deutschland gegen Italien, die *Bild* mit der Formulierung beschreibt: „Der Tor-Protz, der wie ein Krieger posierte" (*Bild*, 30.06.12). Die Tatsache, dass dieses Bild wie kaum ein anderes im Jahr 2012 in das kollektive Gedächtnis der Europäer einging – wir müssen die Details dieser Pose daher hier nicht beschreiben – ist u.a. ein Indiz für die Relevanz und Durchsetzungskraft emotionalisierender Bilder[22].

Nun weisen Emotionsdarstellungen wie die erwähnten für sich selbst genommen keine kollektiv-identitären Bezüge auf. Diese werden erst durch sinnhafte Rahmungen hergestellt. Neben und mit nationalen Symbolen sowie Bildern von Fans, die den Eindruck nationaler Gefühlsgemeinschaften erwecken (sollen), fungiert das narrative Gerüst des Wettkampfs als eine Rahmung, die das allgemeinmenschliche der Emotionen mit Nationalsemantiken verknüpft.

7 Die rituelle Ordnung der Bilder

Im Rahmen transnationaler Wettkämpfe werden Siege und Niederlagen als Achtungsgewinne bzw. -verluste der Nation thematisiert. In den Boulevardmedien ist gar von „Ehre" explizit die Rede: Sie muss von Spiel zu Spiel verteidigt oder errungen werden und kann punktuell als ‚auf dem Spiel stehend' dramatisiert werden – z.B. in einer Headline, die ein Mitglied des italienischen Teams zitiert: „Unsere

---

21 Zu den Pathosformeln des Fußballs vgl. Bredekamp 2007: 169-185.

22 Der Casus Balotelli hat daher zu Recht Eingang in die Jahresrückblicke verschiedener Medienformate und deren Titelseiten gefunden, so z.B. u.a. bei der Süddeutschen Zeitung.

Spieler müssen Italiens Ehre retten"[23] (*Bild*, 10.06.12). Siege lassen sich auf dieser Verstehensbasis als ruhmreiche Ereignisse für die Nation verherrlichen: „Full glory pages 4,5,6" titelt *The Sun* nach dem Sieg des englischen über das schwedische Team (16.06.12). Auch die wörtliche Rede von „Stolz" identifiziert Mannschaften mit Nationen und gibt eine emotionale und kognitive Beteiligung an der kollektiv bedeutsamen Achtungsdimension des Sports zu erkennen: „Löw: ‚Wir können stolz sein auf diese Mannschaft‛" (*Bild*, 23.06.12).

Die mediale Narration zur EM kann demnach als eine Modulation der Interaktionsordnung zwischen anwesenden Akteuren in sozialen Situationen verstanden werden. Denn Letztere ergibt sich maßgeblich durch die auf (Miss-)Achtung eingestellten Handlungs-, Darstellungs- und Kommunikationsmuster, die Erving Goffman als rituelle Ordnung rekonstruiert. Grundlegend für dieselbe ist im Kontext der Berichterstattung zur EM wiederum die Kommunikation der Imagination der Nation, die – personalen Akteuren vergleichbar – um ein gutes Ansehen bemüht ist. Die Form des Selbstlobs und die vermeintliche Erhöhung des eigenen (hier: nationalen) Images durch die Herabsetzung anderer sind zu diesem Image-Zweck in der Boulevardpresse eine häufig gewählte Methode. Die Frage, mit welchen Leistungen ein Team im Einzelnen Achtung erringen oder aufs Spiel setzen kann, fußt dabei auf den *Erwartungen*, die man an die jeweiligen Teams glaubt, stellen zu können. Während der EM 2012 zeigen die deutschen Medien eine deutlich höhere Erwartung als die englischen Medien für die jeweils von ihr in den Mittelpunkt gestellten Mannschaften. Während *Bild* bis zum Ausscheiden der deutschen Elf siegesgewisse Botschaften formuliert wie „Jogi, noch viermal tanzen bis zum Titel" (14.06.12); „Tschüss Griechen, heute können wir euch nicht retten" (22.06.12); „Jogi, wer schießt uns ins Finale Grande?" (26.06.12), gibt sich *The Sun* trotz anfänglicher Positiveinschätzungen („We've got the best back 5 in Europe – that's why we can win this tournament"; *The Sun*, 11.06.12) zurückhaltender. Personalen Images im mikrosozialen Kontext der Interaktion vergleichbar, geben sich Images der Nation im makrosozialen Maßstab der Medienkommunikation als soziale Konstruktionen Vieler zu erkennen. Die Medien können nicht nach eigenem Gutdünken positive Selbstbilder des Nationalen kreieren, sondern sie müssen in ihren Image-Arbeiten von intersubjektiv verfügbaren Informationen und (Fremd-)Einschätzungen ausgehen. Während die englischen Medien u.a. den Sachverhalt problematisieren, dass Roy Hodgson erst sechs Wochen vor Tur-

---

23 Nachdem *Bild* vor dem Halbfinalspiel wünscht „Italien, jetzt rechnen wir ab", lässt sie am Tag darauf ihre Leser wissen „Buffon exklusiv in Bild: Wir wissen, dass ihr Rache wollt." Wie in anderen Fällen dient die Medienbühne also der Inszenierung einer interaktionsanalogen Image-Kommunikation (*Bild*, 27./28.06.12).

nierbeginn die vakante Stelle des Trainers übernahm, ist die mediale Narration zum deutschen Team schon vor der EM von der Idee getragen, dass die vieljährige Zusammenarbeit von Joachim Löw und ‚seinem' jungen Team nunmehr Früchte in Form von Turniersiegen tragen müsse. An der medialen Thematisierung des Ausscheidens des englischen und deutschen Teams geben sich dementsprechend die Image-Balancen im Gefüge von mehr oder weniger realistischen Erwartungslagen einerseits und von Wünschen und Zielvorstellungen andererseits prägnant zu erkennen. Während die englischen Medienformate trotz einiger Kritik am englischen Team nach dessen Ausscheiden im Viertelfinale dessen Leistung als respektable Leistung und entsprechend nicht als Image-Verlust für die Nation werten[24], sind die deutschen Medien erheblicher kritischer. Vor allem *Bild* interpretiert das Ausscheiden des deutschen Teams als eine Blamage der Nation und dekonstruiert am Tag nach dem Spiel in einer abrupten Kehrtwendung die zuvor generierten Positiv-Images: „Jogi und seine Verlierer. Bild rechnet ab. Aus bei der EM! Zeit für eine schonungslose Abrechnung! Bild sagt, was schieflief. Die Fehler von Jogi Löw beim 1:2 gegen Italien. Der schwache Schweini. Die Hymnenverweigerung" (*Bild*, 29.06.12).

Visuelle Kommunikationen spielen nun für die (Re-)Produktion der rituellen Ordnung und deren Anpassung an die aktuellen Ereignisse eine bedeutende Rolle: So kann mit *Bildern von Individuen* die Dimension der Achtungskommunikation *personalisiert* und dadurch *konkretisiert* werden. *The Sun* formuliert zum Auftakt des Wettkampfs einen nationalen Auftrag an einige Spieler, denen sie bildlich ein Gesicht verleiht: „Do your best… England stars Rooney, Terry, Gerrard and Cole" (*The Sun*, 10.06.12)[25]. Ein vergleichbarer Fall ist das Zeigen eines Portraits Rooneys vor dem Viertelfinalspiel gegen Italien mit der Beschwörungsformel „Come on England". Ehre und möglicher Ehrverlust klingt thematisch über das Zeigen des Gesichts als wichtigster „Identitätsaufhänger" (Goffman) und symbolisches Medium von ‚Gesichtsverlust' an. Auch die *Süddeutsche* hat vor Turnierbeginn „Den Titel im Blick". Wenngleich das Wortfeld eines nationalen ‚Wir' vermieden wird, fungiert das Bild des nach vorne blickenden Mannschaftskapitäns des deutschen Teams mit besagtem Kommentar als Ausdruck kollektiver Ziele bzw.

---

24 Wenn „The Sun" ein Bild des trauernden Teams auf der Titelseite mit der Feststellung kommentiert: „Anyone for tennis? England lose on pens again – bring on Wimbledon" (25.06.12), lässt sich der humorvolle Umgang mit der ‚Tragödie' neben und mit einer spezifisch britischen (Humor-)Kultur wohl auch auf die von den Medien unterstellte allgemeine Erwartungshaltung an das national team erklären.

25 Entsprechend erläutern Headline und Unterschrift: „Don't con the Nation! England boss Roy Hodgson told yesterday how he feared being ‚conned' by his players – and urged them to perform at their best for the nation" (*The Sun*, 10.06.12).

Wünsche, indem es am Turnierbeginn auf der symbolisch bedeutsamen Titelseite der Zeitung steht.

Die oben erwähnten *Darstellungen kämpferischer Handlungen* tragen nicht nur (potentiell) zum emotionalen Involvement und der Vergemeinschaftung der Rezipienten bei, sondern sie fungieren zugleich als Generatoren und Indikatoren der rituellen Image-Ordnung zwischen den Nationen. Auf einem seitenfüllenden Bild der *Sun* werden drei Spieler mit angezogenen Beinen (spitzen Knien) gezeigt, während die Headline u.a. über militärische Begriffe die Angriffssymbolik der Darstellung unterstreicht und zugleich über ein Wortspiel humoristisch abmildert: „We are ready for a knees up. Your country kneeds you…England stars prove they won't bent the knee to old enemies France this afternoon. Skipper Steven Gerrard led his troops in training in Donetsk yesterday ahead of the 5pm crunch at the Donbass Arena. (…) Let's hope that by 7 pm, the country is ready for a proper knees-up" (*The Sun*, 11.06.12). Vergleichbare Bilder kommen gerade nach dem Ausscheiden des englischen Teams aus dem Wettbewerb forciert zum Einsatz: Mit ihnen wird nochmals der Kampfgeist der Spieler illustriert, mithin jene Ressource, an der die Einsatzbereitschaft des Einzelnen für die Nation gemessen wird und die in den Medienkommunikationen zum Fußball auch jenseits nationaler Rahmungen als ehrenrühriger Eigenwert thematisiert wird. Bilder ‚beglaubigen' dann Botschaften wie die Folgenden: „But cheers for Roy's battling 3 Lions heroes. (…) 3 Lions go out with heads held high (…) England's battlers gave every last ounce of fight." (*The Sun*, 25.06.12).

Nicht zuletzt spielen Bilder eine Rolle, wenn es den Medien darum geht, die Kopplung der beiden Identitäten ‚Nationalteam' und ‚Nation' zu lockern. Wie erwähnt, tritt dieser Fall nach dem Ausscheiden der Teams im Viertel- bzw. Halbfinale ein. Während die Bilder bis zu diesem Zeitpunkt die positiven Eigenschaften des Teams zum Ausdruck bringen (Kampfgeist, Teamorientierung, fußballerisches Können), werden Bilder nun zur *Dokumentation negativer Eigenschaften* und dementsprechend zur argumentativen Verstärkung der im Text entfalteten Kritik eingesetzt. Trotz der positiven Bilanzierung in *The Sun* macht sich auch hier eine ironische bis abwertende Kommentierung zur ‚eigenen' Mannschaft bemerkbar. So wird im statistischen Vergleich gezeigt, dass Ronaldo ein besseres Torergebnis vorweisen kann als die gesamte englische Mannschaft, wobei die Dramaturgie der Bilder die Leistung des englischen Teams ins Lächerliche zieht: Gezeigt wird ein seitenfüllendes Foto des allegorisch übergroß erscheinenden Ronaldo beim Torschuss, während ein nur sehr kleines Foto Wayne Rooney beim vergeblichen Torschuss zeigt, kommentiert mit der Feststellung: „Our Wayne misses again" (26.06.12). Aber auch in der distanzierteren Qualitätspresse folgt der Bildeinsatz der besagten rituellen Logik der Achtungskommunikation. Auf die Titelseiten des *Guardian* schaffen es bevorzugt Bilder von siegreichen Spielen, mithin von Ereignissen, die als positive Identitätsaufhänger des Nationalen fungieren können (*The Guardian*, 12.06.12 und 20.06.12). Vergleichbares ereignet sich in den deutschen Medien: Zwei Tage nach dem Ausscheiden der deutschen Mannschaft unterstreicht z.b. ein Foto in der *Süddeutschen*, das Löw im Flugzeug umstellt von Mikrofonen im weißen Hemd mit dozierender Gestik zeigt, die in der Überschrift anvisierte Problemdiagnose: „Fehlt ein Schuss Verrücktheit? Coacht der Trainer mit Doktorhut? Die Branche debattiert über Joachim Löw und seine Elf" (SZ, 02.07.12). *Bild* hingegen greift mit ihrer Kritik gleich tief in die Vorratskiste solcher Klischees, die Vorstellungen von Fußball, Kampfgeist, Männlichkeit und nationalem Bewusstsein zu einem Sinnkomplex amalgamieren, und bekräftigt ihren Befund mit einem Foto, das die italienische und deutsche Mannschaft beim Singen der Nationalhymne zeigt. Unter der Überschrift „Memmen gegen Männer" heißt es weiter: „Schon bei der Hymne hatten wir verloren. (...) Auffallend: Die Stars mit Migrationshintergrund (Ausnahme Klose) bleiben generell stumm. Sie haben den deutschen Pass, aber verweigern die Hymne. Das kann's nicht sein. Auch andere zeigten beim Singen keinen Mumm. Kroos und Gomez summten nur ein bisschen mit. Ängstlich, unsicher, gehemmt" (30.06.12).

Die Logik des Sports als eine Orientierung an der Unterscheidung von Sieg und Niederlage ist demnach ein basaler Hintergrund für die massenmediale Identifizierung des Sports mit der Nation. Denn von den sportlichen Ergebnissen hängt ab, ob, inwiefern und inwieweit sich die Medien auf den Sport als eine Identifikationsfolie des sozialen Imaginären der Nation einlassen[26].

8 Schlussbemerkungen

Den vorausgegangenen Überlegungen zufolge lässt sich sagen, dass massenmediale Bilder auf sehr vielfältige und grundlegende Weise an der Konstruktion des Bedeutungszusammenhangs von Fußball und Nationalität beteiligt sind: Als Darstellungsmedien *vergegenwärtigen* sie das reale Spielereignis für breite Bevölkerungsgruppen und tragen als Speichermedien maßgeblich zur Ausbildung eines *kollektiven (Bild-)Gedächtnisses* der (Fußball-)Nationen bei. Allegorisch gewinnen Vorstellungen von nationalen *Kollektivkörpern* über die Visualisierung

---

26 Einen Hinweis in diese Richtung geben nicht zuletzt diejenigen Sportarten, die im Vergleich zum Fußball deutlich weniger Raum in der massenmedialen Berichterstattung einnehmen. Tennis, Schwimmen, Reitsport u.a. Sportarten finden als kulturelle Stellvertreter des Nationalen (fast) nur Beachtung, wenn die jeweiligen Akteure erfolgreich sind.

arbeitsteilig zusammenwirkender Teams Kontur. Für die Konstruktion nationaler *Gefühlsgemeinschaften* ist die Verbildlichung des emotionalen Erlebens beteiligter Akteure vor Ort (insbesondere der Spieler, der Trainer, der Fans) relevant – auch deshalb, weil sie als symbolische Verdichtung von Spielergebnissen (Sieg oder Niederlage) und deren Folgen in Sachen (nationaler) Anerkennung fungieren kann. Schlussendlich ist neben und mit den sprachlichen Rahmungen die *visuelle Markierung* von sozialen Objekten (Dingen, Individuen, Gruppen u.a.) über nationale Zeichen und Symbole zentral. Als äußere Interpretationsklammern legen sie die Zuordnung der anderen genannten Dimensionen als Ausdruck des Nationalen nahe.

Abschließend muss festgestellt werden, dass sich aus diesen Befunden nicht die faktische Bedeutung der Medien für die Herstellung nationaler kollektiver Identitäten schließen lässt. Das gilt zumindest dann, wenn man, wie z.b. Jan Assmann, diesen Begriff an die *Identifikation* von Gruppen mit den symbolischen Konstruktionen eines „Wir-Bildes" bindet[27]. Während die Kenntnis der Idee des Nationalen und spezifischer Nationalsemantiken bei den Rezipienten für das *Verstehen* der Medienkommunikationen gegeben sein müssen, kann die *Akzeptanz* nationaler Erzählmuster oder gar die Selbstidentifizierung der Rezipienten mit diesen keineswegs vorausgesetzt werden. Wohl aber kann man mit guten Gründen annehmen, dass die hier behandelten visuellen Kommunikationen die Wahrscheinlichkeit zu steigern vermögen, dass sich eben jene (Selbst-)Identifikationen ereignen. Ob, wie und in welchem Maße sich dies bei Zuschauern entlang der hier skizzierten Dimensionen ereignet, wäre indessen im Rahmen von Forschungsdesigns der Rezipientenforschung zu untersuchen.

Literatur

Assmann, J. (2002): Das kulturelle Gedächtnis. Schrift, Erinnerung und politische Identität in frühen Hochkulturen. München: C.H. Beck.
Anderson, B. (1983): Imagined Communities. Reflections on the Origin and Spread of Nationalism. London: Verso.

---

27 Assmann hierzu: „Unter einer kollektiven oder Wir-Identität verstehen wir das Bild, das eine Gruppe von sich aufbaut und mit dem sich deren Mitglieder identifizieren. Kollektive Identität ist eine Frage der Identifikation seitens der beteiligten Individuen. Es gibt sie nicht ‚an sich', sondern immer nur in dem Maße, wie sich bestimmte Individuen zu ihr bekennen. Sie ist so stark oder so schwach, wie sie im Bewusstsein der Gruppenmitglieder lebendig ist und deren Denken und Handeln zu motivieren vermag" (Assmann 2002: 132).

Bendix, R. (1991): Strukturgeschichtliche Voraussetzungen der nationalen und kulturellen Identität in der Neuzeit. In: Giesen, B. (Hg.): Nationale und kulturelle Identität: Studien zur Entwicklung des kollektiven Bewußtseins in der Neuzeit. Frankfurt a.M.: Suhrkamp, 39-55.

Bergmann, J. / Luckmann, T. (1999): „Moral und Kommunikation". In: dies. (Hg.): Kommunikative Konstruktion von Moral, Bd.1, 13-36.

Bredekamp, H. (2007): Bilder bewegen. Von der Kunstkammer zum Endspiel. Aufsätze und Reden. Herausgegeben von Jörg Probst. Berlin: Wagenbach.

Bromberger, C. (1995): Le match de football. Ethnologie d´une passion partisane à Marseilles, Naples et Turin. Paris: Maison des Sciences de L'Homme.

Ciompi, L. / Endert, E. (2011): Gefühle machen Geschichte. Die Wirkung kollektiver Emotionen von Hitler bis Obama. Göttingen: Vandenhoeck & Ruprecht, 175-197.

Eisenstadt, S. N. (1991): „Die Konstruktion nationaler Identitäten in vergleichender Perspektive. In: Giesen, B. (Hg.): Nationale und kulturelle Identität: Studien zur Entwicklung des kollektiven Bewußtseins in der Neuzeit. Frankfurt a.M.: Suhrkamp, 21-38.

Giesecke, M. (1998): Der Buchdruck in der frühen Neuzeit. Eine historische Fallstudie über die Durchsetzung neuer Informations- und Kommunikationstechnologien. Frankfurt am Main: Suhrkamp

Goffman, E. (1969): Wir alle spielen Theater. Die Selbstdarstellung im Alltag. München: Piper.

Gebauer, G. (2006): Poetik des Fußballs. Frankfurt am Main: Campus.

Hahn, Alois (1997): Partizipative Identitäten. In: Herfried Münkler (Hg.): Furcht und Faszination. Facetten der Fremdheit. Berlin: Akademie Verlag, 115–158.

Hitzler, R. / Niederbacher, A. (2010): Leben in Szenen. Formen juveniler Vergemeinschaftung heute (3. Aufl.). Wiesbaden: VS.

Horton, D. / Wohl, R. (1956): Mass-Communication and Para-Social Interaction: Observations on Intimacy at a Distance. Psychiatry 2, 215–229.

Klein, G. (2008): Globalisierung, Lokalisierung, (Re.-)Nationalisierung. Fussball als lokales Ereignis, globalisierte Ware und Bilderwelt. In: Klein, G. / Meuser, M. (Hg.): Ernste Spiele: zur politischen Soziologie des Fußballs. Bielefeld: transcript, 31-42.

Kracauer, S. (1963): Das Ornament der Masse. In: ders.: Das Ornament der Masse. Essays. Frankfurt am Main: Suhrkamp, 50-62.

Leggewie, C. (2006): Marke Deutschland. Sport als Medium kollektiver Identität im Globalisierungsprozeß. In: Schwier, J. / Leggewie, C. (Hg.): Wettbewerbsspiele. Die Inszenierung von Sport und Politik in den Medien (Interaktiva– Schriftenreihe des Zentrums für Medien und Interaktivität (ZMI), Gießen, Bd.3). Frankfurt a.M.: Campus, 105-119.

Luhmann, N. (1997): Die Gesellschaft der Gesellschaft. Frankfurt am Main: Suhrkamp.

Müller, M. G. / Kappas, A. (2011): Visual Emotions – emotional visuals: emotion, pathos formulae, and their relevance for communication research. In: Döveling, K. / von Scheve, C. / Elly A. Konijn, E. (Hg.): The Routledge Handbook of Emotions and Mass Media. London/New York: Routledge, 310-331.

Newcomb, H. / Hirsch, P. (1986): Fernsehen als kulturelles Forum. Neue Perspektiven für die Medienforschung. Rundfunk und Fernsehen. Zeitschrift für Medien- und Kommunikationswissenschaften 34 (2), 177-190.

Schwier, J. /Schauerte, T. (2009): Die Theatralisierung des Sports. In: Willems, H. (Hg.): Theatralisierung der Gesellschaft. Band 1: Soziologische Theorie und Zeitdiagnose. Wiesbaden: VS, 419-438.

Speth, R. (1999): Nation und Emotion. Von der vorgestellten zur emotional erfahrenen Gemeinschaft. In: Klein, A. / Nullmeier, F. (Hg.): Masse – Macht – Emotionen. Zu einer politischen Soziologie der Emotionen. Westdeutscher Verlag: Opladen, 287-307.

Weiß, J. (1998): Handeln und handeln lassen: über Stellvertretung. Opladen: Westdeutscher Verlag.

Willems, H. (1998): Inszenierungsgesellschaft? Zum Theater als Modell, zur Theatralität von Praxis In: ders. (Hg): Inszenierungsgesellschaft. Ein einführendes Handbuch. Westdeutscher Verlag: Opladen, 23-79.

Wolf, S. (2011): Textanalyse. In: Bergmann, J. / Ayaß, R. (2011): Qualitative Methoden der Medienforschung (2. Aufl.). Mannheim: Verlag für Gesprächsforschung, 245-273.

Trikotwerbung für den Geldverleiher – der Sündenfall im Fußball-Sponsoring?

Kit Advertising for the Money Lender – The Original Sin in Football Sponsorship?

Jürgen Schraten

Zusammenfassung

Der Artikel analysiert die Berichterstattung des britischen Guardian über einen neuen Sponsorenvertrag des populären englischen Klubs Newcastle United. Dieser Sponsorenvertrag wurde mit einem expandierenden Zahltags-Geldverleiher geschlossen, der sehr viel höhere Zinssätze als ein gewöhnliches Kreditinstitut verlangt, und daher auch in höherem Maße zur Verschuldung von Bürgern beiträgt. Zunächst untersucht der Artikel den massenmedialen Mechanismus, nach dem die Berichterstattung ablief. Dabei spielten Möglichkeiten der Ausweitung der Berichterstattung und ihrer Resonanz eine wichtigere Rolle als die sachliche Redlichkeit der Kritik. Danach widmet sich der Artikel der Angemessenheit der vorgetragenen Kritik. Dafür wird die Geschäftspraxis der Kreditfirma hinsichtlich ihres Einflusses auf die ethischen Ansprüche des professionellen Fußballsports überprüft: Einerseits ist die Verbindung von Fußball und Geld so alt wie die Sportart selbst, andererseits ist das sportliche Spielprinzip auf eine rigorose Abschottung von finanzieller Beeinflussung angewiesen, und öffentliche Debatten wie jene im Guardian entscheiden ganz wesentlich darüber, ob eine solche Abschottung noch als gegeben betrachtet wird. Im Falle von Newcastle United stellte sich nach kurzer Zeit heraus, dass eine unvertretbare Grenzübertretung nicht unterstellt werden konnte, woraufhin die Berichterstattung eine andere Richtung einschlug.

Abstract

This article analyses the reporting in the British *Guardian* about a new sponsorship deal for the popular English club Newcastle United. This sponsorship deal was made with a pay day money lender which is expanding its business. This money lender is demanding much higher interest rates than a normal credit company and is consequently adding in no small measure to the debt problems of individual citizens. Firstly, the article examines how the reporting was carried out in line with the mechanisms operating in the mass media. The possibilities of extending the reporting and its resonance played in the process a more important role than that of the critique's objective honesty. Then the article goes on to gauge the appropriateness of the criticisms being voiced. Following on from this the business practices of the credit company will be critically examined in respect of its influence on the ethical demands of the game of professional football. On the one hand the connection between football and money is as old as the game itself, whilst on the other hand the principle of sport and play requires a rigorous exclusion of financial influences, and public debates such as those in the *Guardian* lead to quite fundamental judgements about whether such exclusion can still be regarded as given fact. In the case of Newcastle United it soon emerged that an unjustifiable crossing of such a boundary could not be proven and at that point the reporting turned to different matters.

1   Einleitung

Der vorliegende Artikel behandelt die Debatte über den neuen Sponsorenvertrag des Premier League-Klubs Newcastle United FC mit dem Kreditgeber Wonga. com in der Online-Ausgabe der englischen Tageszeitung The Guardian im Oktober 2012. Bemerkenswert an dieser Debatte ist, dass im milliardenschweren professionellen Geschäft des Fußballs über die moralische Vertretbarkeit eines Sponsorenvertrags debattiert wurde.

Newcastle United ist ein traditionsreicher Klub des englischen Fußballs mit einer vergleichsweise großen Fangemeinde. Wonga.com ist eine von zwei Südafrikanern in Großbritannien gegründete Firma, die kurzfristige Kleinkredite in einem schnellen, vollständig online abgewickelten Verfahren vergibt.

Erstaunlich war die Debatte aus mindestens zwei Gründen.

Der erste Grund ist mit der Eigenlogik der Massenmedien (Baecker 2007; Luhmann 2009) gut zu erklären. Denn auf den ersten Blick war an der Aufgeregtheit verwunderlich, dass Newcastle United nicht der erste englische Klub ist, der einen Vertrag über Trikotwerbung mit Wonga.com abschloss. Bereits seit 2010 wirbt mit Blackpool FC ein Verein, der bis zum Saisonende 2011/12 ebenfalls der höchsten englischen Spielklasse Premier League angehörte, für Wonga.com. Allerdings genießt Blackpool FC nicht annähernd die Popularität von Newcastle United. Und auch das Fußball-Sponsoring von Wonga.com war bereits wiederholt Thema in The Guardian gewesen. Am 27. und 28. März berichtete die Zeitung über die Initiative der Fußballfans von insgesamt 18 englischen Teams, die ein Ende der Werbung ihrer Klubs für Wonga.com verlangten. Es handelte sich jedoch um Vereine, die in jüngerer Vergangenheit aufgrund mäßigen sportlichen Erfolgs nur noch geringe mediale Aufmerksamkeit auf sich ziehen konnten. Und am 18. Juni 2012 berichtete The Guardian sogar über einen zählbaren Erfolg dieser Faninitiative, als die Football League entschied, einen Sponsorenvertrag mit Wonga.com ohne Verlängerung auslaufen zu lassen. Beide Berichterstattungen erzeugten jedoch keine weitergehende öffentliche Aufmerksamkeit, daran anschließende Nachrichten blieben aus.

Genau dies änderte sich im Falle von Newcastle United. Nun griffen auch andere Massenmedien das Thema auf, Parlamentsabgeordnete meldeten sich zu Wort und wirtschaftliche Akteure, die mit Kreditgebern befasst sind, schalteten sich in die Debatte ein. Der Fußballverein bildete somit den Aufmerksamkeit erzeugenden Knotenpunkt, der The Guardian auch die Wiederanknüpfung an eigene, zuvor vergleichsweise resonanzlos gebliebene Berichterstattung ermöglichte.

Der zweite Grund für Erstaunen über die Debatte liegt darin, dass die Werbung für Wonga.com ab der Saison 2013/14 auf den Trikots von Newcastle United jene von Virgin Money ersetzen wird, einem Anbieter von Kreditkarten, Hypotheken und Versicherungsprodukten. Auf den ersten Blick handelt es sich also bei Wonga.com um einen anderen Vertreter derselben Branche, des Finanzsektors, und es fragt sich, woher die Aufgeregtheit ihren Anlass bezieht.

Zur Klärung dieser Frage werden zunächst Newcastle United und Wonga.com etwas eingehender vorgestellt, bevor die Debatte in The Guardian untersucht wird. Dabei werden die beiden Hauptaspekte der Kritik am Wonga.com-Sponsoring kritisch reflektiert. Der erste Aspekt bezieht sich auf einen ‚Spielkulturpessimismus' (Claussen 2007: 659), der die angeblich zunehmende Kommerzialisierung des Fußballs beklagt. Der zweite Aspekt behandelt den Vorwurf, bei Wonga.com handele es sich um einen legalen Kredithai, der mit etablierten Bankgeschäften nicht gleichgesetzt werden könne. Der Artikel schließt mit einer Bewertung der Frage, ob es sich um eine ungerechtfertigt erzeugte Aufgeregtheit der Massenmedien handelte, oder um eine begründete Besorgnis um die ethische Kultur des Fußballs.

2   Die Akteure des Spiels: Newcastle United und Wonga.com

2.1   Die Vorgeschichte des Newcastle United FC

Newcastle United FC ging aus dem Zusammenschluss zweier kurzlebiger Vorläufer hervor. Dabei wurde der eine der beiden, Newcastle East End bereits im März 1890, kurz nach seiner Gründung in eine Gesellschaft mit beschränkter Haftung umgewandelt. Der ökonomische Aspekt war also bereits vor der Entstehung des späteren Klubs präsent (Newcastle United 2012c). Nach einer Zusammenlegung mit Newcastle West End Football Club wurde der neue Verein am 6. September 1895 als Newcastle United Football Club Limited Company rechtlich eingetragen. Er stieg nach mehrfachen Versuchen zur Saison 1898/99 erstmals in die englische First Division auf.

Seit 2007 ist der Club im Besitz von Mike Ashley, dem Gründer eines großen Sportartikelhandels. Er kaufte den Klub für £134,4 Millionen. Ein vom Verein 2011 selbst herausgegebenes Leitbild verdeutlicht, dass er Newcastle United zu einem sich selbst finanzierenden Unternehmen machen möchte: „We cannot continue to acquire debt year after year and rely on additional financial support from the owner" (Newcastle United 2011)[1]. Offenbar ist der Besitzer in Bezug auf dieses Ziel allerdings skeptisch, denn 2008 und 2009 versuchte er zweimal den Klub zu verkaufen, entschied sich jedoch nach kurzer Frist wieder um. Der zweite Verkaufsversuch Ashleys scheiterte explizit an der Erzielung eines für ihn akzeptablen Preises (BBC 2009a)[2]. Die Suche nach alternativen Geldquellen lag nahe, und im November 2011 wurde Uniteds traditionsreiches Stadion St. James Park mit

---

1   In öffentlichen Statements wird aber auch auf Anforderungen der Fans nach neuen Spielern verwiesen, um den Finanzbedarf zu legitimieren: „The fans want us to buy more players, we need a new striker in January, we'll need replacements in the summer" (BBC 20112b).

2   Der erste Verkaufsversuch war Resultat einer unpopulären Personalentscheidung (BBC 2008).

dem Namen der von Ashley gegründeten Firma versehen (BBC 2011b). Bereits ein erster Versuch der Umbenennung hatte heftige Fanproteste ausgelöst, und auch dieses Mal kam es zum Aufruhr (BBC 2009b; BBC 2011c). Die Umbenennung in Sports Direct Arena war dabei ausdrücklich als beispielgebend für andere Investoren gedacht, um durch diese Form des Sponsoring „significant additional income" (BBC 2011a) zu generieren.

In einem weiteren Schritt, Gelder zu akquirieren, gab Newcastle United am 9. Oktober 2012 den Abschluss eines neuen Sponsorenvertrags mit der Kreditfirma Wonga.com im Umfang von £24 Millionen und einer Laufzeit von vier Jahren bekannt (Newcastle United 2012a). Zur Ironie der Geschichte gehört, dass Wonga.com als erste Maßnahme am 17. Oktober 2012 die Rück-Umbenennung des Stadions in St. James Park bewirkte und mit pathetischen Worten als ‚Wiedergeburt' verkündete. „Newcastle United Football Club's new sponsor wonga. com has today given the club's fans back their home of football by reinstating the stadium's rightful St. James' Park name. [...] The transfer is a gift to fans from the digital finance company [...]. As well as defending the heritage of the club with the reinstated name, Newcastle United and its fans will also benefit from Wonga's investment in the academy and the club's foundation scheme, which helps 15 and 16 year-olds find work" (Newcastle United 2012b). Die Betonung lag somit auf solchen Aktivitäten, die nicht als unmittelbar ersichtliche Motive der Geschäftsverbindung – Generierung von Geldquellen für die Profimannschaft hier, und Werbung für die Kreditfirma dort – angesehen werden konnten. Allerdings sahen sich Wonga.com und Newcastle United einer weit ausgreifenderen Debatte über die Angemessenheit der Sponsoring-Beziehung ausgesetzt.

2.1 Die digitale Finanzfirma Wonga.com

Wonga.com wurde 2006 von den Südafrikanern Errol Damelin und Jonty Hurwitz in London gegründet. Die Firma hat sich auf das Kleinkundengeschäft der Kreditbranche spezialisiert. Sie soll hier als Geldverleiher charakterisiert werden, da ihr Geschäftsmodell, im Unterschied zu einer Bank, keine Geldeinlagen von Kunden vorsieht, sondern sich auf die Vermittlung von Krediten und deren Rückzahlung beschränkt. Spareinlagen dienen bei Banken als wichtige Ressource, die an andere Interessenten in der Form des Kredits weitergereicht wird. Ohne diese Ressource ist das Wachstum des Geschäftsvolumens also auf die zurückgezahlten Kredite beschränkt, sofern die Besitzer nicht das Grundkapital aufstocken (Baecker 2008).

Wonga.com limitiert die Höhe des Kredits und seine Laufzeit strikt. Die kurze Laufzeit ist dabei implizit an den Gedanken der monatlichen Gehaltszahlung geknüpft, so dass Kunden im Bedarfsfall einen kleinen Geldbetrag bei Wonga.com leihen, und ihn am Zahltag ihres Gehalts mit Zinsen zurückgeben. Daraus resultiert die Bezeichnung des Zahltag-Geldverleihers.

Wonga.com operiert in vier Staaten. In England und Wales werden maximal £400 für 45 Tage gewährt, in Kanada $500 für 45 Tage, in Polen 500 Zloty für 30 Tage und in Südafrika ZAR2500 für maximal 30 Tage. Im Folgenden beschränkt sich der Artikel auf die Beschreibung des englischen Geschäftsmodells. Auf der Webseite kann man mit einem Schieberegler den Betrag und die Laufzeit des Kredits im Rahmen der erwähnten Beschränkungen wählen und bekommt umgehend den Auszahlungszeitpunkt und die Kosten am Rückzahlungstag eingeblendet. Beispielsweise versprach eine Anfrage um 15:30 Uhr nach £100 für zehn Tage den Eingang des Geldes auf dem eigenen Konto für 15:55 Uhr, und forderte dafür die Rückzahlung von £115,91 zehn Tage später. Der Preis ergibt sich aus der Summe von Bearbeitungsgebühren und des einfach zu kalkulieren Zinssatzes von 1% pro Tag, mit dem Wonga.com offensiv wirbt. Deutlich sichtbar war auf der Webseite aber auch der Hinweis, dass dies einem effektiven Jahreszins von 4214% entspricht. Dieser Hinweis wiederum ist mit Erläuterungen versehen, da die Absicht, das Geld für ein Jahr zu leihen, nicht vorliege. Dies verschweigt allerdings den Umstand, dass der Jahreszins dennoch den Vergleichsmaßstab mit Kreditkosten bei anderen Geldinstituten bildet.

Im nächsten Schritt der Kreditbeantragung heißt es, man sei sechs Minuten von der Entscheidung und 15 Minuten von der Auszahlung entfernt. Verlangt wird auf dieser zweiten Webseite die Angabe des Namens, mit den Optionen, sich als Doktor oder Reverend titulieren zu lassen; zusätzlich ist die Angabe der Wohnverhältnisse, Arbeitsverhältnisse und der Einkommen der eigenen Person sowie des Haushalts, dem man angehört, erforderlich, und man kann sich auch mit dem sozialen Netzwerk Facebook verbinden, was explizit die Wahrscheinlichkeit erhöht, den Kredit bewilligt zu bekommen. Auch ein Fahrzeugbesitz wird abgefragt. Schließlich werden Adresse und telekommunikative Kontaktdaten angefragt. All diese Angaben – Facebook inklusive – können für das Prinzip des *credit scoring* verwendet werden. Dabei wird die Kreditwürdigkeit nicht aufgrund einer Einschätzung der charakterlichen Vertrauenswürdigkeit und nur minimal durch die Einkommens- und Kredit*geschichte* bestimmt. Bedeutsamer sind die *zukünftigen* Erwartungen von Einkommen, die sich aus Bildungsstand, Wohnort und eben auch Namenstiteln ergeben. Diese werden mit statistischen Wahrscheinlichkeitswerten versehen und in einem Algorithmus berechnet. Die Informationen für die Wahrscheinlichkeitswerte werden von Kredit-Auskunfteien bereitgestellt und fortwährend aktualisiert und optimiert (Burton 2008: 53). Das Verfahren ist soziologisch durchaus gewitzt – hinter der Abfrage, ob der Antragsteller ‚Reverend‘ ist, steckt gewiss die Vermutung, dass ein geistlicher Würdenträger aufgrund seiner moralischen Verpflichtung und guten sozialen Einbettung ein zuverlässigerer Kreditkunde ist als andere Bürger mit dem gleichen Einkommen. Zugleich muss aber auch festgehalten werden, dass das Verfahren in seinem Wesen diskriminatorisch ist, weil von sozialen Verhältnissen auf Charaktereigenschaften und individuelle Leistungsfähigkeit geschlossen wird (Burton 2008: 54). Damit werden soziale Randlagen freilich stabilisiert – wer in einer schlechten Wohngegend lebt, bekommt keinen Kredit und hat damit geringere ökonomische Ressourcen zur Verfügung, um sich aus genau dieser Wohnsituation zu befreien.

Credit scoring wird heute von vielen Kreditinstituten genutzt, die Besonderheit bei Wonga.com besteht darin, dass die Kalkulation online erfolgt und der Kunde das Ergebnis vor dem Bildschirm abwarten kann. Im Falle einer positiven Einschätzung durch Wonga.com ist noch die Erteilung einer Abbuchungsermächtigung von einem bestehenden Bankkonto zu gewähren. Dieser Schritt ist von eminenter Bedeutung, da er eine Machterteilung an Wonga.com bedeutet. Sobald der Kredit bewilligt ist und dem Vertrag vom Kunden zugestimmt wurde, hat Wonga.com den direkten Zugriff auf die Eingänge von dessen Bankkonto. Die Firma braucht für Abbuchungen in Bezug auf den Kredit nicht jedes Mal die Zustimmung des Kunden einzuholen – das gehört zu den Geschäftsbedingungen. Eine solche Machterteilung erfolgt allerdings in der Regel auch bei Krediten durch eine Hausbank. Der Kunde gibt damit autonome Manövrierfähigkeit in Finanzangelegenheiten auf.

3 Diskursanalyse in The Guardian

3.1 Publizistische Beobachtung eines Geldverleihers

Noch bevor Ende März 2012 die ersten Berichte von Protesten der Fußballszene über Werbekontrakte mit Wonga.com erscheinen, publizierte The Guardian zu Beginn desselben Monats einen ausführlichen Artikel über die Geschäftspraxis von Wonga.com in seiner Finanzrubrik. In der Online-Ausgabe der Zeitung wird diesem Artikel retroaktiv große Prominenz zuteil, indem die später diskutierten Berichte über Newcastle Uniteds Sponsorengeschäft stets auf diesen Artikel als zusätzliche Informationsquelle verweisen. Die in ihm enthaltenen Informationen bilden somit die Hintergrundfolie, auf der das spätere Ereignis skizziert werden wird.

Der Bericht leitet mit dem Statement eines Wonga.com-Pressevertreters ein, die höheren Preise ihrer Kredite im Vergleich zu gewöhnlichen Kreditinstituten entsprächen dem Unterschied zwischen einem Busticket und den Kosten einer Taxifahrt – unter bestimmten Umständen sei es einem den Unterschied wert.

Weiter wird berichtet, der Prozess der Kreditgewährung, der online verfolgt werden könne, sei von fröhlich scherzenden Texten begleitet, wie „Great news! We can confirm £100.00 have just left Wonga and is winging its way to your bank account at the speed of light (well, extremely fast anyway)" (The Guardian vom 1. März 2012). Die Firma werbe zwar mit Transparenz, verschweige aber den Jahreszins von 4214% - eine Behauptung, die zumindest ein halbes Jahr später nicht mehr zutraf, als dieser Zinssatz deutlich auf der ersten Webseite des Kreditantragsverfahrens zu sehen war. Dabei kann es sich durchaus um eine Reaktion auf die Berichterstattung gehandelt haben, um einer Zwangsmaßnahme der Aufsichtsbehörden zuvor zu kommen.

Für den hier diskutierten Zusammenhang von Bedeutung ist der Hinweis des Artikels, dass die Ausgaben der Firma für Werbung von £22 000 im Jahre 2009 auf £16 Millionen in 2011 gestiegen seien, denn dies verweist auf zweierlei: Zum einen ist, wie erwähnt, das Geschäftsvolumen eines Zahltags-Geldverleihers von der Anzahl seiner Kunden abhängig, und massiv ausgeweitete Werbung deutet auf eine Expansionsabsicht des Geschäfts hin. Im Falle von Wonga.com war diese Absicht offenkundig erfolgreich, denn es wird ebenfalls berichtet, dass die Gewinnspanne sich zwischen 2009 und 2010 auf £73 Millionen verdreifacht habe. Zum anderen ist Werbung als Selbstdarstellung immer auch Imagepflege, so dass Wonga.com einen erheblichen Teil der neuen Einnahmen in die Beeinflussung seines Ansehens investierte.

Als nächstes merkt The Guardian an, dass die Werbung sich nicht nur auf Londons Verkehrsbussen, sondern auch auf den Trikots des Blackpool FC und der Spieler vom Heart of Midleothian FC aus Edinburgh befinde. Während Werbung auf Verkehrsbussen mit ihrer Alltagsgegenwart als Maßnahme für die Verbreitung der Bekanntheit gesehen werden kann, tritt bei Trikotwerbung im Fußball das gute Ansehen aufgrund der Identifikation von Fans mit ihren Klubs als zweiter Aspekt hinzu.

Wonga.com hebt dem Artikel zufolge seine unbürokratische Vorgehensweise als zukunftsträchtig hervor und vergleicht sich nicht etwa mit Banken, sondern mit Facebook und Amazon. „We see ourselves as an internet technology business first, and a finance business second" (The Guardian vom 1. März 2012). Davon ist auch die Wahrnehmung der Kundschaft geprägt. Wonga.com sehe hier „young professionals, who are web-savvy, fully-banked, have access to mainstream credit and a regular income" (The Guardian vom 1. März 2012) und wisse von einer 95%igen Kundenzufriedenheit zu berichten.

Dies werde federführend von der Labour-Abgeordneten aus Walthamstow, Stella Creasy kritisiert: „They need to think about the idea that it is the technology that people are attracted to, rather than the credit" (The Guardian vom 1. März 2012). Die Kritik Creasys besteht in der Einschätzung, dass die Einfachheit der Kreditbeschaffung vor allem auf jene attraktiv wirke, die Geld benötigen. Auch Schuldnerberatungen und Parlamentsmitglieder hätten eher jene Kunden vor Augen, denen durch Zahltag-Geldverleih finanzielle Probleme entstanden seien, und deren Zahl sei innerhalb von zwei Jahren auf ein Vierfaches angestiegen. Nach Luhmann muss Creasy unbedingt beigepflichtet werden, da „in das Zahlen um des Zahlens willen [...] offensichtlich ein Motivmangel hineinorganisiert" (Luhmann 1994: 59) ist. Das heißt, dass der Bezug eines Kredits durch internet-affine Kunden nur, weil er einfach zu beziehen ist, nicht erwartet werden kann. Es gibt keinen Anlass für jemanden, der problemlos mit einer Bankkarte Geld von seinem Konto abheben kann (sei es vorhandenes Vermögen, oder sei es ein bereits eingeräumter Überziehungskredit), sich dieses Geld zuvor von Wonga. com auf sein Konto überweisen zu lassen – zu einem wahrscheinlich erheblich höheren Preis. Daher kann Creasy beigepflichtet werden, dass die Einfachheit des Wonga-Verfahrens nur jene zur Kreditaufnahme motiviert, die von Geldmangel als Motiv betroffen sind.

Als treffenden Beleg führt der Artikel den Fall eines gut verdienenden 29jährigen an, der aufgrund einer belasteten Kreditgeschichte keine Kreditkarte oder Überziehungskredite von seiner Bank erhält. „He began taking out loans on his iPhone, as he walked into town to meet friends; the money would be in his account before he reached the cash machine" (The Guardian vom 1. März 2012). Dies war einfach und schnell, aber ohne Verweigerung eines Überziehungskredits durch seine Bank wäre sein Kredit nicht nur überflüssig, sondern auch sehr teuer und daher unwahrscheinlich gewesen.

Creasys Argument, dass Wongas neuartiges High-Tech-Produkt von Kurzzeitkrediten mit einem Tagessatz von 1% auf ein Klientel zielt, das von etablierten Kreditinstituten zurückgewiesen werde, ist also stichhaltig. The Guardian nimmt an dieser Stelle erstmals die später wiederholt aufgegriffene Charakterisierung Wongas durch Stella Creasy als ‚legal loan sharks' (The Guardian vom 1. März 2012) auf.

Tiefere Einblicke in die Spannung des Selbstbildes von Wonga.com mit der Wahrnehmung durch die eigenen Kunden werden gewährt, als die Journalistin Amelia Gentleman den Marketingchef von Wonga.com, Darryl Bowman, auf Kunden in Geldnot anspricht: „It's not difficult to find people who have had bad experiences with Wonga.com, and when I explain that I've spoken at length to several very unhappy customers, the company's PR manager is sanguine, remarks that debt is an emotional subject, and says the company accepts that its services will be controversial" (The Guardian vom 1. März 2012). Diese kritische Selbstsicht ist bedeutsam, weil sie bereits verdeutlicht, dass Wonga.com zum Zwecke der Imagepflege auf der Suche nach Werbeverträgen mit populären Fußballklubs ist.

Als Marketingchef Bowman der Journalistin empfiehlt, auch einmal mit zufriedenen Kunden zu sprechen und ihr zu diesem Zweck vier Telefonnummern weitergibt, macht Amelia Gentleman die interessante Begegnung mit einer 53jährigen Arbeitslosen, die auf Sozialleistungen angewiesen ist. Diese Frau passt zwar nicht in das Selbstbild einer gut situierten, internet-affinen jungen Kundin, das Wonga.com in seiner Werbung anpreist – im Gegenteil gibt sie zur Kenntnis, dass sie die Kredite für den Kauf von Nahrungsmitteln ausgab, weil die Sozialleistungen nicht ausgereicht hatten –, aber sie lobt Wonga.com tatsächlich, denn mit Kreditkarten habe sie bereits viel Ärger gehabt und ein Überziehungskredit werde ihr von Banken nicht eingeräumt. Und obwohl sie mehr als 21% ihrer monatlichen Sozialleistungen allein für die Zinsen aufwenden musste, kommentierte sie dies mit Zufriedenheit, denn alternative Leihmöglichkeiten bestünden eben nicht. Und die Journalistin muss konzedieren, dass jeder für kreditwürdig erachtete Kunde denselben Betrag problemlos über seine Kreditkarte hätte borgen können. In einer Gesellschaft, in der Kreditverfügbarkeit als Normalfall gilt, bedeutet der Ausschluss eine diskriminierende Benachteiligung (Burton 2008: 60). Wonga.com verdient sein Geld mit der Befreiung von diesem Ausschluss – bis zum Rückzahlungstermin.

Der technologische Ablauf der Kreditvergabe bei Wonga.com ist freilich nicht bedeutungslos. Er ermöglicht die Kreditgewährung ohne Feierabend und Wochenende und ohne einen einzigen persönlichen Kontakt. The Guardian verweist darauf, dass diese Ausschaltung menschlicher Interaktion zur Popularität des Service erheblich beigetragen habe – neben der allgemeinen ökonomischen Entwicklung sinkender Einkommen und restriktiverer Kreditvergabe durch konventionelle Geldinstitute. Dies bestätigt die Schilderung des bereits erwähnten 29jährigen Kunden: „Because it's done online, there's no human interaction, it is a lot less difficult … it means that I can hide it. The online is a huge aspect of it. I wouldn't want to talk to somebody about it. The web doesn't ask questions. The website wouldn't judge me" (The Guardian vom 1. März 2012). Bowman betont, dass die technische Einfachheit von restriktiver Praxis begleitet sei und Zweidrittel aller Anträge abgelehnt würden. „The reason why we decline them is that we are a responsible lender and we make money when people pay us back. We want people to pay us back. Our model is not built around people not paying us back. Our objective and our need to be responsible are perfectly aligned" (The Guardian vom 1. März 2012). Diese Aussage, mit ihrer wiederholenden Betonung, hat eine durchaus rationale Begründung, da viele Kreditgeber keineswegs auf termingerechte Rückzahlung fixiert sind, weil sich bei Zahlungsverzögerungen höhere Einnahmen erzielen lassen (Burton 2008: 58). Allerdings kontrastiert Bowmans Behauptung der restriktiven Kreditvergabe mit der Aussage eines von The Guardian angeführten 55jährigen Kunden, der gemeinsam mit seiner Ehefrau ein frei verfügbares monatliches Einkommen von £500 hat: „I was surprised that they didn›t refuse me" (The Guardian vom 1. März 2012).

Die Firma wirbt mit Transparenz und setzt dieses Prinzip mit verantwortlicher Kreditvergabe gleich: „When people come to our website they have all the information presented to them in a very transparent, upfront way, and they are able to make a sensible decision about whether this product is right for them. We charge 1% interest per day, which is £1 per £100 borrowed. With us we're telling you exactly what you›re getting into, there›s no small print, no surprises" (The Guardian vom 1. März 2012). Er plädiert gegen gesetzliche Begrenzungen des Zinssatzes, weil gerade die Verteuerung hohen Risikos zur Verantwortlichkeit gehöre. Würden Firmen wie seine das Geschäft nicht betreiben, wichen die Kunden auf illegale Alternativen aus. Die Artikelautorin Amelia Gentleman schlussfolgert, dass Bowman mit dieser Aussage jedoch implizit dem Werbeimage der Firma widerspreche: „Here, for the first time is half an admission that this is a service for people who have nowhere else to go" (The Guardian vom 1. März 2012). Es gehe also nicht um internet-affine Kunden, sondern um teure Angebote für risikobehaftete Schuldner.

Hier wird die Abgeordnete Stella Creasy erneut als Kritikerin ins Feld geführt: „The mistake they make is to assume that people, when faced with a financial penalty, have the option to avoid it. In their mind they have the option of choosing not to extend a loan, when they see the costs. What they don't understand is that they are dealing with a clientele who doesn't have that choice [...] They need to think about the idea that it is the technology that people are attracted to, rather than the credit. [...] Once they've paid back the loan and interest and charges, their money runs out even quicker" (The Guardian vom 1. März 2012). Den von Creasy unterstellten Mechanismus erklärt ein 55jähriger Kunde, der eingangs £400 für 35 Tage geliehen hatte, woraus eine Rückzahlungsverpflichtung von £545,48 resultiert sei. Diese Rückzahlung werde durch die Abbuchungsermächtigung automatisiert. „When they take the money out of your account, that reduces your disposable income for the month; halfway through the month I had no money so I took out another loan with Wonga. Once you start, you don't stop. Unless

something happens, you have to go back to bridge the gap" (The Guardian vom
1. März 2012). Dies verweist auf den Umstand, dass die Inanspruchnahme eines
teuren Kurzzeitkredits normalerweise als letzte Wahl gesehen wird, und somit
konsequenterweise davon ausgegangen werden muss, dass die Rückzahlung des
Kurzzeitkredits am Zahltag das verfügbare Einkommen des Folgemonats so sehr
minimiert, dass die Aufnahme eines nächsten Kurzzeitkredits wahrscheinlich
wird. Man könnte auch sagen: Durch die unwiderrufliche Einzugsermächtigung
erhält Wonga.com die Möglichkeit, durch Abbuchung bereits am Zahltag des Gehalts die Wahrscheinlichkeit einer erneuten Kreditaufnahme durch den Kunden
zu erhöhen. Der 55jährige verweist darauf, dass aufgrund dieses Mechanismus die
zusätzliche Inanspruchnahme anderer Anbieter schnell hinzukäme. Schließlich
habe er insgesamt £1500 an Zinsen für seine ursprüngliche Entscheidung eines
Kredits über £400 gezahlt. Die Verantwortlichkeit sieht er jedoch nicht nur bei
der Firma: „He is unsure about what he feels about Wonga, and he blames himself
as much as them" (The Guardian vom 1. März 2012). Die Auswirkungen für das
Image von Wonga.com werden auch unmissverständlich benannt: „When he sees
the logo on buses and football shirts he thinks: Yes, they are doing this because
they are getting so much money from me" (The Guardian vom 1. März 2012).
Bestätigt wird diese Erfahrung sogar von dem gut verdienenden 29jährigen, der
auf Wonga.com zurückgriff, weil seine Kreditgeschichte ihm keine Alternativen
ließ. Vor allem ergänzt er den Aspekt, dass die kontaktlose Online-Kreditvergabe
nicht nur den Zugriff erleichtere, sondern auch den Überblick erschwere. Auf die
Frage nach der Gesamthöhe seiner Schulden erwidert er: „I'd like to be able to
say this much, but I honestly don't know. […] I'm under no illusion that I'm the
victim. I know I'm the idiot in the scenario" (The Guardian vom 1. März 2012).
   Wonga.com hat laut The Guardian bereits zweimal Werbung wegen Irreführung der Kunden zurückziehen müssen. Bei einem Kunden mit erheblichen
Rückzahlungsschwierigkeiten hatte Amelia Gentleman eine E-Mail gesehen, in
der ihm ein Rabatt auf die Bearbeitungskosten angeboten wurde, wenn er einen
neuen Kredit aufnähme. „Obviously, that's not ideal" (The Guardian vom 1. März
2012) war der lakonische Kommentar des damit konfrontierten Pressechefs Bowman. Aber offenkundig gehört die Vermittlung eines Folgekredits als ‹Lösung› für
die durch schnelle Abbuchung selbst erzeugte Geldnot zum Kalkül von Wonga.
com. Um die Konkurrenz auszustechen, wird auch schon mal auf Bearbeitungskosten verzichtet.
   Schließlich beschreibt The Guardian noch das Unternehmen. Die Firma habe
60 überwiegend junge Beschäftigte „dressed down in internet startup style" (The
Guardian vom 1. März 2012), und 100 weitere in einem Callcenter in Südafri-
ka, von dem aus telefonischer Druck auf säumige Schuldner ausgeübt werde. Die

Büros seien papierarm und digitalisiert, und ein Fitness-Trainer animiere die Beschäftigten zweimal die Woche. „These offices feel very far removed from the homes of the clients who are taking the loans" (The Guardian vom 1. März 2012). Diese Beschreibung der Unternehmenskultur mobilisiert beim Leser Vorbehalte durch den Kontrast gegenüber der Geldnot der Kunden, ist aber freilich irrational – denn mit einem ärmlichen Arbeitsumfeld von Beschäftigten der Finanzbranche wäre den bedrängten Kunden in keiner Weise geholfen. Hier wird eine Verknüpfung provoziert, die auf emotionale statt argumentative Kritik setzt.

Der Artikel war mit dem Vergleich der Kosten eines Bustickets und einer Taxifahrt eingeleitet worden. Gegen Ende des Artikels entlarvt Amelia Gentleman den argumentativen Trick dieses Vergleichs, denn er vernachlässige die Tatsache, dass die meisten Kunden in diesem Falle das Taxi nähmen, weil ihnen kein Busticket mehr verkauft werde.

3.2   Die öffentliche Debatte um einen Sponsorenvertrag

Die Debatte über Sponsorengeschäfte mit Wonga.com begann bereits vor dem Vertragsschluss mit Newcastle United. Auf Initiative von Fußballfans, unter denen der Northampton Town-Anhänger Bob Ward namentlich genannt wird, habe sich die Football League entschieden, bisher geführte Werbung für Wonga. com von ihren Webseiten zu entfernen. Zur Charakterisierung Wongas werden die 4214% Jahreszins angeführt. Ein Sprecher der Liga wird mit den Worten zitiert: „The Football League's website advertising agreement with Wonga.com concluded at the end of the 2011/12 football season. It is not currently envisaged that this agreement will be extended" (The Guardian vom 18. Juni 2012). The Guardian greift hier die Bezeichnung der Labour-Parlamentarierin Stella Creasy des ‚legal loan sharks' wieder auf, und zitiert sie mit ihrer Aufforderung, der Kampagne der FSF (Football Supporters' Federation) beizutreten. Die Kampagne der FSF übernimmt dabei die symbolische Fußballgeste des Platzverweises und fordert „show Wonga the red card" (The Guardian vom 18. Juni 2012).

Bob Ward verweist darauf, dass die Werbung im Web auch für Minderjährige zugänglich sei, die gerade die Seiten des Fußballvereine in überdurchschnittlichem Maße besuchten. Daher komme der geschäftlichen Entscheidung über Sponsoring eine moralische Komponente zu. Wonga.com zeigte sich jedoch zur Gegenoffensive entschlossen: „We will continue to assess all opportunities and sponsorship deals for next season" (The Guardian vom 18. Juni 2012). Nach dem Erfolg bei der Football League kündigt Bob Ward eine Fortsetzung der Kampagne an: ‚There is still a payday lender involvement with football clubs so the campaign still has legs" (The Guardian vom 18. Juni 2012). Er sollte Recht behalten – New-castle United verlieh dem Thema bald zusätzliche Dynamik.

Erste Anzeichen für einen möglichen Aufruhr gab es bereits, als Gerüchte über den neuen Sponsorenvertrag auftauchten. In einem Spielbericht der Partie gegen Manchester United (0:3) mischte sich die Bemerkung, unpopulärer als zu wage-mutige Ankündigungen des Trainers Alan Pardew sei nur das Geschick des Klub-besitzers Mike Ashley in finanziellen Angelegenheiten. Als Ursache der Kritik wird dabei angegeben, das der voraussichtliche neue Sponsor Wonga.com wegen seiner Zinsraten häufiger in der Kritik sei (The Guardian vom 7. Oktober 2012).

Die erste Ankündigung des Sponsorendeals erfolgte dann mit dem Verweis des Klubdirektors Derek Lliambas, dass die Gelder in die Jugendakademie und die lokale Arbeit gingen, „as well as to boost the first team" (The Guardian vom 9. Oktober 2012a). Auch die Namensrechte für das Stadion gingen an Wonga.com, würden aber zur Wiederherstellung des ursprünglichen St. James Park verwendet. Nach dieser, die zentrale Zielsetzung eher verbergenden Aufzählung, enthüllt er dennoch die eigentliche Absicht: „We are building a club that can regularly com-pete for top honours at the highest level. […] As everyone knows, a strong com-mercial programme is vital to this goal and I am delighted to welcome Wonga into the fold as our lead commercial partner" (The Guardian vom 9. Oktober 2012a). Der Artikel verweist sodann auf die 4214% Jahreszins, und den diesbezüglichen Verweis von Wonga.com, dass diese Zahl durch Einrechnung von Zinseszinsen zustande käme, die aber tatsächlich nicht anfielen, weil nur Kurzzeitkredite ver-geben würden. Stella Creasy wird erneut als zentrale Kritikerin von Wonga.com angeführt, die bereits gegen das Spornsorenengagement Wongas protestiert habe und für eine Zinsobergrenze im Geldverleiher-Geschäft eintrete. Allerdings sei-en nun andere Parlamentsmitglieder auf diesen Protest eingestiegen, wie die La-bour-Abgeordneten Ian Lavery aus Wansbeck und Chinyelu Susan Onwurah aus Newcastle upon Tyne Central. Auch der Verweis auf die Forderung der FSF nach Ausschluss von Firmen wie Wonga aus dem Sponsorengeschäft wird wieder auf-gegriffen.

Eine neue Facette bringt das Muslim Council of Britain in die Debatte ein, als es das Recht für jeden muslimischen Spieler fordert, das Trikot auch ohne Spon-sorennamen zu tragen, weil unter der Scharia das Geben und Nehmen von Zin-sen verboten sei. Dieses betreffe die vier muslimischen Spieler Demba Ba, Papiss Cissé, Cheik Tioté und Hatem Ben Arfa. Diese Forderung ist aus zwei Gründen außerordentlich fragwürdig. Zum ersten sind freilich nicht die Spieler an Zins-nahme beteiligt, sondern der Werbeträger des Klubs. Zum zweiten verdient auch der bisherige Trikotsponsor Virgin Money sein Geld mit Zinsnahme, was offen-bar keinen Anlass zur selben Forderung bot. Ginge es dem Muslim Council of

Britain um die strikte Umsetzung seiner Forderung, müsste es auf der Unterbindung von Geschäften zwischen Fußballklubs und nicht-islamischem Finanzsektor bestehen. Die Forderung kann somit im Sinne Claussens als ‚Spielkulturpessimismus' charakterisiert werden, da hier punktuell eine Kommerzialisierung des Fußballs beklagt wird. Da vom Muslim Council of Britain auf eine Anwendung der moralischen Forderung auf alle Fälle des Diskurses verzichtet wurde, kann die Behauptung aufgestellt werden, dass die öffentliche Aufmerksamkeit, die Newcastle United der Debatte garantierte, hier als willkommener Anlass genutzt wurde, um die eigene Sichtweise publikumswirksam zu platzieren. Eine rigorose Anwendung des Grundsatzes war offenkundig gar nicht das Ziel. So kann es auch nicht verwundern, dass die vier genannten Spieler zeitnah verlauten ließen, dass sie ihren Glauben durch die Trikotwerbung nicht bedrängt sähen (The Guardian vom 10. Oktober 2012a).

Am selben Tag der offiziellen Bekanntgabe des Sponsorenvertrags durch die Klubleitung informierte The Guardian in einem weiteren Artikel über „10 things every Newcastle fan should know about Wonga". Die erste wichtige Kenntnis sei, dass Wonga einen Jahreszins von 4214% erhebe. Die Firma wehre sich dagegen, weil sie nur Kurzzeitkredite vergebe und der Jahreszins somit eine verzerrte Angabe sei. Jedoch, so die Autorin Jill Insley, andere Geldverleiher im selben Marktsegment kämen dennoch mit geringeren Zinsraten aus. Sie verschweigt dabei freilich, dass auch sehr viel höhere Zinsraten durchaus gängig sind, und eine Marktübersicht wird nicht gegeben. Zweitens, das ‚Einkommen' der Firma (The Guardian vom 9. Oktober 2012b) – nicht etwa der ‚Unternehmensgewinn' – sei 2011 um 269% auf £45,8 Millionen gestiegen, und der höchstbezahlte Direktor verdiene £635 000. Dieser Punkt verweist somit auf den Erfolg der Firma; allerdings wird durch die Bezeichnung des Unternehmensgewinns als ‚Einkommen' suggeriert, es handele sich hier um rein persönliche Bereicherung, und die Verbindung mit dem Gehalt des Direktors stellt eine recht willkürliche Verbindung mit Verhältnissen im Unternehmen her, die keine rationale Aussagekraft haben. Gerade im Vergleich mit den oftmals immensen Einkünften professioneller Fußballspieler, die hier jedoch unerwähnt bleiben, wirkt dieser Verweis instrumentell. Drittens wird auf die Fehlbarkeit von *credit scoring*-Daten, die über das Internet gewonnen werden, hingewiesen, was von Wongas Unternehmensboss Errol Damlin aber auch freimütig eingestanden werde. Dieser Verweis kann als irrational bezeichnet werden, denn die Erhebung von Zinsen auf Kredite ist ja gerade durch das Risiko der fehlerhaften Einschätzung der Rückzahlungsfähigkeit begründet. Das Tragen dieses Risikos ist das Geschäftsprinzip eines Kreditgebers; könnte er nicht falsch liegen, gäbe es kein Risiko. Viertens berge die Kundschaft bei Zahltags-Geldverleiher Wonga.com die Gefahr in sich, bei anderen, institutionellen Kreditgebern als kreditunwürdig eingestuft zu werden. Als Beispiel wird GE Money zitiert, die auch im Falle eines pünktlich zurückgezahlten Kurzzeitkredits in den drei vorhergehenden Monaten die Kreditwürdigkeit des Kunden prinzipiell verneinten. Dies ist ein verdeckt bleibendes Risiko für die Kunden; die Einschätzung der Kreditwürdigkeit liegt allerdings in der Autonomie jedes Kreditgebers und kann Wonga.com nicht angelastet werden. Fünftens habe Wonga eine Abmahnung des Office of Fair Trading erhalten, weil man 2010 in Briefen an säumige Schuldner ungerechtfertigt von ‚Betrug' gesprochen und mit der Polizei gedroht habe. Dies verweist auf eine eindeutig rechtswidrige Praxis, für die insbesondere aufgrund der Abbuchungsermächtigung zugunsten von Wonga.com kein Grund besteht. Sechstens, Wonga sei wegen der gezielten Bewerbung von finanziell bedürftigen Studenten auffällig geworden, was die Firma nach öffentlicher Thematisierung eingestellt habe – womit sie die Unvertretbarkeit indirekt auch eingestanden hat. Siebtens werbe Wonga mit den lediglich 15 Minuten, die zwischen Online-Antragstellung und Überweisung des gewährten Kredits vergingen, aber einige Kunden hätten den Verdacht einer Vernachlässigung der Datensicherheit geäußert. Dazu muss angemerkt werden, dass Wonga.com in seiner Privacy Policy explizit darauf verweist, dass alle Daten zur Absicherung der Rückzahlung umfassend ausgewertet und verwendet werden. Das mag man als unfreundlich bezeichnen, ist aber soweit legal. Dass ein Geldverleiher mit besonders risikoreicher Kundschaft die Rückzahlung nachdrücklicher absichert als vorsichtigere Konkurrenten, liegt – wie der höhere Zinssatz – in der Eigenlogik des Geschäfts begründet. Achtens, die Advertising Standards Authority habe einige Werbemaßnahmen Wongas wegen irreführender Inhalte untersagt. Dies ist verwerflich, aber kein Alleinstellungsmerkmal von Wonga.com. Die Entscheidung über Irreführung in der Werbung bleibt eine Gratwanderung, da eine Beschönigung von Produkt- und Firmenimage freilich die Absicht von Werbung ist. Neuntens, die Labour-Abgeordnete Stella Creasy habe Zahltag-Geldverleiher als ‚legal loan sharks' (The Guardian vom 9. Oktober 2012b) bezeichnet und leite, wie auch ein Fußballfan des ebenfalls Wonga-gesponsorten Klubs Northampton Town, eine Kampagne dagegen. Die Fans werden hier auf Referenzen für die Verwerflichkeit des Wonga-Vertrags verwiesen. Im zehnten Punkt wird mit der Satzsequenz „First step, Wonga sponsorship on the shirt. Second step, the Wonga stadium ..." (The Guardian vom 9. Oktober 2012b) suggeriert, der neue Sponsor werde bald die gesamte symbolische Umwelt der Fußballfans dominieren.

Insgesamt verbindet dieser Artikel also stichhaltige Kritik an der Geschäftspraxis Wongas, die von The Guardian bereits thematisiert war, mit zahlreichen fragwürdigen Vorwürfen, und zielt somit eindeutig auf eine Polarisierung ab. Inhaltliche Zusammenhänge zwischen Sponsoring und Profifußball werden nicht hergestellt. Newcastle United-Fans sollen gegen den Werbevertrag ihres Vereins mobilisiert werden. The Guardian beteiligt sich hier implizit selbst an den Protesten der Abgeordneten und der Fan-Initiativen, was den funktionalen Zweck erfüllt, die öffentliche Debatte lebendig zu erhalten, deren Bestandteil die eigenen Artikel sind. Letztlich zielt The Guardian hier auf die Erhöhung der Nachfrage nach dem eigenen Produkt ab.

Ein weiterer Kommentar an diesem ersten Tag der Berichterstattung verweist auf die seit zwei Jahren währende Kampagne gegen Zahltags-Geldverleiher der Labour-Abgeordneten Stella Creasy und ihren Slogan des legalen Kredithais, und zitiert sie mit der Begründung: „It is only through preying on families struggling to make ends meet that Wonga has made enough money to be able to sign this deal with Newcastle" (The Guardian vom 9. Oktober 2012c). Auch dieser Kommentar muss eher als Mobilisierung öffentlichen Protests gewertet werden.

In einem weiteren Artikel desselben Tages begründen politische Akteure der Labour-Partei, warum sie gegen den Sponsorendeal sind. Eingeleitet wird mit dem Hinweis einer Beratungsfirma für insolvente Bürger und Firmen, dass der Nordosten Englands die höchste Überschuldetenrate des Landes aufweise. Der Präsident der Firma, Lee Manning, weist darauf hin, dass es für Wonga.com einen anderen Grund als die relative Popularität von Newcastle United für den Vertragsschluss geben könnte: „Wonga has chosen to target a region that has comparatively high numbers of people experiencing financial difficulty. Our experience tells us that many of those seeking high cost credit need professional advice for their financial problems, rather than accruing further debt" (The Guardian vom 9. Oktober 2012d). Wonga.com habe demnach auf Popularität in einer Region mit vielen potenziellen Kunden gezielt. Dem pflichtet später im Artikel der Labour-Abgeordnete Ian Lavery bei, der eine rigorose Trennung verlangt: „A city like Newcastle and the region should not have any ties with an organization like Wonga" (The Guardian vom 9. Oktober 2012d).

Einen weitaus stärkeren Kontrast zwischen der Stadt Newcastle upon Tyne und dem Klub zieht der Leiter des City Councils, Nick Forbes: „We see devastating consequences of people getting into financial difficulty and we spend a lot of money each year helping people who are in debt through companies like this. […] It's a sad indictment of the profit at any price culture at Newcastle United. […] We are fighting hard to tackle legal and illegal loan sharking and having a company like this right across the city on every football shirt that's sold undermines all our work" (The Guardian vom 9. Oktober 2012d). Auch wenn die argumentative Spitze, dass bereits die Trikotwerbung jedes Engagement gegen Überschuldung entwerte, übertrieben erscheinen mag, bildet Forbes hier eine bedenkenswerte Verknüpfung: Politikern und Fußballklubs ist gemeinsam, dass sie für ihren Erfolg auf den Zuspruch der regionalen Bevölkerung angewiesen sind. Wenn sich nun die politische Exekutive der Stadt ausdrücklich darum bemüht, auch legalen Geldverleih-Geschäften Einhalt zu gebieten – was darauf hinausläuft, deren Reputation als unbedenkliche Wettbewerber im Kreditgeschäft zu attackieren – dann ist die Werbetätigkeit des lokalen Fußballvereins tatsächlich eine kontraproduktive Aktion. Das Argument Forbes' läuft also darauf hinaus, von Newcastle United neben der Gewinnerzielungsabsicht auch regionale soziale Verantwortung zu übernehmen. Da der Verein auch soziale Einrichtungen unterhält, unterläuft er dieses Engagement in den Augen Forbes› durch den neuen Sponsorendeal. Dem hält der Klubverantwortliche Derek Lliambas die sozial ausgerichtete Sponsorentätigkeit Wongas entgegen: „Throughout our discussions Wonga's desire to help us invest in our young playing talent, the local community and new fan initiatives really impressed us and stood them apart from other candidates" (The Guardian vom 9. Oktober 2012d). Dieses Image des mildtätigen Unternehmens wurde von ihm durch den unmittelbar vorhergehenden Satz jedoch bereits entwertet: „We are building a club that can regularly compete for top honours at the highest level" (The Guardian vom 9. Oktober 2012d). Dieser Zielsetzung zufolge dürfte das soziale Engagement Wongas kaum den Ausschlag gegeben haben.

Dies bestätigt sich, als am Folgetag die sportlich Verantwortlichen des Klubs zu Wort kommen. Der Coach Alan Pardew verteidigt den Vertrag mit der sportlichen Erfolgsabsicht: „It's about building the first team and it›s about having the financial muscle to have improving the academy" (The Guardian vom 10. Oktober 2012a), womit der soziale Aspekt auf die fußballerische Nachwuchsarbeit beschränkt wird. Nach beschwichtigenden Äußerungen über Wonga.com wird Pardew sehr deutlich in seiner Ablehnung der Kritik, die er für eine Überreaktion hält, und spielt auf die Widersprüchlichkeit und Inkonsequenz der Angriffe an: „You see other companies, whether it is Standard Chartered, who are the same type of business as Wonga, or betting companies sponsoring football clubs and nothing gets said" (The Guardian vom 10. Oktober 2012a). Diese Sichtweise selbst ist allerdings strategisch, denn zum einen handelt es sich bei Standard Chartered um eine Bank, und nicht um einen Geldverleiher, und zum anderen entschuldet verwerfliches Handeln anderer das eigene nicht. Die Frage der Vertretbarkeit des Fußball-Sponsorings wird hier zwar adressiert, aber nicht argumentativ geklärt.

Zwei Tage später positioniert sich The Guardian etwas unentschiedener als Berichterstatter unterschiedlicher Meinungen. Es werden Fans zitiert, die den neuen Sponsorenvertrag rigoros ablehnen, aber auch solche, die auf Inkonsequenzen der Kritiker verweisen, weil beispielsweise niemand die jahrelange Werbung für eine Biersorte mit dem Verweis auf Verführung zum Alkoholismus moniert habe. Ergänzt wird diese Unentschiedenheit mit dem Verweis auf die Präsenz anderer

Geldverleiher und ebenfalls teurer, etablierter Kreditinstitute in Newcastle upon
Tyne. Die Kritik der Vortage findet ihren Ausdruck im Zitat eines Passanten, der
in der Trikotwerbung eines Legitimierung des Geldverleihers sieht: „These footballers are their heroes, if they say Wonga›s good, they'll just assume it's okay"
(The Guardian vom 12. Oktober 2012). Der Artikel endet mit den resignierten
Statements, dass Profifußballern in Finanzangelegenheiten ohnehin nicht zu
trauen sei und dass Wonga.com auch vor dem neuen Sponsorenvertrag bereits in
der Bandenwerbung von Newcastle United präsent gewesen sei.

Diese Unentschiedenheit spiegelte offenbar das Meinungsbild bei den Fans,
wie es in einer Umfrage einer Faninitiative zutage trat. Deren Sprecher Michael
Thewes wird von The Guardian eine Woche nach der Bekanntgabe des Sponso-
renvertrages zitiert: „It is clear from the initial results from our survey that this
isn't a simple black or white issue and that there are many factors impacting on
fans' opinion about this deal" (The Guardian vom 16. Oktober 2012). Unter die
Einsicht, dass Finanzquellen für erfolgreichen Profifußball essenziell seien, mi-
sche sich Skepsis über das Ansehen des neuen Sponsors. In der Umfrage unter
1000 Fans hätte sich nur ein Fünftel in Bezug auf den Vertragsschluss als „sehr
unglücklich" bezeichnet, und die Zufriedenheit mit den Aktivitäten des Besitzers
Mike Ashley und des Managers Derek Lliambas sei sehr hoch, und als Gründe
werden vornehmlich sportliche Erfolge genannt. Somit ist die Hauptbotschaft der
Fanvereinigung, dass sich die Zufriedenheit der Fans vor allem am fußballeri-
schen Erfolg bemisst, und die politischen Proteste keine durchschlagende Wirkung auf die Wahrnehmung ihres Klubs hatten.

Dies hieß offenbar auch für The Guardian, das immense Engagement in der
Berichterstattung umzulenken. Wonga.com blieb zwar im Visier der Zeitung,
und Stella Creasy der prominente Ankerpunkt der Berichterstattung. Zunächst
fand auch das Sponsorship für Newcastle United noch kurze Erwähnung. In einer
Attacke auf Wonga.com, nachdem ein Regierungsberater in die Führungsebene
des Geldverleihers gewechselt ist, wird Creasy mit den Worten zitiert: „They have
used their profits to target our football clubs and Saturday night TV, and now
they are targeting the highest echelons of government" (The Guardian vom 30.
Oktober 2012). Und einige Wochen später skandalisiert The Guardian einige an
Creasy adressierte Beschimpfungen über den Nachrichtendienst Twitter. Erwähnung findet dabei auch, dass Kritik an Wonga.com aus Wikipedia-Artikeln entfernt worden sei, scheinbar von einem Computer der Firma aus. Zu der entfernten
Kritik gehörten auch Bemerkungen über den Sponsorenvertrag mit Newcastle
United (The Guardian vom 20. und vom 21. November 2012). Im dritten Artikel
über diesen Skandal fallen dann jedoch die Hinweise auf Newcastle Uniteds Geschäft mit Wonga.com und den manipulierten Wikipedia-Artikel weg. Nun ist es

die – auch im Zuge der Berichterstattung erzeugte – Prominenz von Stella Creasy, die als Anknüpfungspunkt für die öffentliche Aufmerksamkeit präsentiert wird. Die akute Debatte über den Sponsorenvertrag von Newcastle United mit Wonga.com endete hier.

4   Das teuflische Geld im göttlichen Fußball

Die Bildungen schlaglichtartiger Fokussierungen ist ein wichtiges Mittel von Massenmedien, um in einem Umfeld von Informationsüberflutung die Aufmerksamkeit der Leser auf sich zu ziehen. Im Zuge der Berichterstattung gelangten mehrere Personen zur Prominenz, wie der Wonga-Pressesprecher Bowman, der Blackpool FC-Fan Ward und schließlich Creasy. Wonga.com selbst ist ebenfalls ein solcher Aufmerksamkeitsfänger, was an zwei Punkten verdeutlicht werden kann. Denn die zur Berühmtheit gelangenden 4214% Jahreszins sind kein Extremwert in der Branche, wie The Guardian mit der Nennung der 16.381% des Geldverleihers Peachy selbst bekannt gibt (The Guardian vom 1. März 2012); somit geht es eher um die Wiederholung eines bekannten Symbols als um die Entlarvung einer Extremposition. Zum anderen wurde Wonga.com im Jahre 2011 von The Guardian mit dem Digital Entrepreneurs Awards ausgezeichnet (The Guardian 2011). Das öffentliche Interesse an Wonga.com wurde durch diese Preisverleihung teilweise selbst erzeugt.

Und schließlich muss auch Newcastle United als ein solches Schlaglicht für potenziell interessierte Leser gesehen werden. Die auffällige Häufung einer mitunter sehr engagierten Berichterstattung ebenso wie das schnelle Abflauen deuten darauf hin, dass auch für The Guardian die relative Popularität des Newcastle United ein Hauptgrund für die Fokussierung war, und weniger ein substanzielles Problem, dass dem Profifußball aus dem Sponsorenvertrag entstünde.

Die ethische Kritik eines Sponsorenvertrags des Fußballklubs mit einem Geldverleiher hat zwar ein argumentatives Fundament, das für eine delegitimierende Kritik jedoch nicht ausreicht. Das Verhältnis zwischen Geld und Fußball ist historisch alt und vielschichtig, es zieht jedoch öffentlich sehr leicht Empörung auf sich, weil es mit dem Grundgedanken des Sports konfligiert.

Bereits vor der Bildung einer höchsten Spielklasse in England im Jahre 1888 gab es Fußballer, die mit ihrem Spiel ihr Geld verdienten, auch Preisgelder, Eintrittsgelder der Zuschauer, Investitionen in die Fußballklubs und Fußballwetten waren üblich (Curry 2004; Garnham/Jackson 2003; Claussen 2007). Obwohl also finanzielles Engagement für den Erfolg von Fußball von Beginn an bedeutsam war, kann man den Sieg im Spiel nicht kaufen, ohne den Sport zu zerstören. Die

Ethik des Spiels verlangt eine Suspension finanzieller Vorteilnahme und strategischer Beeinflussung des Spiels. Den populärsten Ausdruck findet dies im Prinzip des *fair play*, verkörpert in den Schiedsrichtern (Claussen 2007: 656f.), die bezeichnenderweise bis heute von den immensen Gehaltssteigerungen im Profifußball ausgeschlossen zu sein scheinen, als könnte ihre Regelauslegung durch Geldzahlungen kontaminiert werden.

Obwohl also das Umfeld des Fußballs von Geldzahlungen geprägt wird, muss das Spielprinzip davon entschieden frei gehalten werden. Dieser Spannungspunkt findet in der Trikotwerbung, die deutlich sichtbar auf der Brust eines jeden Spielers angebracht ist, eine symbolische Verdichtung.

Mit Wonga.com wird im Falle von Newcastle United eine Firma diesen Platz besetzen, die gerechtfertigte Kritik für ihre Geschäftspraxis auf sich zieht. Auch andere Kreditgeber, wie der Vorgänger im Sponsoring in Newcastle, Virgin Money, verdienen an der Geldnot ihrer Kunden. Der Zahltags-Geldverleiher ist jedoch dem begründeten Verdacht ausgesetzt, diese Geldnot mit seiner eigenen Geschäftspraxis wissentlich zu verschärfen, und auf diesem Wege sein Geschäftsvolumen und seine Einnahmen zu erhöhen.

Dieses politische, soziale, ökonomische und ethische Problem hat jedoch keine direkte Auswirkung auf den Fußball. Die Verhaltensweise von Newcastle United, trotz dieser vielschichtigen Bedenken die Geschäftsbeziehung zu Wonga.com aufzunehmen, ist gegenüber zahlreichen Bürgern ihres regionalen Umfeldes, unter denen gewiss auch einige Fans sind, mindestens fragwürdig. Gegenüber lokalen politischen Akteuren, die sozial schädliche Geschäfte der Geldverleiher bekämpfen, ist es ein Affront. Aber im Verlaufe der Berichterstattung von The Guardian wurde – scheinbar auch den Berichterstattern selbst – schnell klar, dass dies für den Fußballklub Newcastle United irrelevant bleiben kann, da seine Popularität am sportlichen Erfolg hängt. Dieser wiederum ist auf finanzielles Sponsoring in ganz erheblichem Maße angewiesen. Ein unpopulärer Trikotsponsor mag finanzielle Einbußen im Absatz von Merchandising-Produkten und bei Eintrittsgeldern bedeuten. Aber die Alternative bestünde darin, durch finanzielle Engpässe verursachten sportlichen Misserfolg und im Extremfall eine Versenkung in der Bedeutungslosigkeit zu riskieren.

Literatur

Baecker, D. (2007): Form und Formen der Kommunikation. Suhrkamp: Frankfurt am Main.
Baecker, D. (2008): Womit handeln Banken? Suhrkamp: Frankfurt am Main.

Burton, D. (2008): Credit and Consumer Society. Routledge: London.
Claussen, D. (2007): On Stupidity in Football. In: Football and Society 8 (4), 654-662.
Curry, G. (2004): Playing for money. James J. Lang and emergent soccer professionalism in Sheffield. In: Soccer and Society 5 (3), 336-355.
Garnham, N. / Jackson, A. (2003): Who Invested in Victorian Football Clubs? The Case of Newcastle-upon-Tyne. In: Soccer and Society 4 (1), 57-70.
Gratton, C. (2000): The peculiar economics of english professional football. In: Soccer and Society 1 (1), 11-28.
Luhmann, N. (1994): Die Wirtschaft der Gesellschaft. Suhrkamp: Frankfurt am Main.
Luhmann, N. (2009): Die Realität der Massenmedien. VS Verlag: Wiesbaden.

Medienberichte

BBC (2008): Ashley calls off Newcastle sale. news.bbc.co.uk/sport2/hi/football/teams/n/newcastle_united/7801792.stm. Zugriff am 8. Dezember 2012.
BBC (2009a): Ashley takes Newcastle off market. news.bbc.co.uk/sport2/hi/football/teams/n/newcastle_united/8329055.stm. Zugriff am 4. Dezember 2012.
BBC (2009b): news.bbc.co.uk/sport2/hi/football/teams/n/newcastle_united/8342406.stm. Zugriff am 4. December 2012.
BBC (2011a): Newcastle remane St James' Park the Sport Direct Arena. www.bbc.co.uk/sport/0/football/15668207. Zugriff am 4. Dezember 2012.
BBC (2011b): Newcastle's naming rights worth up to £10m a year – Derek Lliambas. www.bbc.co.uk/sport/0/football/15670830. Zugriff am 8. Dezember 2012.
BBC (2011c): Freddy Sheppherd says renaming St Jame's Park will deter investors. www.bbc.co.uk/sport/0/football/15672054. Zugriff am 8. Dezember 2012.
Newcastle United (2011): Newcastle United FC Mission Statement. www.nufc.co.uk/articles/20111016/newcastle-united-fc-mission-statement_2281670_2483862. Zugriff am 8. Dezember 2012.
Newcastle United (2012a): Newcastle Agree Four-Year Wonga Deal. www.nufc.co.uk/articles/20121009/newcastle-agree-four-year-wonga-deal_2281670_2944166. Zugriff am 8. Dezember 2012.
Newcastle United (2012b): Toon Fans Celebrate as St. James Park Reborn. www.nufc.co.uk/articles/20121017/toon-fans-celebrate-as-st-james-reborn_2281670_2951302. Zugriff am 8. Dezember 2012.
Newcastle United (2012c): www.nufc.co.uk/page/Club/History/ClubHistory/0,,10278~2108980,00.html. Zugriff am 10. Dezember 2012.
The Guardian (2011): Winners 2011 (des Digital Innovations Awards). www.guardian.co.uk/megas/winners-2011. Zugriff am 17. Dezember 2012.
The Guardian vom 1. März 2012: 'Wonga: the real cost of a payday loan', von Amelia Gentleman.
The Guardian vom 27. März 2012: 'We want Wonga off our clubs' websites', in der Rubrik 'Letters'.
The Guardian vom 28. März 2012: 'Football fans seek removal of Wonga ads from club websites', von Jill Insley.

The Guardian vom 18. Juni 2012: 'Football League stop wearing Wonga adverts', von Jill Insley.

The Guardian vom 7. Oktober 2012: 'Newcastle United short on audacity but maybe not payday loan cash', von Louise Taylor.

The Guardian vom 9. Oktober 2012a: 'MPs attack Newcastle's Wonga deal, dubbing company „legal loan shark"', von David Conn.

The Guardian vom 9. Oktober 2012b: '10 things every Newcastle fan should know about Wonga', von Jill Insley.

The Guardian vom 9. Oktober 2012c: 'Newcastle United risk damaging their reputation with Wonga deal', von David Conn.

The Guardian vom 9. Oktober 2012d: 'Newcastle United sponsorship by Wonga critisised by insolvency experts', von James Callow.

The Guardian vom 10. Oktober 2012a: 'Alan Pardew: Wonga can propel Newcastle into Premier League top four', von Louise Taylor.

The Guardian vom 10. Oktober 2012b: 'Rising costs of Premier League TV rights „could have a knock out effect"', von Owen Gibson.

The Guardian vom 12. Oktober 2012: 'Wonga's Newcastle United link has high interest rate – for wrong reasons', von Zoe Williams.

The Guardian vom 16. Oktober 2012: 'Newcastle fans criticise acceptance of Wonga sponsorship', Press Association.

The Guardian vom 30. Oktober 2012: 'Cameron adviser to become lobbyist for Wonga', von Nicholas Watt.

The Guardian vom 20. November 2012: 'MP demands apology after abusive tweets are traced to Wonga employee', von Mark King.

The Guardian vom 21. November 2012: 'Wonga apologises to Stella Creasy over abusive Twitter messages', von Mark King.

The Guardian vom 23. November 2012: 'Wonga promotes Walthamstow debt event as apology to MP', von Mark King.

Professioneller und Amateurfußball in Deutschland und England: Diskursverschränkungen, Praktiken und implizite Kollektivität

Professional and Amateur Football in Germany and England: Discourse Interconnections, Practices and Implicit Collectivity

Kristian Naglo

Zusammenfassung

Der Artikel beschäftigt sich mit der Frage, ob sich in Zeiten des globalisierten, vermeintlich postmodernen Fußballspiels noch von unterscheidbaren, spezifisch *nationalen Fußballkulturen* sprechen lässt. Damit schließt er direkt an die übergreifende Fragestellung des Sammelbandes an. Betrachtet werden vor allem Entwürfe und Konstruktionszusammenhänge nationaler Fußballkulturen im medialen Diskurs, die sich sowohl im Bereich des Profifußballs sowie auf den untersten Ebenen des Amateurfußballs nachvollziehen lassen. Dabei wird die Frage nach eventuellen Verschränkungen der beiden Ebenen in den Mittelpunkt gerückt.

Abstract

This article deals with the issue of whether one can still speak of discrete, specifically national football cultures in the age of globalized and assumed postmodern football. In this way it links directly with the all-embracing question addressed by this volume. In particular it will look closely at conceptions of national football cultures in media discourse and the contexts in which these are constructed and understood both in professional football as well as at the lowest levels of amateur football. In so doing the questions of possible interconnections at both levels will be foregrounded.

Welche kulturellen und sozialen Einflüsse des professionellen Fußballspiels lassen sich auf den lokalen Ebenen des nicht-professionellen Vereinsfußballs für den deutschen Fall identifizieren und entsprechend dem englischen gegenüberstellen? Welche routinisierten Interaktionsprozesse sind in Vereinen der relativ untersten Ebenen nachzuvollziehen, die wiederum Vorstellungen der Teilnahme an einem größeren nationalen, kulturellen Zusammenhang erzeugen? Inwiefern bleiben umgekehrt lokale Spezifika erhalten – entweder in traditionellen oder überformten Ausprägungen?

Die hier fokussierte Verbindung zwischen professionellem und nicht-professionellem Fußball ist so vielschichtig, dass eine Annäherung über eine kombinierte Herangehensweise der Interpretation medialer Diskurse und der Beobachtung spezifischer Praktiken besonders sinnvoll erscheint. Auch in theoretischer Hinsicht ist eine mehrdimensionale Basis erforderlich. Es wird eine Verbindung des Glokalisierungsansatzes mit dem der *social imaginaries* herangezogen. Der Ländervergleich zwischen Deutschland und England dient vor diesem Hintergrund zur Auslotung von Zwischenräumen einerseits, und um andererseits Genaueres über die einzelnen Fälle zu erfahren.

Mit dem hier vertretenen Ansatz wird ein Desideratum der Forschung zu *Fußballkultur* angegangen, das in der Globalisierungstheorie des Fußballs von Giulianotti und Robertson (2009) aufscheint. In Übereinstimmung mit deren Grundkonzept wird davon ausgegangen, dass der Globalisierungsprozess parallel verlaufenden, gegenseitigen Beeinflussungen des Universalen und Partikularen unterliegt, und dass sich die kulturelle Globalisierung sowohl als Homogenisierung als auch als Heterogenisierung niederschlägt. Da sich das Konzept vornehmlich auf den Profifußball bezieht, bleibt die Bezugsebene der darin beschriebenen Beispiele des Lokalen letztlich immer das Globale oder Nationale, der Amateurfußball als das eigentlich Lokale wird darin nicht repräsentiert. Hier steht er hingegen gleichwertig im Mittelpunkt des Interesses.

1   Nationale Fußballkulturen?

Grundsätzlich erscheint die analytische Auseinandersetzung mit dem modernen Fußballspiel als kulturellem Phänomen aus sozialwissenschaftlicher Perspektive in verschiedener Hinsicht vielversprechend: Als medial und global präsente, (populär)kulturelle Form ist es verbreitet wie keine andere Sportart und wird als entsprechend bedeutsam für Globalisierungs- und Nationalisierungsprozesse betrachtet (Giulianotti/Robertson 2009; Tomlinson/Young 2006 a u. b). Fußball wird beispielsweise als ernstes Spiel interpretiert: durch kompetitive Elemente des modernen Sports, vor allem aber durch politische und kulturelle Verflechtungen, komplexe Interpenetrationen von Gemeinschaftsidentitäten, Kodierungen sozialer Verhaltensweisen, Glaubenssysteme und durch die Symbolisierung von In- bzw. Exklusion sowie sozialer Hierarchien (vgl. Klein/Meuser 2008).

Dies gilt sowohl für den professionellen als auch für den nicht-professionellen Bereich des Spiels. Während jedoch der professionell betriebene Fußball vor allem mit dem Leistungsprinzip und wirtschaftlichen Elementen in Verbindung gebracht wird, ordnet man dem nicht-professionellen Spiel in Alltagsdiskursen automatisch sich davon unterscheidende Aspekte wie Geselligkeit, soziale Anerkennung, langfristige Bindungen, wertvermittelte Traditionen in dörflichen Gemeinschaften usw. zu. Demgegenüber argumentiert der vorliegende Beitrag, dass die mediale Verfassheit und Bedeutung des Fußballs insgesamt es als unzureichend erscheinen lässt, den nicht-professionellen Fußball einzig als lokales Phänomen zu untersuchen. Amateurvereine und deren zentrale Akteure sind in der hier vertretenen Sichtweise vielmehr einerseits in die Emergenz einer Vorstellung des medial – insbesondere durch das Fernsehen – vermittelten globalen und nationalen Profifußballs einbezogen, indem in ihren alltäglichen Sportpraktiken Versatzstücke und Vorstellungen zu finden sind, die aus der *kulturellen Zirkulationssphäre* des Profifußballs stammen. Andererseits bleiben sie durchaus auf bestimmte Organisationsformen, lokal spezifische Praktiken, Selbstverständnisse (Werte, Traditionen, Mythen) und Gemeinschaften verwiesen[1].

Ziel des Beitrags ist es, der Frage nach gegenseitigen Einflüssen des globalisierten, professionellen Fußballspiels und lokalen Ebenen des vielschichtigen nicht-

---

1   Der Amateurfußball ist dabei klassisch vornehmlich in den regionalen Zeitungen präsent, wenn auch nur ab einer bestimmten Spielklasse und nur auf wenigen Seiten. In den letzten Jahren hat sich diese Situation allerdings stark zugunsten des Internets und dort auftretender Magazine zum Amateurfußball in bestimmten Regionen verändert. Dieses Phänomen ist vor allem in Deutschland verbreitet (vgl. 11Freunde, Juli 2010), vergleichbares lässt sich für England nicht zeigen.

professionellen Vereinsfußballs, der unter dem Sammelbegriff *Amateurfußball*[2] firmiert, nachzugehen. Außerdem soll die Frage nach dem Erhalt lokaler Spezifika – entweder in traditionellen oder überformten Ausprägungen – bearbeitet werden. Daran anschließend wird ein Konzept zur Einbeziehung des Profi- *und* des Amateurfußballs in die Analyse nationaler Fußballkulturen am Beispiel der Repräsentationen des Spiels in Deutschland und England entwickelt[3]. Es geht hier also – zusammengefasst – um eine Verbindung des massenmedialen und spektakulären Wesen des Profifußballs der Gegenwart mit der auch methodologisch und theoretisch zu beantworteten Frage nach den lokalen Operations- und Aneignungsweisen medialer Kreisläufe im Amateurfußball, wo mit einer Vorstellung gearbeitet wird, welche die lokale Ebene weit hinter sich lässt.

In Vorbereitung dieser kontrastierenden Differenzierung der Konzepte Profi- und Amateurfußball in den beiden Ländern geht es zunächst um den Entwurf eines theoretischen Rahmens, der die Konzepte *Glokalisierung* und *social imaginaries* zur Thesengenerierung zusammenführt, ergänzt durch den Begriff des *Post-Fans*, der vermeintlich postmodernen Entwicklungen Rechnung trägt. Es bietet sich diesbezüglich eine ethnografische Vorgehensweise an[4], die hier zur punktuellen Illustration der vor allem konzeptuellen Herangehensweise herangezogen wird.

Zur weiteren Verdeutlichung wird ein Vergleichsrahmen aus englischem und deutschem Fußball genutzt, dem die Annahme gegenläufiger Tendenzen, hier formuliert als Arbeitshypothesen, zugrunde liegt:

Für den deutschen Fall wird von stärkeren Kontinuitäten und Gemeinsamkeiten bzw. Diskursverschränkungen zwischen professioneller und Amateurebene ausgegangen. Das zunehmende Eintreten von Amateurvereinen in die kulturelle Zirkulations- und Diskurssphäre des Profifußballs hilft ihnen zugleich bei einer verstärkten Konturierung, Modernisierung und Neubestimmung der Vereins-

---

2 Hier geht es vor allem um den Bereich des Männerfußballs. Frauen- und Jugendfußball spielen insofern eine wichtige Rolle im Rahmen der Analyse, als entsprechende Mannschaften einen Teil der *Figuration Fußballverein* darstellen.

3 Allgemein legt die vergleichende Betrachtung der beiden Länder Deutschland und England bezüglich des Fußballs die Annahme unterschiedlicher, einflussreicher kultureller und sozialhistorischer Prozesse nahe (vgl. Eisenberg 1999; Pfister 2003; Waine 2007; Tomlinson/Young 2006a; Schulze-Marmeling 2000; Pyta 2006).

4 Das hier verwertete Datenmaterial wurde im Rahmen teilnehmender Beobachtungen, von Spielbeobachtungen und Experteninterviews in Deutschland und England im Jahr 2012 in unterschiedlichen Spielklassen zusammengetragen. Fokussiert wurden dabei vornehmlich Amateurligen am unteren Ende der jeweiligen nationalen Pyramide (Kreisligen/ Oberbergischer Kreis; North Lancashire Premier League/District League).

grenzen, führt aber gleichzeitig auch potentiell zur Schließung und Standardisierung des eigentlich per se öffentlichen Raums Amateurfußball.

Für den englischen Kontext wird hingegen eine stärker betonte Trennung zwischen professionellem (Elite-) und nicht professionellem Fußball angenommen, die mit einer stärkeren Orientierung an traditionellen und mitunter stereotypen Werten des englischen Spiels einhergeht, welche auch im massenmedialen Diskurs des Profifußballs prävalent sind. Außerdem lässt sich im englischen Kontext eine Betonung des ‚Lokalen' (*local football*) ausmachen, die den Amateurfußball als *public arena* der Nähe reproduziert.

2   Theoretischer Analyserahmen zu Medien und Praxis: Glo*k*alisierung, Social Imaginaries und Post-Fans

Es gilt die Annahme für den Fußball *on and off the field*, dass Medien bzw. mediale Diskurse sowohl Prozesse globaler Standardisierung als auch der nationalen Differenzierung des Spiels bewusstseinsbildend vermitteln und über unterschiedliche Formen der Rezeption verschiedene globale, nationale und lokale Praktiken nach sich ziehen[5]. In diesem Sinne ist die Thematisierung des Profifußballs immer auch eine der Medien (Stichwort: Mediensport, vgl. Schwier 2000 u. Schauerte/ Schwier 2008), die bestimmte Inhalte (Symbole, Kommunikationen, Materialisierungen) zu niedrigeren, lokalen Ebenen transportieren. Wie diese durchaus auch ambivalenten Inhalte des globalen und nationalen, mediatisierten Profifußballs auf den untersten (lokalen) Ebenen des nicht-professionellen Vereinsfußballs aufgenommen und in Praktiken umgesetzt bzw. über Vermittlungsinstanzen weitertransportiert werden, ist jedoch eindimensional nicht ableitbar und differiert in den unterschiedlichen, national ungleich organisierten Systemen des Fußballs üblicherweise stark.

Die zu Beginn entwickelte Fragestellung legt in theoretischer Hinsicht zunächst die Einbeziehung von Robertsons Glo*k*alisierungskonzept (vgl. 1992)

---

5   „Sprachliche und nicht-sprachliche Praktiken können als Materialisierung von kollektivem, sozial erzeugtem und bereitgestelltem Wissen verstanden werden. Einzelne Individuen sind Träger und Interpreten der gesellschaftlich konventionalisierten Praktiken, auch wenn solche Interpretationen mitunter nur als ‚körperliche Reaktionsweisen' erscheinen. Praktiken sind als typisierte Handlungsmuster Bestandteil der kollektiven Wissensvorräte. Von den Individuen werden sie in Prozessen der Sozialisation und des Lernens als Routinekompetenzen des Handelns und Be-Deutens zugleich inkorporiert, ohne dass dies notwendig eine im starken Sinne bewusst-reflexive Zuwendung zum jeweiligen Handlungsakt erfordert" (Keller 2005: 61f.).

nahe, welches anschließend von Giulianotti und Robertson (vgl. 2009) explizit auf den globalen Fußball angewendet wurde. Glokalisierung beschreibt entsprechend, wie lokale Akteure globale Prozesse und Phänomene interpretieren, damit diese ihren partikularen Vorstellungen und Bedürfnissen entsprechen. So organisieren nationale Systeme den Fußball beispielsweise nach (global) standardisierten Prinzipien, nämlich in einem Ligasystem, jedoch interpretieren sie das Spiel in diesem System jeweils national und massenmedial unterschiedlich (vgl. Giulianotti/Robertson 2009, 62)[6]. Das Image des FC Bayern München beinhaltet beispielsweise die ökonomische Einbindung der Vereinsmarke in den Weltmarkt bei gleichzeitiger Betonung des Lokalkolorits (*Mia san mia, Finale dahoam* usw.). Ein weiteres glokalisiertes, (pop)kulturelles Versatzstück ist das zur Hymne des FC Liverpool umfunktionierte *You'll never walk alone*: Komponiert und getextet für das Broadway-Musical *Carousel* im Jahr 1945 wurde das Lied als Coverversion ein Nummer-Eins-Hit der britischen Charts im Jahr 1963, gesungen von Gerry & the Pacemakers, und fand so den Weg in die Fußballstadien der Swinging Sixties. Dem Mythos folgend wurde das Lied im Stadion an der Anfield Road gespielt, als plötzlich die Lautsprecher ausfielen. Die Fans sangen einfach weiter und schufen so ihre eigene Erkennungsmelodie im lokalen Kontext mit einem Versatzstück aus der globalen Musikindustrie (vgl. hierzu auch Irwin 2006: 173ff.). Mittlerweile wird das Lied quasi in jedem Stadion der Erde abgespielt und es existieren unzählige weitere Coverversionen (z.B. von den Toten Hosen), was wiederum eine (Rück)Beeinflussung des Globalen durch das Lokale andeutet.

Ähnliches ließe sich beispielhaft mit beliebig vielen Versatzstücken aus dem Profifußball illustrieren (vgl. Giulianotti/Robertson 2007). Davon, dass der Profifußball als offensichtlicher Teil der Kulturindustrie (vgl. Eisenberg/Gestrich 2012) also – der klassischen These folgend – vor allem Perspektiven von Homogenität produziere (vgl. Horkheimer/Adorno 2003), in denen kollektive Vorstellungen den Kräften der Kommodifizierung bzw. des Kapitalismus unterworfen würden, was wiederum zu einer generellen Reglementierung bzw. Säkularisierung gesellschaftlicher Zusammenhänge führe (Appadurai 1996: 6f.), kann keine Rede sein[7]. Vielmehr existiert eine Vielzahl unterschiedlicher und gegenseitiger

---

6 Bezogen auf den Ländervergleich könnte man zur Konkretisierung etwa die Einrichtung der Winterpause nennen, die in England nicht existiert, wo Spiele sogar am zweiten Weihnachtsfeiertag (Boxing Day) und an Silvester stattfinden.

7 Ohnehin gilt dies nur für das deutsche Konzept der Kulturindustrie. „The English term ,cultural industries', by contrast, takes for granted that both areas of culture are dependent on the market, and that it therefore applies to both classical and pop music, good books and cheap literature, educational valuable sporting events and dubious computer killer games alike" (Eisenberg/Gestrich 2012: 4).

Beeinflussungen und Interdependenzen der globalen, nationalen und lokalen Ebenen, die wiederum – insbesondere im stark ausdifferenzierten Amateurbereich des Fußballs, wo sich im Verein als dörflicher Gemeinschaft heute traditionale und posttraditionale Werte vermischen (Klein/Meuser 2008: 10f.) – eine Vielzahl diverser Praktiken nach sich ziehen und unterschiedliche Sinnbezüge und Wissensdimensionen enthalten. Angelehnt an Appadurai wird hier davon ausgegangen, dass die Massenmedien und insbesondere das Fernsehen nicht vor allem passive, willenlose und manipulierbare Konsumenten erzeugen (vgl. auch Gebauer 2003b), sondern eher Handlungen und Praktiken in unterschiedlichen Ausprägungen provozieren. „This is not to suggest that consumers are *free* agents, living happily in a world of safe malls, free lunches, and quick fixes. As I suggest (…), consumption in the contemporary world is often a form of drudgery, part of the capitalist civilizing process. Nevertheless, where there is pleasure there is agency" (Appadurai 1996: 7).

Das gemeinsame Rezipieren der Massenmedien kann in dieser Sichtweise vorgestellte Gemeinschaften (Anderson 1983) erzeugen, die nicht mehr zwingend auf explizite Kommunikation über fußballspezifische Diskurse und Narrative angewiesen sind, obwohl diese insbesondere im Bereich Fußball noch eine bedeutsame Rolle spielen. Dies entspricht dem Gedanken, „dass auch Praktiken, die nicht als Sinngebungen angelegt sind, einen für Identitäten und Grenzen inhaltlich relevanten Sinn haben" (Langenohl 2010: 50; vgl. auch Reckwitz 2003) können, also gleichsam implizit imaginäre Grenzen und damit ‚Innen' und ‚Außen' etablieren.

Appadurai (1996:8) hebt in diesem Kontext generell den Bereich des Sports hervor. Hier wird nun argumentiert, dass es sich insbesondere für das Fußballspiel gut darstellen lässt, wie als möglicherweise nicht bewusst intendierte Folge dieser Praktiken auf der lokalen Ebene imaginäre Grenzen des Lokalen, Nationalen und Globalen entstehen (Langenohl 2010: 51). Diese social imaginaries (Taylor 2004) können als implizites Hintergrundwissen verstanden werden, welche gemeinschaftliche Praktiken wiederum möglich machen und mit Legitimität ausstatten[8]. Praktiken können dann beispielsweise als agonistische, ritualisierte körperliche Fähigkeiten bedeutsame Bestandteile im Kontext der Herstellung und

---

8   „They are first-person subjectivities that build upon implicit understandings that underlie and make possible common practices. They are embedded in the habitus of a population or are carried in modes of address, stories, symbols, and the like. They are imaginary in a double sense: they exist by virtue of representation or implicit understandings, even when they acquire immense institutional force; and they are the means by which individuals understand their identities and their place in the world" (Gaonkar 2002: 2).

Erhaltung moderner imagined communities darstellen[9]. Diese nehmen parallel zu den Mechanismen des *Medienkapitalismus* auf Prozesse der Vergemeinschaftung Einfluss und werden von den elektronischen Medien transportiert (Appadurai 1996: 112; siehe Kautt in diesem Band). So werden über alltägliche Routinen neue Vorstellungen imaginierter Welten möglich (ebd.: 3).

Während also die Glokalisierungsthese, die dem Globalen und Lokalen ein gegenseitiges Abhängigkeitsverhältnis unterstellt, in dem lokale Praxis Einfluss auf den inhaltlichen Niederschlag der Massenmedien hat (vgl. Klein 2008: 33), im Rahmen des professionellen Fußballs aufgrund der massenmedialen Verfasstheit desselben direkt beobachtbar ist, ist sie für den Amateurbereich nur über die Kommunikation der teilhabenden Akteure und Beobachtung vor Ort entsprechender Praktiken greifbar. Begründet ist dies durch die deutlich komplexere Rolle des globalen, massenmedialen Einflusses, der im Amateurbereich nicht direkt, sondern vielmehr indirekt wirkt. So ist zu zeigen, inwiefern der nationale Fernsehfußball, der – gemäß dem Konzept der *Glokalisierung* – Angebote des globalen Medienfußballs ja bereits kulturell kontextualisiert hat, auf der Amateurebene durch entsprechende Akteure und ihre partikularen Interessen unter Umständen re-interpretiert wird.

Im Hinblick auf die analytische Verbindung von professionellem und Amateurfußball ist hier noch das kontrovers diskutierte Konzept des *Post-Fans* – in Anlehnung an John Urrys *Post-Tourist* (1988) – zu erwähnen. Dieser muss beispielsweise nicht mehr das Haus verlassen, um an einem professionellen Fußballspiel als Zuschauer teilzunehmen, da vor allem das Fernsehen, und mittlerweile natürlich das Internet, zahlreiche Gelegenheiten bieten, dies von zu Hause aus zu tun. Die Hauptspielart des Post-Fans ist demzufolge Mitglied einer neuen Mittelschicht in seinen unterschiedlichen Formen, welche sich populärkulturellen Erscheinungen gegenüber einerseits offen, andererseits reflexiv und kritisch-ironisch bzw. distanziert verhält und ein Bewusstsein für die mediale Durchdringung des modernen Sports ausbildet, in welchem Inhalte stark selektiv verbreitet und Atmosphäre weitgehend simuliert wird (Redhead 1997; Giulianotti 1999). Ob sich tatsächlich, wie mit dem Konzept unterstellt, die soziale Basis des Fußballpublikums seit den 1990ern hin zur Mittelschicht verschoben hat, oder ob es sich hierbei lediglich selbst um ein medial konstruiertes Phänomen handelt, ist unklar (siehe Fürtjes in diesem Band sowie Taylor 2008: 360ff.). Jedoch deuten sich ins-

---

9 Appadurai etwa arbeitet dies für den indischen Fall am Beispiel des Cricket heraus (vgl. 1996: 89ff.).

besondere im deutschen Fußball Modernisierungs- bzw. Elitenbildungsprozesse an, die potentiell Auswirkungen auf der Amateurebene zeitigen[10].

Gerade aber die Flexibilität der Kategorie des Post-Fans ist hier von hervorgehobenem Interesse, weil sie eine Betrachtung unterschiedlicher Praktiken und Diskurse konzeptuell vorbereitet und entsprechend die Untersuchung eines Niederschlags des populärkulturellen Phänomens Fußball im Lokalen ermöglicht. Post-Fans partizipieren in dieser Sichtweise in der Regel in ihrer Funktion als Spieler, Trainer, Funktionäre, Schiedsrichter, Vereinsmitglieder- oder -angestellte, Fans, Beobachter usw. am professionellen *und* nicht-professionellen Fußballspiel.

3   Profifußball als Fernsehfußball im medialen Kontext

Als populäre Kultur des Globalen und Nationalen ist Fußball stark medial inszeniert und ohne die modernen Massenmedien schlechthin nicht vorstellbar. Im Profifußball, der sich vor allem am Prinzip der Wirtschaftslogik orientiert und sportliche Leistung vermeintlich absolut setzt[11], ist die Rolle des Fernsehens und seine zunehmende Kommerzialisierung und Standardisierung hervorzuheben. „Was wir über Fußball sagen, denken und fühlen können, ist eine Koproduktion von Fußball und Fernsehen" (Adelmann/Stauff 2003: 104f.). Dies stellt eine Entwicklung dar, die McLuhans These vom *global village* (vgl. 1964) im Bereich des Fußballs zu bestätigen scheint. Andererseits lassen sich bereits seit dem Heimsieg Englands über Westdeutschland bei der Weltmeisterschaft 1966 Stimmen vernehmen (siehe Porter/Wagner in diesem Band), die solche Wettbewerbe und allgemein den professionellen Fußball zunehmend kritisch als globale Events betrachten, welche ausschließlich durch und für die Massenmedien konzipiert würden (vgl. Redhead 1997: 37), die letztlich hyperreal (vgl. Baudrillard 1993) seien und zusätzlich – als moderne Form der Gladiatorenkämpfe – von der Realität ablenk-

---

10 Vgl. etwa die Jugendförderung des Deutschen Fußball-Bundes an Gymnasien als Exzellenz- und Eliteschulen des Fußballs unter http://talente.dfb.de/index.php?id=519149. Zugriff am 14.2.2013.

11 Obwohl der Fußball allgemein zunehmend Tendenzen der wissenschaftlichen und vermeintlich objektiven Messung der Leistungsfähigkeit unterliegt, existieren offensichtlich Kontingenzen, die das Spiel unberechenbar und unüberschaubar machen, unabhängig von der rein physischen Leistungsfähigkeit. Hier wird dann häufig die Frage nach dem ‚Charakter' der Spieler oder der ‚Ansprache' der Trainer gestellt – wobei auch diese mittlerweile deutlich über das reine Motivieren hinausreicht (etwa beim Einsatz von Power Point in der Halbzeitpause etc.) (vgl. Müller 2008: 210f.).

ten (Eco 1987) und in denen die professionellen Fußballspieler entsprechend als
Bewohner eines stark protektionierten, geradezu mythischen *Über-Raums* (Gebauer 2003b) entworfen werden (siehe Wagg und Hacker/Waine in diesem Band).
Fraglos hat die Form der Darstellung des professionellen Fußballs im Fernsehen
wesentliche Auswirkungen darauf, wie die Beteiligten das Spiel wahrnehmen,
was sie darüber wissen, und auch, wie sie sich dem Spiel gegenüber verhalten (vgl.
Gebauer 2003b).

Im Rahmen eines historischen Vergleichs lässt sich in den beiden hier be-
trachteten Ländern von ähnlichen Entwicklungen im Bereich einer umfassenden
medialen Fußball-Berichterstattung ausgehen, obwohl die Gründung der ersten
Profiliga (*Football League*) in England bereits im Jahr 1888 und damit sehr früh
erfolgte, während die deutsche *Bundesliga* als professionelle Liga erst spät, nämlich 1963 eingeführt wurde. Sowohl in Deutschland als auch in England beginnt
die Hochzeit der medialen Verbreitung des Fußballs schwerpunktmäßig in den
1960er Jahren in mittlerweile klassischen Sendungen, die gleichsam als Schlüssel-
komponenten der jeweiligen *Fernseh*-Fußballkulturen zu begreifen sind und seit
ihrem Erscheinen erheblichen Einfluss auf die Art und Weise haben, wie Fußball wahrgenommen wird (siehe Turner in diesem Band). Zu nennen sind hier
die Sportschau (ARD, seit 1961) bzw. *das aktuelle sportstudio* (ZDF, seit 1963) auf
deutscher sowie *Match of the day* (BBC, seit 1964) auf englischer Seite (vgl. Mikos
2006: 145 u. Taylor 2008: 275). Seit den 1980ern und dem Aufkommen des Privat-
fernsehens, vor allem aber mit Beginn der 1990er Jahre sind mit der Übernahme
der Übertragungsrechte des Profifußballs durch die ‚Kirch Mediengruppe‘ im
deutschen und im britischen Fernsehen durch den Sender ‚British Sky Broadcasting‘ weiter ähnliche Entwicklungen zu beobachten, die Kommerzialisierungs-
prozesse im Fußball beschleunigen (vgl. Mikos 2006 u. Porter 2012; siehe Elliott
in diesem Band). Neben den öffentlich-rechtlichen und privaten Sendern (mo-
mentan *Kabel 1* und *Sport 1* in Deutschland bzw. *ITV* in England) wird der Fußball heute in beiden Ländern vor allem durch den Pay-TV-Sender *Sky* via Abon-
nement zugänglich gemacht. *Sky* ist immer (‚24/7‘) auf Sendung, was tendenziell
den Eindruck einer allgegenwärtigen und grenzenlos bedeutsamen Fußball- bzw.
Sportwelt vermittelt, in der sich ständig Ereignisse von öffentlichem Interesse
zutragen. Gleichzeitig verdeutlicht dieses Überangebot den *sozialkonservativen*
Charakter des Fußballs, dessen Grundprinzip das der ständigen Wiederholung
ist[12]. Der Einfluss von *Sky* etwa auf die deutsche Fußball-Medienberichterstattung
ist nicht zu unterschätzen, da hier mit eingespielten medial-kulturellen Eigen-

---

12 Vgl. etwa die treffende Parodie auf http://www.youtube.com/watch?v=VF_uOgyBK1c.
Zugriff am 27.2.2013.

arten gebrochen wird, insbesondere hinsichtlich der Einführung von *Experten-runden* anstatt nur eines Experten bzw. der Idee, dem Kommentator eines Spiels einen Experten zur Seite zur stellen; dies sind Aspekte, die einer Standardisierung der Berichterstattung insgesamt Vorschub leisten.

Neben den dargestellten ähnlichen Ausprägungen der Fußball-Medien in Deutschland und England soll im Folgenden auf unterschiedliche Entwicklungen im professionellen Fußball der jüngeren Vergangenheit eingegangen werden, die m. E. die Wahrnehmung unterschiedlicher Fußballwelten in den beiden Ländern als wirkmächtige Diskurse nachhaltig prägen. Dabei geht es um jeweils krisenhafte Entwicklungen der jüngeren Vergangenheit.

Zunächst gelten die 1980er Jahre als das Krisenjahrzehnt des englischen Fußballs schlechthin. Als Hauptprobleme können zum einen der ausgeprägte *Hooliganism* einerseits sowie die schlechte Stadien-Infrastruktur andererseits genannt werden, die zu diversen Tragödien führten[13] (vgl. Taylor 2008: 338ff.). Als am 15. April 1989 im Hillsborough-Stadion in Sheffield 96 Besucher beim FA-Cup Halbfinale zwischen dem Liverpool F.C. und Nottingham Forest ums Leben kamen, nachdem die Polizei durch diverse Fehlentscheidungen die Fanströme in besonders enge Teile des Stadions leitete, so dass viele der Fans in der entstehenden Massenpanik erdrückt wurden, stieß dies grundlegende Änderungen im englischen Profifußball an. Die offizielle Untersuchung wurde im Anschluss von Lord Justice Taylor durchgeführt. Dessen im Januar 1990 publiziertes Gutachten, der sog. *Taylor report*, legte den Schwerpunkt auf Aspekte der Sicherheit und verlangte nicht weniger als ,a new ethos in football' (ebd.: 340). Die äußerst vielfältige und komplexe Debatte im Anschluss sei hier auf zwei wesentliche Punkte reduziert und damit stark verkürzt: Der *Taylor report* forderte die Einführung reiner Sitzplatzstadien (*all seater stadia*), was den englischen Profi-Vereinen im Anschluss zur Auflage gemacht wurde. Dies führte zweitens dazu, dass sich die führenden englischen Vereine von der Football League abspalteten, vor allem auch um höhere TV-Einnahmen zu erzielen, um die geforderten Stadien-Umbauten oder Neubauten stemmen zu können. Im Jahr 1992 fand dann die erste Spielzeit einer neuen Liga unter dem Namen *FA Premier League* statt, die heute als finanzstärkste nationale Liga weltweit gilt (siehe auch Elliott in diesem Band).

---

13 Neben den Fußballkatastrophen in Bradford und dem Brüsseler Heysel-Stadion (beides 1985), letztere hervorgerufen durch englische Hooligans, mit jeweils 55 und 41 Todesfällen trugen auch zivile Unfälle zur Wahrnehmung extremer Defizite der britischen Infrastruktur bei. Zu nennen sind beispielsweise das Sinken der Fähre Herald of Free Enterprise und das Feuer in der Londoner U-Bahn (King's Cross) (beides 1987), bzw. das Feuer am Flughafen in Manchester (1985) sowie der Lockerbie-Absturz (1988) (Taylor 2008: 338f.).

Die hier als bedeutsam erachtete Krise des deutschen Fußballs lässt sich demgegenüber zwischen den Jahren 2000 und 2006 verorten. Zunächst wurde das
klägliche Ausscheiden der deutschen Nationalmannschaft in der Vorrunde der
Europameisterschaft in Belgien und den Niederlanden als Kulminationspunkt
einer fatalen Entwicklung gesehen, die sich bereits in den Jahren zuvor angekün-
digt hatte. Als zentrales Problem wurde dabei eine generelle Konzeptlosigkeit
im Jugendbereich benannt, die in der öffentlichen Wahrnehmung zu taktischen
Defiziten und einer Überalterung der Mannschaft führten (vgl. Schulze-Marmeling 2004). Dies leitete eine Phase der Neuorientierung beim DFB ein, der zügig
(2001) ein neues Jugendkonzept entwickelte, in dessen Zentrum seitdem die sogenannten Leistungszentren stehen[14]. Parallel hierzu ist der Kollaps des Kirch-
Medienimperiums im Jahr 2002 zu nennen, der die Bundesligamannschaften
mit einer erheblichen Finanzierungslücke konfrontierte (vgl. Mikos 2006: 152).
Dies forcierte, trotz der Liberalisierung des Spielermarktes durch das Bosman-
Urteil[15], eine verstärkte Bereitschaft der deutschen Lizenzvereine, in den Jugendfußball zu investieren. In Bezug auf den deutschen Profifußball kann also von
einer doppelten Krise ausgegangen werden, auf die mit einer strategischen Neuausrichtung des Gesamtsystems reagiert wurde. Die von deutschen Jugend- und
Seniorenmannschaften erreichten Erfolge seitdem (vgl. dfb.de) legen nahe, von
einer sehr erfolgreichen Anwendung der neuen Strategien zu sprechen[16]. So stellte Deutschland bei der Europameisterschaft 2012 in Polen und der Ukraine mit
einem Durchschnittsalter ca. 25 Jahren die jüngste aller Mannschaften, ganz im
Gegensatz zur EM des Jahres 2000, was vor allem auch in der Eigendarstellung
des DFB positiv hervorgehoben wird[17].

---

14 Vgl. http://talente.dfb.de/index.php?id=519152. Zugriff am 17.2.2013.

15 Das Bosman-Urteil geht auf die Klage des gleichnamigen Spielers vor dem Europäischen
    Gerichtshof im Jahr 1995 zurück, der darin argumentierte, dass die Transferregeln des
    belgischen Fußballverbands, der UEFA und FIFA die freie Wahl des Arbeitsplatzes ver-
    hinderten. Der Erfolg des Spielers in diesem Verfahren bedeutete die Aufhebung der
    geltenden Beschränkungen für ausländische Spieler, bekannt als '3+2'-System, und er-
    laubte fortan die freie Wahl des Arbeitsplatzes für Spieler, deren Verträge auslaufen,
    ohne das eine Transfersumme von dem neuen Verein zu zahlen wäre (vgl. Taylor 2008:
    396).

16 In England kursiert etwa seit der WM 2010 die Rede vom German model, dem man
    nacheifern solle (vgl. http://www.guardian.co.uk/football/david-conn-inside-sport-
    blog/2012/dec/01/german-fan-owned-clubs-bundesliga?INTCMP=SRCH. Zugriff am
    17.2.2013).

17 Vgl. http://talente.dfb.de/fileadmin/pdf/ft10_09_06_13.pdf. Zugriff am 17.2.2013.

Parallel zum internen Diskurs des DFB wurde der entsprechende öffentliche Diskurs vornehmlich angestoßen durch den 2004 berufenen Nationaltrainer Jürgen Klinsmann und dessen *Aufbruchsrhetorik* rund um die WM 2006 in Deutschland, die sich u.a. in einer zunehmenden Beschäftigung mit Taktik und moderneren Strukturen, sich von den alten deutschen Fußballtugenden wie ‚Rennen, Kämpfen, Effizient-Sein‘ abhebend, niederschlug, und generell einen vermeintlichen ‚Intellektualisierungsschub‘[18] im deutschen Fußball auslöste: Wurde der damalige Bundesligatrainer Ralf Rangnick 1998 beispielsweise noch von der *Bild* als ‚Fußball-Professor‘ verhöhnt, als er die taktische Abwehrformation ‚Vierer-Kette‘ im *aktuellen sportstudio* des ZDF erklärte[19], ist die journalistische und akademische Auseinandersetzung mit dem Thema Taktik heute weitgehend üblich (vgl. Biermann 2002 u. 2010; Wilson 2011). Im Gegensatz zu anderen Ländern wurde dieser Prozess in Deutschland jedoch relativ spät und top-down initiiert, was sich in der Fokussierung kognitiver und sozialer Lernziele parallel zu den sportlichen niederschlug. Damit eröffnen sich zusätzlich diskursive Anschlüsse an die Bereiche *Schule* und *Arbeitswelt*, die ja häufig auch in einer netzwerkartigen Verbindung zur Vereinswelt stehen. In diesem Kontext hat sich in seiner Zeit beim DFB insbesondere der ehemalige Spieler und Trainer *Matthias Sammer* hervorgetan, der mit einem Konzept im Jahr 2006 eine Schuloffensive zur Eliteförderung einforderte, die mittlerweile als mehr oder weniger umgesetzt gelten kann[20].

Die beiden skizzierten, krisenhaften Entwicklungen im Bereich des Profifußballs der beiden Länder verdeutlichen die jeweils unterschiedlichen Auswirkungen auf das Gesamtsystem. Während in Deutschland eine sportliche und finanzielle Krise zu einer kompletten und erfolgreichen Neugestaltung des Systems Jugendfußball auf der höchsten Ebene (DFB, Profivereine) mit entsprechenden öffentlichen Diskursen und den Schlagworten *Verjüngung, Elite, Fußball in Schulen* und *Taktik* führte, ging es in England eher um den Aspekt Sicherheit in all seinen Facetten und eine Neuordnung des Profifußballs, der Tendenzen weiterer Kommerzialisierung Vorschub leistete, und in der sich die Premier League selbst als Weltmarke bzw. als beste Liga der Welt propagierte. Hier stehen nunmehr weniger die eigene Ausbildung von Talenten als internationale Stars im Fokus der

---

18 Ein Indiz hierfür sind eine Reihe von erfolgreichen Bundesligatrainern in Deutschland, die nicht auf allerhöchstem Niveau selbst gespielt, dafür aber studiert haben, was mittlerweile als nicht unwesentliche Kompetenz in einem zunehmend wissenschaftlichen Methoden unterworfenem Spiel gilt, zumindest in Deutschland (z.B. Tuchel, Klopp, Rangnick u.a.).

19 Vgl. ‚Die Demokratie der Doppel-Sechs‘, Süddeutsche Zeitung 5.8.2011.

20 Vgl. http://www.faz.net/aktuell/sport/fussball/bundesliga/fussball-sammer-praesentiert-elite-konzept-1382542.html. Zugriff am 16.2.2013.

Aufmerksamkeit. Die Abspaltung unterstrich die Eigenständigkeit des professionellen Elite-Fußballs und vor allem der *Premier League* bzw. deren relative Unabhängigkeit vom nationalen Gesamtsystem.

Vor diesem Hintergrund und an das oben Gesagte anschließend, wird der analytische Blick nun auf den Fußball-Amateurbereich gerichtet.

4   Amateurfußball: Versuch einer Differenzierung

Etymologisch enthält der *Amateurbegriff*, der zurückzuführen ist auf das lateinische *amator*, von dem im 17./18. Jahrhundert das Altfranzösische *l'amateur* abgeleitet wurde (Bretschneider 2008: 58), einerseits Inhalte wie Liebhaberei, Passion, Verehrung usw. Andererseits transportiert er Konnotationen wie Limitation und Dilettantismus. Bereits hier wird die paradoxe Natur des Begriffs mitsamt seinem Potential zur Ideologisierbarkeit deutlich. Insofern ist er als einer der häufigen neuzeitlichen Kollektivsingulare zu begreifen, „die viele ausdifferenzierte Bedeutungen abstrakt zusammenfassen" (Koselleck 2006: 66).

Ursprüngliche Unterscheidungen zwischen Amateur- und professionellem Status sind auf das 19. Jahrhundert zurückzuführen, als *Gentlemen* mit Zeit, Geld und dem Bedürfnis, ihren sportlichen Interessen nachzugehen, zunehmend von den arbeitenden (auch bürgerlichen) Schichten herausgefordert wurden, die aus unterschiedlichen sportspezifischen, vereinspolitischen und gesellschaftlichen Gründen nunmehr eine Vergütung für die Ausübung des Sports erhielten (vgl. Eisenberg 1999; Curry 2004). Die Idee, dass der *Gentlemen-Amateur* höher angesehen sein sollte als der bezahlte Profi, wurde spätestens in der Mitte des 20. Jahrhunderts als zunehmend unzeitgemäß wahrgenommen[21].

Generell orientierten sich historische Definitionen von Amateur- und Profifußball an Klassen-und Statuskategorien, die sich im Laufe der Zeit wandeln konnten. Prinzipiell erwartete man von einem Amateur, dass er aus ‚Liebe zum

---

21 Die Idee eines ‚guten Amateurfußballers', dessen Kerneigenschaften Loyalität, Solidarität und Gemeinschaftsglaube sind, wird aber auch heute noch im deutschen Amateurfußball bemüht, und zwar ex negativo: So werden Spieler, denen unterstellt wird, vornehmlich des Geldes wegen den Verein zu wechseln, häufig abwertend als *Söldner* adressiert. Mit dem gleichen Begriff werden auch Profifußballer, die häufig den Verein wechseln, bezeichnet. Während das Konzept im Profifußball jedoch eher in Diskussionen mit sozialromantischen Zügen auftritt, da Profifußballer per definitionem in der Regel dort spielen, wo am meisten bezahlt wird, beinhaltet der Begriff im Amateurbereich mitunter den impliziten Vorwurf an den Spieler, die Vereine durch das häufige Wechseln in den Ruin zu treiben und nicht ‚wirklich' Loyalität zu empfinden.

Spiel' am selbigen teilnimmt, während bei einem professionellen Spieler eine Entlohnung in irgendeiner Form vorausgesetzt wird (vgl. Porter/Smith 2000: viii f.). Tatsächlich spiegelt dieser grobe Dualismus nicht die Komplexität der Thematik wider, da auch der gegenwärtige Amateurfußball – abhängig von der jeweiligen Spielklasse – in den hier fokussierten Beispielländern in der Regel äußerst kompetitiv ist: Trainerentlassungen bei Misserfolg gehören bis in die untersten Spielklassen zum Alltag, Spieler beziehen Gehälter und werden auf einem Transfermarkt gegen entsprechende Summen ,verkauft'. Dies sind allerdings eigentlich Inhalte der kulturellen Zirkulationssphäre des Profifußballs, dessen zentrale Charakteristika mit den Schlagworten *Leistung, Wirtschaftlichkeit* und *Wissenschaft* umrissen werden können. Somit lässt sich bereits an dieser Stelle festhalten, dass sich die kulturellen Zirkulationssphären bzw. die Funktionssysteme von Amateur- und Profifußball nicht sauber voneinander trennen lassen. Die Bezeichnung Amateurfußball bringt als Sammelbegriff, der in der Regel synonym für *unbezahlt, nicht-kommerziell* bzw. *nicht-professionell* verwendet wird, die real bestehenden Differenzierungen also nicht adäquat zum Ausdruck[22] (vgl. hierzu auch Bretschneider 2008: 55ff.). Dennoch ist das lokale bzw. regional beschränkte Interesse ein wesentliches Charakteristikum des Amateurfußballs. So entsteht, trotz der Einflüsse des professionellen Fußballs, ein System, das einer von den maßgeblichen Akteuren – etwa Vereinsfunktionäre, die gleichzeitig *Post-Fans* sind – bestimmten Eigenlogik folgt und in dem etwa finanzielle Aufwendungen und öffentliches Interesse stark auseinanderdriften können[23]. Auch im Amateurfußball spielt also der Kreislauf von Personen (z.B. Transfersystem für Spieler und Trainer) und Waren (z.B. Fanartikel) eine wesentliche Rolle für die Ausbildung relevanter Kollektivvorstellungen und damit der Herstellung imaginärer Grenzen des Lokalen und Nationalen. Gleichzeitig findet auf diesen Ebenen eine Betonung klassischer Gemeinschaftsformen im Sinne von exklusiven, traditionell verankerten Bindungen statt (vgl. Tönnies 1979), die mit den zentralen Funktionslogiken des Fußballsports, nämlich Leistungsvergleich, Konkurrenz, Wettbewerb und Austausch auf einem durch das Ligasystem und die Zirkulationssysteme festgelegten Markt kollidieren und den nicht-professionell betriebenen Fußball so zu einem nur schwer deutbaren und facettenreichen System werden lassen.

---

22 Der Sporthistoriker Dilwyn Porter stellt daher die Bezeichnung Amateur generell in Frage, die man ihm folgend, freilich nur im englischen Kontext aufgrund der strukturellen Unterschiede zum deutschen Fall, durch *recreational football, parks football* oder *grass-roots football* ersetzen sollte (aus einem persönlichen Gespräch).

23 Insbesondere in höheren Klassen des Amateurfußballs in beiden Ländern sind die finanziellen Aufwendungen oft erheblich, während die Zuschauerzahlen eher auf einem niedrigen Niveau verbleiben.

In vergleichender Perspektive lassen sich bezüglich der Fallbeispiele Deutschland und England nun deutliche historisch-geprägte Gegensätze, etwa in Bezug auf Vereinstraditionen konstatieren[24]. Ferner ist der englische Fußball insgesamt deutlich dezentraler organisiert[25]. Bereits der Begriff *local football* – eine sprachliche Wendung, zu der im Deutschen keine treffende Entsprechung existiert – verweist auf die im Englischen stärker betonten Konnotationen wie Spontaneität, Nähe, Vertraulichkeit oder Unmittelbarkeit sowie Bezüge auf eine gemeinschaftlich geteilte, erholsame Beschäftigung in kleineren, meist nachbarschaftlich geprägten Räumen. Diese zunächst theoretische Betonung des *playing for fun* sowie des physischen Ausdrucks ist historisch charakteristisch für den englischen Fall und lässt sich in der englischen Sprache unter den konsensfähigen Begriff *popular culture* subsumieren. Im deutschen Kontext war die bildungsbürgerliche Kritik des Populären (Stichwort: Kulturkritik) im Zeitalter des Aufkommens moderner Massenmedien in der zweiten Hälfte des 19. und in der ersten des 20. Jahrhunderts historisch ausgeprägter als in anderen Gesellschaften (vgl. Hecken 2007 u. 2009)[26]. Darüber hinaus musste sich der Fußball in Deutschland bekanntlich als ,englische Krankheit' gegen die starke traditionelle und zeitweise stark nationalistisch geprägte Konkurrenz der Turnerbewegung durchsetzen, und schaffte dies zunächst, nämlich zu Beginn des 20. Jahrhunderts, durch die Verankerung des Fußballs in den Ausbildungsplänen des Militärs (vgl. Eisenberg 1999: 178ff.).

---

24 Nathaus (2012: 78) schreibt: „Unlike in Britain, where sport had grown out of pre-modern contexts before it became organised in clubs, in Germany modern associativity preceded sports. As a consequence of this, the influence of commerce on the early development of sport in Germany was weaker than in Britain, and this meant that sports enthusiasts often depended on the goodwill of patrons like politicians, members of the economic elite and other honoraries who supported clubs primarily in order to preserve local hierarchies, not to sponsor entertainment for the common people".

25 Die Dachverbände sind der Deutsche Fußball-Bund (DFB) und die englische Football Association (FA). Es existieren unter dem Dach der englischen Football Association – im Sinne einer quantitativen Unterscheidung – 43 Regionalverbände (County FAs), wohingegen der DFB lediglich in 21 Landesverbände untergliedert ist. Hier stellt sich weniger die Frage nach der genauen Funktionslogik des Gesamtsystems – das Grundprinzip hier wie dort ist dasjenige des Auf- und Abstiegs (vgl. zum deutschen Fall Bretschneider 2008) – als vielmehr die Frage nach dem relevanten Feld für die empirische Untersuchung und Beobachtung kultureller Praktiken.

26 Bezüge im Kontext populärer Kultur verweisen seitdem auf unterschiedliche Konzepte, wie etwa Unterhaltung, Freizeit, Alltagskultur, Volkskultur usw. Hinsichtlich des Begriffs der Volkskultur schwingt im deutschen Kontext immer auch der Terminus ,Kultivierung des Volkes mit' (vgl. Waine 1997: 15ff.), der sich auch in der engen inhaltlichen Verbindung der Konzepte Bildung und Kultur widerspiegelt (vgl. Koselleck 2006: 105ff.).

Im deutschen Amateurfußball (und hier insbesondere im Jugendfußball) sind Hinweise auf disziplinierende und pädagogische Zielsetzungen immer noch allgegenwärtig[27]. So benennen heutige Entscheidungsträger von Amateurvereinen der untersten Klassen nicht selten ihre Vereinsidentität als Ausbildungsverein[28], wobei Aspekte wie Disziplin, Spielsysteme oder taktische Ausbildung in den Vordergrund gerückt werden. Gleichzeitig sind Professionalisierungstendenzen (Stichworte: Sponsoren, Mäzenatentum, Gehälter, Transferzahlungen, vgl. hierzu Bretschneider 2008: 71ff.) im nicht-professionellen Fußball der höheren Ebenen, wie bereits angedeutet, üblich. Bemerkenswert ist für den deutschen Fall, und hier im starken Kontrast zum englischen, dass diese Tendenzen der Professionalisierung auch auf den untersten Ebenen (Kreisligen) nachweisbar sind. Die teilnehmenden Beobachtungen und Experteninterviews legen dabei Anschlüsse an den Erneuerungsdiskurs im deutschen Profifußball nahe (vgl. 4.), insbesondere im Kontext des Baus von *Kunstrasenplätzen* (siehe 5.).

Bemerkenswert im englischen Kontext ist wiederum eine sprachliche Besonderheit. Dabei geht es um die Bezeichnung der Mannschaften, die sich knapp unterhalb der professionellen Ligen (*Premier League, The Championship, League One, League Two*) in der Pyramide des nationalen Systems einordnen lassen. Diese werden als *Non-League Clubs* deklariert, da sie professionellen oder semiprofessionellen Fußball außerhalb der ausgewiesenen Profiligen (insgesamt 92 Mannschaften) betreiben, obwohl die FA seit 1974 offiziell jeden Spieler nur noch

---

27 In einer Broschüre, die sich an die Eltern der Spieler richtet, erläutert der Jugendvorstand des SSV Bergneustadt (Oberbergischer Kreis, Fußballverband Mittelrhein) beispielsweise den Aspekt Disziplin folgendermaßen: „Fußball ist ein Mannschaftssport und fordert darum sehr viel Disziplin. Disziplin von den Trainern und Betreuern, aber auch von den Spielern und deren Eltern. Daher an dieser Stelle eine generelle Bemerkung: Fußball zeichnet sich dadurch aus, dass die ganze Mannschaft letztendlich zum Training oder am Spieltag „an Bord" sein muss. Wenn ein Spieler überhaupt nicht zum Training oder zum vereinbarten Treffpunkt erscheint ohne dass dies dem Trainer bekannt ist, so ist dies eine besondere Situation. Der Trainer hat für die Zeit der Trainingseinheit die Aufsichtspflicht, wie ein Lehrer in der Schule. Er muss sich also vergewissern, ob dem Kind nichts passiert ist. Dieses kostet in der Regel viel Zeit und Nerven. Schwierigkeiten mit Absagen zu Spieltagen, haben die Trainer und Betreuer, wenn ein Spieler – oder seine Eltern – am Freitagabend beim Trainer anrufen und diese dann völlig überraschend am Samstag auf eine Hochzeit müssen".

28 Hier aus einem Experteninterview mit einem Vertreter eines Amateurvereins (Kreisliga) aus dem oberbergischen Kreis. Der Begriff ‚Ausbildungsverein' impliziert zum einen die Existenz eines – ähnlich den Strukturen des professionellen Fußballs – hochwertigen Marktes für entsprechend ausgebildete Spieler. Gleichzeitig dient der Verweis auf die Ausbildung zur Betonung der produktiven Funktion des Vereins im nationalen Gesamtsystem.

als *footballer* betrachtet, von denen manche bezahlt werden, andere eben nicht (vgl. Porter 2011). Dies beinhaltet eine Trennung des professionellen vom vermeintlichen Amateursystem, die das deutsche System so nicht kennt und zeigt sich beispielsweise, wenn man die Internetauftritte der Ligen vergleicht: Während in England jede Liga ihren eigenen Internetauftritt mit eigener Organisation und eigenem Sponsor aufweist (siehe etwa den Auftritt der *North Lancashire Premier League* unter *http://www.nlfl.org.uk*), treten die einzelnen Ligen in Deutschland immer als Teil des DFB auf (siehe etwa die offiziell vom DFB initiierte Internet-Seite *fussball.de*).

Zusammenfassend lässt sich, bezogen auf die Diskussion des schwer greifbaren Raumes Amateurfußball, formulieren, dass dieser, wegen des überragenden Einflusses der globalen Massenmedien, nicht als isoliertes und rein lokales Phänomen betrachtet werden kann. Gleichzeitig herrschen hier lokale Aspekte, Interpretationen und Netzwerke vor, die den Raum insgesamt als eher intransparent erscheinen lassen.

5   Empirische Aspekte

Der ethnografische Zugang und die Beobachtung von Praktiken im deutschen und englischen Amateurfußball verdeutlichen nun unterschiedliche Aspekte *spielbezogener Rituale*, die Einflüsse aus dem Profifußball aufweisen und teilweise anhand offensichtlicher Praktiken nachzuvollziehen sind: das Tragen bestimmter Kleidung (etwa von personalisierten Trikots mit Namenszug und eigener, nicht wechselnder Rückennummer; ‚bunte‘ Schuhe) oder entsprechender Frisuren (vgl. den Begriff des *Schönheitshandelns*, siehe Gros und Degele in diesem Band) bzw. Tattoos wären hier zum einen zu nennen, zum anderen auch der Versuch von Amateurspielern, Verhaltensweisen von Profispielern auf dem Platz zu imitieren (Bewegungsabläufe wie Laufstil, Auslaufen, Jubeln, ‚Schwalben‘ usw., die sich an medial vermittelten nationalen/globalen Vorgaben orientieren). Üblich sind auch Motivationsrituale wie das Hören bestimmter Musik vor dem Spiel in der Kabine oder das gemeinsame ‚Einschwören‘ in einem zu diesem Zweck aus den Körpern der Spieler gebildeten Kreis. Ferner enthält die Ansprache des Trainers häufig motivationale Aspekte, die in der Regel aus dem professionellen Bereich übernommen werden. Diese Elemente sind im deutschen Kontext deutlich ausgeprägter als im englischen[29].

---

29 Um die Analyse noch genauer vorantreiben zu können, müsste man zwei Vereine detailliert beschreiben und gegenüberstellen, vor allem auch in Hinblick auf das zweck-

Begrüßungsrituale sind im Fußball ‚als gruppenspezifischer Zugehörigkeits-gruß' (Müller 2008: 152) bedeutsam und zeigen Inklusion und Exklusion an, unterliegen aber in England und Deutschland unterschiedlichen kulturspezifi-schen Ausprägungen. So ist das Händeschütteln bzw. Abklatschen in den hier be-trachteten unteren Ebenen unter englischen Spielern eher unüblich, im deutschen Kontext hingegen sehr verbreitet. Für beide Länder kann festgehalten werden, dass, während die Intensität von Berührungsritualen im Profifußball insgesamt als relativ hoch bezeichnet werden kann, dies in eher abgeschwächter Form für den Amateurbereich gilt.

Auch der Ablauf *off the field* lässt, anschließend an die bisherigen Ausführun-gen, insbesondere für den deutschen Amateurfußball eine stärkere Annäherung an die Zirkulationssphäre im Profifußball vermuten. Selbst in relativ niedrigen Spielklassen (nach Spielbeobachtungen in Kreisligen im oberbergischen Kreis, aber z.B. auch der Mittelrheinliga) werden im deutschen Kontext die aus dem Pro-fibereich bekannten Lieder (z.B. ‚Hells Bells'; ‚Champions League Erkennungs-melodie'; ‚Fluch der Karibik-Theme' usw.) vor den Spielen in unterschiedlichen Abfolgen als Erkennungsmelodie abgespielt. Demgegenüber werden mit dem offiziellen und standardisierten Einlaufen der Mannschaften oder der Kontrolle von Spielerpässen vor den Spielen auch routinierte Praktiken durch den Landes-bzw. nationalen Verband vorgegeben, die explizit den Zweck erfüllen sollen, einen gemeinsamen Raum abzustecken. Im englischen Amateurfußball der untersten Ebenen finden sich weder das Abspielen von Musik noch die Kontrolle von Spie-lerpässen oder standardisierte Regelungen bezüglich des Einlaufens der Mann-schaften. Die Verpflichtungs- und Freigabeprozeduren (*signing*) sind in England deutlich unkomplizierter, Spielerpässe mit Lichtbildern existieren in der hier fo-kussierten Liga (*North Lancashire Premier League*) nicht, was die generelle Wahr-nehmung der *Offenheit* im englischen Kontext verstärkt.

Ein weiterer wichtiger Komplex sind *Formen von Geselligkeit* und spezifische *Praktiken*, die mit materiellen Veränderungen wie etwa der jeweiligen Sportan-lagen einhergehen. Sie beziehen sich beide auf das Fußballspiel als räumliches Ereignis. In England ist in Bezug auf Geselligkeitsformen vor allem der *local pub* als zentraler Ort für Geselligkeit in den verschiedensten Formen (Jubiläumsfei-ern, Sitzungen, fund raiser usw.) zu nennen (vgl. Nathaus 2012, 79). Im deutschen Amateurfußball ist in der Regel das sog. *Vereinsheim* oder *Clubheim* der Ort, an dem sich das Vereinsleben im Wesentlichen abspielt (*Vereinsidentität*) und in das

---

orientierte sprachliche Handeln der beteiligten Akteure. Ein solches Projekt ist bereits begonnen, und zwar mit den Vereinen BSV Bielstein (Oberbergischer Kreis) auf deut-scher und Storeys F.C. (District League) auf englischer Seite.

erheblich investiert wird, im starken Kontrast zu den mitunter stark herunter-gekommenen Anlagen im englischen local football[30]. Dies weist auf die hervor-gehobene Bedeutung der *eigenen Anlage* als Prestigeobjekt im deutschen Kontext hin[31].

Der deutsche Amateurfußball unterliegt auch in den hier fokussierten unters-ten Ebenen des Ligasystems zunehmend Ansätzen der Modernisierung, die Orientierungen am mediatisierten professionellen Fußball – insbesondere seit der WM 2006 bzw. mit dem Neubau und der Renovierung vieler Bundesligasta-dien – erkennen lassen. Dies zeigt sich beispielsweise in dem zunehmenden Bau von *Kunstrasenplätzen*, die häufig durch gemeinschaftliche Aktionen wie Party-Events, Spendenläufe, Patenschaftsmodelle mit Quadratmeterverkauf usw. durch den jeweiligen Verein mitfinanziert werden[32]. Im Fußball als räumlichem Ereig-nis steht der Kunstrasenplatz zunehmend im Mittelpunkt des Geschehens des deutschen Amateurfußballs[33] (vgl. Schroer 2008: 155). Der Kunstrasenplatz als Bewegungsraum, der in FIFA-Präsident Joseph Blatter einen prominenten Für-sprecher hat, bedeutet eine Rationalisierung alltagskultureller Räume (vgl. Inglis 2005: 50) und beinhaltet zwei Komponenten: Zum einen unterstellt er eine zu-nehmende Attraktivität des Spiels, dass vermeintlich ‚schneller‘ und ‚sauberer‘ wird und damit einen Prozess der Zivilisierung einleitet[34] (vgl. Elias 2006), in dem das unwägbare Element (sowie der Schmutz) weiter zurückgedrängt wird (vgl. Alkemeyer 2008: 90). Damit stellt er das ideale Umfeld für die zunehmende kommunikative und rituelle Modernisierung und Professionalisierung des Spiels auch in den untersten Amateurbereichen dar. Die Gleichartigkeit dieser neuen Plätze betreibt vor allem aber eine Standardisierung, also Homogenisierung des Raums, die dem Stadionprinzip im professionellen Fußball nahe kommt. Wie die

---

30 Vgl. hierzu auch http://www.guardian.co.uk/football/david-conn-inside-sport-blog/2012/dec/01/german-fan-owned-clubs-bundesliga?INTCMP=SRCH. Zugriff am 17.2.2013.

31 Dies gilt selbst dann, wenn die Anlage Eigentum der Kommune und nicht des Vereins ist.

32 Der Hauptteil der Finanzierung wird in der Regel – auch aus versicherungstechnischen Gründen – von der jeweiligen Kommune getragen.

33 Dies gilt vor allem für Regionen, in denen sog. Tennenplätze, also Plätze mit steinigen, granularen Oberflächen historisch vorherrschend waren, wie etwa in Deutschland in den Bundesländern Nordrhein-Westfalen oder auch Rheinland-Pfalz.

34 Mitunter wird die gesamte Existenz von Vereinen von der Realisierung solcher Kunst-rasenprojekte abhängig gemacht, da diese Beläge von Spielern bzw. den Eltern von Nachwuchsspielern mittlerweile eingefordert werden (vgl. Kölner Stadtanzeiger, 17.07.2012/Oberbergischer Kreis: „Der Kunstrasen als Existenzsicherung").

Stadien im professionellen Fußball symbolisieren die neuen Kunstrasenplätze einen exklusiven Ort der Disziplinierung: Da sich die Plätze nach einigen Jahren abnutzen, werden sie in der Regel komplett eingezäunt, was die Frage nach der Partizipation dringlich werden lässt. Zugang besteht in der Regel nur noch für Vereinsmitglieder, Teilnahme wird dann zunehmend zum Privileg. Dies hebt sich stark ab von den offenen Anlagen der ,Vor-Kunstrasen-Ära'[35], die als öffentliche Arenen in der Regel weit weniger begrenzt waren. Die Aktivierung des gemeinschaftsbildenden Vereins und seiner lokalen, expressiven und exklusiven Elemente (Müller-Jentsch 2008: 479) durch den Bau von Kunstrasenplätzen betont die lokale Gemeinschaft und stellt Mitgliedschaften und vereinsinterne Partizipation in den Vordergrund. Gleichzeitig werden Bezüge zum direkten Umfeld des Vereins (Schule, Kommune) und darüber hinaus zum leistungsorientierten Fußball möglich[36].

6   Ausblick

Fußballkulturen wurden hier sowohl definiert als spezifische Diskursräume und solche der Zirkulation von Symbolen, die geprägt, geformt und kreativ konstruiert werden durch regional (lokal), national und global agierende Medien, sowie als lokal spezifische Praktiken, Selbstverständnisse und Gemeinschaftsformen. Entsprechend sind sie zu verstehen als Ausprägungen eines *Imaginären*.

---

35 Fußball nähert sich somit tendenziell dem ,Feldhockey' an, ein klassisches Beispiel für einen Sport der Mittelschichten. Ein weiteres Indiz für die ,Mittelschichtsthese' ist die Zunahme von ,Fußballschulen', die Fußballstunden nach dem ,Nachhilfeprinzip' anbieten. Vgl. etwa http://www.anstoss-fussballschule.de/index.php?option=com_content&view=frontpage&Itemid=1. Zugriff am 27.2.2013 . Weiterhin sind hier die bereits erwähnten Kooperationen zwischen Bundesligavereinen und Gymnasien, die als ,Fußball-Exzellenzschulen' firmieren, zu nennen.

36 In einer Werbebroschüre fasst der Verein BSV Bielstein (Oberbergischer Kreis) die Vorteile des Kunstrasenprojektes unter dem Titel ,Ein Kunststück für Bielstein' beispielsweise wie folgt zusammen:
    „Zukunfts- und Existenzsicherung des BSV; Schulsportplatz; Sozialisierung und Förderung der Jugend; Kunstrasen unempfindlich gegenüber Wind und Wetter, dadurch: können Spiele und Trainingseinheiten (fast) immer stattfinden und es ergeben sich erhebliche Nutzungs- und Pflegevorteile; gleich bleibende gute Qualität des Kunstrasens erlaubt eine langfristige bessere technische Ausbildung; Vorbeugung von schweren Verletzungen; visuelle Attraktivitätssteigerung des Freizeit- und Sportgeländes in Bielstein; keine Staubbelastung für Anlieger" (vgl. http://www.bielsteiner-kunstrasen.de/).

Im deutschen Fall werden Diskursverschränkungen zwischen professioneller und Amateurebene deutlich, die gleichzeitig Standardisierungs- und Schließungstendenzen mit sich bringen. Das englische Beispiel deutet in eine eher gegenteilige Richtung, nämlich einen Amateurbereich der untersten Klassen, der offener und lokal ausdifferenzierter ist und deutlich weniger Standardisierungstendenzen unterliegt. Es bestätigten sich also potentiell gegenläufige Entwicklungen und somit die These lokaler und nationaler Spezifika bzw. *glokaler* Formen und Praktiken, die reinen Homogenisierungstendenzen auch auf der Ebene des Amateurfußballs entgegenstehen.

Die gewählte, vornehmlich konzeptuelle Herangehensweise liefert somit eine Grundlage für weitere, detaillierte historische und empirische Untersuchungen, zum einen, um die hier aufgeworfenen Thesen überprüfen, zum anderen, um weitere und spezifischere Thesen generieren zu können. Darüber hinaus liegt das hier als wesentlich identifizierte Desiderat in der verstärkten Einbeziehung auch sprachlicher Praktiken des Profi- und Amateurfußballs, die eine vergleichende Darstellung der jeweiligen strategischen Bezüge verdeutlichen könnte.

Literatur

Adelmann, R. et al. (2003): Querpässe. Beiträge zur Literatur-, Kultur- und Mediengeschichte des Fußballs. Heidelberg: Synchron.

Adelmann, R./Stauff, M. (2003): Die Wirklichkeit in der Wirklichkeit. Fernsehfußball und mediale Wissenskultur. In: Adelmann et al., 103-124.

Alkemeyer, T. (2008): Fußball als Figurationsgeschehen. Über performative Gemeinschaften in modernen Gesellschaften. In: Klein/Meuser, 87-112.

Althoff, M./Nuboer, J. (2008): Fußball, Spiel und Kampf. Zur politischen Dimension des Hooliganismus. In: Klein/Meuser (Hg.) (2008), 135-154.

Anderson, B. (1991): Die Erfindung der Nation. Zur Karriere eines folgenreichen Konzepts. Erweiterte Neuausgabe. Frankfurt a. M.: Campus.

Appadurai, A. (1996): Modernity at Large. Cultural Dimensions of Globalization. Minneapolis: University of Minnesota Press.

Baudrillard, J. (1993): The Transparency of Evil. Essays on Extreme Phenomena. London: Verso.

Biermann, C./Fuchs, U. (2002): Der Ball ist rund, damit das Spiel die Richtung ändern kann. Köln: Kiepenheuer & Witsch.

Biermann, C. (2010): Die Fußball-Matrix: Auf der Suche nach dem perfekten Spiel. Köln: Kiepenheuer & Witsch.

Böhnisch, L./Brandes, H. (2006): ‚Titan' und ‚Queen von Madrid' – Fußball zwischen Männlichkeitspraxis und Kommerz. In: Holger Brandes et al.: Hauptsache Fußball. Sozialwissenschaftliche Einwürfe. Gießen: Psychosozial-Verlag.

Bretschneider, C. (2008): Geld für Amateure – Vereine für Jugendliche? Eine Untersuchung zur Jugendarbeit im so genannten Amateurfußball. Schorndorf: Hofmann-Verlag.

Curry, G. (2004): Playing for money: James J. Lang and emergent soccer professionalism in Sheffield. In: Soccer & Society, 5:3, 336-355.

DFB.de.

Donnelly, M. (2005): Sixties Britain. Culture, Society and Politics. Edinburgh: Pearson/ Longman.

Eco, U. (1987): Travels in Hyperreality. London: Picador.

Eisenberg, C. (1999): ‚English Sports' und deutsche Bürger. Eine Gesellschaftsgeschichte 1800-1939. Paderborn: Schöningh.

Eisenberg, C./Gestrich, A. (Hg.) (2012): Cultural Industries in Britain and Germany. Sport, Music and Entertainment from the Eighteenth to the Twentieth Century. Augsburg: Wißner Verlag.

Elias, N. (2006): Der Fußballsport im Prozeß der Zivilisation (1983). In: Norbert Elias: Gesammelte Schriften. Sinzheim: Nomos, 360-374.

Gaonkar, P. D. (2002): Toward New Imaginaries. An Introduction. In: Public Culture 14(1), 1-19.

Gebauer, Gunter (2003a): Nationale Repräsentationen durch Fußball. In: Adelmann et al., 13-26.

Gebauer, Gunter (2003b): Fußball als Spiel der symbolischen Macht. In: Adelmann et al., 91-102.

Giulianotti, R. (1999): Football. A Sociology of the Global Game. Cambridge: Polity.

Giulianotti, R. (2005): Sport. A Critical Sociology. Cambridge: Polity.

Giulianotti, R./Robertson, R. (2007): Globalization and Sport. Oxford: Blackwell.

Giulianotti, R./Robertson, R. (2009): Globalization & Football. London: Sage.

Halm, D. (2006): Turkish immigrants in German amateur football. In: Tomlinson/Young (2006a), 73-92.

Hecken, T. (2009): Pop: Geschichte eines Konzepts 1955-2009. Bielefeld: transcript.

Hecken, T. (2007): Theorien der Populärkultur. Dreißig Theorien von Schiller bis zu den Cultural Studies. Bielefeld: transcript.

Hitzler, R. (1998): Posttraditionale Vergemeinschaftung. In: Berliner Debatte INITIAL 9, 1998, 81-89.

Horkheimer, M./Adorno, T. W. (2003): Dialektik der Aufklärung. Frankfurt a. M.: Fischer.

Hörning, K. H./Reuter, J. (Hg.) (2004): Doing Culture. Neue Positionen zum Verhältnis von Kultur und sozialer Praxis. Bielefeld: transcript.

Inglis, D. (2005): Culture and Every Day Life. London: Routledge.

Keller, R. (2005): Wissenssoziologische Diskursanalyse. Grundlegung eines Forschungsprogramms. Wiesbaden: VS Verlag.

Klein, G. (2008): Globalisierung, Lokalisierung, (Re-)Nationalisierung. Fußball als lokales Ereignis, globalisierte Ware und Bilderwelt. In: Klein/Meuser, 31-42.

Klein, G./Meuser, M. (Hg.) (2008): Ernste Spiele. Zur politischen Soziologie des Fußballs. Bielefeld: transcript.

Koselleck, R. (2006): Begriffsgeschichten. Studien zur Semantik und Pragmatik der politischen und sozialen Sprache. Frankfurt a.M.: Suhrkamp.

Langenohl, A. (2010): Imaginäre Grenzen. Zur Entstehung impliziter Kollektivcodierungen in EU-Europa. In: Berliner Journal für Soziologie, 1, 2010, 45-63.

Lee, B. (1997): Talking heads. Durham/London: Duke University Press.

Lee, B./Li Puma, E. (2002): Cultures of circulation: the imaginations of modernity. Public Culture, 14, 191-213.

McLuhan, M. (1964): Understanding Media. New York: Mentor.

Mikos, L. (2006): German football – a media-economic survey: the impact of the KirchMedia company on football and television in Germany. In: Tomlinson/Young, C. (2006a), 143-154.

Müller, M. (2008): Fußball als Paradoxon der Moderne. Zur Bedeutung ethnischer, nationaler und geschlechtlicher Differenzen im Profifußball. Wiesbaden: VS Verlag.

Müller-Jentsch, W. (2008): Der Verein – ein blinder Fleck der Organisationssoziologie. In: Berliner Journal für Soziologie, 3, 2008, 476-502.

Nathaus, K. (2012): Between Club and Commerce: Comparing the Organisation of Sports in Britain and Germany from the Late Nineteenth to the Early Twentieth Century. In: Eisenberg/Gestrich, 77-92.

Pfister, G.: Fußball als Erinnerungsort. Zur Globalisierung des Fußballsports an der Wende vom 19. Zum 20. Jahrhundert. In: Adelmann et al., 27-48.

Pyta, W. (2006): German Football: a Cultural History. In: Tomlinson/Young (2006a), 1-22.

Redhead, S. (1997): Post-Fandom and the Millenial Blues. The Transformation of Soccer Culture. London: Routledge.

Robertson, R. (1992): Globalization: Social Theory and Global Culture. London: Sage.

Schauerte, T./Schwier, J. (2008): Soziologie des Mediensports. Köln: Sportverlag Strauß.

Smith, A./Porter, D. (2000): Amateurs and Professionals in Post-War British Sport. London: Frank Cass Publishers.

Schroer, M. (2008): Vom ‚Bolzplatz‘ zum ‚Fußballtempel‘. Was sagt die Architektur der neuen Fußballstadien über die Gesellschaft der Gegenwart aus? In: Klein/Meuser, 155-174.

Schulze-Marmeling, D. (2000): Fußball. Zur Geschichte eines globalen Sports. Göttingen: Die Werkstatt.

Schulze-Marmeling, D. (Hg.) (2004). Die Geschichte der Fußballnationalmannschaft. Göttingen: Die Werkstatt.

Schwier, J. (2000): Sport als populäre Kultur. Hamburg: Czwalina Verlag.

Tomlinson, A./Young, C. (Hg.) (2006a): German Football. History, Culture, Society. London: Routledge.

Tomlinson, A./Young, C. (Hg.) (2006b): National Identity and Global Sports Events. Culture, Politics, and Spectacle in the Olympics and the Football World Cup. New York: State of University of New York Press.

Taylor, C. (2004): Modern Social Imagineries. Durham/London: Duke University Press.

Taylor, M. (2008): The Association Game. A History of British Football. Harlow: Pearson.

Tönnies, F. (1979): Gemeinschaft und Gesellschaft. Grundbegriffe der reinen Soziologie. Darmstadt: Wissenschaftliche Buchgesellschaft.

Urry, J. (1988): The Tourist Gaze. London. Sage.

Wagg, S. (Hg.) (2011): Myths and Milestones in the History of Sport. Basingstoke: Palgrave Macmillan, 57-79.

Waine, A. (2007): Changing Cultural Tastes. Writers and the Popular in Modern Germany. New York: Berghahn.

Wilson, J. (2011): Revolutionen auf dem Rasen. Eine Geschichte der Fussballtaktik. Göttingen: Verlag die Werkstatt.

Danksagung

Für Kommentare und Anregungen zu diesem Text sowie die Gelegenheit zur ausführlichen Diskussion danke ich Anne Sophie Krossa und Tony Waine.

Zeitleiste des modernen englischen und deutschen Fußballs

Andreas Stolz

Im 18. Jahrhundert besteht ,Deutschland' aus hunderten von kleineren und größeren Einzelstaaten. Im Gegensatz zu Großbritannien findet die Industrialisierung erst in der zweiten Hälfte des 19. Jahrhunderts statt. Auch die *Nationenbildung* ist sehr zögernd. Dies bedeutet unter anderem, dass sich das Nationalgefühl – also die Identifikation mit ,Deutschland' – erst weitaus später entwickelt, als beispielsweise in England. Man fühlt sich eher badisch oder preußisch, denn als ,deutsch'.

1860er Jahre: Der Prager Hygieneprofessor Ferdinand Hueppe spielt mit englischen Schülern in der Lehranstalt Neuwied Fußball.

Ab 1750   1800   Um 1850   1860

Im 18. Jahrhundert war Großbritannien weltweit die führende Imperialmacht und die Geburtsstätte der Industriellen Revolution. Die bürgerlichen und aristokratischen Eliten genossen, organisierten und kodifizierten alte und neue Freizeitgestaltungsmöglichkeiten.

1840er Jahre: Der Beginn der Geschichte des modernen Fußballs. Es gibt lediglich mündlich tradierte Regeln. Seit den 1840er Jahren beginnen die privaten Schulen Regelsysteme festzulegen.

1848: Erste Versuche der Universität Cambridge die bisherigen Fußballregeln zu vereinheitlichen.

24. Oktober 1857: Gründung des ältesten heute noch existierenden Fußballvereins der Welt. Der FC Sheffield wird von Sir Nathaniel Creswick und William Prest gegründet. Ihnen geht es vor allem um die Etablierung eines regelmäßigen Spielbetriebs und die Vereinheitlichung der Regeln. Ihre Sheffield Rules sind das erste moderne Fußballregelwerk.

1860er Jahre: Erste ernsthafte Versuche, die Regeln des Fußballs zu kodifizieren.

Zwischen 1750 und 1850: Der Fußball wandelt sich vom Volks- zum Sportspiel. Es handelt sich aber immer noch um eine relativ raue und ungeordnete Aktivität.

1860

1870

1880

1874: Einführung des Fußballs in Deutschland. Fußball wird in Deutschland meist auf Gymnasien und höheren Schulen gespielt. Konrad Koch, Pionier des deutschen Fußballs und Gymnasialprofessor am Martino-Katharineum in Braunschweig bringt das Spiel nach Deutschland. Es wird zunächst nach den Regeln des Rugbys gespielt.

1875: Veröffentlichung des ersten deutschen, dem heutigen Fußball sehr ähnlichen, Regelsatzes.

30. November 1872: Erstes offizielles Länderspiel zwischen England und Schottland in Glasgow. Endergebnis: 0:0

14. Oktober 1878: Erstes Spiel unter Flutlicht. Der FC Sheffield trägt an der Sheffielder Bramall Lane das erste Spiel unter Flutlicht aus. Das Spielfeld wird von vier Bogenlampen in helles Licht getaucht.

1870er und 1880er Jahre: Im Anschluss an die Gründung der FA in England gründeten Wales, Schottland und Irland eigene nationale Fußballverbände.

26. Oktober 1863: Gründung der F.A. als ersten Fußball-Verband der Welt. Festlegung eines offiziellen Regelwerks. Neben der Festlegung von verbindlichen Regeln, bei denen unter anderem das Treten des Gegners und das Rennen mit dem Ball in der Hand verboten werden, wird mit der Gründung der Football Association eine Aufsichtsbehörde geschaffen, die in Streitfällen entscheidet.

1866: Einführung der modernen Abseitsregel. Bereits Bestandteil der ursprünglichen Fußballregeln von 1863, unterscheidet sie sich allerdings stark von der heutigen Regel. Der englische Fußballverband trifft 1866 mit der Einführung der "Drei-Spieler-Regel" eine wichtige Entscheidung, die vorsieht, dass ein Angreifer dann im Abseits steht, wenn er sich näher zur Torlinie befindet als der Ball und der drittletzte Gegner. Erst jetzt kann sich das Passspiel entwickeln.

5. März 1870: Erstes inoffizielles Länderspiel zwischen England und Schottland.

1871: Einführung eines jährlich ausgetragenen Pokalwettbewerbs zwischen den Klubs der FA. Nun können auch indirekte Leistungsvergleiche zwischen den Mannschaften erfolgen und es entsteht eine Kontinuität an ausgetragenen Spielen, die auch für die Entstehung einer eigenen Geschichte und Erzählkultur sorgt.

1880er und 1890er Jahre: Vermehrte Gründung von Vereinen, die nach den F.A. Regeln spielen. Mitglieder dieser Vereine kommen zumeist aus dem gegenüber Neuerungen aufgeschlossenen Bildungsbürgertum.

13.11.1886: Aufruf Roland Kochs zur Gründung eines deutschen Fußball-Bundes, welcher jedoch erfolglos bleibt.

1882: Billigung des Spiels an deutschen Schulen durch das preußische Unterrichtsministerium.

15.04.1888: Gründung des Vereins Berliner FC Germania 1888. Er gilt als ältester noch bestehender Verein, in dem von Anfang an Fußball mit einem runden Ball gespielt wurde.

04.11.1890: Gründung des Bundes deutscher Fußballspieler.

1890: Austragung der 1. Deutschen Meisterschaft. Erster Sieger ist der Berliner FC Germania 1888.

19.11.1891: Gründung des Deutschen Fußball- und Kricket-Bundes.

Anfang der 1890er Jahre entwickelt sich eine nationalistische Bewegung, die sich gegen die „Engländerei" wehrt. Viele von ihnen stehen dem chauvinistischen Jungdeutschlandbund nahe und „germanisieren" in Kooperation mit dem Allgemeinen Deutschen Sprachverein und den Fußballoffiziellen das englische Fußballvokabular. So wird aus „corner" Eckball. Außerdem halten Worte aus dem deutschen Militärsprachgebrauch Einzug in den Fußball. „Feld", „Flanke", „Flügel", „stürmen", „abwehren" und weitere werden seit dieser Zeit verwandt.

1898: Veröffentlichung des Pamphlets: „Fußlümmelei: Über Stauchballspiel und englische Krankheit". Der Fußball wird darin als "[...]ein Zeichen der Wegwerflung, der Geringschätzung, der Verachtung, des Ekels, (und) des Abscheus [...]" beschrieben. [Bouvier 2006, S. 32]

1880

1890

1900

1870er bis 1890er Jahre: Mit der Verbreitung des Fußballspiels in ganz England ist gleichzeitig eine Veränderung seiner sozialen Basis verbunden. Viele Mitglieder der neu gegründeten Klubs gehören nicht mehr wie die Initiatoren der FA der bürgerlichen Mittel- oder Oberschicht an, sondern kommen aus der unteren Mittelschicht oder Arbeiterklasse.

1888: Legalisierung des Berufsfußballs unter der Aufsicht der FA.

1888: Gründung der weltweit ersten nationalen Liga, der Football League. Dieser gehören zu Beginn zwölf Profimannschaften an, die in Heim- und Auswärtsspielen miteinander konkurrieren. Die Einführung des Ligabetriebs führt zu einer Intensivierung von Wettbewerb und Training und resultiert schließlich in weiteren Leistungssteigerungen von Spielern und Mannschaften.

1891: Einführung des Elfmeters. Angesichts des zunehmenden Wettbewerbs wird 1891, neben einer ganzen Reihe weiterer wichtiger Änderungen an den Spielregeln, der Strafstoß eingeführt.

1896: Die ersten modernen Olympischen Spiele finden in Athen statt.

1899: Erste offizielle Auslandstournee einer englischen Mannschaft in Deutschland.

1899: Legalisierung von Spielertransfers. Der Höchstbetrag beträgt zehn Pfund.

1900 — 1910 — 1915 — 1918

28.01.1900: Gründung des DFB im Leipziger Mariengarten. Deutschland schließt mit der Gründung eines nationalen Verbandes zu anderen Nationen auf, die ihrerseits bereits deutlich früher nationale Fußballverbände ins Leben riefen.

1899: Erste offizielle Auslandstournee einer englischen Mannschaft in Deutschland.

1898: Spiele einer deutschen Mannschaft gegen Auswahlen von „Frankreichbriten" in Paris.

1910: Übernahme des Fußballspiels in die Ausbildungspläne der Armee.

1908: Erstes Länderspiel des DFB gegen die Schweiz in Basel. Endstand 3:5.

1912: Die Nationalmannschaft nimmt erstmals am Olympischen Fußballturnier teil. In der Trostrunde besiegt Deutschland Russland mit 16:0 – bis heute der höchste Sieg einer deutschen Nationalelf.

1911: Beitritt des DFB zum paramilitärischen Jungdeutschlandbund.

1913: Aufhebung des Fußballverbots an bayrischen Schulen.

1914: Der Vorstand des DFB sieht zu Beginn des Krieges eine wichtige Aufgabe darin, Meisterschaftsspiele auszutragen, um die jungen Männer, welche noch nicht an der Front kämpfen, auf den Kampf gegen den Feind vorzubereiten.

05. April 1902: Während des Länderspiels zwischen Schottland und England stürzt die Westtribüne im Ibrox-Park in Glasgow ein. 25 Zuschauer sterben, 500 werden verletzt.

1904: Gründung der FIFA.

1906: Die FA tritt der FIFA bei.

1908 Bei den IV. Olympischen Spielen in London wird erstmals Fußball gespielt. Erster Turniersieger ist England, das Dänemark mit 2:0 besiegt.

1914: Ausbruch des Ersten Weltkriegs. England und Deutschland gehören verfeindeten Bündnissen an.

1918: Ende des ersten Weltkriegs.

1920

1925

1930

1920:   Gründung der Fachzeitschrift „Kicker" durch Walter Bensemann. Bis zu seiner Absetzung wegen seiner jüdischen Herkunft 1933 ist er Chefredakteur des Blattes.

27.06.1920:   Erstes Länderspiel des DFB nach dem Ersten Weltkrieg in Zürich gegen die Schweiz. Obwohl sich die Spieler auf dem Feld in Freundschaft die Hand reichen, brechen durch diese Austragung alte politische Ressentiments wieder auf. Belgien, Frankreich und Großbritannien drohen der Schweiz mit einem Fußballboykott.

1924:   Spiel des Karlsruher FV gegen Bastidienne Bordeaux. Der DFB nutzt hier eine sich bietende Chance zur Völkerverständigung und um die bestehenden Ressentiments gegenüber dem Erbfeind abzubauen und schickt eine Mannschaft nach Frankreich.

1927:   Erste Rundfunkübertragung eines Fußballspiels (FC Arsenal gegen Sheffield United). Es ermöglicht einem Großteil der Bevölkerung die Teilnahme an einem aktuell laufenden Spiel über das Medium Radio.

1928:   Die FA tritt aus der FIFA aus, da es zu einem Disput über den Amateursport kam. Die Olympischen Spiele sollen nur mit Amateurteams bestritten werden. In England ist der Fußball jedoch längst professionalisiert. Die Mannschaft Großbritanniens hätte einen großen Vorteil gegenüber den Amateurteams anderer Nationen gehabt, so das Argument.

1929:   Erste Rundfunkübertragung eines Länderspiels (Italien gegen Deutschland in Turin).

1930

1935

Sommer und Herbst 1930: Verzicht Deutschlands auf Teilnahme an der ersten Fußball-Weltmeisterschaft.

1930: Die Spieler von Schalke 04 werden zu Berufsspielern erklärt und aus dem Westdeutschen Verband ausgeschlossen.

Januar 1933: Zu der angekündigten Legalisierung des Berufsfußballs kommt es auch nach drei Jahre andauernden Verhandlungen nicht.

1933: *Adolf Hitler wird Reichskanzler.*

Mai 1933: Erlass des „Arierparagraph" durch den DFB und zahlreiche andere Verbände. Es folgt eine systematische Ausgrenzung aller Juden und Marxisten aus den Vereinen.

1933 - 1935: Das Ziel der Gründung einer Profiliga scheint 1933 in greifbare Nähe gerückt zu sein, denn Adolf Hitlers Ziel, die Arbeitslosigkeit zu senken, spielt den Befürwortern des Profifußballs in die Karten. Diese bieten bis zu 8000 Menschen ein unregelmäßiges bis festes Einkommen. Der DFB sieht dadurch eine erhebliche Beschneidung seiner Macht und wehrt sich erfolgreich dagegen.

1934: Beginn der Auflösung der sieben Landesverbände, die unter dem Dach des DFB ein bis dato großes Maß an Eigenständigkeit genießen. An ihre Stelle treten 16 Gaue.

1934: Schalke 04 gewinnt als erster Arbeiterverein die Deutsche Meisterschaft.

1934: Deutschland gelingt bei der zweiten WM-Teilnahme ein Achtungserfolg.

14. November 1934: Battle of Highbury. Im Highbury-Stadion vom FC Arsenal treffen England und der amtierende Weltmeister Italien zum Freundschaftsspiel aufeinander. Das Match England gegen Italien gilt auch außerhalb des Fußballplatzes als internationaler Machtkampf. Zeitweise gleicht das Spiel mehr einer Massenschlägerei, denn einem Fußballspiel.

1935: Einführung des DFB-Pokalwettbewerbs für Vereinsmannschaften. In Düsseldorf wird der 1. FC Nürnberg erster deutscher Pokalsieger.

30. Januar 1937: Sepp Herberger wird „Reichstrainer".

1937: Weiterer wesentlicher Schritt voranschreitender Medienpräsenz des Fußballs: Ausschnitte des FA-Cup-Finales Preston North End gegen Sunderland werden erstmals im Fernsehen gezeigt.

1935

1936: Olympische Spiele in Berlin. Gegen Norwegen ist auf der Tribüne nahezu die gesamte NS-Prominenz versammelt. Goebbels, Göring, Heß, Rust und auch Hitler sitzen auf den Rängen. Deutschland verliert 0:2 und scheidet aus dem olympischen Turnier aus.

1939: Ausbruch des Zweiten Weltkrieges. England und Deutschland stehen sich wieder als Feinde gegenüber.

1942: Die deutsche Nationalmannschaft besiegt die Slowakei mit 5:2. Es ist für acht Jahre das letzte Länderspiel. Deutschland wird wenig später aus der FIFA ausgeschlossen.

09. März 1943: Burnden Park Disaster. Im FA Cup treffen die Bolton Wanderers und Stoke City aufeinander. Das Rückspiel im Burnden Park ist mit 65.000 Besuchern restlos ausverkauft. 20.000 Menschen versuchen dennoch in das Stadion zu gelangen. Kurz vor dem Anpfiff geben die Einlasssperren nach und die Menge drängt in den Zuschauerraum. 33 Menschen finden den Tod, mehr als 500 werden zum Teil schwer verletzt. Als Reaktion ordnet das britische Innenministerium strengere Kontrollen sowie Betriebsgenehmigungen für Stadien an. Zudem gibt es eine offizielle Untersuchung des Vorfalls, an deren Ende eine deutliche Reduzierung der Zuschauerkapazität empfohlen wird.

1940

18. Juli 1944: Austragung des letzten Endspiels um die deutsche Meisterschaft. Der Dresdner SC besiegte den Luftwaffen-Sportverein Hamburg vor 70.000 Zuschauern im Berliner Olympiastadion mit 4:0.

1945: Ende des Zweiten Weltkriegs. Deutschland wird in vier Besatzungszonen unterteilt.

1946: In den Besatzungszonen werden Regionalmeisterschaften ausgetragen.

1948: Die Besatzungsbehörden genehmigen die Durchführung einer Deutschen Meisterschaft. Erster Nachkriegsmeister wird der 1. FC Nürnberg.

1947: In England wird mit dem FA-Cup-Final Charlton Athletic gegen Burnley (1 0) erstmals ein Fußballspiel vom Fernsehen in voller Länge live übertragen.

1945

1950

1955

1960

1949: Gründung der Bundesrepublik Deutschland (BRD) und der Deutschen Demokratischen Republik (DDR).

23. September 1950: Wiederaufnahme des DFB in den Fußball-Weltverband.

1. Juli 1949 Wiedergründung des DFB nach dem Zweiten Weltkrieg. Die FIFA hebt das Spielverbot gegen deutsche Mannschaften auf. Gründung der *DDR-Oberliga.*

22. November 1950: Erstes offizielles Nachkriegs-Länderspiel gegen die Schweiz (1:0).

1951: Die verstärkte Präsenz des Fußballs im Medium Fernsehen übt Einfluss auf die Farbe des Balles aus: Um den Ball in den Fernsehübertragungen und bei Flutlichtspielen sichtbarer zu machen, wird ein schwarz-weißer oder ganz weißer Ball verwendet.

26. Dezember 1952: Das DFB-Pokalspiel zwischen dem FC St. Pauli und den Sportfreunden Hamborn 07 (4:3) ist das erste im deutschen Fernsehen übertragene Fußballspiel.

1952: Aufnahme der DDR in die FIFA.

30. Juli 1955: Der DFB beschließt auf seinem Bundestag den Frauenfußball zu verbieten. Den Vereinen des DFB drohen drastische Strafen, wenn sie ihn dennoch erlauben oder zulassen, dass Frauenmannschaften auf ihren Plätzen spielen. Als Begründung für das Verbot schreiben die Funktionäre unter anderem: „Im Kampf um den Ball verschwindet die weibliche Anmut, Körper und Seele erleiden unweigerlich Schaden und das Zurschaustellen des Körpers verletzt Schicklichkeit und Anstand."

1954: Gewinn der WM in der Schweiz. Gegner im Finale ist Ungarn. Sechs Minuten vor Spielende erzielt Rahn das 3:2. Deutschland ist erstmalig Fußballweltmeister.

4. Juni 1961: Erstausstrahlung der Sportschau. Zunächst wird gar nicht über Fußball berichtet, denn die Bundesliga existiert noch nicht. Erst 1963 wird die „Sportschau" auf den Samstag verlegt.

1958: Gründung des Deutschen Fußball Verbands der DDR (DFV).

25. November 1953 England verliert erstmals ein Heimspiel. Im eigenen Land noch ungeschlagen, spielt es gegen die zu jener Zeit stärkste kontinentale Mannschaft, die seit drei Jahren unbesiegten Ungarn, und verliert mit 3:6.

April 1954: Mit „Sportsview" geht die erste Fußballshow beim BBC auf Sendung.

6. Februar 1958: Munich Air Desaster. Bei diesem Flugzeugunglück kommen insgesamt acht Manchester United-Spieler ums Leben. Der Tod der so genannten Busby Babes stürzt die Fußballwelt in tiefe Trauer.

11. Oktober 1958: Die BBC geht mit „Grandstand" auf Sendung. Die Show ist eine der bekanntesten im britischen Fernsehen. Sie wird am Samstagnachmittag auf dem Hauptkanal der BBC ausgestrahlt und überträgt fast jedes große Sportereignis in Großbritannien, wie das FA-Cup-Finale, Wimbledon, das Grand National, und das University Boat Race.

1961: Tottenham Hotspur holt als erster englischer Verein im 20. Jahrhundert das *double.*

24. August 1963: Einführung der Bundesliga und Manifestation des Berufsspielertums. Zuvor gab es heftige Debatten um die Zusammensetzung des 16er-Feldes und über die Statuten. In keiner der führenden Fußball-Nationen Europas wird der Profi-Fußball so spät eingeführt wie in Deutschland. Die misslungene WM 1962 gab den letzten Anstoß zur Gründung. Sonst könne Deutschland nicht mehr mit den anderen Nationen mithalten, heißt es.

28. Juli 1963: Bundestag des DFB an dem „die Einführung einer zentralen Spielklasse mit Lizenzspielern unter Leitung des DFB" beschlossen wird.

1963

10. Oktober 1963: Als am 10. Oktober 1963 zum ersten Mal „You´ll never walk alone" von Gerry & the Pacemakers an der Anfield Road in Liverpool durch die Lautsprecher hallt, ahnt noch niemand, dass dieses Lied bald eines der bedeutendsten Fan-Lieder der Welt sein wird.

22. August 1964: „Match of the Day" geht auf Sendung. Das Programm wird jeden Samstag während der englischen Fußball-Meisterschaft ausgestrahlt und zeigt Highlights aus der höchsten englischen Spielkasse. Regelmäßig werden Fußballexperten eingeladen, die versuchen, die aktuellen Geschehnisse aus professioneller Sicht einzuordnen und zu bewerten.

1964: Erster Deutscher Meister der Bundesliga wird der 1. FC Köln. Erfolgreichster *Goalgetter* der Auftaktsaison ist Uwe Seeler.

1965: Der erste Bundesliga-Skandal: Hertha BSC soll an Spieler u.a. Handgeld und höhere als die festgelegten Gehälter ausgezahlt haben. Der DFB ermittelt und Hertha wird in die Regionalliga Berlin zurückgestuft.

Um 1965: Aufkommen der britischen Hooligan-Bewegung. In Großbritannien entsteht eine Fankultur, die in dieser Form bis dahin unbekannt ist. Auf Auswärtsfahrten kommt es vermehrt zu Delikten von Vandalismus und zu stark gewalttätigem Auftreten. Dies führt zu einem gesteigerten Medieninteresse, so dass bald eine intensive Diskussion über die neu entstandene jugendliche Gewalt entbrennt.

11. bis 30. Juli 1966: Die FIFA Weltmeisterschaft wird in England ausgetragen und der Gastgeber wird zum ersten Mal Weltmeister. Die vier vorausgegangenen Turnierteilnahmen waren für die Engländer wenig erfolgreich. Doch im eigenen Land wird es ein überaus erfolgreiches und spektakuläres Turnier. Im Finale kommt es zum Spiel gegen Deutschland. Vor 96.924 Zuschauern im Wembleystadion und den Augen der Queen wird das Finale durch das berühmteste und umstrittenste Tor der WM-Geschichte entschieden. England gewinnt 4:2.

1970: Einführung der gelben und roten Karte.

31. Oktober 1970: Der DFB hebt das Verbot des Frauenfußballs auf. Ende der 1960er Jahre ändert sich die politische Stimmungslage in der BRD. Neue Strömungen, wie die Frauen- und Studentenbewegung, lösen eine Reihe von Veränderungen des bisher eher autoritären Systems aus. Um ein Ausufern verschiedener neugegründeter Verbände zu unterbinden und um keine Konkurrenz im Damenfußball aufkommen zu lassen, entschließt sich der DFB, sein Damenfußball-Verbot zurückzunehmen.

1970

29. Mai 1968: Manchester United gewinnt als erster englischer Klub den Europapokal der Landesmeister durch ein 4:1 Sieg über Benfica Lissabon.

02. Januar 1971: Tote beim Old-Firm Derby. Im Old-Firm Derby gegen die Glasgow Rangers schießt Celtic Glasgow in der 89. Minute das 1:0. Tausende Rangers-Fans verlassen daraufhin das Stadion. Als kurz darauf der Ausgleich fällt kehren sie plötzlich um, strömen wieder in das Stadion und prallen mit den ihnen entgegenkommenden aufeinander. 66 Menschen sterben.

1971: Aufdeckung des Bestechungsskandals in der Bundesliga. Im Kampf gegen den Abstieg kassieren Spieler *Schmiergelder*.

1973: Einführung der Deutschen Meisterschaft im Frauenfußball

1972: Die Begrenzungen der Gehaltszahlungen an Spieler werden abgeschafft.

Sommer 1973: Beginn der ersten Spielzeit der Frauen-Bundesliga.

1972: Gewinn der EM in Belgien.

1974

1980

1990

1974: Gewinn der WM in Deutschland.

15. Mai 1974: Der FC Bayern München gewinnt als erster deutscher Verein den Landesmeister-Pokal.

1980: Beginn der Austragung des DFB-Pokals der Frauen.

1980: Gewinn der EM in Italien.

1982: Erstes Länderspiel der Frauen-Nationalmannschaft. In Koblenz wird die Schweiz mit 5:1 besiegt.

28. Juni bis 02. Juli 1989: Gewinn der EM der Frauen in Deutschland und erstmalige Live-Übertragung eines Frauen-Länderspiels.

1989: Fall der Berliner Mauer.

1990: Wiedervereinigung Deutschlands.

1990 Gründung der zweigleisigen Frauen-Bundesliga.

1990: Letztes Länderspiel der Nationalmannschaft der DDR (2:0 gegen Belgien). Als Folge der Wiedervereinigung löst sich der DFV auf.

1990 Gewinn der WM in Italien.

1990: Erste gesamtdeutsche Bundesligasaison. Die ehemalige DDR wird in der Bundesliga durch Hansa Rostock und Dynamo Dresden vertreten.

1991 Gewinn der Frauen-EM in Dänemark.

02. Juni 1991: Der FC Hansa Rostock wird erster und einziger Gewinner des NOFV-Pokals.

1979: Zum ersten Mal in der Geschichte der englischen Fußball-Liga wird eine Ablöse von einer Million Pfund für einen Spieler gezahlt: Nottingham Forest kauft Trevor Francis für diese Summe.

13. März 1985: „Kenilworth Road Riot". Der wohl längste Platzsturm der achtziger Jahre geht als „Kenilworth Road Riot" in die englische Fußballgeschichte ein. Vor, während und nach der Pokalpartie zwischen Luton Town und dem Millwall FC im Jahr 1985 kommt es zu Auseinandersetzungen zwischen den Zuschauern.

11. Mai 1985: Valley-Parade-Katastrophe. Der Bradford City Football Club spielt gegen den Lincoln FC. Kurz vor der Halbzeit wird durch die Tribünen aufsteigender Rauch bemerkt. Binnen kurzer Zeit entsteht ein offenes Feuer auf der Haupttribüne, welches am Ende 56 Menschenleben und mehr als 265 zum Teil schwer Verletzte fordert.

29. Mai 1985: Heysel Stadium Desaster. Als vor dem Landesmeister-Pokal-Endspiel gegen Juventus Turin im Brüsseler Heysel Stadion die eigenen Fans den Block der Juventus-Anhänger nach beiderseitigen Provokationen stürmen und in der sich ausbreitenden Massenpanik 39 Menschen den Tod finden, wird der FC Liverpool für sieben Jahre von internationalen Wettbewerben ausgeschlossen.

15. April 1989: Hillsbrorough-Katastrophe. Kurz vor Anpfiff des Spiels FC Liverpool gegen Nottingham Forest versuchen noch ca. 10 000 zu den Eingängen zu gelangen. Um den Druck zu mildern, entscheidet die Polizei einen Ausgang zu öffnen. Hunderte Fans gelangen in kürzester Zeit ins Stadioninnere. Durch die von oben einströmenden Fans wird der Druck nach unten weitergegeben und Menschen gegen Gitter und Zäune gepresst. Durch den großen Druck bricht schließlich der Zaun und die Fans gelangen auf das Spielfeld. Auf Anweisung der Polizei wird das Spiel in der 6. Spielminute unterbrochen. 96 Menschen sterben, 766 erleiden zum Teil schwere Verletzungen.

1990

1995: Gewinn der EM der Frauen. Austragung ohne Gastgeberland, da im gleichen Jahr die WM der Frauen in Schweden stattfindet.

1995: Einführung der Drei-Punkte-Regel, wonach ein Sieg mit drei Zählern belohnt wird. Ein Remis bringt einen Punkt, eine Niederlage keinen.

21. November 1990: Vereinigung des deutschen Fußballsports in Leipzig. Der aus dem tags zuvor aufgelösten Deutschen Fußball-Verband der DDR entstandene Nordostdeutsche Fußball-Verband tritt als neuer Regionalverband mit seinen sechs Landesverbänden dem DFB bei.

1995

1997: Gewinn der EM der Frauen in Norwegen und Schweden. Es folgen weitere Siege der Frauen bei EM und WM bis zur WM 2007 in China.

1997: Einführung der sog. *Rückpassregel*.

1997: Mit Borussia Dortmund gewinnt erstmals eine deutsche Mannschaft die Champions League.

1996: Gewinn der EM in England.

2000

2001: Gründung des Ligaverbandes, der mit der Deutschen Fußball-Liga (DFL) als operativer Einheit weitgehend unabhängig agiert und doch eng mit dem DFB verzahnt ist.

30 September 2000: Verselbstständigung des Profifußballs.

01.Januar 1999: Inkrafttreten der 50+1 Regel. Die 50+1-Regel in den Statuten der Deutschen Fußball Liga soll verhindern, dass Investoren die Mehrheit an den als Kapitalgesellschaften organisierten Klubs erlangen.

2006: Ausrichtung der WM in Deutschland.

2010

14. März 2010: Erste Live-Übertragung eines Bundesliga Spiels (Bayer 04 Leverkusen vs. Hamburger SV) im 3D-Format.

30.August 2011: Abschwächung der 50+1 Regel. Klubs erhalten fortan die Möglichkeit, eng verbundenen Finanziers, Sponsoren oder Mäzenen nach 20 Jahren Engagement im Verein die Kapitalmehrheit und Stimmenmehrheit an der Fußball-Kapitalgesellschaft zu übertragen. Diese Ausnahme war bisher nur den beiden Werksvereinen Bayer Leverkusen (Bayer AG) und VfL Wolfsburg (Volkswagen AG) gestattet

---

01. August 1989: Veröffentlichung des Taylor Reports. Der Taylor Report wird unter der Aufsicht von Lord Taylor of Gosforth erstellt und behandelt die Auswirkungen und Ursachen der Hillsborough-Katastrophe. Der Untersuchungsbericht kommt zu dem Ergebnis, dass die Hauptursache für die Hillsborough-Tragödie ein Versagen der Sicherheitskräfte war. Ein Straf- und etliche Zivilrechtsprozesse im Laufe der Jahre ziehen niemanden zur Verantwortung. Sie enden allesamt mit dem Urteil „Tod durch Unfall".

1989: Einführung des Satellitenfernsehens in Großbritannien. Zwei Medienrivalen, BSB und Sky, schließen sich zusammen.

1992: Rupert Murdochs Sky Television gewinnt die Rechte für die Übertragung der Premier League-Spiele.

14. Februar 1995: Der Londoner Sender „Talk Sport Radio" geht mit seinem 24-stündigen Dauerfachgespräch auf Sendung. Das Programm enthält Sportgespräche, Liveschalten, Diskussionen und Telefondebatten rund um die Uhr.

1995: *Der Europäische Gerichtshof fällt sein Urteil im „Fall Bosman", das erhebliche Auswirkungen auf das Transfersystem und den gesamten professionellen Fußballbereich hat.*

2005: Übernahme des Vereins Manchester United durch die amerikanische Glazer-Familie.

1996: Sky bezahlt die Premier League 690 Millionen Pfund für einen 4-Jahres-Deal.

28. Januar 2007: Die legendäre BBC-Fernsehsendung „Grandstand" wird nach fast 50 Jahren eingestellt.

12. September 2012: 23 Jahre nach der Hillsborough-Katastrophe, die 96 Todesopfer forderte, belegen nun veröffentlichte Dokumente, dass die Liverpool-Fans zu Unrecht beschuldigt wurden. Die unabhängige Untersuchungskommission enthüllt Vertuschungsmanöver der Polizei.

31. Januar 2010: Erste Live-Übertragung eines Premier League Spiels (Arsenal London vs. Manchester United) im 3D-Format.

A B

Bpb (Hrsg.) (2007): Verlacht, verboten und gefeiert - Zur Geschichte des Frauenfußballs. Audio-CD 72 Minuten, mit O-Tönen des Deutschen Rundfunkarchivs.

Bouvier, B. (Hrsg.) (2006): Zur Sozial- und Kulturgeschichte des Fußballs. Studienzentrum Karl-Marx-Haus der Friedrich-Ebert-Stiftung. Trier.

dfb.de

D E F G

Doh, M. (2001): Als der Fußball laufen lernte – Das für und Wider einer englischen Sportart aus Sicht von Konrad Koch und Carl Planck. In Wieland, H. (Hrsg.), Fußball - Strategien des Siegens. Stuttgart: Naglschmid, 23-33.

Eisenberg, C. et al. (2004): FIFA 1904 – 2004. 100 Jahre Weltfußball. Göttingen: Verlag die Werkstatt.

Eisenberg, C. (1999): „English sports" und deutsche Bürger. Eine Gesellschaftsgeschichte 1800-1939. Paderborn: Schöningh.

H

Grengel, R. (Hrsg.) (2000): 100 Jahre deutscher Fußball. Berlin: Schirner-Sportfoto.

Eisenberg, C. et al. (2004): FIFA 1904 – 2004. 100 Jahre Weltfußball. Göttingen: Verlag die Werkstatt.

Havemann, N. (2005): Fußball unterm Hakenkreuz. Der DFB zwischen Sport, Politik und Kommerz. Bonn: Bundeszentrale für politische Bildung.

Hörstmann, M. (Hrsg.) (2012): 11 FREUNDE Spezial. Football´s coming home. Die Geschichte des britischen Fußballs. Berlin: 11 FREUNDE Verlag.

Frech, S. (2006): Fußball und Politik. In: Der Bürger im Staat. Landeszentrale für politische Bildung Baden-Württemberg/LpBBW (Hrsg.), 56. Jahrgang, Heft1 / 2006.

K L M

Koch, K. 1895/1983: Die Geschichte des Fußballs im Altertum und in der Neuzeit. 2. Auflage. Berlin: Gaertner / Nachdruck: Münster: Lit, Münster.

Koller, C. (2006): Von den englischen Eliteschulen zum globalen Volkssport: Entstehung und Verbreitung des Fußballs bis zum Ersten Weltkrieg. In: Bouvier, B. 2006, 14-36.

Mason, T. (1997): Großbritannien. In: Eisenberg, C. (Hrsg.): Fußball, soccer, calcio. Ein englischer Sport auf seinem Weg um die Welt. München: dtv, 22-40.

Lanfranchi, P. / Taylor, M. (2001): Moving with the Ball: the Migration of Professional Footballers. Oxford: Berg.

N W Z

Müller, M. (2009): Fußball als Paradoxon der Moderne. Zur Bedeutung ethnischer, nationaler und geschlechtlicher Differenzen im Profifußball. Wiesbaden: VS Verlag.

Nadler, M. (2008): Fußball & Religion: Eine dokumentarische Bestandsaufnahme. München: GRIN Verlag.

Wilson, J. (2011): Revolutionen auf dem Rasen. Eine Geschichte der Fußballtaktik. Göttingen: Verlag Die Werkstatt.

thefa.com

Timeline of Modern Football Game in England and Germany

Anthony Waine

From 1750 onwards

'Germany' consists of hundreds of independent states, many small and some larger, in the eighteenth century. In contrast to Great Britain the process of industrialisation does not take place until the second half of the nineteenth century. The formation of these different states into one nation is only very gradual. One of the consequences is that feelings of national belonging, in other words being able to identify with 'Germany', develop much later, for example, than is the case in England. People instead feel they belong more to Baden or to Prussia than to Germany.

Great Britain was the world's foremost imperial power in the eighteenth century and the cradle of the industrial revolution. The aristocratic and middle class elites organised, codified and indulged in older as well as newer modes of leisure activity.

1800

1840s: The history of modern football begins. The rules are still only passed on orally. Private schools start to establish rules systematically from the 1840s onwards.

Around 1850

1848: Cambridge University tries to unify the different sets of rules used hitherto.

1860

1860s: The Prague Professor of Hygiene, Ferdinand Hueppe, plays football with English pupils in the educational establishment of Neuwied.

24 October 1857: The oldest football club in the world, Sheffield FC, is founded by Sir Nathaniel Creswick and William Prest. Their particular aim is to set up a regular system for matches and to standardise the rules. Their Sheffield Rules are the first modern set of football rules.

1860s: Serious endeavours are undertaken to produce a code of football rules.

Football changes from being a folk sport to becoming a game of sport. But the game is still fairly primitive and unruly.

1860

1870

1880

26 October 1863: The FA becomes the world's first football association. An official code is agreed on. As well as the establishment of binding rules which include prohibiting kicking an opponent and running whilst holding the ball, the founding of the Football Association creates a supervisory authority which adjudicates in cases of dispute.

1866: The modern offside rule is introduced. Although it was already included in the original football rules of 1863, it is very different from today's rule. With the introduction of the "Three-Player-Rule" in 1866 the English FA enacts a crucial decision, for it means that an attacker is offside when he is closer to the goal line than the ball and the third from last opposing player. Only now can the passing game develop.

1874: Football is introduced into Germany. It is mainly played in grammar schools and academies. Konrad Koch, a pioneer of German football and a grammar school teacher at the Martino-Katharineum in Brunswick, brings the game to Germany. Initially the game is played according to the rules of rugby.

5 March 1870: The first unofficial international match between England and Scotland.

1871: The first annual cup competition between clubs belonging to the FA is introduced. From now on one can begin to make indirect comparisons between the performances of individual teams, and a more continuous round of matches is established which leads to clubs creating their own individual histories and thus to a culture narrated around stories of a team's record.

1875: Publication of the first German set of rules which are very similar to today's rules.

30 November 1872: The first official international game between England and Scotland in Glasgow. It ends 0-0.

14 October 1878: The first floodlit game. Sheffield FC plays for the first time under floodlights. The pitch is lit up by four arc lights.

1870s and 1880s: Following the formation of the English FA, Wales, Scotland and Ireland found their own national associations.

At the beginning of the 1890s a nationalistic movement develops which resists "the vogue of aping the English". Many adherents support the chauvinistic ideology of the 'Jungdeutschland' Association and, in collaboration with both the General Society for the German Language and football officials, they 'germanicise' English football vocabulary. Thus football becomes 'Fußball', penalty is 'Strafstoß' and corner is 'Eckball'. In addition, words taken from German military usage make their way into football. 'Feld' (field), 'Flanke' (flank), 'Flügel' (wing), 'stürmen' (attack) 'abwehren' (defend) and others start to be used from this time onwards.

1900

1890

1880

1880s and 1890s: Increasing numbers of clubs being founded who adopt FA rules. Members of these teams come mainly from the more outward-looking sections of the well-educated middle classes.

13 November 1886: Roland Koch appeals for the foundation of a German football association. It falls on deaf ears.

15 April 1888: The Berliner FC Germania 1888 club is founded. It is regarded as the oldest surviving club in which football was played with a round ball from the very beginning.

1882: The Prussian Ministry of Pedagogy approves the playing of the game in German schools.

4 November 1890: The Association of German Football Players is founded.

1890: The first German championships take place. The first victors are the Berliner FC Germania 1888.

19 November 1891: The German Football and Cricket Association is founded.

1898: Publication of the pamphlet entitled 'Foot loutishness: On the Thrust-Ball Game and English Disease'. In it football is described as "[...] a symptom of wastefulness, disdain, contempt, disgust (and) repulsion" [...] (Bouvier 2006, p.32)

1870s through to 1890s: As the game of football spreads throughout the whole of England, its social base also changes. Many members of the newly founded clubs no longer belong to the middle and upper middle classes, like the men who created the FA, but come from the lower middle class and the working class.

1888: Professional football is legalised under the supervision of the FA.

1888: The world's first national league, the football league, is founded. Initially twelve professional clubs belong to it who compete against one another in home and away games. The introduction of a league system leads to increased competition and training, and ultimately results in both players and teams raising their levels of performance.

1891: The introduction of the penalty. In view of increased competitiveness the penalty is introduced along with a whole series of additional changes to the rules.

1896: The first modern Olympic Games take place in Athens.

1899: The first official foreign visit made by an English team to Germany.

1899: The transfer of players is made legal.

28 January 1900: The DFB is founded in Leipzig's Mariengarten. Through the founding of a national association Germany catches up with other nations, after lagging behind for years.

1899: The first official foreign tour of an English team in Germany.

1910: Football is incorporated into the training courses of the army.

1898: A German team plays matches against teams made up of British ex-pats in France and Paris.

1908: The first international match of the DFB against Switzerland in Basle. The game ends 3-5.

1912: The national team takes part in the Olympic football tournament for the first time. In the consolation round Germany beats Russia 16-0. Until this day it remains the highest score of any German team.

1911: The DFB joins the paramilitary 'Jungdeutschland' Association.

1913: The ban on playing football is lifted in Bavarian schools.

1914: The executive of the DFB regards it as an important task at the outbreak of war to organise championship matches in order to steel young men who have not yet fought on the front lines and to prepare them for doing battle with the enemy.

1900

1910

1915

1918

5 April 1902: During an international game between Scotland and England the West stand at Ibrox Park, Glasgow collapses. 25 spectators die, and 500 more are injured.

1904: FIFA is founded.

1906: The FA joins FIFA.

1908: Football is included for the first time in the Olympic programme when the Games are held in London. The first winners are England, defeating Denmark 2-0.

1914: The outbreak of the First World War. England and Germany are enemies.

1918: End of the First World War.

1920: The specialist journal 'Kicker' is founded by Walter Bensemann. He remains editor-in-chief until he is dismissed in 1933 on grounds of his Jewish origins.

27 June 1920: The first international match of the DFB after the First World War against Switzerland. Although the players shake hands on the pitch in a gesture of friendship, old political resentments are triggered by the game. Belgium, France and Great Britain threaten to boycott Swiss football.

1920

1924: Karlsruhe FV play Bastidienne Bordeaux. The DFB uses the occasion to improve French-German relations and break down resentments felt towards the traditional enemy by sending a team to France.

1925

1927: The first radio broadcast of a football match (Arsenal FC versus Sheffield United). The medium of radio enables many people to be part of a live game.

1928: The FA resigns from FIFA because of a dispute regarding amateur sport. Only amateur teams are to be allowed to compete at the Olympic Games. Football in England, however, has long since been professionalised. It is claimed that the British team would enjoy a huge advantage over the amateur teams from other nations.

1929: The first radio broadcast of an international match (Italy versus Germany in Turin).

1930

1930

1933: Adolf Hitler is elected Imperial Chancellor.

Summer and Autumn 1930: Germany refuses to take part in the first football World Cup.

1930: Schalke 04's players are declared professionals and excluded from the regional West German Association.

January 1933: Even after three years of negotiations the legalisation of professional football, that has long been proclaimed, does not come about.

May 1933: The 'Aryan Clause' is enacted by the DFB and numerous other associations. There follows a systematic exclusion of all Jews and Marxists from clubs.

1934: The start of the process of dissolving the seven regional associations which until now enjoy a considerable degree of autonomy. They are replaced by 16 so-called 'Gaue', i.e. administrative districts created specifically and controlled by the Nazi party.

1933-1935: The aim of setting up a professional league seems very close to reality in 1933 since Adolf Hitler wishes to reduce unemployment, and this gives leverage to the proponents of professional football. These are offering up to 8,000 men an income ranging from irregular to fixed. The DFB views this as a serious curtailing of its authority and successfully resists the move.

1934: Germany achieves a respectable result at the second World Cup.

1934: Schalke 04 is the first working class club to win the German championship.

1935

14 November 1934: The Battle of Highbury. England and the world champions Italy meet at Arsenal's Highbury Stadium for a friendly. Observers see the game as an international battle for supremacy. At times the game resembles more a mass brawl than a game of football.

1935: Introduction of the DFB cup competition for club teams. 1 FC Nuremberg are the first German cup winners in Düsseldorf.

30 January 1937: Sepp Herberger becomes 'imperial team coach'

1936: Olympic Games in Berlin. For the match against Norway almost the entire Nazi top brass are assembled in the main stand. Goebbels, Göring, Heß, Rust and Hitler too sit in the gallery seats. Germany loses 0-2 and is eliminated.

1939: Outbreak of the Second World War. England and Germany face each other once more as enemies.

1942: The German national team defeats Slovakia 5-2. It is the last international played for another eight years. Shortly afterwards Germany is expelled from FIFA.

18 July 1944: The final game to decide the German league championship. Dresdner SC beats the Air Force Sports Club of Hamburg 4-0 in front of 70,000 spectators in the Olympia Stadium Berlin.

1945: End of the Second World War. Germany is divided into four zones of occupation (American, British, French and Soviet).

1946: Regional championships are held again in the zones of occupation. South Germany sets up the first regional upper league.

1948: The occupying powers allow a German championship to be established. The first post-war champions are 1 FC Nuremberg.

1935

1940

1945

1937: A further significant step taken by football into the new media. Parts of the FA Cup final between Preston North End and Sunderland are shown on television for the first time.

9 March 1943: The Burnden Park Disaster. Bolton Wanderers and Stoke City meet in the FA Cup. The replay at Burnden Park is sold out. 65,000 spectators watch the match. 20,000 more want to gain entry. Just before kick-off the barriers give way and the crowd swarms into the ground. 33 people are killed, with more than 500 seriously injured. The British Home Office reacts by ordering stricter ground controls as well as stadia operating licenses. In addition there is an official enquiry into the incident the outcome of which is a recommendation that crowd capacity at grounds be reduced.

1947: The whole of the FA Cup final between Charlton Athletic and Burnley (1-0) is televised live for the first time.

1949: Founding of the Federal Republic of Germany (FRG) and the German Democratic Republic (GDR).

23 September 1950: The DFB is allowed to re-join the World Football Association.

22 November 1950: The first official post-war international match against Switzerland (1-0).

1 July 1949: The DFB is founded anew after the Second World War. FIFA lifts the ban on German teams. The East German upper league is formed.

26 December 1952: The DFB cup game between FC St. Pauli and the Sportfreunde Hamborn 07 (which ends 4-3) is the first televised football game on German TV.

1952: The GDR (East Germany) is admitted to FIFA.

1951: The increased prominence of football in the medium of television influences the colour of the ball. In order to make the ball more visible in television broadcasts and in floodlight matches a black and white or white ball is used.

30 July 1955: At its annual conference the DFB decides to prohibit women's football. Clubs who belong to the DFB face severe punishment if they get involved in women's football or allow women's teams to play on their pitches. Reasons given by the officials to justify the ban include the following: "When fighting to win the ball female gracefulness disappears, body and soul inevitably suffer harm, and the deliberate flaunting of the body offends against seemly and respectable values."

1954: World Cup victory in Switzerland. The opponents in the final are Hungary. With six minutes to go Rahn scores the winning goal to make it 3-2. Germany are world champions for the first time.

4 June 1961: The original broadcast of the 'Sportschau'. At first there are no reports on football, as the Bundesliga does not yet exist. It is not until 1963 that the 'Sportschau' is moved to Saturdays.

1958: The German Football Association of the GDR is founded (DFV).

1960

25 November 1953: England's unbeaten home record ends. They are defeated for the first time on home soil by the then strongest continental side, Hungary, who have not lost for three years. The result is 6-3 for Hungary.

April 1954: The BBC's 'Sportsview' is the first football show on TV.

6 February 1958: The Munich Air Disaster. Eight members of the Manchester United team are killed. The death of the so called Busby Babes throws the football world into grief.

11 October 1958: The first broadcast of the BBC's 'Grandstand'. The programme is one of the best known in British broadcasting. It is shown on a Saturday afternoon on the main channel and transmits almost every major sporting event in Great Britain, including the FA Cup final, Wimbledon, the Grand National and the University Boat Race.

1961: Tottenham Hotspur becomes the first English team in the twentieth century to do the double.

1955

1950

1963

24 August 1963: Start of the Bundesliga and first moves towards players becoming professionals. Prior to that there were heated debates about the composition of 16 teams and the statutes. Professional football is brought in earlier in every other leading football nation than in Germany. The failure at the 1962 World Cup is the impetus needed to found the league. It was claimed that otherwise Germany could not compete successfully with the other nations.

28 July 1963: The Annual Conference of the DFB takes the decision to "introduce a central division with licensed players and supervised by the DFB."

10 October 1963: When "You'll never walk alone" by Gerry & the Pacemakers is broadcast for the first time through the loudspeakers at Anfield Road in Liverpool, nobody at the time realises that this song will soon become one of the most significant football anthems in the world.

22 August 1964: The original broadcast of 'Match of the Day'. It is shown every Saturday during the English football season on BBC. 'Match of the Day' shows highlights from the top division of English football. Soccer experts are regularly invited to explain current events from a professional point of view and give their assessment.

1964: 1. FC Cologne are the first German champions. The top goal scorer in the inaugural season is Uwe Seeler.

1965: The first Bundesliga scandal. Hertha BSC are alleged to have handed their players lump sum payments and paid higher than permitted wages. The DFB investigates and Hertha are relegated to the regional league of Berlin.

Circa 1965: The rise of the British hooligan movement. A type of fan culture emerges in Great Britain which is unheard of until then. On trips to away games there are increasing cases of vandalism and violent behaviour. These lead to greater media interest so that heated debates quickly ensue about the new phenomenon of young people's violence.

11-30 July 1966: The FIFA World Cup is hosted by England for the first time. The previous four tournaments had brought English teams little success. But on home soil the tournament proves to be spectacular and successful. The final becomes a clash between England and Germany. The Queen joins 96,924 spectators in Wembley Stadium and they witness how the most famous and disputed goal in the history of the World Cup decides the outcome of the game. England win 4-2.

1970

1970: The yellow and red card is introduced.

31 October 1970: The DFB lifts the ban on women's football. The national mood in the FRG changes at the end of the 1960s. New movements such as feminism and the student movement, lead to a series of changes to the hitherto authoritarian system. To prevent the proliferation of various newly constituted associations and to thwart any rivals in women's football, the DFB decides to withdraw its ban on women's football.

29 May 1968: Manchester United become the first English club to win the European Cup with a 4-1 victory over Benfica, Lisbon.

2 January 1971: Fatalities at the Old Firm derby, Glasgow Rangers are beaten in the last minute of the derby by a goal from Glasgow Celtic. Thousands of Rangers' fans promptly start leaving the ground. When the equaliser is scored minutes later they turn back round, stream back into the stadium and crush those coming towards them. 66 people die.

1971: The bribery scandal in the Bundesliga is uncovered. Players accept bribes in games which decide relegation.

1973: The German women's championship is introduced.

1972: Caps on players' salaries are removed.

Summer 1973: The first season of the women's Bundesliga begins.

1972: West Germany become European Champions in Belgium.

1974

1974: Germany win the World Cup, held in their country.

15 May 1974: FC Bayern Munich become the first German side to win the European Cup.

1980

1980: The DFB Cup competition for Women is inaugurated.

1980: Germany win the European Championships hosted by Italy.

1982: The German women's team play their first international game in Koblenz. They beat the Swiss 5-1.

1989: Fall of the Berlin Wall

28 June to 2 July 1989: The German women's team become European champions on home ground. It marks the first live coverage of a women's international match.

1990

1990: The Reunification of Germany

1990: A two tier Women's Bundesliga is created.

1990: The GDR national side plays its final international game (2-0 against Belgium). The DFV is dissolved following reunification.

1990: Germany wins the World Cup in Italy.

1990: The first Bundesliga season following reunification. The former GDR is represented by Hansa Rostock and Dynamo Dresden in the united German league.

2 June 1991: The FC Hansa Rostock become the first and only winners of the NOFV Cup.

1991: German women are crowned European champions in Denmark.

1979: For the first time in the history of the English game one million pounds is paid for a player. Nottingham Forest buys Trevor Francis for this sum.

13 March 1985: Kenilworth Road Riot. Probably the longest pitch invasion in the eighties enters English football history as the 'Kenilworth Road Riot'. Brawls between rival fans take place before, during and after the cup game between Luton Town and Millwall FC.

11 May 1985: Valley Parade Catastrophe. Bradford City Football Club is playing against Lincoln FC. Just before half time smoke can be seen rising from the stands. Within a short time the main stand is engulfed in flames resulting in the deaths of 56 people with more than 265 injured, many seriously.

29 May 1985: Heysel Stadium Disaster. Before the start of the European Cup final between Juventus Turin and Liverpool FC in the Heysel Stadium, Brussels, fans from Liverpool invade the section with Juventus supporters, after both sets of fans have been provoking one another. A mass panic breaks out and 39 people are killed. Liverpool FC are banned from international competitions for seven years.

15 April 1989: The Hillsborough Disaster. Just before the kick off in the cup match between Liverpool FC and Nottingham Forest about 10,000 fans are crowded outside the stadium and try and reach the entrances. In order to relieve the pressure, the police decide to open an exit gate. Hundreds of fans quickly get inside the ground. Through these fans pouring in from above, the pressure is exerted on those below and people are pressed up against the railings and fencing. Due to the huge force exerted the fence is broken and fans spill on to the pitch. The police instruct the game to be stopped in the sixth minute. 96 people die and 766 suffer often severe injuries.

1995: The women's team become European champions, but there is no host country for the tournament since the women's World Cup is held in the same year in Sweden.

1995: The three point rule is brought in, meaning that a win gains three points, a draw one point and a defeat no points.

21 November 1990: The unification of German football sport takes place in Leipzig. The German Football Association of the GDR, which had been disbanded the day before, is re-named the North East German Football Association. It joins the DFB as a new regional association consisting of six federal regional associations.

1997: German women win the European championships held in Norway and Sweden. Further victories of the women in major international championships (World and European Cups).

1997: The new back pass rule comes into force.

1997: Borussia Dortmund become the first German side to win the Champions League.

1996: Germany become European champions in England.

2001: The League Association is formed which operates as a unit largely independently with the German Football League (DFL) but is also closely connected with the DFB.

30 September 2000: Professional football gains its independence.

1 January 1999: The 50 + 1 rule comes into force. This rule is incorporated in the statutes of the German Football League and is intended to prevent investors gaining the majority of shares in clubs which are joint stock companies.

2006: Germany hosts the World Cup. Its team wins third place.

30 August 2011: The 50 + 1 rule is watered down. It is now possible for clubs to transfer the majority of shares and majority of votes in football stock corporations to financiers, sponsors or patrons who have been closely involved with the club for at least twenty years. Hitherto only the two company teams, Bayer Leverkusen (belonging to Bayer p c) and VfL Wolfsburg (belonging to Volkswagen plc), were the exceptions to the 50 + 1 rule.

14 March 201C: First live broadcast of a Bundesliga ma·ch (Bayer 04 Leverkusen versus Hamburger SV) in 3D.

1990   **1995**   **2000**   **2010**

---

1 August 1989: The Taylor Report is published. This report is drawn up under the chairmanship of Lord Taylor of Gosforth and looks into the causes and consequences of the Hillsborough Disaster. The inquiry report concludes that the main cause of the Hillsborough tragedy is a failure of the security forces. Criminal proceedings and several civil actions fail to bring any one to account. All end with the verdict of 'accidental death'.

1989: The advent of satellite television in Great Britain. Two media rivals, BSB and Sky, merge.

August 1992: The Premier League is inaugurated. Rupert Murdoch's Sky Television gains the rights to show Premier League games.

14 February 1995: The London broadcaster Talk Sport Radio begins a 24 hour round the clock show consisting of sport reports, live transmissions, discussions and phone-in debates.

1995: *The European Court of Justice makes its judgement in the 'Bosman Case' which has repercussions for the system of transfers and for the whole area of professional football.*

2005: The American Glazer family buy Manchester United football club.

1996: Sky pays the Premier League £670 million pounds for a four year deal.

28 January 2007: The legendary BBC TV programme 'Grandstand' ends after 50 years.

31 January 2010: First live broadcast of a Premier League match (Arsenal versus Manchester United) in 3D.

12 September 2012: 23 years after the Hillsborough Disaster, which cost the lives of 96 people, newly published documents prove that Liverpool fans were not responsible. The independent commission of inquiry reveals a police cover-up.

Autorenverzeichnis / Contributors

Editors / Herausgeber

Kristian Naglo, Dr., studierte Politikwissenschaft, Psychologie sowie Spanische Philologie in Trier und Madrid. Promotion in Politischer Sprachsoziologie / Angewandter Sprachwissenschaft an der LMU München. Seit 2007 Lehrbeauftragter und wiss. Mitarbeiter u.a. in Innsbruck, Gießen und Lancaster in Soziologie, Politikwissenschaft und Germanistik. Forschungsinteresse: Soziale und kulturelle Herstellung von Einheit und deren politische Instrumentalisierung unter Bedingungen von Europäisierung und Globalisierung.

Anthony Waine, Dr, studied German in Newcastle-upon-Tyne and Jesus College, Oxford, where he began his PhD thesis. From 1972 till 2009 he taught German Studies at Lancaster University. He has written books on Martin Walser, and co-edited volumes on Bertolt Brecht and on Culture and Society in the German Democratic Republic. His later publications dealt frequently with German cultural history, often linking it to Anglo-American societies. In 2007 he published *Changing Cultural Tastes: Writers and the Popular in Modern Germany* (New York and Oxford).

Contributors / Autoren

Nina Degele, Prof. Dr., ist seit 2000 Professorin für Soziologie und Gender Studies an der Uni Freiburg. Forschungsschwerpunkte: Soziologie der Geschlechterverhältnisse, Modernisierung, Körper, Sport, qualitative Methoden. Zuletzt erschienen: *Fußball verbindet – durch Ausgrenzung*. Wiesbaden: Springer VS (2013).

Richard Elliott, Dr, is Associate Professor at Southampton Solent University, UK and Director of the Lawrie McMenemy Centre for Football Research. He completed his doctorate at Loughborough University. His research primarily revolves around globalisation and migration in professional football where he has published widely. He provides academic support for the Football Association, education programmes and research for the League Managers Association, and has worked in conjunction with the Premier League and professional clubs. He also provides expert support for the media, appearing in print, on radio and television.

Oliver Fürtjes, Dipl.-Soz., ist wissenschaftlicher Mitarbeiter am Institut für Sportsoziologie, Deutsche Sporthochschule Köln. Forschungsschwerpunkte: Sozialstruktur- und Ungleichheitsforschung, Publikumsforschung, Mediensoziologie. Veröffentlichungen: *Fußballfans im sozialen Wandel*. Bremen, 2009; Der Fußball und seine Entproletarisierung. Kölner Zeitschrift für Soziologie und Sozialpsychologie 63, 2011; Der Fußball und seine Kontinuität als schichtenübergreifendes Massenphänomen. SportZeiten 12, 2012.

Eva Gros studierte Soziologie, Pädagogik und Psychoanalyse in Gießen und Frankfurt am Main. Seit 2007 wissenschaftliche Mitarbeiterin am Institut für Soziologie der JLU Gießen. Schwerpunkte in Forschung und Lehre: Soziologische Perspektiven auf Holocaust

und Nationalsozialismus, Soziologische Theorie, Antisemitismustheorie, Theorien sozialer Ungleichheit, Gender Studies, Queer Theory.

Vivien Hacker, Dr, studied Germanistik and Amerikanistik at Frankfurt University, where
she was awarded her PhD in 2002 for a thesis on German-Italian cultural relations. She
taught contemporary German culture at Lancaster University 1998 – 2003. Subsequently she switched careers, founded her own business consultancy, Eureko Associates Limited, advising British firms on marketing their products in Europe.

York Kautt, Dr., ist wissenschaftlicher Mitarbeiter am Institut für Soziologie, Justus-
Liebig-Universität Gießen. Forschungsschwerpunkte: Medien- und Kultursoziologie,
Theorie und Analyse visueller Kommunikation, qualitative Sozialforschung. Publika-
tionen (Auswahl): *Image. Zur Genealogie eines Kommunikationscodes der Massenmedien*, Bielefeld (2008). „Televisuelle Koch-Formate: zur Kulturbedeutsamkeit eines Be-
reichs der Massenmedien", in: Sociologia Internationalis, 2/2010, S. 211-247.

Dilwyn Porter, Prof Dr, is Professor of Sports History and Culture at De Montfort University and is also Visiting Professor at Boston College's Centre for Irish Studies. He has
published extensively on twentieth-century British history and on the history of sport
and is currently working on a history of amateur football in England. From 2004-08 he
edited the journal *Sport in History*.

Jürgen Schraten, Dr., studierte Politikwissenschaft, Mittlere Geschichte und Soziologie.
Gegenwärtig ist er Postdoctoral Fellow des Human Economy Programmes an der Universität Pretoria. Seine Arbeitsfelder sind Wirtschaftssoziologie und Rechtssoziologie,
und er arbeitet zur Entwicklung der Finanzialisierung in der südlichen Hemisphäre.

Andreas Stolz studierte Dipl. Sportwissenschaften an der Sporthochschule Köln. Derzeit
Studium der Fächer Sport, Politik und Wirtschaft an der JLU Gießen (Lehramt an Gymnasien). Interessenschwerpunkte: Sport- und bewegungsorientierte Prävention und Re-
habilitation von orthopädischen und neurologischen Krankheiten, sportartspezifisches
Kraft-, Ausdauer- und Koordinationstraining, Entwicklung und Professionalisierung
der Trainingsmethoden im Profi- und Amateurfußball.

Mark Turner is Senior Lecturer in Sociology of Sport and a member of the Southampton
Solent Centre for Health, Exercise and Sport Science (CHESS) Research Cluster. He was
awarded his BSc undergraduate degree from the University of Lancaster and his MA
postgraduate degree from the University of Brighton. His main teaching interests are
located in the areas of sport sociology and cultural studies.

Stephen Wagg, Prof Dr, is a Professor in the Carnegie Faculty of Leeds Metropolitan University in the UK. He writes regularly on the politics of sport, of childhood and of leisure. His most recent books are *Myths and Milestones in the History of Sport* and (with
Helen Lenskyj) *The Palgrave Handbook of Olympic Studies* (both Basingstoke: Palgrave
Macmillan, 2012). With Brett Lashua and Karl Spracklen he will shortly publish *Sounds
and the City: Music, Place and Globalisation* and (with Jane Pilcher) *Thatcher's Grand-
children?: The Politics of Childhood in the Twenty First Century* (both Palgrave Macmillan, forthcoming in 2014).

Christoph Wagner is a student at De Montfort University, Leicester, where he is writing a
thesis on Anglo-German football rivalry as reflected in the press. He writes about his
thesis at http://donotmentionthewar.wordpress.com. He is the editor of the football blog
http://anoldinternational.co.uk. and a regular contributor for http://footballrepublik.
com and for the German football magazine OstDerby.